THE POLITICS OF PROPERTY RIGHTS

POLITICAL INSTABILITY, CREDIBLE COMMITMENTS, AND ECONOMIC GROWTH IN MEXICO, 1876–1929

This book addresses a puzzle in political economy: why is it that political instability does not necessarily translate into economic stagnation or collapse? In order to address this puzzle, this book advances a theory about property rights systems in many less developed countries. In our theory, governments do not have to enforce property rights as a public good. Instead, they may enforce property rights selectively (as a private good) and share the resulting rents with the group of asset holders who are integrated into the government. We then use the theory to explore how systems such as this operate as an empirical matter. We focus on Mexico, from 1876 to 1929. We explain how the property rights system was constructed during the Porfirio Díaz dictatorship (1876–1911) and then explore how this property rights system either survived or was reconstructed during the long period of political instability that followed, 1911–29. The result is a book that offers, on the one hand, an analytic economic history of Mexico under both stability and instability and a generalizable framework about the interaction of political and economic institutions.

Stephen Haber is A. A. and Jeanne Welch Milligan Professor at Stanford University, where he teaches political science and history. He is also the Peter and Helen Bing Senior Fellow of the Hoover Institution. Haber also serves as Director of Stanford's Social Science History Institute. He is the author of numerous books and articles and editor of many others.

Armando Razo is a Ph.D. candidate in the Department of Political Science at Stanford University. He has published articles in *World Politics* and the *Journal of Latin American Studies*.

Noel Maurer is Assistant Professor of Economics at ITAM. He has been a lecturer at Stanford University and is the author of *The Power and the Money: The Mexican Financial System, 1876–1931*, as well as the author of articles for journals such as the *Journal of Economic History* and the *Journal of Latin American Studies*.

POLITICAL ECONOMY OF INSTITUTIONS AND DECISIONS

Series Editors

Randall Calvert, Washington University, St. Louis
Thrainn Eggertsson, Max Planck Institute, Germany, and University of Iceland

Founding Editors

James E. Alt, Harvard University
Douglass C. North, Washington University, St. Louis

Other Books in the Series

Continued on page following index

THE POLITICS OF
PROPERTY RIGHTS

*Political Instability, Credible Commitments, and
Economic Growth in Mexico, 1876–1929*

STEPHEN HABER
Stanford University

ARMANDO RAZO
Stanford University

NOEL MAURER
CIE, ITAM

CAMBRIDGE
UNIVERSITY PRESS

PUBLISHED BY THE PRESS SYNDICATE OF THE UNIVERSITY OF CAMBRIDGE
The Pitt Building, Trumpington Street, Cambridge, United Kingdom

CAMBRIDGE UNIVERSITY PRESS
The Edinburgh Building, Cambridge CB2 2RU, UK
40 West 20th Street, New York, NY 10011-4211, USA
477 Williamstown Road, Port Melbourne, VIC 3207, Australia
Ruiz de Alarcón 13, 28014 Madrid, Spain
Dock House, The Waterfront, Cape Town 8001, South Africa

http://www.cambridge.org

© Stephen Haber, Armando Razo, Noel Maurer 2003

First published 2003

Printed in the United States of America

Typeface Sabon 10/13 pt.   *System* LaTeX 2_ε [TB]

A catalog record for this book is available from the British Library.

Library of Congress Cataloging in Publication data

Haber, Stephen H., 1957–
    The politics of property rights : political instability, credible commitments, and
    economic growth in Mexico, 1876–1929 / Stephen Haber, Armando Razo,
    Noel Maurer.
        p.   cm. – (Political economy of institutions and decisions)
    Includes bibliographical references and index.
    ISBN 0-521-82067-7
    1. Mexico – Economic policy.   2. Right of property – Mexico – History.
    3. Mexico – Politics and government – 19th century.   4. Mexico – Politics and
    government – 20th century.   I. Razo, Armando, 1971–   II. Maurer, Noel.
    III. Title.   IV. Series.
    HC135 .H173   2003
    320'.6'0972'0904 – dc21   2002031354

ISBN 0 521 82067 7 hardback

To Our Families
Marsy and Natalie
Micaela, Dante, and Michael
Diana, Paige, and Amanda

Contents

List of Illustrations and Tables

List of Abbreviations

AGN	Archivo General de la Nación, Mexico City
AHBNM	Archivo Histórico del Banco Nacional de México, Mexico City
APPM	Association of Petroleum Producers in Mexico
ASARCO	American Smelting and Refining Company
Banamex	Banco Nacional de México
Banxico	Banco de México
BLM	Banco de Londres y México
CNB	Comisión Nacional Bancaria
COCACO	Confederación de Cámaras de Comercio (Federation of Chambers of Commerce)
CONCAMIN	Confederación de Cámaras Industriales
CPOI	Caja de Préstamos Para Obras de Irrigación
CROM	Confederación Regional Obrera Mexicana
LDC	Less Developed Countries
MSOA	Miners and Smelters Owners' Association
PLM	Partido Laborista Mexicano
PRM	Partido de la Revolución Mexicana
PNR	Partido Nacional Revolucionario
PRI	Partido Revolucionario Institucional

Acknowledgments

One of the truly wonderful features about having great colleagues is that they sometimes recognize the implications of your work in ways that never occurred to you. This book is an example of that phenomenon, and the person whom we would like to thank for encouraging us to explore our own insights is Douglass North. We had written a series of papers that demonstrated that the Mexican Revolution did not produce the impact on the country's manufacturing sector that one would expect from the extant theories about political instability and economic performance. We presented one of those papers at a seminar at the Hoover Institution in 1998. After the seminar, North suggested that we explore the subject further by looking at the property rights systems that underpinned economic activity in other sectors of the economy. He also suggested that we should write a "short book" about our results. We took all of his advice, except the part about the book being short.

As the project grew, so too did the number of colleagues, friends, students, and institutions who contributed to it. First, we want to thank Scott Wilson and Marie Toney, the associate director and administrator, respectively, of Stanford's Social Science History Institute. Their hard work helped move this project along in innumerable ways. We also had seven extraordinary research assistants on this project. Moramay López Alonso and Betsy Carroll helped gather financial data on mining and petroleum companies. Jonathan Morgenstein helped us gather much of the qualitative and quantitative evidence for the mining chapter. Jean Kim did endless hours of data entry and now knows more about Mexico's mining censuses than she ever wanted to. Maite Careaga helped gather data on Mexico's agricultural exports. She also read the penultimate draft of the book in its entirety and made valuable comments. Belinda Yeomans and Derek Fears helped us prepare the final manuscript. We particularly want to thank Belinda for the careful manner in which she double-checked each and every table in the manuscript.

Research assistants do not, of course, pay for themselves. We therefore want to thank the following institutions and individuals who provided the financial support necessary for data collection and data processing. Some of the funding for this project, particularly in its earliest stages, came from a grant from the National Science Foundation, SBR 34-3163-00-79-483, administered through the National Bureau for Economic Research. Additional support, particularly for the funding of graduate student research assistance, came from a grant to Stanford's Social Science History Institute from the William and Flora Hewlett Foundation. We would like to thank the foundation and its program officer, David Lorey, for their support. Most of the funding for this project came from the Hoover Institution at Stanford University. We would like to thank its director, John Raisian, for his generous funding of a Hoover Scholar Account, which funded research trips to Mexico and research assistants at Stanford. We would also like to thank him for providing office space for this project, as well as for providing an intellectual environment that encourages the free exchange of ideas among scholars from a broad range of disciplines.

Much of the writing of this book was done during academic year 2000–1 while one of us (Haber) was Moore Distinguished Scholar at the Division of Humanities and Social Sciences of the California Institute of Technology. The experience there enriched this book in innumerable ways. Its faculty, particularly Fiona Cowie, Lance Davis, Jean Ensminger, Phil Hoffman, Jonathan Katz, and Jim Woodward, provided a sounding board for many of our ideas and provided endless amounts of very useful feedback. We would also like to thank the people at Caltech who made Haber's visit possible, and who, more importantly, provide the leadership that makes Caltech such a truly remarkable place: its president, David Baltimore; its provost, Steve Koonin; and the division head of Humanities and Social Sciences, John Ledyard. We would also like to thank the HSS division administrator, Susan Davis, for making Haber's visit there run smoothly and for helping to make Caltech a home, in the fullest sense of the word, for Haber and his family during their year there.

Our students at Stanford University and the Instituto Tecnológico Autónomo de México (ITAM) also contributed to this project in ways large and small. Over the past six or seven years, there has developed a de facto program at Stanford in what might be called the New Latin American Political Economy. At the core of that program has been a series of seminars, some convened as formal classes, some convened as informal workshops, that has brought together students from various departments who are interested in problems of credible commitment, political organization, and economic development. We have been fortunate to be able to participate in those seminars and workshops, to learn from our fellow participants, and to benefit from the useful criticism that they have given us on chapter drafts. We note that some of the students we thank here have gone on to very successful academic careers in their own right since leaving Stanford. We want, in particular, to thank the following individuals who have participated in those seminars in recent years: Norma Alvarez, Edward Beatty, Maite Careaga, Gustavo del Angel, Moramay López Alonso, Francisco Monaldi, Aldo Musacchio, and Mary Speck. At ITAM an informal group of undergraduate honors thesis students with similar interests provided input and criticism of chapter drafts far above and beyond the call of duty. We would especially like to thank Carlos Puente, Ricardo Rivera, and Miriam Rubalcava, of whom the latter two are currently graduate students at the University of Chicago and Harvard, respectively.

Some chapter drafts have been presented at various conferences and seminars over the past several years. These include the economic history seminars at Harvard University; Yale University; Columbia University; the University or Pennsylvania; Stanford University; the Universidad Torcuato di Tella; the Universidad de la República, Uruguay; the University of California, Davis; the University of California, Los Angeles; and the University of California, Berkeley. Chapter drafts were also presented at the Center for U.S.-Mexican Studies at the University of California, San Diego; the Public Choice Seminar at the Hoover Institution; the Division of Humanities and Social Sciences of the California Institute of Technology; the Department of Economics and Centro de Investigación Económica of the Instituto Tecnológico Autónomo de México; the Economic History Association; the All University of California Group in Economic History; and UCLA's Center for Comparative and Global Research. We also obtained feedback at an earlier stage of this project from participants at the Third Annual Conference of the International Society of New Institutional Economics. We thank the conveners of those seminars and conferences, as well as the audiences who provided much useful feedback.

Numerous individuals also gave generously of their time. The useful conversations we had with them at various stages of this project enriched this book in many ways. We would, in particular, like to thank David Abernethy, Daron Acemoglu, Terry Anderson, Jon Bendor, Luis

Bértola, Tim Bresnahan, Bruce Bueno de Mesquita, Enrique Cárdenas, Gary Cox, Gerardo della Paolera, Alan Dye, Stanley Engerman, Judith Goldstein, Aurora Gómez Galvarriato, Andrei Gomberg, Avner Greif, Tim Guinnane, David Kaplan, David Kennedy, Anne Krueger, David Laitin, John Londregan, Chris Mantzavinos, César Martinelli, Carlos Marichal, Graciela Márquez, Gary Miller, Joel Mokyr, Ian Morris, Naomi Lamoreaux, Kevin Middlebrook, Robert Packenham, Joyce Sadka, Tom Sargent, Paul Sniderman, Kenneth Sokoloff, Alan Taylor, Peter Temin, Aaron Tornell, Eric Van Young, and Gavin Wright. We would also like to express our very deep gratitude to the group of scholars and friends who, in addition to sharing their ideas with us, also read chapter drafts (sometimes multiple times!) and provided detailed comments. Our thanks in this regard go to Edward Beatty, Jeffrey Bortz, Herbert Klein, Melvin Reiter, Tridib Sharma, William Summerhill, and Barry Weingast. We would also like to thank the two anonymous referees from Cambridge University Press, who provided very helpful feedback on an early draft of the book.

Five great scholars, and even better friends, Ted Beatty, Phil Hoffman, Sandra Kuntz Ficker, Jim Robinson, and Jean-Laurent Rosenthal, read the book manuscript in its entirety. Their detailed comments on issues of fact, on data analysis, on historical interpretation, on analytic models, and on many other issues proved invaluable in the crafting of this book. We owe them far more than our thanks.

We have dedicated this book to our families: Marsy and Natalie Haber; Micaela, Dante, and Michael Razo; and Diana, Paige, and Amanda Maurer. We are certain that there were many times when they wished we were doing something other than writing this book. We are also certain that they simultaneously understood why we got so much joy from this project. For their understanding, we dedicate this book to them with love.

THE POLITICS OF PROPERTY RIGHTS

POLITICAL INSTABILITY, CREDIBLE COMMITMENTS, AND
ECONOMIC GROWTH IN MEXICO, 1876–1929

I

Introduction

We began this book in order to address a puzzle in political economy: why is it that political instability does not necessarily translate into economic stagnation? In the process of answering this question, we found that we had to draw on methods and approaches from what are usually thought of as three distinct disciplines: political science, economics, and history.

First, we had to develop a theory. That theory had to explore the conditions under which political violence, coupled with unpredictable and recurring change in the identity of the government, did not affect the underlying property rights system. Constructing that theory required, in turn, that we develop a theory about how governments can specify and enforce property rights as private (not public) goods. It also required that we explore the mechanisms that would make such selective commitments by governments credible – even if the identity of the government changed repeatedly.

Second, we needed to test that theory. Testing the theory required that we explore the functioning of a real-world case of such a selective property rights system under conditions of political stability and political instability. We therefore focused on Mexico, which created a selectively enforced property rights system during the long dictatorship of Porfirio Díaz (1876–1911) and which then underwent a prolonged period of revolutions, civil wars, political assassinations, and coups from 1911 to 1929. Our empirical exploration of the Mexican case required, in turn, that we learn about the specific features of the property rights system in individual economic sectors, and how that property rights system evolved over time, under both conditions of political stability and political instability.

Third, we had to measure the performance of those economic sectors. That meant, in turn, that we had to construct firm- and industry-level data sets that spanned the decades of Porfirian peace and revolutionary instability. We also had to employ quantitative tools drawn from micro-economics in order to analyze those data sets.

The result is a book that offers, on the one hand, a generalizable frame-work about the interaction of political and economic institutions and, on the other, a detailed, microeconomic history of Mexico from 1876 to 1929. We realize that this means that different readers are likely to approach this book in different ways. We therefore think it appropriate to provide a guide as to how we came to write this book, a discussion of the concepts and methods we employ, and an explanation of the argument we advance.

THE PARADOX OF GROWTH AMID INSTABILITY

Our motivation in writing this book is the lack of fit between the political science and economics literatures on the political determinants of economic growth. One of the logical implications of the theoretical literature on the interaction of political and economic institutions is that political instability should have a strongly negative impact on growth. The empirical literature on the determinants of growth cannot, however, detect the predicted relationship.[1]

The origins of this paradox can be traced to the political science literature on the commitment problem. Basically stated, the problem is as follows: any government strong enough to define and arbitrate property rights is also strong enough to abrogate them for its own benefit. Unless the government can give the population strong reason to believe that it will not act in its own short-run interest (by seizing property or taxing away all of the income it produces), the population will not invest. If there is no investment, there will be little economic activity, and hence there will be insufficient tax revenues for the government. In short, governments face a dilemma: if they do not find a way to tie their own hands, they will not have sufficient resources to insure their own survival.[2]

---

[1] As we discuss in detail later, to the degree that any relationships can be detected, they are not statistically robust; are not causally linked; are sensitive to even modest alterations in data sets, conditioning variables, and regression specifications; and are weak tests of the instability–negative growth hypothesis.

[2] The problem of commitment has been around since the creation of the first state systems in the ancient Near East. It regularly weighed on the minds of medieval kings, who were especially concerned with the problem of making credible commitments to foreign merchants, who feared the king would expropriate their wealth. (See, e.g., Greif, Milgrom, et al. 1994, p. 747.) The commitment problem loomed throughout the debates surrounding the writing of the U.S. Constitution. Indeed, it figures as

The extant theoretical literature offers two solutions to the commitment problem: stationary banditry and limited government.[3] The stationary bandit solution is based on the notion that a truly self-interested despot will not abrogate property rights or tax all of the income those property rights generate.[4] If he sets taxes too high (or engages in the outright theft of property), he will create disincentives to invest or exchange. There will therefore be less to tax. A self-interested despot therefore has an incentive to set taxes at the "revenue maximizing" rate.[5] What is more, a revenue-maximizing despot has an incentive to provide public goods (roads, bridges, stable currencies, standard weights and measures, and the like), because these will raise the total income of society and hence his own tax income. He will spend his own funds to provide public goods up to the point that the marginal cost of providing those goods equals

a major theme in Madison's writings in the Federalist Papers. In the modern social science literature, the commitment problem reemerged in North's discussion of the neoclassical theory of the state (in North 1981, chap. 3). The problem was discussed even more explicitly in North and Weingast (1989) on the economic effects of the Glorious Revolution, and was later pursued by Weingast (and various coauthors) in a series of articles. Hence, the commitment problem is sometimes referred to as Weingast's dilemma. There exists now a broad literature on various problems related to credible commitment. For representative works, see Barro and Gordon (1983); Levi (1988); Root (1989); North (1990); Shepsle (1991); Miller (1992); Greif, Milgrom, et al. (1994); Hoffman and Norberg (1994); McGuire and Olson (1996); Alston, Eggertsson, et al. (1996), pp. 129–33; Weingast (1997a, 1997b); Qian and Weingast (1997); North, Summerhill, et al. (2000); Olson (2000), chap. 1; and Bates (2001).

[3] There are other institutions that work in special cases without governments. This type of commitment mechanism, however, can only function if the number of parties involved is small and if the costs of transmitting information among the parties are low. There are historical cases of such mechanisms at the city-state level. The ability of these mechanisms to produce credible commitments breaks down as the size of the state increases, because it becomes increasingly difficult to monitor and enforce agreements as geographic dispersion and the heterogeneity of actors increases. For a discussion of a wide variety of institutions that sustained trade before the development of nation-states, see Greif (1989, 1997, 1998); and Greif, Milgrom, et al. (1994).

[4] This discussion is drawn from Olson (2000), chap. 1; McGuire and Olson (1996); and North (1981), chap. 3. In North's discussion, the despot acts as an efficient monopolist, practicing discriminatory pricing for his services. Implicit in this discussion is the notion that the despot might provide protection for only some members of society. In McGuire and Olson, and Olson, the despot–stationary bandit provides property rights protection as a public good. In both cases, however, it is assumed that the ruler is a long-run revenue maximizer.

[5] For example, if an increase in taxes from 50 percent to 51 percent causes economic activity to decline from 100 to 98, then the despot would receive an income of 49.98 (0.51 times 98) rather than 50 in income (0.50 times 100).

the marginal income he receives in increased tax revenues from increased economic activity. The same logic of self-interest also means that a despot will have strong incentives to police and arbitrate property rights, because secure property rights will create incentives for the population to invest, and thereby maximize the despot's tax income.

There are two problems with the stationary bandit-despot solution, one practical and one theoretical. The practical problem is that no one lives forever. The time horizons of despots are not infinite. In fact, the older a despot grows, the more he will discount the future. As his discount factor decreases, the despot will increase taxes, cut spending on public goods, and become increasingly likely to seize property. Hereditary monarchy is an attempt to solve this problem. Historically, this solution does not work as well in practice as it does in theory.[6] Consider England, an archetypal "stable" monarchy. Between 1066 and 1715, 18 out of 31 royal successions produced a political crisis.[7]

The theoretical problem is that the despot's commitment to protect property rights is purely volitional. No real mechanism constrains the despot other than his own goal of long-run revenue maximization. Historical evidence, however, indicates that despots cannot usually see how the exercise of their own power diminishes their own accumulation of wealth. Moreover, even a despot who gains a reputation for protecting property rights, in order to encourage investment, may later on have strong reasons to behave in an opportunistic or predatory fashion. The longer a despot is in power, the greater is the stock of accumulated assets on which he can prey. Simultaneously, the longer he is in power, the older he will be, and the higher the rate at which he will discount the future. Ultimately, the predatory incentives are huge, and the despot either seizes property or taxes away all of the income it produces. In short, just like mutual funds, under despotism past performance is no indication of future returns.[8]

The other well-known solution to the commitment problem is limited government. Limited governments respect individual rights as a matter of law, are bound by self-enforcing institutions to respect their own laws, and cannot arbitrarily alter the laws that constrain them. They can only alter the law by following due process, which is itself clearly and transparently defined by the law.

[6] See Olson (1993).
[7] See DeLong and Shleifer (1993).
[8] See Veugelers (1993).

4

The literature is just beginning to specify the exact configuration of the institutions that force limited governments to respect their own laws regarding individual political and economic rights. There are numerous models but, as yet, no general theory. The literature suggests, however, that what is key is that individual political actors cannot exceed the authority granted to them by the law. If they do so, they are subject to sanctions that are imposed by other branches or levels of government or, in the case of democracies, by the electorate.[9] These sanctions are not imposed in an arbitrary or ad hoc fashion: the sanction mechanisms are themselves prescribed by the law. In the United States, for example, the president is limited by a bicameral legislature, an independent judiciary, state and local governments, and a professionalized civil service that staffs executive federal agencies. Thus, the U.S. president cannot arbitrarily violate the rights of a citizen because he or she would be subject to sanctions from other branches and levels of the government.[10] Precisely because the government cannot act in an arbitrary manner – because its own political institutions prevent the government from arbitrarily confiscating assets and the economic returns from those assets – asset holders will invest. They do not fear government predation.[11]

Limited government is the theoretically optimal solution to the commitment problem. First, commitment no longer depends on individual volition. Commitments are made credible by the self-enforcing nature of the institutions that underlie limited government. Second, because limited governments involve more than one actor, they will bear more of the deadweight costs of their own rent-seeking behavior than would a

---

[9] Limited governments and democracies are not identical sets. Any government that cannot act arbitrarily because of the nature of its own political institutions – that is to say, whenever the rule of law exists – is a limited government. The United States, for example, was a limited government from 1789 onward, but universal white male suffrage did not become widespread until the 1820s, and universal suffrage did not become effective until 1965. For a discussion of the evolution of suffrage in the United States, see Sokoloff (2002).

[10] In the specific case of the United States, an additional feature prevents any actor in the government from abrogating the rights of citizens: sets of multiple, overlapping veto points in the decision structure of the polity (e.g., bicameral legislatures, an executive branch of government, and judicial review of legislation). This means that an actor in the U.S system is not just subject to sanctions ex post but is also blocked ex ante from abrogating a citizen's rights. For a discussion of multiple, overlapping veto points in the U.S. case, see McCubbins, Noll, et al. (1987a, 1987b).

[11] The literature on limited government is exemplified by North (1981), pp. 154–57, and (1990); Levi (1988); Weingast (1997a, 1997b); North and Weingast (1989); North, Summerhill, et al. (2000); and Bates (2001), chap. 3.

despotic government. In fact, the actors that make decisions within a limited government may have or represent interests that are harmed by rent seeking and opportunism. Thus, the self-interest of many individuals, interacting through a set of formal institutions that govern decision making, serves to check and balance the opportunistic inclinations of any individual actor.[12]

For both theoretical and empirical reasons, the group of countries that are typically characterized as unstable and the group of countries that are ruled by limited governments do not overlap. Unstable polities are implicitly defined in the empirical growth literature as those in which governments change hands in an unconstitutional, unpredictable, recurring, and violent manner. This recurring violence may be localized (e.g., political assassinations), more widespread (e.g., coups), or more generalized (e.g., civil war or revolution).[13] As a theoretical matter, unstable polities cannot be ruled by limited governments. In a limited government, by definition, the selection mechanism for choosing government officials is based on the rule of law. If you can shoot your way into office, the mechanisms of limited government have ceased to function. As an empirical matter, until the 1990s the set of limited governments was very small, and the set of limited governments that fell into instability was even smaller still. As a matter of history, limited government is, in fact, a very rare phenomenon.

Countries ruled by stationary bandits and countries that are usually characterized as unstable are overlapping sets. Once a country ruled by a stationary bandit becomes unstable, however, the stationary bandit can no longer provide a credible commitment to protect property rights. The result should be economic collapse, stagnation, or, at best, very slow growth. The reason is that stationary bandits can only provide a credible commitment to protect property rights when the despot – and the population he rules – believes that he will be in power for a long time. If a despot comes to the realization that his reign is about to end, he has every incentive to steal everything he can while he still can. The higher the probability that his government will fall, the shorter will be his time horizon, and thus the greater the incentive to abrogate property rights. In fact, the logic of political instability will force a stationary bandit to abrogate property

---

[12] See McGuire and Olson (1996). Also see McCubbins and Schwartz (1984).
[13] The empirical growth literature measures instability using instrumental variables such as assassinations, coups, and revolutions. See Barro (1991), p. 432; Alesina, Özler, et al. (1996), pp. 191–92.

rights and behave like a roving bandit. If he does not become predatory, someone else will, and will use those resources to overthrow him.

In point of fact, any government, despotic or not, facing a violent threat to its existence has strong incentives to abrogate property rights because it needs resources to fight its enemies. The threat of violence shortens the time horizons of governments (and of factions aspiring to be governments). They must seize property or tax away all of its income, or be overthrown. The leader of such a government knows, of course, that seizing assets and production today will mean less production (and therefore taxes) tomorrow. The advantage is that he will live to see tomorrow.

The logical implication of the extant solutions to the commitment problem is that political instability should be inversely correlated with growth. In the first place, unstable countries will not be ruled by (economically efficient) limited governments. In the second place, it is not possible to make credible commitments to protect property rights via stationary banditry if the polity is unstable. This causal link between instability, the inability to make credible commitments, and economic stagnation is explored by North, Summerhill, and Weingast as an explanation for the differences in the economic performances of the United States and Latin America in the nineteenth century. In their model there is an endless feedback loop between political disorder and economic stagnation: authoritarianism produces politicized property rights systems designed to produce rents for some select group, which produces strong incentives for other groups to capture the state, which produces political disorder, which produces slow growth, which produces incentives for some group of agents to capture the state, establish an authoritarian system, and establish a property rights system designed to provide them with opportunities for rent seeking, ad infinitum.[14]

Given what seemed like a straightforward connection between political instability and economic stagnation, economists engaged in cross-country growth accounting exercises began to code their data sets for unstable countries. Their goal was to determine the exact costs, in terms of forgone growth, of having an unstable political system. They expected to find that growth was not only inversely correlated with instability, but that causality runs from political instability to no growth, rather than from no growth to political instability.

The results they obtained, however, did not match their expectations. First, the studies that searched for a correlation between instability and

[14] North, Summerhill, et al. (2000).

slow growth did not all reach the same conclusion. Some studies detected a correlation between political instability and slow economic growth; other studies, which used different data sets, regression specifications, and instrumental variables, failed to replicate those results.[15] Second, subsequent work employing sensitivity analysis found that whatever correlations had been detected were extremely fragile. As Levine and Renelt put it: "Almost all identified relationships are very sensitive to slight alterations in the conditioning set of variables and many publicized coefficients change sign with small changes in the conditioning set of variables.... In particular, the broad array of fiscal expenditure variables, monetary-policy indicators, and political-stability indexes considered by the profession are not robustly correlated with growth."[16] Third, work that used time series econometric techniques to test Granger causality failed to find a causal relationship between political instability and economic growth. As Campos and Nugent state it: "[T]he evidence that SPI [sociopolitical instability] causes a decrease in the growth rate of per capita income seems much weaker than generally believed. In addition, such a negative and causal relation seems to be largely confined to the Sub-Saharan Africa sample."[17] Londregan and Poole obtained similar results.[18] Related work on the impact of instability on investment did find a causal relationship, but that relationship, contrary to expectations, was *positive*: an increase in the level of instability caused an increase in investment.[19]

Even had the growth accounting literature detected a statistically robust relationship between political instability and slow growth, that result would have been a very weak test of the empirical implications of the literature on the commitment problem. Political instability should produce stagnation or economic collapse, not just slow growth. The reason is not hard to divine. The more unstable a polity, the shorter will be the time horizon of governments and potential governments. They must prey on assets (or the revenues they produce) today in order to have a chance of remaining in power tomorrow. Thus, the more unstable the situation, the

---

[15] Seminal work in this field includes Londregan and Poole (1990, 1992); Alesina, Özler, et al. (1996); Barro (1991, 1997), especially chap. 2.

[16] Levine and Renelt (1992), p. 943. Brunetti obtains similar unstable results when using Extreme Bound Analysis to test for the sensitivity of various measures of instability and the sensitivity of various regression specifications. See Brunetti (1997), especially pp. 60–79.

[17] Campos and Nugent (2002), pp. 164–65.

[18] Londregan and Poole (1990), p. 174.

[19] Campos and Nugent (2000).

more governments, factions, and the general population will discount the future.

Two interrelated results follow from this increase in discount rates. First, there will be fewer economic transactions. The more uncertain the political situation, the less certain the population can be about economic policies. The population will find it increasingly difficult to predict future rates of inflation (monetary policies may change dramatically), future levels of taxation, or even whether there will be a government in place that will protect property rights and enforce contracts. Private parties will therefore abstain from contracting, because it is far from certain that contracts will or can be honored. Second, as instability increases, investment in new fixed assets will decrease. Only those investments in which the rate of return exceeds the discount rate of investors will be made. If instability gets severe enough, and discount rates get high enough, then new investment will fall to zero. At the same time that there is little or no new investment, existing fixed assets are depreciating. If the rate of new investment is only high enough to replace assets that are being used up in production, then the outcome will at best be economic stagnation. If the rate of new investment is lower than the rate of depreciation of existing fixed assets, then the outcome will be economic contraction.

METHODS AND APPROACHES

The lack of fit between theoretical predictions and empirical results produces a curious puzzle: we should be able to observe a strong (and robust) relationship between political instability and economic performance, but the expected empirical results are elusive. All other things being the same, the economies of unstable countries do not collapse, stagnate, or even grow more slowly than stable countries.

Clearly, it would be an overstatement to say that political instability has no effect on growth. In fact, one can point to numerous cases of unstable countries that grew slowly or that did not grow at all. The evidence does strongly indicate, however, that there must be conditions under which political instability hinders growth, and conditions under which growth is unaffected by instability.

Our goal in this book is to explore those conditions. This requires, however, that we depart from the standard theoretical and empirical approaches. As a theoretical matter, we have to depart from the extant solutions to the commitment problem, because those solutions (as we discuss in this introduction) logically imply that instability should produce slow growth, economic stagnation, or complete collapse.

The solution we propose, and that we develop in full in Chapter 2, draws on the literature on the microeconomic analysis of contract and property rights.[20] We integrate this literature with the related (but distinct) literature on credible commitments and the political foundations of growth. In so doing, we expand upon an insight in both literatures that is frequently made but whose implications have not yet been fully explored: investors, first and foremost, care about the sanctity of *their* property rights; they do not require governments to protect property rights as a public good in order for investment to take place.[21] Once the requirement that property rights enforcement be a public good is relaxed, there are a number of mechanisms that can create the necessary credible commitment to a select group of asset holders. These mechanisms neither require the rule of law nor a stable polity. What they require is credible threats of retaliation by investors. These credible threats may come from the possibility of intervention by a foreign state on behalf of its citizens, a financial hostage, or the existence of a powerful political group whose interests have been aligned with investors through the formation of a rent-seeking coalition. Indeed, as we shall show in both theory and practice, there are circumstances under which these mechanisms work better when the polity is unstable.

We also realized that we had to depart from the traditions in the empirical literature on growth of employing cross-country regressions to test our model. Our reasoning was that in the real world there is a complex set of relationships between political and economic institutions. It

---

[20] For an introduction to this literature, see Barzel (1997); Eggertsson (1990); and, Mantzavinos (2001).

[21] The idea that governments can enforce property rights selectively (i. e., as a private good) is implicit in North (1981), chap. 3. It is explicitly made in Weingast (1997a, 1997b) and in North, Summerhill, et al. (2000). In these treatments, however, the focus tends to be on the disadvantages created by the selective enforcement of property rights. In North, Summerhill, et al. (2000), for example, the selective enforcement of property rights is assumed to lead to political disorder and economic stagnation. The coup traps that North, Summerhill, and Weingast have in mind are certainly a very real possibility. They are not, however, a necessary outcome of a selective property rights system. World history suggests numerous cases in which selective property rights systems permitted the development of authoritarian regimes of long duration. Examples would include Mexico under Díaz, Taiwan under Chiang Kai-shek, the Dominican Republic under Trujillo, the Philippines under Marcos, Indonesia under Suharto, Brazil under Vargas, Haiti under the Duvaliers, and Zaire under Mobuto.

is not possible, at least given the current state of theory and technique, to capture these relationships with cross-country regressions – the other well-known problems with the approach notwithstanding. In fact, even if the other problems with cross-country regression analysis could be solved, that approach would still not be appropriate to testing the model we develop. Cross-country regression techniques analyze growth as a short-run macroeconomic problem. The approach relies on representative agent models that aggregate institutional and political variables. Our model, however, focuses on the formation of rent-seeking coalitions made up of subsets of political and economic elites and on their ability to weather political instability. In short, cross-country regressions, even when they rely on panel data, are too blunt an instrument to understand the formation and functioning of political coalitions over the long term.

The need to analyze economic performance and institutional change over time, comparing growth under both stability and instability, required that we take an explicitly historical approach. We focused on Mexico, which after 35 years of political stability (1876–1910) endured 19 years of extreme instability (1911–29). The long-standing dictatorship of Porfirio Díaz fell to an armed insurgency in 1911. The reformists that deposed Díaz tried to institute limited government, but were themselves overthrown by Díaz's generals in 1913. That counterrevolutionary government was, in turn, overthrown by a broad coalition of reformists and radicals in 1914. The constituent groups that made up that coalition, however, soon fell to fighting among themselves because they had very different visions of the institutions that should govern the polity and the economy. Some of them wanted only moderate political reforms. Others wanted the widespread redistribution of land and other productive assets, as well as a complete overhaul of the political system. They therefore fought a long and extremely violent civil war from 1914 to 1917.

Even after a new constitution was written in 1917, Mexico continued to be unstable. The first president under the Constitution of 1917, Venustiano Carranza, was overthrown and assassinated by his own generals in 1920. His successor, Alvaro Obregón, was himself assassinated the day after he was reelected to a second term. The other leaders of the revolution were assassinated as well: Emiliano Zapata in 1919 and Francisco (Pancho) Villa in 1923. On three occasions during the 1920s the army, at times allied with politically ambitious cabinet members, tried to overthrow the government (1923, 1927, and 1929). The 1923 rebellion came very close to success and involved four months of pitched battles between various factions. In addition, from 1926 to 1929 there was a church-state civil war, led by Catholics who opposed the anticlerical elements of the Constitution of 1917 allied to landowners who feared agrarian reform. At both the state and federal levels, violence or the threat of violence played a central role in determining who would rule. Not until 1929, when the last serious violent threat to the government was defeated and a political party (the Partido Nacional Revolucionario, or PNR) was formed in order to provide a nonviolent forum for Mexico's generals to choose the federal executive, was a stable polity achieved.

The extant theories of credible commitment would predict that from 1911 to 1929 the Mexican economy should have performed badly. In order to see whether the extant theories or the one we develop in Chapter 2 better fits the evidence, we constructed an analytic economic history of Mexico from 1876 to 1929. Chapter 3 provides an overview of the political and institutional history of Mexico during the period 1876–1929. Chapters 4 through 8 present historical analyses of each of Mexico's most important economic sectors: banking, manufacturing, petroleum, mining, and agriculture.[22]

In each chapter, we proceed in three steps. First, we discuss the institutional arrangements that sustained investment and growth before the polity became unstable in 1910. Second, we discuss how those institutional arrangements either weathered the impact of extreme political instability after 1910 or were replaced by institutional arrangements that were robust to instability. Finally, we present a systematic analysis, employing tools from microeconomics, of the structure and performance of that economic sector both before and during instability.

---

[22] The only economic sector that we do not study in detail is transport. The reason is that Mexico's railroad system, which was the only economical mode of long-distance transport until the highway system was constructed beginning in the late 1920s, was a white elephant that was effectively nationalized by the government even before the polity became unstable. Mexico's railroads created huge social savings (Coatsworth's estimates range from 25 to 39 percent of GDP in 1910), but virtually all of the savings were captured by shippers of freight, not the companies that owned the railroads. This may have been because there was cut-throat competition among trunk lines. It may have been because the Díaz government reserved for itself the right to set freight rates as part of its agreement to provide railroad companies with construction subsidies. It may have been because freight densities on Mexican railways were extremely low. Whatever the cause, one thing is clear: Mexico's major railroads lost large sums of money and were going bankrupt. The Díaz government therefore bought out the stockholders of the companies that operated the major trunk lines in 1907 and created the Mexican National Railways. For the history of Mexico's railways, see Kuntz Ficker (1995, 2000); Kuntz Ficker and Riguzzi (1996); Grunstein (1994); Maurer (1999); and Coastworth (1981).

Introduction

In each chapter, we use the data sets we have developed to test three hypotheses: (1) investment and output should not have grown in absolute terms after 1911 (and likely would have shrunk); (2) instability should have slowed the rate of growth of that economic sector relative to the 10-year period before 1911; and (3) rates of investment and output growth might have continued at a high rate relative to the period prior to 1911, but they were slow relative to what Mexico could have accomplished in the absence of an unstable polity. We assess hypotheses 1 and 2 on the basis of time series analysis of economic data from Mexico. That is, our counterfactual case is Mexico itself before 1911. Assessing hypothesis 3 is more difficult, because it requires the comparison of Mexico with a country that was like Mexico in every respect but that did not undergo a long period of instability. There is, of course, no such country. As a second-best method, we can assess this hypothesis by comparing lines of economic activity in Mexico against those same industries in countries where those industries resembled Mexico's. We do this, for example, in the mining industry, where Mexico and the southwestern United States had very similar geologic endowments. We also do it for export agriculture, where we compare Mexico's performance against other countries that exported tropical products to the United States.

Some readers may wonder why we confined our empirical analysis to a single case. Why not construct multiple economic histories of unstable polities? We recognize that there are advantages to such multicountry historical case studies, and there is a sizable social science literature that employs this approach.[23] There is, however, a disadvantage to this approach that outweighs the advantages. As a practical matter, retrieving and analyzing primary source data are not enterprises characterized by increasing returns. Thus, multiple case studies must rely on the extant historical literature. This creates a serious problem because the extant historical literature tends not to bring to bear much in the way of systematically gathered quantitative evidence about economic structure and performance. Most of the historical literature is also not written with a set of questions in mind that are of direct interest to political scientists and economists. The end result is that much of the comparative history written by social scientists pays a steep price: they are hampered by the lack of systematic quantitative and qualitative data. The resulting economic analysis therefore tends to be haphazard.

[23] See, for example, Skocpol (1979); Moore (1967); Goldstone (1991); Levi (1988).

13

We therefore decided that there would be a high marginal return to writing an analytic economic history of a single case that was designed to answer questions of interest to the social sciences. Our strategy was to build on the extant secondary literature on Mexico's political and economic history. We then used primary sources to develop a detailed institutional history of the property rights system that underpinned growth in each economic sector and to develop quantitative data sets that would allow us to measure the economic performance of those sectors under both stability and instability.

Some readers may ask why we went to the trouble of writing a primary source-based, analytic history. Why not instead just look at published series on Mexican gross domestic product (GDP), or some similar measure of performance, and then compare how the economy did under both stability and instability? Unfortunately, there are no estimates of Mexican GDP for the period 1911–20. In addition, the GDP estimates that we have for the periods 1900–10 and 1920–29 are of doubtful reliability, drawn from imputed values and controlled conjectures rather than large bodies of empirical evidence. Mexico did not, in fact, carry out its first comprehensive industrial and agricultural censuses until 1930. The first input-output matrices for Mexico were not constructed until 1950. What researchers appear to have done in estimating GDP for earlier years was to use the limited data available on the output or export of particular commodities and plug them into the 1950 input-output matrix. The accuracy of these historical projections is anybody's guess. Much the same can be said, incidentally, about the estimates of GDP for most LDCs, or less developed countries, prior to 1950.

We therefore have constructed detailed economic histories of Mexico's most important economic sectors. Essentially the same pattern has appeared in every sector: output and investment fell sharply during the civil war of 1914–17 but in most sectors quickly recovered their former levels and rates of growth – even though the political system continued to be unstable until 1929. One partial exception to this pattern is banking. The banking system grew more rapidly in the politically turbulent 1920s than ever before but failed to regain its 1911 absolute size before 1929. This is because the growth of the 1920s began from an extremely low base, due to widespread predation on bank assets during 1914–17. The other exception is the petroleum industry, in which output and investment rose even during 1914–17. Mexican petroleum output during the period 1921–29 was twice that of the decade 1911–20, and 87 times that of the (politically stable) decade 1901–10.

In an ideal world, we would be able to aggregate the data on individual industries and sectors into a composite measure of economic performance. That would require, however, knowledge of the weights of the inputs and outputs. Our point is simply this: if investment and output rose in petroleum, manufacturing, mining, banking, and agriculture, then in the aggregate the economy was growing.

In short, we advance two arguments in this book. One is a substantive argument about the way that political and economic elites form coalitions to sustain economic activity and about how those coalitions can endure the effects of revolution, civil war, and political assassination. We argue that there is no *necessary connection* between political instability and economic stagnation.

We wish to be particularly clear that we are not arguing that political instability is never bad for growth. Rather, we are arguing that there are conditions under which political instability is bad for growth, and conditions under which it might actually be good for growth. Those conditions essentially fall into three categories: the degree to which the polity is unstable, the particular characteristics of individual industries, and the particular characteristics of the political coalitions that enforce property rights in any individual industry.

First, although the cross-country regression literature tends to code instability as a binary variable (either stable or not stable), not all unstable polities are alike. There is, to put it bluntly, a world of difference between an economy in which changes in the federal executive are characterized by recurrent bloodless coups and an economy in the throes of a civil war that destroys productive assets and interdicts markets. Our empirical results indicate that, in most sectors, economic activity was little affected by instability until the point at which a full-scale civil war broke out. The civil war of 1914–17 destroyed the country's rail system and hence prevented factor and product markets from operating. Once the rail system was restored, economic activity resumed at its old levels and rates of growth, even though political instability, in the sense of coups, political murders, military rebellions, and even civil wars, persisted for another decade.

Second, instability will affect different industries to varying degrees depending on the specific technological and organizational features of those industries. In fact, there are circumstances under which asset holders have a stronger bargaining position against the government when the polity is unstable. As we explore in Chapters 6 and 7 (on petroleum and mining, respectively), such cases occur under the following set of conditions: an industry provides a significant portion of government tax revenues, the government cannot nationalize and run the industry in the short run because there is knowledge of specific technologies that cannot be easily obtained, and the owners of firms can easily coordinate their actions. In this situation, asset holders can easily mitigate attempts to reduce their property rights or increase taxes. In the cases we examine, in fact, they actually persuaded the government to ignore constitutionally mandated property rights reforms and to lower their tax rates.

Third, political instability does not necessarily translate into instability of the property rights system. The specific features of the political coalitions that enforce property rights in different industries will have an important effect on whether changes in government can have any effect on the policies that affect property rights and the income from property rights. In a system in which all property rights are enforced as private goods, the commitment mechanism that constrains government opportunism is the threat that crucial political supporters of the government will defect from the coalition because their rents have been interrupted or reduced. If it is the case that any government that may come to power needs the political support of that particular group, then asset holders who share rents with that group can rest assured that no government, regardless of its stated ideology, will try to reduce their property rights. From their point of view, governments may come and go, but the underlying property rights system will be unchanged.

The other argument we make in this book is a methodological statement about history and the social sciences. The social sciences are fundamentally about the study of social processes – the ways that human beings interact and the institutions that structure those interactions *over time*. Thus, social scientists do not really have a choice regarding the use of history – their interest in change over time gives them little choice but to make historical arguments. The real choice for social scientists is whether the historical arguments they make are supported by systematically gathered and carefully analyzed evidence, or whether they are supported by "stylized facts."[24]

At the same time, coherent history requires a theoretical framework and set of analytic tools that draws from the social sciences. Historians do not really have a choice regarding the use of quantitative evidence and the analytic tools necessary to analyze that evidence. At some point, the construction of historical narratives requires the discussion of trends,

---

[24] "Stylized facts" are facts that may or may not be true, but are taken as true for the sake of the argument.

frequencies, and distributions. The real choice they confront is whether the inferences they draw are the product of systematic methods or vague impressions. Similarly, historians do not really have a choice regarding the use of theory. Writing a coherent narrative requires them to adopt a scheme by which to order facts and events and explain the causal relationships among them. Whether they realize it or not, the scheme they employ to do this constitutes a theory. The real choice historians face is whether the theory they employ is implicit or explicit, vague or clearly specified, confused or logically consistent. In sum, we argue that the study of social processes requires the integration of tools and methods from what have come to be thought of as distinct disciplines. We would submit that there is much to be gained by the integration of these disciplines into a single, coherent approach to historical social science.

2

Theory

Instability, Credible Commitments, and Growth

All governments – stable and unstable – face a commitment problem: if they are strong enough to arbitrate property rights, they are also strong enough to confiscate them. If the population does not believe that the government will refrain from exercising its power, then it will not invest. If there is no investment, there will be little economic activity, and there will be insufficient tax revenues to sustain the government.[1]

The commitment problem is essentially a problem of contract enforcement. In a stable political system, a sovereign government offers property rights protection in exchange for some kind of benefit, typically a stream of tax revenues, from the holders of those property rights. The government and the asset holders assume contractual obligations, much in the same way that any two individuals or corporate bodies can. In a contract between two private parties, of course, the government, typically through the court system, ultimately serves as the third-party enforcer of the contract.[2] A thorny problem arises, however, when the government is itself a party to the contract: the government has a monopoly over the enforcement of property rights but will only enforce those rights when it is in its interest to do so. Even if there is a promise of full enforcement, a sovereign government will be tempted to break it afterward. Private actors can, of course, anticipate government opportunism and therefore choose to invest less or not at all. In short, the crux of the commitment problem

---

[1] For a discussion of the commitment problem, and an introduction to the literature, see Chapter 1, especially note 2.

[2] There are limits, of course, even to the effectiveness of the government as an enforcer of contracts. The cost of enforcing contracts, even when a court system is available, is one of the reasons why firms exist. It is also one of the reasons why firms vertically integrate. We return to the logic of vertical integration, and its implications for government-private contracts, later in this chapter.

is precisely the enforcement of the contractual obligations assumed by a government.

Political disorder exacerbates the commitment problem. In contrast to political stability, governments under siege, or factions aspiring to be governments, cannot afford to tie their hands. This produces two problems for asset holders. First, they cannot know with any degree of certainty the content of government policies in the future. Second, asset holders know that the government has strong predatory incentives concerning property rights – regardless of its stated ideology. If the government is not predatory, someone else will be, and will then use those resources to overthrow the government.

The implication is that political instability should bring economic activity to a halt. Yet as Chapter 1 discussed, the cross-country regression literature cannot find a statistically significant and robust relationship between instability and growth. Political instability does not produce economic collapse or even economic stagnation. Some studies detect a correlation between instability and *slow growth* (a very weak form of the hypothesized relationship between instability and growth), but those results are extremely fragile to even the most minor alterations in data sets, conditioning variables, and regression specifications. Tests of Granger causality cast further doubt on whatever correlations can be detected, producing a result contrary to expectations: there is a *positive* relationship between instability and investment.

The empirical paradox of growth amid political instability suggests that there must be solutions to the commitment problem other than the two standard models presented in the literature to date: stationary banditry and limited government. As we discussed in Chapter 1, a growing economy with an unstable polity could not fall into either of these two categories.

What solution to the commitment problem could be robust to instability? How would such a system function? To answer that question we draw on two related, but distinct, literatures: the literature on the microeconomic analysis of contract and property rights; and the literature on the commitment problem.[3] Both recognize that there is no strict requirement that governments enforce property rights universally (as a public

---

[3] Representative works on the commitment problem can be found in Chapter 1, note 2. Representative works on the microeconomics of property rights include Barzel (1997); North and Thomas (1973); Brennan and Buchanan (1985); Eggertsson (1990); Mantzavinos (2001); Pejovich (1990); and Kasper and Streit (1999).

good). Nevertheless, the political and economic implications of selective property rights enforcement have not been fully explored to date. The extant models tend to be of special cases, such as North, Summerhill, and Weingast's discussion of the relationship between selective enforcement and political disorder in 19-century Latin America, and Weingast's discussion of the sovereign debt problem.[4] We are, in short, a long way from any general theory about the economics and politics of governance systems in which property rights enforcement is selective rather than universal.

We therefore build upon the extant literatures on property rights and credible commitments in order to explore how a governance system in which property rights are enforced as a private good can produce positive rates of investment and growth. We also explore the conditions under which such a system would be robust to political instability.

We note that the extant literature on the microeconomics of property and contract rights stresses that systems that lack universal enforcement of property rights will be economically inefficient.[5] We are in complete agreement with that insight. The system we propose – which we call vertical political integration (VPI) – is clearly a theoretically second-best solution to the commitment problem. Indeed, the system we have in mind requires the creation of rent-seeking coalitions, is economically inefficient, has negative consequences for the distribution of income, implies political authoritarianism, and requires that the government be an inefficient provider of public services. We note, however, that these theoretical implications mirror the empirical reality of many countries around the world. Thus, our task is to understand why such systems are so common, and why they are able to reproduce themselves even when they are perturbed by political revolution.

---

[4] See North, Summerhill, et al. (2000); Weingast (1997a).

[5] For example, Pejovich (1998), pp. 39, 60–61, requires that all citizens be subject to the same laws and, by implication, to the same protection of property rights. In fact, property rights are conceived as being a "constitutional guarantee." Eggertsson (1990), p. 59–60, notes that the state becomes the single agent of society in a contract in which the state protects property rights for the rest of society. A similar view is held by Brennan and Buchanan (1985), who argue that agreements between the state and citizens must be inclusive. Pejovich (1990) also notes that, except for providing public goods and solving externalities, the role of the state is to maintain a competitive environment, which requires, inter alia, private ownership of all resources. Moreover, he argues that entrepreneurs need indiscriminate protection of property rights to invest (pp. 29, 79). Kasper and Streit (1999) argue that if "the principle of universality is abandoned ... property users will incur rapidly rising transaction costs. ... A legal order that erodes property rights tends to clash with a competitive economic order."

Theory

CREDIBLE COMMITMENTS AS PRIVATE CONTRACTS

We begin by making clear what we mean by property rights and the associated role of government. A property right consists of three, conceptually distinct rights: the right to use an asset, the right to earn income from an asset and contract with other individuals regarding that asset, and the right to alienate or sell the asset. From the point of view of asset holders, all three rights are important – all three have an impact on the value of their property. Governments play two roles regarding these rights: they specify property rights, and they enforce property rights.

Governments have strong incentives to *specify* property rights as private goods. All other things being equal, the more clearly defined are the rights to use, earn income from, and alienate an asset, the greater the value of that asset – and the greater the stream of tax revenues that can be produced by that asset. Not surprisingly, governments tend to specify property rights as private goods. When a government specifies a property right, it is, in essence, defining what belongs to one actor or group of actors, precisely to exclude the public from having rights over that asset. That is, it is assigning an exclusive right over a given asset to a particular economic agent. This is not to say that there are not occasions when the specification of property rights leaves some elements of those rights in the public domain.[6] When governments pass laws that affect generic groups of economic agents, as opposed to a particular asset holder, property rights will have some public goods characteristics.[7] It is also not to say that there are not occasions when governments specify property rights that overlap, where more than one economic agent has a usufruct right to an asset.[8] It is to say, however, that, with the exception of socialist economies, property rights are *first and foremost* specified in nearly all property rights systems as private goods.

When it comes to the *enforcement* of property rights, however, the strategy of the government is less clear. Governments can enforce property rights as a public good by protecting the rights of asset holders indiscriminately, without consideration of the identity of the particular asset holder. They can also choose to enforce property rights selectively, enforcing the

---

[6] For a full discussion, see Barzel (1997).

[7] An example would be an import tariff. Barring some other action by government to limit competition, the effects of the tariff are nonexcludable – they enhance the value of the assets of all domestic producers in that industry.

[8] A right of way on an otherwise private parcel of land is a common example of an overlapping set of rights.

21

rights of only some special group of asset holders. In this case, property rights enforcement is a private, not a public good.

We make the following four assumptions about the interaction between governments and asset holders. First, governments may chose to enforce property rights as a private good. This may be because a particular government is not able, as a practical matter, to protect everyone's property rights. Alternatively, governments may manipulate the level of enforcement to fit their needs. Indeed, under certain circumstances, a government might find it in its interest to protect only some subset of society's property rights, even if the government had the ability to protect property rights universally.

Second, asset holders do not demand that the government protect everyone's property rights. Indeed, it is not clear that an individual asset holder should always demand the universal protection of property rights. On the one hand, an asset holder can receive utility from the universal protection of property rights, because this makes her assets more liquid, and therefore more valuable. On the other hand, if selective enforcement grants the asset holder market power, then it may be more profitable to demand less than universal enforcement. Between these two possibilities, we suggest that it is realistic to assume that asset holders care first and foremost about their own property rights. Any profit-maximizing actor would readily accept the exclusive protection of her property rights, providing that it produced net benefits to that actor.[9]

Third, asset holders do not make binary choices between production and no production, implying that they face either a certain or a null risk of predation on their property rights. Rather, asset holders make decisions based on a continuum of risk assessments. This means that asset holders will tolerate a certain level of predation risk as long as they expect some positive level of profits in compensation. In short, some asset holders will invest even when they are not operating with absolute certainty that the government will enforce their property rights as a private good.

Fourth, we assume that asset holders cannot perfectly monitor the impact of the government's actions or policies upon their property rights. In other words, we assume the existence of information asymmetries between the government and asset holders. The reason for these asymmetries

---

[9] Asset holders may, in fact, have an incentive to influence government to offer such protection on a selective basis. This is reminiscent of the literature on captured agencies, in which economic agents use the power of the state for private gain. See Stigler (1971) and Peltzman (1976).

is that there are numerous margins on which governments can tinker with property rights and the revenues they generate. Governments do not have to redefine the rules regarding the possession, use, and transfer of property in order to reduce property rights. They can do so through a broad range of policies or regulations that affect the ability of those who hold property rights to earn returns from that property. These include tax regimes, tariffs, labor laws, monetary policies, exchange rates, and a whole host of other regulations that can effectively reduce the returns to property rights. From the point of view of asset holders, these are crucial because an asset that provides no revenue is, by definition, valueless – even if the putative right to the property has not been abrogated.[10] As a practical matter, it is difficult for asset holders to monitor the government on every policy dimension that affects the value of their property rights.[11] Both the intent of reforms and their actual economic consequences can be difficult for asset holders to determine ex ante. This is especially the case if the government is simultaneously reforming multiple regulatory institutions, some of which potentially enhance the value of property rights and some of which reduce them.

Implications

Our assumptions imply that the commitment problem is *not necessarily* about the interaction between a government and all of society. Governments can offer selective property rights protection in exchange for some type of economic benefit (typically tax revenues) from a particular asset holder or organized group of asset holders.[12] The government can

---

[10] Permit us a discussion of import tariffs to make the distinction between property rights and the returns from property clear. Imagine a situation in which a particular industry has grown under a protective tariff. Industrialists own the factories and the related assets (buildings, land, and the like) *and* they earn a stream of revenues from those assets. Now imagine that the government eliminates the tariff, pushing product prices down below the level where industrialists can earn a positive rate of return on their assets. The property rights of industrialists have not been abrogated – they still own the factories. Their returns, however, have been reduced, and this, in turn, reduces the value of the factories.

[11] We also assume that these property rights are defined for specific domains. Governments, of course, define property rights in various domains. The informational asymmetries can therefore be characterized as the asset holder's lack of complete knowledge about how government operates in its entirety.

[12] We assume that in cases where the government is making a contract with a group of asset holders that those asset holders can solve coordination problems within the group. Thus, one would expect in such a system to observe the formation of various producers' associations, commissions, conventions, or other organizations.

protect property rights in much the same way as a mafia: it can protect some individuals' property rights (in exchange for a share of the rents generated by those selective rights) at the same time that it abrogates the property rights of others.[13]

From the point of view of asset holders, this selective arrangement has a potential disadvantage: their assets are less liquid (and hence less valuable) than they would be if property rights were universally protected. As noted earlier, asset holders may nonetheless prefer such selective arrangements to obtain market power or other types of rents. These rents may be generated by the government, either by using its regulatory powers to constrain competition or by providing a subsidized input to production. What is crucial, however, is that the government must make a credible commitment to protect whatever set of property rights arrangements allows the asset holders to earn these rents.

Even if selective enforcement is promised, why should an individual asset holder believe that the government will honor that promise after the asset holder has deployed her wealth in productive assets? What keeps the government from unilaterally altering the terms of the contract (e.g., raising the tax rate), or abrogating it entirely by seizing the assets?

There are three ways that a selectively enforced contract between the government and an asset holder can be made credible. The first is when the government earns more from imposing the profit-maximizing tax rate than it would earn from abrogating the asset holder's property rights and running the industry itself.[14] This occurs, for example, when the asset holder has specialized knowledge of technologies or markets that the government cannot replicate. The government is already taxing at the profit-maximizing rate for that industry, so it will not raise the *tax rate* any further. The government will also refrain from abrogating property rights because it would earn less from running the industry itself than from taxing it at the profit-maximizing rate.[15]

---

[13] For a discussion of property rights and mafias, see Gambetta (1993). Curiously, Olson (2000) draws on Gambetta's insight about the mafia to argue that "stationary bandits" will protect property rights as a public good.

[14] We assume that governments incur costs in protecting property rights and that taxes create deadweight losses by distorting the incentives of producers. A government will therefore raise taxes only to the point that marginal increases in tax rates will yield marginal increases in *net* tax revenues.

[15] This self-enforcing solution to the commitment problem does *not* depend upon the government's desire to preserve its reputation among other potential domestic entrepreneurs. One might argue that governments that can profitably confiscate rather than tax assets might be constrained from confiscating them to preserve their

This type of self-enforcing solution to the commitment problem fundamentally depends on the superior technical know-how of the asset holder. To the extent that the government can overcome this asymmetry by learning over time, the incentives to refrain from ex post opportunism will diminish. Contracts would have an expected lifetime equal to the amount of time necessary for the government to replicate enough of the asset holder's knowledge that running the industry itself would produce more revenue for the government than leaving it in the asset holder's hands and applying the revenue-maximizing tax rate. Note that the government does not have to be able to run the industry as efficiently as the asset holder. It simply needs to be able to run the industry *efficiently enough* that the stream of revenues it earns through expropriation exceeds the stream of revenues it can earn through taxation. This implies that self-enforcing mechanisms in a system of selective property rights contracts are going to be difficult to sustain.

This means that governments and asset holders must devise mechanisms to constrain the government. One such mechanism is the proffering by the government of a hostage – an asset that would be seized by the asset holders in the event that the government reneged on its promises under the contract.[16] As a practical matter, such hostage mechanisms are very difficult to create. First, the value of the hostage would have to be sufficiently large that it exceeded the value of the stream of income that would be earned by the government from expropriating the asset holder and running the industry itself. Second, by virtue of the fact that the government is the sole arbitrator of property rights within the borders of its own territory, the assets that compose the hostage would have to be held abroad.[17]

A final – and, we shall argue, quite common – mechanism to constrain the government is a third party that can punish the government. In

reputation among other asset holders. That argument, while correct, depends on the assumption that these *other* asset holders possess some type of asset that the government cannot replicate. For an interesting discussion of this problem, in the context of foreign multinationals, see Veugelers (1993).

[16] Such hostages were quite common in antiquity, as a way to maintain peace between two rival states. The hostages in this case would often be the children of the king or other nobles, who would reside in the household of the king of the rival state. Their fate, quite literally, would be linked to their father not reneging on his agreement to keep the peace. In the modern social science literature the use of a hostage as a commitment device was first addressed by Schelling (1956).

[17] For an interesting discussion of a case where a hostage actually meets these conditions, and therefore works as a commitment mechanism, see Monaldi (2002), chaps. 4 and 5.

contracts between individuals or corporations, third-party enforcement occurs all the time: the government, usually through its judicial system, serves as the third party. A third-party enforcer is a more complicated matter when one of the parties to the contract is the government. Unless we are talking about the special (and historically rare) case of a limited government, the third party cannot be the government. If it were, the government would be acting as both party to and enforcer of the same contract.

Third-Party Enforcement

In a system in which the government is not limited by its own institutional structure, the government's conflict of interest implies that some other group or entity must fulfill the role of third-party enforcer. This third party must have both the incentive and the ability to punish the government. For that to be the case, the third party's interests must be aligned with those of the asset holder. That is, the third party's payoffs must directly depend on the ability of asset holders to obtain favorable treatment from the government. Otherwise, the third party will not have an incentive to monitor and punish the government should it behave opportunistically against the asset holder.

One requirement of such a system is that it must be incentive-compatible for all three parties – the government, the asset holder, and the third-party enforcer. The creation and distribution of rents to all three parties is the most obvious way to align the interests of all the members of the coalition. The government offers selective protection of property rights and other favorable policies to a particular group of asset holders. This property rights system allows this group of asset holders to earn returns above the competitive level. Some of the returns to the asset holder's investment are also diverted to the government, in the form of tax revenues. An additional share of the rents must also be apportioned to the third party, which will enforce the contract in exchange for this stream of rents. In short, the system we have in mind not only permits rent seeking; it requires it.

An additional requirement for this property rights system to be stable is that the third party will always be able to police and enforce the arrangements between the other parties to the contract. This requirement has three implications. First, a third party that is well organized – that is to say, when the individuals who compose a third party can coordinate their actions – will be more effective than an unorganized third party whose actions must be coordinated by moves of the asset holders. Second, an institutionalized third party (or third parties) will be more effective than a group of individuals. If the third party was an individual or set of individuals, asset holders would not necessarily believe that government predation could be deterred in the future when key individuals passed away. An institutionalized third party, however, will exist beyond the life-span of its individual members. It will therefore increase the expectation of other actors that third-party enforcement will be long-lasting. Finally, a third party that is embedded into the governance structure will be more effective than one that exists outside of it. Such a third party will not only be able to punish the government if it reneges on the contract, but it may even be able to prevent the government from even contemplating making such a move. The most effective third parties will therefore be institutionalized bodies directly linked to decision makers (or *the* decision maker) inside the government.[18]

Who could the third party be? In some cases, the third party could be a foreign state. This tends to occur when one party to the contract is a citizen of that foreign state (usually a very wealthy and influential citizen) or is the foreign state itself. Of course, the foreign government must meet the requirements of being able to exert punishment. It is more common, however, that the third party be a domestic group that is not itself an asset holder and can credibly threaten the government if its rents are interrupted. Two crucial elements will determine the effectiveness of this third party. First, the third party must be a group that is politically essential for the government. Second, asset holders must align the third party's interests with their own. That is, the stream of rents earned by the third party must come *directly* from the asset holders.

A system such as the one we describe will involve a complicated balance between third parties, governments, and asset holders. Asset holders need third parties to balance the threat posed to their property rights by the government. The government, paradoxically, needs third parties as well. If there were no third parties to enforce the property rights system, commitments made by the government would not be credible and there would be little or no investment. A logical implication of this system is

---

[18] Paradoxically, the more effective third-party enforcers are, the more difficult it will be for a society with a selectively enforced property rights system to make the transition to limited government. The reason is simple: an institutionally embedded third-party enforcer will have the incentives and the ability to thwart reforms of the political system that will diminish the revenues it receives for providing property rights enforcement.

that there will be circumstances under which it is in the interests of both the government and the asset holders that third parties be extremely powerful. The cost of government opportunism must increase as the value of the assets vulnerable to expropriation increases.[19] This, in turn, produces another paradox: extremely powerful governments cannot make credible commitments through the use of a third-party enforcer. For this system to work, third parties must be able to lodge credible threats. If the government is so powerful that no third party (or group of third parties) can credibly threaten it, then asset holders will not take the government's commitments as credible.

The balance between third parties, governments, and asset holders is made even more complicated by the fact that a very powerful third party (vis-à-vis the government) will also be a threat to asset holders. If the third party is too powerful, it can replace the government and itself become a predatory threat to asset holders. In that case, the commitment problem remains. Only the identity of which group is predatory will have changed. This implies that there are strong incentives for asset holders to avoid potential third-party enforcers who can easily eliminate the government. It also implies that asset holders will want to constrain the rents earned by the third party – lest it use those rents to grow in strength.

Even if the third party and government are of roughly equal strength, there is a danger that they will collude and jointly expropriate the asset holders. Two factors mitigate – but do not entirely preclude – this possibility. The first is that third-party enforcers have a strong incentive to provide protection across a wide array of industries or economic sectors. The more asset holders they protect, the more rents they will receive. If a third-party enforcer colludes with the government and allows predation in one industry, its promises to provide protection in other industries will lose credibility. Asset holders in those other industries would therefore break the implicit contracts with the third party and would recruit a new third party to protect their property rights. Unless the payoff from collusion in the first industry is larger than the stream of rents a third party would earn by providing protection across a broad number

---

[19] This insight parallels a similar insight that Weingast had about the sovereign debt problem. In his formulation, the greater the punishment that lenders could levy on a sovereign, the more confident lenders would be, and hence the more funds they would lend. In his discussion, the costs imposed by lenders on a sovereign who transgresses are produced by sets of formal institutions. See Weingast (1997b).

of industries, the third party would refrain from accepting a collusion offer from the government. In sum, competition by third-party enforcers to offer "protection" in various markets minimizes – but does not entirely eliminate – the incentives to collude with the government.[20]

A second factor mitigating the possibility of collusion between the government and the third party is that they have strong incentives not to let one another get too powerful, lest one of them later turn on the other and seize its share of the rents. Collusion by them against the asset holder may, perversely, produce exactly that result. The problem is that the government is almost always going to have better information than the third party about the value of the rents that are being retained by the asset holder. The third party knows this and thus may assume that any collusion offer made to it likely entails a disproportionate share of the asset holder's rents being awarded to the government. This disproportionality will, in a future stage, produce an imbalance in the total resources available to the government and the third party, allowing the former to move successfully against the latter and cut it out of the game entirely. A metaphor from Brooklyn may illustrate the point. Imagine two small-time gangs, each skimming off 5 percent of the gross income earned by a candy store. The first gang may tell the other that it won't have to go around to the candy store anymore because the first gang will insure that the second will get its 5 percent. The problem is that the second gang knows that the first would not make such an offer unless it was going to get substantially more than its original 5 percent – which it could use to buy more guns and recruit more gangsters and eventually cut the second gang out of the picture altogether.

VERTICAL POLITICAL INTEGRATION

The system we have just described (a rent-seeking coalition made up of asset holders, a government too weak to establish a despotic state, and a group that receives rents in exchange for enforcing the contract between the asset holders and the government) assumes that the asset holders and the third party can easily monitor the government. Such monitoring may, however, be quite costly and imperfect. As a practical matter, asset holders

---

[20] Even if a third party monopolized protection across all markets, it would take an extremely powerful government to be able to expropriate all industries simultaneously. Piecemeal expropriation – even in collusion with the third-party enforcer – would only prompt all remaining asset holders to cease investment and liquidate their assets in advance of expropriation.

may find it difficult to estimate the consequences of government policy changes ex ante, particularly when the government is engaging in multiple institutional reforms simultaneously. In other words, there are information asymmetries that provide the government with numerous margins to behave opportunistically vis-à-vis asset holders.

In such a situation, it may be difficult for asset holders to assess the net impact of multiple reforms of the laws that govern their property rights and revenues from those property rights. They will only be able to do so ex post, and even then their analyses will be clouded by any number of intervening events that will affect their revenues. In addition, the consequences of these simultaneous changes in property rights may affect different asset holders in varying degrees. Some may be better off as a result of the reforms. Some may be worse off. In short, the government may well know that it is behaving opportunistically, but the asset holders *as a group* can at best only know this ex post. Finally, precisely because such behavior takes place on the margin, the use of a third party to threaten the government over the new property rights system may be too blunt an instrument for the task facing asset holders.

How can asset holders check marginal opportunistic behavior by the government in the presence of information asymmetries? An insight into this problem is provided by the literature on transactions and contracts between private firms. Private firms often possess incentives to engage in opportunistic behavior vis-à-vis one another.[21] Often the scope for opportunistic behavior depends upon whether the contracting firms can monitor each other. If information asymmetries between the two firms are high, then firm A can never be certain whether firm B is behaving opportunistically, or is just trying to renegotiate the contract because of events beyond its control. Under these circumstances, vertical integration between the two firms can reduce the incentives for opportunistic behavior because information asymmetries are lower within a single, merged firm than between two separate ones.[22]

---

[21] Such opportunism typically occurs when firms have formed specialized relationships, especially where a monopolist provides a crucial input to a second monopolist. Moreover, both firms have made substantial sunk investments in specific assets that cannot be redeployed to another use. Both firms, therefore, have an incentive to engage in opportunistic behavior to appropriate the value produced by the specialized assets – *even after they have signed a contract.* Under such circumstances, the costs of contract enforcement are very high. See Klein, Crawford, et al. (1978); Williamson (1985); and Hart (1995). A classic case is the sugar industry. See Dye (1998).

[22] See Arrow (1974); Green and Porter (1984); and Riordan (1990).

Obviously, it is not possible for a government and an asset holder to form a "firm." It is possible, however, for the line between the government and private asset holders to become blurred – so blurred, in fact, that as a practical matter it is difficult to distinguish precisely where the government ends and the asset holders begin.

The exact form that this "vertical integration" takes will vary. Governments may ask private bodies to write policies or the heads of the government's executive agencies might be drawn from the most prominent asset holders in the country. It is not a strict requirement, however, that there be formal organizational innovations for effective integration between government and asset holders. In authoritarian polities such integration might be accomplished informally. If a dictator can specify property rights by decree and enforce them at his whim, then all that needs to happen is that a group of asset holders is close enough to him that they have his ear.

Asset holders gain three things from integration. First, they gain the opportunity to shape the policies that govern *their* own activities. That is, they obtain the ability to specify the property rights system in their industry. Second, they obtain the ability to monitor the government to ensure that it is not trying to alter these policies. That is, they increase the probability that the government will enforce *their* property rights. Third, they gain the ability to signal the government if they detect attempts at opportunistic behavior. What the government gains is the confidence of a select group of asset holders that *their* property rights are secure. These asset holders will now be more likely to deploy more of their wealth in productive investment, thereby generating tax revenues for the government.

The process of vertical political integration – the blurring of the lines between the asset holders and the government – is not in and of itself a commitment mechanism. VPI is an institutional innovation that redefines the interaction (i.e., contract) between governments and asset holders. Like all contracts between a government and an asset holder, VPI must be enforceable if it is to be credible. After all, what would keep the government from simply dissolving the organizations that allowed asset holders to shape and monitor the policies that affect their property rights? Enforcement of these arrangements would have to come from the same mechanisms that we discussed earlier in regard to other contracts between the government and the asset holders: asset holders' specialized knowledge of markets or technology, the proffering of a hostage, or third-party enforcement.

Before discussing the full implications of VPI, we wish to stress that there is nothing inevitable about its evolution. Obviously, a VPI agreement that is enforced by an institutionally embedded third-party enforcer will provide the most credible commitment of any of the options available. This is not to say that this combination of monitoring and enforcement mechanisms is a unique solution to the commitment problem when governments are not required to provide property rights on a universal basis. There are, in our view, multiple possible outcomes, some of which will involve VPI and some not, some of which will involve third parties and some not.

Both VPI and the development of institutionally embedded third parties will likely come out of an iterative process in which asset holders learn how to constrain the government from behaving opportunistically. It is, in short, a historical process in which each of the players in the game – the government, the asset holders, and (where applicable) third parties – continually try to garner for themselves larger shares of the available pool of revenues generated by the property rights system.

Characteristics of Vertical Political Integration

What are the political and economic implications of a fully developed VPI system? How are VPI systems different from limited government and stationary banditry?

In stark contrast to limited government, under VPI the security of property rights is a function of the amount of rent earned and distributed. Rent seeking may occur in limited government but is not essential to its functioning. In VPI, on the other hand, the asset holders must receive a stream of rents in order to induce investment. The government must receive a portion of these rents, in order to finance its own operations. Rents must also be transferred to the third-party enforcers; otherwise they will have no incentive to check the government should it attempt to abrogate or reduce the property rights of the asset holders.

In further contrast to limited government (and stationary banditry), in VPI systems the sanction mechanisms that constrain opportunistic behavior by the government are ad hoc. All governance systems require sanction mechanisms that force the government to obey its own laws: the law is never, in and of itself, a commitment device. Under stationary banditry, the sanction mechanism is very weak: it is simply the ruler's own long-run self-interest in maximizing his wealth. Because he is already taxing at the profit-maximizing rate, increases in taxes (or reductions in property rights on other margins) will automatically produce a drop in tax revenues in the long run. Under limited government, the sanction mechanisms are legally codified: The limits on the authority and discretion of government actors is specified in the law; the sanction mechanisms for actors who exceed these limits are specified in the law; and the content of the sanctions themselves are specified in the law. The government, in such a system, is forced to obey its own laws because different actors in the government have the authority (and the incentive) to sanction one another in legally prescribed ways. In a VPI system, however, neither the sanctions nor the mechanisms for their application are legally codified. They are ad hoc, created out of the interaction of coalition members. Sanctions might include the open rebellion of the third party against the government. They might also simply be a threat by the third party that it will defect from the coalition, leaving the government vulnerable to challenges by political competitors. What is key, however, is that these sanctions do not rely on the ruler's long-run interest in the maximization of his own wealth (such a mechanism would require the ruler to have a very long time horizon, but that would require that he has eliminated all potential political competitors), and they do not rely on self-enforcing formal institutions. The sanctions are, instead, sets of implicit and explicit threats.[23]

The fact that the sanction mechanisms of VPI systems are not legally codified does not mean, however, that the law is completely meaningless. The government and the integrated asset holders will almost inevitably need to codify legally the property rights of the latter. What then keeps everyone else in society from taking advantage of the codification of the property rights system and investing their wealth precisely in those sectors where property rights have been most clearly drawn – the very sectors dominated by the integrated asset holders? Why won't the positive externalities generated by the codification of the integrated asset holders' property rights produce market entry that dissipates their rents?

Such positive externalities will be minimized in a VPI system for two reasons. First, property rights can be specified so as to limit competition. Governments, of every variety, do this all the time when they award temporary monopolies through the patent system. In a VPI system, however, other options to limit competition are available to create barriers to entry to potential competition. One common technique is a monopoly on some crucial input of production. This can be especially effective if that input

---

[23] This is not to say that VPI is characterized by omnipresent violence. Quite the contrary, violence only occurs in a stable VPI system when the government breaches the contract with asset holders. Because the government knows that the outcome of such a breach will be violence, it does not breach the contract in the first place.

has to be imported and can be made subject to import permits. Another common technique is preferential tax treatment. The following heuristic example illustrates the point. Suppose that an asset holder makes a deal with a government that she will receive tariff protection in exchange for founding a new industry. The government is also interested in obtaining some of the rents generated from protection for itself, so it establishes an income or excise tax on the industry. The asset holder knows that the existence of the import tariff will generate domestic competitors, so she obtains a full or partial exemption from the income or excise tax. New competitors, however, will be subject to the full effect of these taxes. The result would be higher than normal returns for the integrated asset holder, trade protection for the unintegrated asset holders, and a stream of tax revenues for the government.

Second, it may be the case that the government and the integrated asset holders cannot successfully *specify* property rights so as to eliminate all competition. This is particularly the case in economic activities that are geographically dispersed, that have small minimum efficient scales of production, that do not rely on proprietary technology or imported inputs to production – agriculture being the most obvious example. The point is that they may not need to *specify* property rights so as to eliminate all positive externalities. Remember that the government must also *enforce* property rights and can do so on a selective basis. Other individuals may be tempted to deploy their capital in a particular industry that has been opened up by an integrated asset holder, but they have no reason to believe that the government will enforce their property rights. In fact, they have every reason to believe that the government will do exactly the opposite. The greater the degree to which they compete with the integrated asset holder the more likely it will be that that asset holder will demand that the government abrogate their rights, tax away all of their income, or transfer their property to the asset holder.

It is unclear whether VPI is more, or less, efficient than stationary banditry. Neither stationary bandits nor VPI coalitions are trying to maximize the polity's total economic output. Stationary bandits are trying to maximize the ruler's total tax revenues. VPI coalitions are trying to maximize the rents earned by multiple individual players (some of which are diverted to the ruler as tax revenues). Whether VPI will create fewer distortions than stationary banditry will depend on whether the integrated asset holders (as a group) realize that the net effect of all their rent seeking is to make their customers poorer, and that there will be a point at which the losses from having poorer customers outweigh the gains from extracting additional rents. The exact results will most probably depend on how many different VPI coalitions, spread across different industries, there are in any given polity.

What is clear, however, is that VPI is less economically efficient than limited government. First, the requirement that rents be generated and distributed through the political system means that there will be a serious misallocation of resources in the economy. Industries will exist that would not exist otherwise, monopolies and oligopolies will exist in industries that should be more competitive, and opportunities will be denied to entrepreneurs with the required skills and assets but without political access or protection. Second, the rents necessary to sustain VPI must come from somewhere: usually everyone and anyone outside the coalition.[24] Thus, VPI has negative distributional consequences. Third, VPI coalitions will only be stable when the government earns rents above and beyond the cost of providing public services. If the government is not earning such rents, then it will have an incentive to abrogate property rights. Because the government protects property rights at a less than socially optimal rate, and it charges a higher price for that protection (in terms of rents), this implies that the government will be an inefficient provider of public services.

VPI also has negative political consequences compared with limited government. The very nature of VPI – a series of contracts between select economic agents and the government – means that the particular features of those contracts cannot be debated and revised through a transparent and open process. The government must be able to make deals in smoke-filled rooms without the necessity of public review and approval. This is especially crucial because VPI governments are inefficient providers of public services. In a democratic system, the electorate would remove the government and replace it with a government that was more efficient. In addition, electoral democracy and its accoutrements make it easier for the losers from rent seeking to mobilize and defend their interests. In short, VPI is not consistent with high levels of political democracy.

Readers may ask how VPI is different from "crony capitalism." The answer is that crony capitalism is a particular variant of VPI. In both crony systems and VPI the government enforces property rights as a private good. In both crony systems and VPI there is a blurring of the

---

[24] We assume that not all groups in society can solve the coordination problems involved in making credible threats against the government, and therefore rents can be extracted from them with impunity.

lines between asset holders and the government. The difference between a crony system and VPI is that the third-party enforcers under a crony system are individuals who are themselves members of the government, whereas under VPI they may be any group in society that provides the government with crucial political support.

The distinction is crucial in three senses. First, as we pointed out earlier, the problem of collusion between the third party and the government always looms. In VPI it is mitigated (but not completely eliminated) by mutual distrust between the government and the third party, as well as by the third party's desire to obtain protection rents across a broad number of markets. In a crony system, however, the element of mutual distrust is attenuated because there is substantial overlap between the government and the third party. From the point of view of the asset holder, they may not even appear to be independent entities. Precisely because the government and the third party may be overlapping sets, collusion is easy. They do not fear the growth of one another's power because they are, in many senses, one and the same. They can therefore demand continually larger shares of the rents held by the asset holder. As the histories of the Philippines under Marcos, Nicaragua under Somoza, and Indonesia under Suharto make clear, this is not just a theoretical possibility. Second, it means that crony systems are more fragile. In a crony system, the enforcement of the contracts between government and asset holders are dependent upon the existence of *particular individuals* (who are members of the government or of their families), rather than organized groups. Obviously, institutionalized groups are more durable than individuals, who have finite life-spans and whose power may be tied to particular idiosyncratic factors. Finally, precisely because third-party enforcement in a crony system is performed by particular individuals in the government, crony systems are less robust to instability than VPI. Once those individuals have been eliminated from the game (by being deposed, assassinated, or forced into exile), there is no longer third-party enforcement of the property rights system. There may be particular features of particular industries that check the government's predatory behavior, which we discuss in detail later, but, in the absence of these features, property rights are in the public domain.

VPI AND POLITICAL INSTABILITY

Are VPI contracts credible if governments continually change hands violently and unpredictably? The answer is yes – provided certain conditions hold.

There are, in fact, conditions under which political instability may actually make the government's commitment to asset holders more credible. This occurs if all three of the following conditions hold: if asset holders have private knowledge of technologies or markets that makes it difficult for the government to expropriate and run the industry in the short run; if the revenues provided by the asset holders are so crucial to the government that even their brief interruption could cause the government to fall; and if the asset holders can coordinate their actions, allowing them to simultaneously shut down production and its associated tax revenues.[25] In the context of an unstable polity, these conditions mean that opportunistic behavior on the part of the government will translate into a collapse in tax revenues – and the replacement of the government by a competing faction. The government, of course, knows this. It therefore refrains from opportunistic behavior. Asset holders in that industry also know it and therefore take the government's commitments to them as credible.

Even if these conditions do not hold, commitments made by governments can still be credible – provided that one condition holds regarding third party enforcement: any *potential government* requires the political support of the existing third-party enforcer. Changes in the identity of the government – even sudden and violent changes – under this circumstance will have no effect on the property rights system. Presidents, prime ministers, and cabinets may be shuffled willy-nilly. In fact, they may even be shuffled at gunpoint. From the point of view of the integrated asset holders, however, there will have been no change in the institutions that govern the specification and enforcement of their property rights. They will behave as if the polity was stable.

Is there a threshold of instability at which VPI no longer functions? VPI breaks down when third-party enforcement is no longer credible. This breakdown occurs if any of three conditions holds. The first is when the government's time discount increases to the point that it is willing to risk sanction by the third-party enforcer. This happens when the government comes to perceive that the probability of being overthrown is above a certain threshold unless it confiscates assets and uses those assets to defend itself. In that case, the value of the stream of rents declines relative to the stable value of immediate confiscation. If this decline is of sufficient magnitude, the government will switch from honoring the deal with the asset holders (and implicitly with the third party) and will confiscate the assets.

---

[25] For an example of this type of asymmetric holdup, see Chapter 6, on the oil industry in Mexico during the 1910s and 1920s.

It is no longer concerned about the loss of the third party's support (or a rebellion by the third party), because it perceives that the probability of losing power – even with the support of the third party – has risen too high.

The second condition is if asset holders or third-party enforcers can no longer coordinate their actions. If political violence should eliminate their coordination mechanisms, then battling factions can prey on assets with impunity. Once that happens, asset holders will no longer invest, although fixed assets that cannot be redeployed elsewhere will continue to be operated. The assets may be run either by the old owners, or by the political factions that have confiscated them. (See Chapters 5 and 8 for examples.)

The third condition under which extreme violence may disrupt VPI is if a new government does not need the support of the previous third-party enforcer. Obviously, threats of punishment by this third party will no longer constrain the government. This situation most intuitively occurs when the third-party enforcers are dead on the battlefield. A less extreme case occurs when the new government is invulnerable to the previous third-party enforcer used to threaten the government. For example, third-party enforcement by a dictator's cronies may no longer be effective once the dictator loses power.

Without third-party enforcement, or a self-enforcing solution based on the kind of private production knowledge we discussed earlier, property rights can no longer be protected. Investment will contract or will not occur. Only those investments in which the rate of return exceeds the rate at which investors discount the probability of expropriation will take place. The result of the decline of investment will be a contraction in economic activity. This will, in turn, mean that there will be diminished rents for political combatants to extract. Without access to rents, the only source of resources to finance military action is the further confiscation of assets. Confiscation will, in turn, provoke its victims to back opposing factions – which will need to prey on further victims to finance their military activities, ad infinitum. In short, the society could become locked into a coup trap: a self-replicating cycle of violence, predation, and zero growth.[26]

What options are available to exit a coup trap? Limited government is not an option. The historical record provides *no* examples of a polity that made a direct leap from political instability to limited government. The reason is not hard to divine. If a political faction violently fighting for its existence creates institutions to tie its hands and prevent predation, a less scrupulous faction that does not hesitate to use predation in order to gain

---

[26] The logic of such coup traps is discussed in Londregan and Poole (1990).

resources to direct against its opponents will defeat it. Hence, any promise made by a government not to become predatory is known in advance not to be credible. Everyone knows that political contenders under instability must engage in predation in order to remain in the game.[27]

Despotism is also a problematic exit from political instability. One faction may engage in widespread predation and use the resulting resources to slaughter all potential sources of opposition and seize uncontested power. The problem is that in order to make a credible commitment to protect property rights the new government would have to accomplish two very difficult tasks: it would have to eliminate *all* of its enemies and establish a regime that is perceived by the populace to have an extremely long time horizon. Satisfying both conditions is not impossible, but it is a rare feat in world history. Despotic governments are common following periods of political instability. Very few, however, have succeeded in producing growth at anything more than a very modest level.

It is easier to reconstitute a VPI system that has been disrupted by extreme instability than it is to create a despotic government capable of sustaining economic growth. Unlike establishing despotism, reconstituting VPI does not require the government to eliminate all its political enemies. Nor does it require the populace to perceive that the government will be long-lived. As long as asset holders perceive that there will be enforcement by a third party of the property rights system, the identity, ideology, and expected duration of the government do not matter. Both of the essential preconditions of economic growth under despotism are therefore relaxed.

The only essential requirement to reconstitute VPI is that there be a shared belief system about how a VPI coalition is formed. As long as this condition holds, VPI can be reconstituted even if the identities of the government, the asset holders, and the third-party enforcers have changed. Third-party enforcers can be eliminated by military action. Some subgroups of asset holders can be eliminated as a social class. Nevertheless, it

---

[27] It may appear that the Glorious Revolution of 1688 and the American Revolution of 1775–83 violate this prediction. Close examination reveals that the transition from instability to limited government was slow and characterized by governments that were neither despotic nor limited. In England the constitutional arrangement of 1688 did not immediately spring into its final form. Rather, it came at the end of 50 years of decreasing civil strife. In 1660, Charles II was restored to the throne by a "convention" rather than the full Parliament. The designers of the 1688 arrangement also admitted that their convention was, in fact, "irregular."

The American case is even clearer. The Peace of Paris was signed in 1783, but limited government was not established until the Constitution came into effect in 1789. See Wood (1998), p. 311.

is not a secret to any of the consequential actors in society about how to constitute a viable coalition to govern the country and mobilize resources. In short, because everyone understands the rules of the game, asset holders, political factions, and groups that are politically crucial will all seek out one another. A new coalition will emerge, but the basic structure of the political and economic system will be reconstituted. The result will be the resumption of economic activity in fairly short order.

A VPI coalition formed under instability must provide large rents to asset holders and third-party enforcers. The reason is that the presence of uncertainty, even calculable uncertainty, means that asset holders and third-party enforcers that choose to integrate under instability face a first-mover problem. The first groups to integrate assume the risk that the government will fall, or the faction with which they are integrating will fail to take power, leaving them at the mercy of enemies who will need to punish them in order to maintain their own credibility. The rewards from restoring order, however, are not excludable, unless the integrating asset holders and third parties earn rents to compensate them for this ex ante risk.[28]

One might argue that all of this rent seeking must necessarily push economic activity below the point that existed before instability. That argument misses the key point: polities that are characterized by political instability are almost never governed by limited governments before they become unstable. What is being reconstituted is a rent-seeking coalition much like the one that governed before instability. The rate of growth of this economy will certainly be modest by the standards of limited government. Limited government is not, however, the appropriate counterfactual, as it is not a feasible option. The appropriate counterfactuals are despotism without growth (a despotic government that cannot convince the population that it has a long time horizon), stationary banditry, or anarchy. For all of its shortcomings, VPI is easier to establish (and may be more efficient) than stationary banditry. It is also more efficient than despotism without growth or continued anarchy.[29]

---

[28] Governments (or factions aspiring to be governments) may also increase the amount of rents they require in order to finance political and military actions against their enemies.

[29] We make no claims about how long VPI must last. VPI systems may, in fact, provide the basis for limited government in the future. Recent history certainly offers numerous examples of polities that appear to have made the transition from being governed by VPI coalitions to being ruled by limited governments. We only contend that after severe episodes of political instability a direct jump to limited government is impossible.

3

VPI Coalitions in Historical Perspective

Mexico's Turbulent Politics, 1876–1929

In the previous chapter we explored how, as a theoretical matter, governments and some *subgroup* of asset holders can create an economic system in which property rights are specified and enforced as private goods. We also explored how the implicit contract between the government and these select asset holders can be made credible via the creation of a coalition with a third group, which receives a stream of rents from the asset holders and provides the government with crucial political support. Finally, we explored why the property rights system laid down by such a coalition might be impervious to changes in the identity and ideology of the government.

Empirical reality is, of course, inevitably messier than any model of it.[1] In order to make models tractable, it is necessary to assume that the actors are behaving as if they are playing a game whose rules and strategies are common knowledge. In the real world, however, it is often the case that some actors have a good sense of the game at hand, while others do not. (Indeed, casual empiricism suggests that many actors in social situations do not even know that there is a game.) Even those who ultimately figure out the rules of the game and the strategies for winning do not start out with that knowledge. They learn the game as they play.

The metaphor of a game whose rules and strategies became clear during the course of play is particularly apt in the cases of Porfirian (1876–1911)

---

[1] This is not to say that models are not useful. Indeed, without a clearly specified theory of social interaction it is not possible to order the facts and events of empirical reality in a coherent fashion. One purpose of models is to guide empirical research by providing testable hypotheses – logical implications of the model that are empirically falsifiable. These, in turn, guide researchers in the retrieval of evidence relevant to those hypotheses. As we pointed out in Chapter 1, all historians, whether they realize it or not, are guided by models.

and Revolutionary (1911–29) Mexico. In both cases, asset holders were interested in obtaining protection of their property rights and generating income from those property rights for as long a period as possible. In both cases, Mexico's generals turned politicians were interested in obtaining economic rents and establishing political order so that they could continue to receive those rents. That is, their goals were money and political survival. In both cases, the players were operating in the context of a highly unstable polity with weak formal political institutions. Their only guides were the moves of other players, their relentless self-interest, and their knowledge of what had been tried before in Mexico. As we shall see, some players made bad moves and were eliminated from the game. Others figured out winning strategies. Even these players, however, did not hit on the optimal strategy right away: they had to figure it out as they played the game.

THE POLITICAL ECONOMY OF PORFIRIAN MEXICO

Prior to the rise of Porfirio Díaz, Mexico was a classic case of a country locked in a coup trap. In the 55 years from independence in 1821 to the beginning of the Porfiriato in 1876, Mexico had 75 presidents. For every constitutional president there were four interim, provisional, or irregular presidents. One military figure, Antonio López de Santa Ana, occupied the presidential chair on 11 different occasions.

The constant shuffling of federal executives was only one reflection of the absence of anything resembling stable political institutions. Although there were two dominant ideologies, one conservative and centralist, the other liberal and federalist, these lacked a national structure that could organize them as unified political movements. Moreover, despite the guidelines of a liberal constitution enacted in 1857, there were no well-defined mechanisms for political interaction. Thus, interests and ideologies were promoted through the use of military force or the threat of military force. The result was that by 1876 Mexico had fragmented into a number of de facto subnational polities ruled by local political and military bosses. The political reality of late 19th-century Mexico was similar to contemporary Russia: "a crumbling, peripheralized federalism."[2]

---

[2] For a comparison of contemporary Russia and Porfirian Mexico, see Robinson (forthcoming). Robinson's concept of a "crumbling, peripheralized federalism" is adapted from Shleifer and Treisman (2000), p. 135. The concept of a peripheralized federalism – one in which there exists no military goal or system of incentives for local politicians to stay within the federation – was first developed by Riker (1964).

Díaz, like many of Mexico's presidents before him, came to power through a military insurrection. He had presidential aspirations dating back to his celebrated role in the liberal army that had resisted the French occupation in the 1860s. As early as 1871, Díaz had challenged the popular liberal president Benito Juárez, but Díaz's revolts and subsequent electoral challenges failed. Publicly humiliated, Díaz returned to private life but remained secretly active, building up political connections and support for an eventual return to public life. His opportunity came when Sebastián Lerdo de Tejada, another liberal lieutenant, became president in 1872 after Juárez's death. Lerdo de Tejada was unable to secure political alliances to contain popular discontent and was accused of centralizing political power. Four years later, Díaz led a successful insurrection against the reelection schemes of the president. Lerdo de Tejada was overthrown in 1876 and forced into exile in 1877. Díaz, who had assumed temporary power in 1876, was formally elected president for his first term the following year.

Díaz inherited an economy that had not grown since independence. Near as it can be measured (and the estimates are admittedly crude), Mexico's per capita GNP (in 2000 dollars) was $522 in 1800 and $443 in 1877.[3] The absence of a robust economy meant that Díaz faced a serious impediment to restoring political order. He faced, on the one hand, state governors and local political bosses with their own militias who governed their states independently and in defiance of the federal government. On the other, he faced opposition from other political actors with national political ambitions, whose movements were fueled by Díaz's unconstitutional rise to power.[4]

Díaz, like his predecessors, had a limited set of instruments to cope with political disorder and a stagnant economy simultaneously. If he concentrated on the problem of disorder, he would need to borrow heavily from the private sector, because of the lack of an administrative structure that could effectively tax the country's slim economic base. Given Mexico's long history of government defaults, the private sector was not

---

[3] See Coatsworth (1978). The figures in 1950 dollars as computed by Coatsworth were $73 in 1800 and $62 in 1877. We have recalibrated Coatsworth's 1950 estimates by changing the base year of the index to 2000.

[4] Two opposition figures loomed particularly large. The first was former president Sebastian Lerdo de Tejada, who maintained an important support base even while in exile. The second was José María Iglesias who, like Díaz, had opposed the centralist tendencies of Juárez and Lerdo de Tejada. Iglesias would not support Díaz, however, because he wanted to become president himself. See Perry (1978), pp. 307–37.

willing to lend sufficient funds to the government, leaving Díaz with two options: predation (forced loans, arbitrary extortions, and confiscations of property) or collapse. If he instead tried to promote economic activity by making commitments to respect property rights, then he would have no resources to fight his political opponents.

Essentially, Díaz accomplished both goals by abandoning the goal of protecting property rights globally. Instead, he specified and protected the property rights of a select group of asset holders and used the rents generated from this selective protection to subdue or seduce his political opponents.

We should be careful to emphasize that Díaz did not come to power with a clearly thought-out strategy in mind. In fact, Díaz's first term (1876–80) could suggest that he would be just another in a long line of Mexican presidents who came to power by military force, ruled for a time, and were then driven out of power by another ambitious political-military strongman. Thus, during his first term Díaz behaved like many of his predecessors, even resorting to political murder. For example, in 1879 Díaz asked his ally, Governor Luis Mier y Terán of the state of Veracruz, to break up a rumored conspiracy of former officials of the Lerdo de Tejada government. Governor Mier promptly assassinated nine key suspects.[5] Knowing just how fragile his rule was, Díaz was careful not to violate openly the constitutional provisions regarding the reelection of the president. Thus, in 1880, in order to preserve the veneer of constitutionality, he stepped down from the presidency in favor of one of his allies, Manuel González.

When Díaz formally reassumed the presidency in 1884 (all evidence indicates that he pulled the strings during the González presidency), he was no longer just another caudillo. Rather, the evidence indicates that he returned to power with a long-term strategy to consolidate power and gradually to undermine the governors of states that stood outside his control. One form this took was the creation of the post of *jefe político* (literally, political boss or chief), a federal appointee assigned to the major cities in each state, whose job essentially was to exert federal control at the municipal level.[6] Another form it took was Díaz's practice of gradually

---

[5] The resulting legal charges against Mier were dismissed after several months of deliberation by the federal and Veracruz legislatures.

[6] State governors also played a role in the selection of *jefes políticos* (political bosses), but Díaz paid close attention to their selection as well. See Knight (1986a), pp. 24–30.

appointing men loyal to him to state-level posts and then slowly promoting them into the governorship when the moment seemed propitious. These handpicked appointees – who were often from outside the state and had few local ties – remained in power for decades and owed that power to Díaz. The state of Guerrero provides a good example. The perhaps aptly named Antonio Mercenario (the name translates as mercenary) only knew the state as the local manager for a mining operation owned by Díaz's wife before becoming governor. Mercenario's successor hailed from distant Puebla (see map of Mexico). By the end of the Porfiriato, over 70 percent of the state governors were presidential favorites "imported" from outside.

In those states where Díaz could not eliminate or undermine a potentially recalcitrant governor, he followed a strategy of seduction. Autonomous state political bosses were rarely overthrown during the Porfiriato; rather, they were co-opted. For example, Governor Enrique Creel of Chihuahua (of the Terrazas-Creel clan, which had ruled the state as a fief even before Díaz came to power) was named Díaz's foreign minister. Another example is provided by Governor Olegario Molina of independence-minded Yucatán, who was named minister of development.[7]

Díaz's mix of carrots and sticks – *pan o palo* in Spanish – to get his way meant that he had to engage in a very delicate balancing act. For example, Díaz feared the independence and power of the northeastern elite in Nuevo León. He therefore simultaneously rewarded incumbent power brokers, such as the powerful Treviño and Naranjo families, with lucrative federal concessions at the same time that he appointed the ambitious young General Bernardo Reyes to be the local military chief. Shortly thereafter, he elevated Reyes to the governorship, where he remained almost continuously for more than two decades (1885–1908). Díaz then played the Treviño-Naranjo clan and Reyes off against one another, in order to prevent either one from becoming too powerful. In fact, when Reyes proclaimed his interest in the presidency in 1908, Díaz responded by appointing the semiretired General Jerónimo Treviño (of the Treviño-Naranjo clan) to be military commander of the Northeast. Reading the political tea leaves, Reyes stepped down as governor and accepted a sinecure as a military envoy in France.[8]

---

[7] See Knight (1986a), p. 16.
[8] Knight (1986a), p. 17.

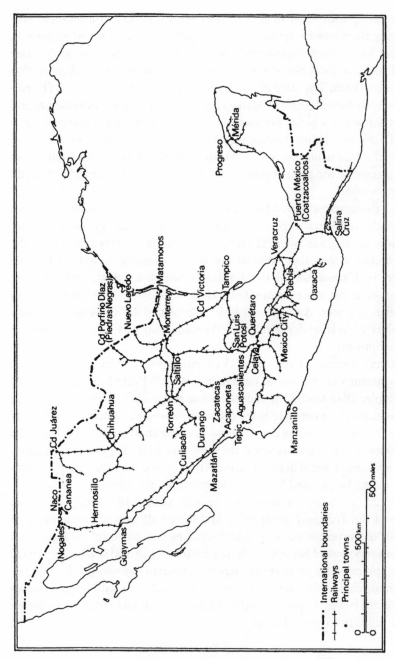

MEXICO: 1910. *Source*: Knight (1986b).

International boundaries
Railways
Principal towns

500 km
500 miles

Progreso
Mérida
Puerto México
(Coatzacoalcos)
Salina Cruz
Veracruz
Oaxaca
Puebla
Tampico
Cd Victoria
Querétaro
Mexico City
Celaya
San Luis Potosí
Matamoros
Monterrey
Nuevo Laredo
Cd Porfirio Díaz
(Piedras Negras)
Saltillo
Aguascalientes
Zacatecas
Acaponeta
Tepic
Torreón
Durango
Chihuahua
Culiacán
Mazatlán
Manzanillo
Cd Juárez
Naco
Cananea
Nogales
Hermosillo
Guaymas

Private Interests and Public Policy during the Porfiriato

Díaz realized that in order to co-opt potential opponents he needed to reward them with rents. He also realized that in order to generate those rents he needed to promote investment. Promoting investment necessarily required that Díaz specify and enforce property rights as private, not public, goods. It also required that Díaz make a credible commitment to those select asset holders that he would not change the policies that provided them with rents.

In this task Díaz had an advantage that was not available to any previous Mexican president: the ability to integrate with the U.S. economy. In the mid-19th century, the U.S. economy, from Mexico's perspective, was a distant theoretical abstraction. By the time Díaz seized power, however, the U.S. economy, and its railroad system, had moved westward. Mexico no longer faced a desert on its northern frontier; it faced one of the largest economies in the world. In addition, the sharp depreciation of the Mexican silver peso against gold-backed currencies during the 1890s produced real exchange rate depreciation. As international trade theory would predict, real exchange rate depreciation provided a tremendous boost to Mexican exports. The fall in transportation costs, the westward shift in the U.S. economy, and real exchange rate depreciation meant that it was now possible for Mexico to trade with the United States in ways that were previously unimaginable. The possibility of trade, in turn, meant that it was now profitable for foreigners to invest in those sectors where tradable goods were produced – particularly mining, ranching, and export-oriented agriculture.

What Díaz needed to do in order to take advantage of this opportunity was to find ways to induce investors to deploy their resources in Mexico. Clearly, Díaz did not have the capacity to offer global protection of property rights. He could, however, find ways to make selective commitments to privileged groups of asset holders. As we shall see in Chapters 4 through 8, the Díaz regime was notable for its creative approach to the specification of property rights. Essentially, the government found ways to specify property rights so as to create barriers to entry, thereby producing monopoly rents for those asset holders who were fortunate enough to receive a special privilege.

Díaz also had to find ways to give asset holders the ability to monitor the government and enforce their special privileges – otherwise the government's commitment would not be credible. In order to accomplish this, Díaz did two things. First, he integrated economic elites directly into the governing process. That is, he allowed a subset of asset holders to play a role in fashioning the policies that governed their own economic activities. Second, he encouraged regional political leaders to go into businesses dependent upon the continuing stability of the federal government. That is, he turned potential political enemies into third-party enforcers of the property rights system he was creating with Mexico's asset holders.

One implication of this strategy was that the Porfirian economic system was characterized by cronyism. Companies that received special privileges from the government routinely put local and national politicians on their boards of directors, thereby transferring rents to them via director's fees and stock distributions. For example, the nation's privately owned dynamite monopoly owed its lock on the market to federal support exempting it from import tariffs and federal excise taxes. In return, President Díaz's son, Governor (and, later, Foreign Minister) Creel of Chihuahua, and Undersecretary of the Treasury Núñez all received seats on the board of directors.[9] A similar situation prevailed in the cigarette industry. El Buen Tono, the country's largest producer and a beneficiary of federal patent protection, included on its board Díaz's son, a treasury undersecretary, the secretary of war, and the president of Congress.[10] The board of the Mexican Eagle Petroleum Company (also known as El Águila), the largest oil company in Mexico and a beneficiary of extensive federal concessions, included Díaz's son, the governor of Chihuahua, the president of Congress, and the governor of the Federal District. (We return to these cases in detail in Chapters 5 and 6.)

State governors were one of the most important sources of third-party enforcement in Porfirian Mexico, particularly those who were strong enough to stand up to the Díaz government. These governors controlled militias that outnumbered the federal garrisons in their states and, therefore, posed two threats to political stability. First, a group of governors acting in concert could have deposed Díaz had he chosen to end the arrangements that provided them with rents. Second, there were holdouts (such as the Terrazas clan in the state of Chihuahua, the Díez Gutiérrez brothers in the state of San Luís Potosí, the Molina-Montes clan in Yucatán, and the Rabasas clan in the state of Chiapas) who had survived Díaz's centralization, ran their states as virtual fiefs, and were powerful

[9] Haber (1989), pp. 91–93. See also *Mexican Year Book*, 1909–10, p. 421; 1912, p. 418; *Economista Mexicano*, December 17, 1903, p. 918.
[10] Haber (1989), pp. 99–100. See also *Mexican Year Book*, 1909–10, p. 420; 1908, p. 531.

enough to compete for executive power. For example, when the federal executive wanted to reform the tax system in 1883, it did not present its plans to Congress. Rather, it called a conference of state governors to ratify the federal project, even though the Constitution of 1857 contained no reference to such a body. When the governors indicated their displeasure with the tax reform, the federal government quickly backed down.[11] State governors were instrumental in enforcing contracts between the Díaz regime and selected asset holders. For example, the majority of banks in Mexico appointed the local governor to their board of directors, which entitled the governor to receive director's fees and stock distributions. (We return to this in detail in Chapter 4.)

The role of the state governors was not just restricted to banking. In the state of Puebla, for example, the textile industrialists went into business with Governor Martínez, forming a partnership with him to run several large agricultural estates. Martínez then appointed members of this group to his cabinet or the mayoralty of Puebla City.[12] Chihuahua provides another example of the blurring of the lines between governors and the business elite. In fact, as Mark Wasserman has shown, the Terrazas-Creel clan ran the state as practically a family business enterprise. Luis Terrazas served as governor from 1860 to 1873, 1879 to 1884, and 1903 to 1904, and his son-in-law Enrique Creel followed in the governorship from 1904 to 1910. Their holdings ran across banking, ranching, agriculture, manufacturing, food processing, mining and smelting, dry goods retailing, railroads, and public utilities. By 1910 they were the single largest employer in the state. They also controlled 70 percent of the flour market and 50 percent of meat-packing operations.[13] Needless to say, if the Díaz government threatened to undermine the property rights of Chihuahua's elite, it would also undermine the property rights of Terrazas-Creel. As detailed in Chapter 8, Creel was actually called on to play the role of enforcer of the property rights arrangements between the state's landowners and the Díaz government – with great success.

The frequency with which powerful political actors (state governors, cabinet members, congressional deputies, and senators) received seats on boards of directors in Porfirian Mexico was high even by the standards of other Latin American countries. Network analysis of the boards of directors of large, public corporations in Brazil and Mexico, carried out

---

[11] Carmagnani (1994), pp. 268–69.
[12] Gamboa Ojeda (1985), pp. 192–94.
[13] Wasserman (1984), chap. 3.

by Aldo Musacchio and Ian Read, produces two striking results. The first is that a small group of Porfirian insiders – particularly Pablo Macedo, Guillermo de Landa y Escandón, Enrique Creel, Porfirio Díaz Jr., Roberto Núñez, and Luis Elguero – appeared on numerous boards. Indeed, it was as common to find one of these politicians on a corporate board as it was to find one of the country's major financiers. The second striking result is the centrality of political actors in Mexico's business networks was unusual even by Latin American standards. Musacchio and Read do not find the Mexican patterns replicated in Brazil.[14]

The Díaz regime was not a kleptocracy, despite the special relationship between government and elite groups. There were limits to how far Díaz would let things go. Díaz rarely granted favors to his political allies that would alienate competing groups of powerful entrepreneurs and the governors of the states in which those entrepreneurs resided. For example, as Edward Beatty has shown, Díaz did not arbitrarily dispense industrial subsidies under the "New Industries" program. In fact, he regularly turned down applications from political allies. To cite one example, Díaz's own Development Ministry turned down an application for a federal tax exemption and protective tariff for a mechanized shoe factory whose principals included Díaz's son and the sons of the governors of Nuevo León and Oaxaca. The reason was that the governors of a number of states challenged the application, arguing that there already existed shoe factories within their borders.[15]

Vertical political integration (VPI) may have been a theoretically second-best solution to the commitment problem, but it produced economic growth and political stability for the first time since Independence. Foreign investors poured nearly 2 billion into Mexico during the Porfiriato, investing in railroads, ports, urban tramways, export agriculture, ranching, mining, smelting, and petroleum, and the banking sector. On the heels of investment by foreigners came a wave of investment by local entrepreneurs in manufacturing, agriculture of all types, ironworking and steelmaking, banking, commerce, and urban real estate. In 1876 Mexico had only five banks, a minuscule manufacturing sector, and a railroad system that consisted of 400 miles of track, of which 71 used mules rather than steam engines to pull the trains. By the time Díaz went into exile in 1911, Mexico had a sizable, if concentrated, banking system,

---

[14] Musacchio and Read (2001).
[15] The impact of political connections on the "New Industries" Program has been systematically studied by Beatty. See Beatty (2001), chaps. 6, 7.

a relatively modern manufacturing industry producing a broad range of consumer and intermediate goods, and a railroad system of 17,000 miles that united all the major cities. Mexico had also just begun a major petroleum boom and was also a major producer of various precious and industrial metals. The available (admittedly crude) estimates of per capita GDP indicate that Mexico's long moribund economy achieved real rates of growth of 2.2 percent per year from 1900 to 1910.[16] Finally, Mexico had a government that, for the first time in its history, was well-enough funded that it did not have to engage in predatory behavior – such as forced loans, debt defaults, and confiscations. The available estimates indicate that (in dollar terms), federal revenues grew by 5 percent per annum from 1895 to 1911.[17]

The fact that Díaz's VPI coalition produced laws and regulations that were codified and the fact that those laws and regulations produced growth do not mean, however, that the rule of law existed in Porfirian Mexico. The existence of laws in and of themselves does not bind governments to obey them. Credible commitments only exist when governments have to obey their own laws even when it is not in their short-run interest to do so. Something more than words on paper is necessary. A commitment mechanism must force the government to adhere to the law. The form that mechanism took in Porfirian Mexico was most certainly *not* limited government. Rather, commitments were based on the generation and sharing of rents among a coalition of economic and political elites. When maintaining the coalition required the Díaz government to obey its own laws, it did. When it was not in the interest of the coalition for the government to obey its own laws, the law meant nothing. In fact, as we discuss in Chapter 8, the Díaz government even disregarded its own laws regarding birth and citizenship requirements for state governors. It also allowed state governors to enact and enforce laws that were clearly in violation of the federal constitution.

THE REVOLUTION BEGINS, 1910–1914

The Pax Porfiriana contained the seeds of its own collapse. Díaz's policies re-specified property rights in land, encouraging the development of

---

[16] Reynolds (1970), pp. 21–22.
[17] There was a real depreciation of the peso against the dollar, meaning that a measurement of federal revenues in real pesos would be even larger than 5 percent per year. Carmagnani (1994), p. 303.

large-scale agriculture at the expense of small farmers. This redistribution of land produced an increasingly vocal peasantry. When these peasants clamored for the return of lands they considered theirs, Díaz often granted their petitions, but the balancing act proved increasingly hard to sustain. Similarly, the nation's rapid industrial growth produced an urban working class that began, tentatively and slowly, to organize and strike. Because industrial workers were not yet an important constituency, many strikes were met with federal bayonets.

Disagreement extended beyond disaffected peasants and workers. The alliance with private economic interests had been an exclusive and selective one, centered on Díaz's supporters and foreign investors. Preferential access to economic and political power prevented other elite economic groups from participating directly, although they often benefited from Mexico's rapid growth. Nevertheless, growing discontent with the distribution of political power and economic resources led the commercial and agricultural elite of the northern border states to begin seeking limited political reforms.[18]

These various disaffected groups at first made their demands peacefully. Díaz had made public statements in 1908 about his intention to retire in 1910. Encouraged by what appeared to be a window of opportunity for political opposition, Francisco I. Madero, a moderate reformer from the northeastern state of Coahuila, published an influential book on the issue of presidential succession and helped organize the Antireelectionist Party.[19] In the election of 1910, this new party nominated Madero as its presidential candidate. When it appeared that Madero could be a contender, Díaz threw him in jail and reelected himself in an election riddled with blatant fraud. Madero escaped and fled to the United States and, in October 1910, began calling for revolution from his exile in San Antonio, Texas.

Madero's call for revolution succeeded. Multiple groups threw their support behind him. Although the federal army was never defeated on the battlefield in a decisive way, an elderly and demoralized Díaz decided to negotiate a transition of power and go into exile in France. On May 26, 1911, Díaz resigned and left the country with the prophetic

---

[18] For discussion of the origins of the Mexican Revolution, see Knight (1986a); Gilly (1994); Hart (1987); Womack (1969, 1986); and Katz (1981). We note that our discussion of the political history of Mexico during the revolution draws heavily on the exhaustive history of the period by Knight. See Knight (1986a, 1986b).

[19] See Madero (1911).

words, "Madero has unleashed the tiger. Now let's see if he can control it."[20]

The elite group of northeasterners that had backed Madero was not of one mind regarding the changes Mexico required now that Díaz was out of the picture. Some of them hoped for the continuation of the existing political system on a somewhat broader, more inclusive basis. Others had been educated in American universities and viewed American liberal democracy with unbridled admiration. Madero himself appears to have held the view that Mexico could now make the transition to a limited government and liberal democracy.

Unfortunately, the movements allied with the Maderistas did not share Madero's views regarding democracy and limited government. Madero's own grandfather was well aware of the pitfalls that his grandson faced and advised him "to repress any new movement which seeks to introduce disorder."[21] This was advice that Madero could not always heed. Madero took control as part of a negotiated settlement with the Porfirian political elite, who retained a prominent and numerically significant presence in the cabinet.[22] In addition, the negotiated settlement left intact the Porfirian army and its leadership. Finally, many of the rebel movements that sprang up in Madero's name lacked any connection with the main thread of his ideology. As the American journalist John Reed noted, "The soldiers all look up to some General under whom they are recruited, as to their feudal lord. They call themselves his *gente* – his people; and an officer of anybody else's gente hasn't much authority over them."[23] Thus, at the time of the May 1911 peace settlement, there were 60,000 armed rebels scattered about the country under only the most tenuous control from Mexico City.[24]

One serious problem that Madero could not get around was that he had rallied peasant support with promises to return lands that had been, in Madero's own words, "illegally" stolen by wealthy landowners in cahoots with the local political bosses. Once in power, however, Madero reneged on his earlier promises, arguing that the promises were practically and legally impossible to carry out.[25]

---

[20] As quoted in Meyer, Sherman, et al. (1999), p. 493.
[21] Knight (1986a), 228.
[22] Méndez Reyes (1996), p. 70.
[23] Reed (1969), p. 81.
[24] Knight (1986a), p. 232.
[25] See Méndez Reyes (1996), pp. 50–54, 73–80.

Madero's inconsistency spurred military insurrections throughout the country. Emiliano Zapata, a charismatic leader from Morelos (the state just south of Mexico City), was the first to pronounce his opposition to the new government through the famous Plan de Ayala of November 1911, calling for the return of lands to peasant communities. Zapatista rebels were already in effective control of much of the state of Morelos, and suppressing them meant that federal troops had to engage in a costly and violent antiguerrilla war in the tossed and crumpled terrain of the region.

Madero quickly discovered that his dream of limited government could not become reality. In fact, he found that the only way to maintain his power was to continue the Porfirian system under a different name, parceling out patronage, judicial leeway, and economic benefits semiformally, just as had Porfirio Díaz.[26] This eroded his support among both liberals and ex-soldiers, who felt he had broken his promises.

In the Northwest, serious rebellions erupted against Madero. Sinaloa became plagued with almost constant violence, which needed to be repressed. Middle-class liberals in the states of Durango and Coahuila discussed revolt when the promised free elections failed to materialize. Ultimately, violent clashes broke out between local and federal authorities in the region.[27] Chihuahua soon joined Durango and Sinaloa in disorder, as an odd coalition of disaffected liberals and angry ex-rebels who wanted land grants began an increasingly violent rebellion under the leadership of Pascual Orozco.[28] Defeating the rebellion required Madero to send federal troops led by General Victoriano Huerta, a former Porfirian army officer.

Madero had unleashed forces that he could not control and expectations that he could not fulfill. No one believed that other factions would obey Madero's dictates, and no one believed that Madero could fulfill promises made to them, and therefore no one cooperated with Madero's regime. The Porfirian equilibrium could not be recreated without alienating middle-class liberals, southern peasants, and northern rural ex-soldiers. The liberals, peasants, and ex-rebels could not be satisfied, however, without risking an economic depression or a counterrevolution

---

[26] Knight (1986a), pp. 266–67.

[27] Knight (1986a), pp. 281–83.

[28] Orozco's plan concentrated almost completely on the issues of redistributing land to ex-soldiers, improving labor conditions, and holding real elections. Orozco had worked for American companies, called for foreign investment as a way to create jobs and raise wages, and made continual references to "our sister republic" and "sacred American soil." See Knight (1986a), pp. 294–96.

led by the old Porfirian elite. Eventually, Madero had to depend on the federal army to contain the peasants and rural workers whom he had mobilized to defeat Díaz. This meant, however, that he needed the support of the army, loaded with reactionary (and ambitious) generals.

Fifteen months after taking office, Madero was overthrown and murdered by General Victoriano Huerta, the same man whom Madero had deployed against the Orozco rebellion. On February 9, 1913, a military faction (led by General Manuel Mondragón) revolted against the Madero government. The rebels released Bernardo Reyes (the Porfirian governor from Nuevo León) and Félix Díaz (Porfirio Díaz's nephew) from jail and assaulted the National Palace in Mexico City. Madero ordered Huerta to put down the rebels. Huerta did not comply. Rather, on February 18 Huerta signed a pact with the rebels in the American Embassy and arrested Madero, who was "shot while trying to escape" three days later. Huerta then dissolved Congress.

Huerta found himself facing a nearly empty treasury and a rapidly deteriorating military situation. Governor Venustiano Carranza of Coahuila, supported by other northern governors, dedicated himself to the overthrow of the Huerta regime and declared himself the *primer jefe* (first chief) of the revolutionary army. The Carrancistas, as the followers of Carranza would come to be called, were joined by the rural army of the División del Norte, under the command of Francisco (Pancho) Villa, which began marching south toward Mexico City. In the southern and central parts of the country, centered around the state of Morelos, the Zapatistas (the followers of Emiliano Zapata) reorganized their command structure, rejecting all moves by General Huerta to co-opt them and forcing the Huerta regime to engage in a vicious, costly, and ultimately unsuccessful counterinsurgency effort. To complicate matters still further for Huerta, the United States invaded and occupied the port city of Veracruz, in order to prevent Huerta from receiving arms shipped from Germany. The motivation for this action was the belief that Huerta was sympathetic to the German cause in World War I.

If Madero's military efforts strained the treasury, Huerta's definitely broke it. At first, the Huerta government resorted to foreign loans. The revenue from these loans, however, went to repay two short-term loans incurred by Madero (totaling $20 million): little went to current expenditures. Thus Huerta had to issue domestic debt. Ever growing deficits caused the private sector to lose confidence in the government and withdraw its credit accordingly. Huerta then resorted to forced loans, asset confiscations, and inflation. (See Chapter 4 for a full discussion.) These steps, along with the imposition of a military draft, did almost as much to defeat his regime as the revolutionary armies rampaging across the countryside. Predation failed to produce sufficient resources to prevent defeat, at the same time that it eroded the credibility of the Huerta government.

Throughout 1914 the various factions allied against Huerta won victory after victory in their drive toward Mexico City. On July 15, 1914, Huerta fled the country. His successor, Francisco Carbajal, followed Huerta into exile on August 12. Venustiano Carranza spurned all the efforts of the collapsing Carbajal government to set the terms of the transfer of power. The surrender signed by the governor of the Federal District – the highest-ranking member of the Huerta regime who had not already left for Paris – set only the terms under which federal forces would submit themselves to the new authorities. General Álvaro Obregón (who led the Carrancista military forces) "entered upon a free and disentailed inheritance."[29] He and the other fighters who had overthrown Huerta held themselves beholden to no promises made by the Porfirian, Maderista, or Huerta governments – and no one knew what they might do.

CIVIL WAR, 1914–1917

What the winning factions did almost immediately was to begin fighting among themselves. As Friedrich Katz has noted, "the bloodiest phase of the Mexican Revolution occurred not when the revolutionaries were fighting the old regime, but when they began to fight one another."[30] Almost as soon as Huerta fled Mexico City for exile in France, the victors split into two camps, one led by Venustiano Carranza and the other led by Francisco "Pancho" Villa. Carranza clearly had a less revolutionary agenda than Villa. He was, in fact, a major landowner and former Porfirian politician. He was essentially a reformist, somewhat akin to Madero, but without Madero's commitment to democratic principles.

Villa was more of a populist, but he was also a pragmatist. His policies changed depending on which way the wind was blowing. Thus Villa gathered around him a number of conservative elements. Some of these were ex-Maderistas. Others included representatives of several important families from the old Porfirian commercial class.[31] Villa's coalition also

[29] Knight (1986b), p. 171.
[30] Katz (1998), p. 433.
[31] Knight (1986b), p. 289.

included large numbers of rural farm workers and tenants who wanted land of their own. One thing papered over this internal contradiction in Villa's base of support: opposition to Carranza.

In early 1914 Villa appeared to be the most likely future president of Mexico. Even before Huerta's defeat, opinion was growing among the educated elites in Mexico City that Villa was the only man capable of restoring order in Mexico.[32] Villa also had the backing of the United States, which saw him as more amenable to American interests than Carranza.[33]

In an attempt to assert control over Villa, Carranza called a national convention on September 1, 1914, to be held in Mexico City. Carranza's attempt failed, as he quickly lost control of the agenda. Villa issued a manifesto calling for the "re-establishment of constitutional order through proper elections" and accused Carranza of assuming "the role of dictator."[34] On October 5 the convention moved from the capital to Aguascalientes – closer to Villa's power base in Chihuahua. On October 15 the Villistas engineered the invitation of Zapatista delegates to the convention and then approved their land redistribution program, enraging the Carrancistas. On October 30 the convention deposed Carranza, and the next day appointed Eulalio Gutiérrez provisional president. Villa and Zapata jointly occupied Mexico City. Elites welcomed the new regime. There were no expropriations, save for the capital residences of a few Porfirian aristocrats. The revolutionary government even allowed Porfirian bureaucrats to reassume their old positions.[35] The United States, figuring a Villa-Zapata victory a done deal, ended its six-month occupation of Veracruz on November 23, 1914.[36]

No sooner had the last Marine departed from Mexican soil than the Carrancistas occupied Veracruz and established a provisional government – in opposition to the Villistas and Zapatistas who continued to control Mexico City. Meanwhile, in the capital, feuding between Villistas and Zapatistas led to the outbreak of a political terror that killed 200 people in the final weeks of 1914. His authority collapsing, President Gutiérrez fled the capital on January 16, 1915. Roque González Garza took over as provisional president and declared martial law. The Villista-Zapatista government, now known as the Convention, bogged down in

---

[32] *Mexican Herald*, July 1 and 3, 1914.
[33] Womack (1986), pp. 110–11.
[34] Knight (1986b), p. 290.
[35] *Mexican Herald*, November 26, 1914.
[36] Womack (1986), p. 111.

academic debates over the new government's structure.[37] On January 28, 1915, Álvaro Obregón, the most talented of the military leaders allied with Carranza, marched into Mexico City. With the city's economy collapsing, Obregón imposed a variety of new taxes, which did nothing to enamor him to the capital's elite.[38] On March 15, 1915, Obregón evacuated Mexico City under American pressure, allowing Convention troops to reoccupy it, only to return yet again in August.

Beginning in early 1915 two factions fought a total war for control of the state: the Carrancistas (also known as the Constitutionalists) and the alliance of the Villistas and the Zapatistas (also known as the Convention). The Carrancistas ultimately prevailed on the battlefield. Their victory was largely based on the ability of Álvaro Obregón (Carranza's most able general) to master the weapons and tactics of the First World War. Villa's cavalry charges, which been effective against the equally old-fashioned General Huerta, were tragically ineffective against Obregón's use of foxholes, barbed wire, and machine guns. The result was a series of slaughters beginning with the first battle of Celaya on April 6, 1915. Villa eventually learned how to fight a defensive war, but by then the backbone of his army had been broken.

From April 1915 onward, the Villistas gradually saw their initial military might erode. Villa then turned to terror tactics, including forced loans, robberies, intimidation, and press ganging, as well as burning down the houses of resisters.[39] The most infamous use of this tactic was the attack on Columbus, New Mexico, which prompted President Wilson to order General Pershing to blunder around northern Mexico with three American brigades in search of Villa. Skirmishing continued throughout 1917–19, with several attacks on major cities. Villa continued to be a threat until 1920, when he was granted a pardon and his army was allowed to come down from the hills. He remained a source of potential opposition until assassins riddled his Chevrolet with bullets in 1923.[40]

The Zapatistas never suffered the sort of crushing defeat to which Obregón subjected the Villistas. They learned quite well how to defend themselves within the mountainous state of Morelos. At the same time,

---

[37] *Mexican Herald*, January 17, 1915.
[38] *Mexican Herald*, February 3, 1915.
[39] Knight (1986b), p. 341.
[40] The negotiated settlement that allowed Villa to retire was carried out by interim president Adolfo de la Huerta. De la Huerta pardoned Villa over Obregón's objections, causing a brief split between Obregón and his underling. For a full discussion of the settlement, see Katz (1998), chap. 19.

however, the nature of their peasant army meant that they could not organize sustained offensives. By mid-1915 allied peasant movements in the contiguous states of Hidalgo, Puebla, and Tlaxcala switched sides and joined the Carrancistas.

Throughout 1916 Carrancista forces interdicted Zapata's supply lines and slowly starved his guerrilla army. In April 1916 the Carrancistas unleashed the full panoply of modern weaponry against Zapata, using airplanes to spot and strafe guerrilla positions, running up barbed wire to break up the countryside, and defending their positions from guerrilla attacks with trenches and machine gun fire. The assault was impressive but fleeting: the guerrillas fled to the hills, surrounded the towns, and now it was their turn to starve out the Carrancistas. The stalemate dragged on, and by 1918 Carrancista soldiers complained that "every settlement, every hamlet, every county, every county seat is a center of active conspiracy and an inexhaustible source of men ready to mobilize at the harsh sound of the war-horn."[41] Zapata's forces, could not, however, hold out forever. The Zapatista movement began to suffer defections. Zapata himself was assassinated in 1919.[42] Nonetheless, the Zapatistas were never defeated on the battlefield in Morelos, and the organized Morelos peasantry remained a potent force throughout the 1920s and 1930s.

All sides in the civil war engaged in predatory behavior. The Carrancistas initially kept records of their confiscations for an eventual return of some of this property to their owners. In practice, individuals closely allied to the Carrancistas seized property for themselves.[43] In fact, Carranza used widespread corruption to reward his supporters, exemplified by the popular saying "Constitucionalistas – con las uñas listas [with fingernails at the ready] and the coinage of the slang term *carrancear*, meaning "to steal." At a larger scale, the Carranza government carried out a de facto nationalization of the banking system in 1915–17 in an effort to finance the war against Villa and Zapata – a subject to which we return in the next chapter. The Villistas, for their part, sacked bank vaults and demanded forced loans. They also commandeered the agricultural properties of the Porfirian oligarchy and used the income generated from those estates to finance the war against Carranza (see Chapter 8).

Neither side in the civil war kept its goals constant. The need to create alliances and build coalitions meant that policies had to evolve

---

[41] Knight (1986b), p. 367.
[42] Knight (1986b), pp. 365–72.
[43] Womack (1986), p. 108.

in an ad hoc fashion, and as alliances dissolved and new ones formed, a faction's policies could shift 180 degrees. For example, neither Villa nor Carranza began as partisans of extensive land redistribution. Villa moved in that direction in 1914 in order to satisfy the demands of his soldiers and cement his alliance with Zapata. When in 1915 it looked like he might be victorious, he looked for and gained allies from the old Porfirian elite and northern middle class and moved away from his more radical stance. Once Carranza forced him out of Mexico City on the run, he moved back in a radical direction. Villa, in fact, never really committed himself to a particular program, instead being all things to all men and following different policies in different times and places.[44] In short, Villista policy was confused, wildly changing, and unpredictable.

Volatility in policy and program was as pronounced among the Carrancistas. A military-civil split divided the entire movement. This split paralleled – but did not completely mirror – other divisions cleaving the Carrancistas: northwestern/northeastern, moderate liberal/radical nationalist, pro-German/pro-Allied, localist/carpetbagger, Obregón/Carranza.[45] To give one example, after 1915 many Carrancista soldiers were recruited from unemployed urban workers in central Mexico to form the Red Battalions, whose radicalism clashed with the liberalism of the northeastern middle-class political leadership. These worker-soldiers had been organized by the anarchist Casa del Obrero Mundial (House of the World Worker), in exchange for which Carranza allowed the anarchists to organize workers in the areas that fell under Carrancista control. By 1916 it was clear that this bizarre coalition of anarchist workers and conservative businessmen and landowners was unsustainable.[46] The alliance came apart: Carranza turned on the anarchists, employing martial law and the death penalty in order to break strikes called by his former allies.[47]

These internal divisions within the Carrancista movement created a great deal of unpredictability regarding policies. Carranza wished to build alliances with Mexico's industrialists and landowners, realizing that they would be important partners in building a new governing coalition. The problem was that his generals, who served as the military governors of the states under Carrancista control, had every incentive to build alliances with local farm and factory workers, in order to carve out their own

---

[44] Knight (1986b), pp. 285–99.
[45] Knight (1986b), pp. 450–53.
[46] For a discussion of why the anarchists chose to ally with the Carrancistas, see Lear (2001), chap. 6.
[47] Hall and Spalding (1986), pp. 351–52.

political fiefdoms. The result was that these military governors carried out labor reforms at the state level that went far beyond what Carranza envisioned or sanctioned. In September 1914 in the state of Puebla, for example, General Pablo González, commander of the Army of the Northeast, established a legal minimum wage and a maximum legal workday of eight hours. González also decreed that employers who violated this decree would be subject to fines administered by state inspectors and that employers who closed their workplaces in order to avoid the new wage and hour laws would have their properties confiscated.[48] Similar decrees, with some variance as to the exact details of wages and hours, were soon promulgated by the military governors of Tlaxcala, Tabasco, Michoacán, México State, the Distrito Federal, and Veracruz.[49]

At times, these reforms reached extreme levels. In September 1914 in the state of Puebla, for example, Brigadier General Francisco Coss, who served as military governor of the state, decreed that henceforth no farm or factory could employ Spanish nationals in supervisory positions because of their long history of maltreatment of Mexican workers. He also established a schedule of fines and jail terms for the owners of firms who violated the law. This decree struck at the heart of Puebla's textile industry: the vast majority of the textile firms in the state were owned by Spanish nationals, and they, or their family members, administered the mills. A delegation of factory owners traveled to Mexico City to appeal this decree to Carranza, who refused to see them. Coss was, however, quietly replaced by Carranza with a more conservative military governor, who suspended Coss's decrees.[50] The point was clear, however, regardless of what Carranza might say, and regardless of his policies in the past, it would be difficult to predict what the local representatives of the Constitutionalist government might do.

POST–CIVIL WAR INSTABILITY, 1917–1929

By 1917 it was clear who would ultimately win the civil war. Obregón's military campaign against Zapata, Villa, and their allies would drag on until 1920. Nevertheless, the Carrancistas had sufficient scope of action in 1917 that they could credibly begin to negotiate coalitions with asset holders. Carranza intended to signal asset holders that he wanted to recreate

[48] Ramirez Rancaño (1987), pp. 152–53.
[49] Ramirez Rancaño (1987), pp. 154–74; Bortz (2002).
[50] Ramirez Rancaño (1987), pp. 150–53.

the old Porfirian coalition. He therefore called a constitutional convention with the intention of writing a conservative governing document for the country.

Just as in the previous Convention of Aguascalientes in 1914, Carranza lost agenda control to the radicals at the constitutional convention of 1917. In two areas in particular, Carranza's conservative proposals became transformed into far-reaching, and extremely radical, articles of law: property rights and labor relations. The result was Articles 27 and 123 of the Constitution of 1917.

Article 27 of the Constitution of 1917 nominally re-specified property rights in land, water, and petroleum. The private ownership of these assets was no longer considered a right. Rather it was a privilege granted by the government (the residual claimant on rights to these assets) that could be terminated at any time. The obvious targets of these reforms were Mexico's agrarian elite and the foreign companies that dominated petroleum extraction, but their implications were not lost on the holders of other assets, who feared that the government was signaling its intentions to expropriate their property as well.

Article 123 established a maximum workday of eight hours (seven for night work), set limits on the work of women and children, established a six-day week, and placed restrictions on the right of employers to fire workers. It also endorsed the principles of a minimum wage, equal pay for equal work, job security, profit sharing, and the indemnification of accidents. Perhaps most fundamentally, it gave workers the right to organize and strike. Finally, it outlined a system of municipal and state labor boards (the Juntas de Conciliación y Arbitraje) that would resolve disputes, determine the minimum wage, and set the appropriate level of profit sharing for each state. In short, the government assumed broad new powers that reduced the ability of asset holders to earn income from their property. Much to the unhappiness of Mexican employers, Article 123 left the process of creating enabling legislation up to the states. This allowed governors to carry out reforms that went far beyond what Carranza or his successors had in mind. Indeed, the incentives for state governors to do so were obvious: a politically mobilized working class could provide a governor with the support he might need to challenge attempts by the federal government to curtail his considerable de facto political autonomy.[51]

---

[51] Bortz (1997), pp. 256–57; Hall and Spalding (1986), p. 352; and Sterret and Davis (1928), pp. 91–92.

What Carranza did achieve at the 1917 Constitutional Convention, however, was a governing document that gave the president quasi-dictatorial powers. The Constitution of 1917 should not be understood as an attempts to establish a limited government, as it did little to constrain the president. This meant that the president could (and did) sit on attempts to craft enabling legislation to Articles 27 and 123.

Congress could not legislate independently. The Constitution ostensibly granted Congress the ability to override a presidential veto by two-thirds of both chambers. In reality, however, a constitutional loophole granted the president an absolute right of veto. Article 89 proclaimed that no law could take effect until it was published in the *Diario Oficial* (federal register), which was the president's responsibility. Therefore, should he refuse to publish the law, it could not take effect. No congressional override was possible.[52]

The President not only had an irrevocable veto, he could also initiate legislation himself.[53] Congress opened its session with new presidential initiatives, which had priority over other legislation. With a three-month congressional session fixed by Article 66, this did not leave a great deal of time for other matters. The Constitution also explicitly empowered the president to issue "executive orders" to enforce sanitary laws, control public expenditures, revoke franchises, forfeit land grants, and expel pernicious foreigners.

Mexico's president could also expand his powers of decree by using Article 29 of the Constitution. This article gave the Congress the ability to confer emergency powers on the president, during times of national emergency. The president did not, however, have to bother with the full Congress in order to invoke Article 29. The Permanent Commission of Congress – 14 senators and 15 federal deputies – could grant the president the power to legislate whenever Congress was not in session, which was nine months out of the year.[54]

---

[52] Weldon (1997), p. 237. Because Congress failed to override any presidential vetoes before 1935, this provision was not used until Lázaro Cárdenas invoked it in that year to suppress a congressional override of a veto of a pension bill.

[53] The Constitution of the United States, in contrast, does not authorize the president to introduce legislation. He or she must find a representative or senator willing to introduce the bill, according to rules set by Congress. In contrast, bills introduced by the Mexican president go directly to committee, bypassing Congress's internal rules "and implicitly the agenda control of the chamber leadership." Weldon (1997), p. 235.

[54] The Permanent Commission was later enlarged to 18 senators and 19 deputies. Weldon (1997), pp. 239–40.

Article 29 was used repeatedly to sidestep Congress and to allow the president to govern by decree. The very first piece of legislation passed by the new Congress in 1917 used Article 29 to grant President Carranza the authority to enact the budget by decree.[55] His successor, President Álvaro Obregón, did not enjoy this power after he assumed the presidency, and he was unpleasantly surprised to find that the Chamber of Deputies had modified his 1921 budget proposal. He therefore pressured Congress into reauthorizing the president's budgetary authority. The 1921, 1922, and 1924 budgets were all unilaterally decreed by Obregón under the power *granted in 1921.* Congress was given a chance to vote on the 1923 budget – *but it had to do so before President Obregón introduced it.*[56] The president's decree powers under Article 29 extended far beyond the budget: between 1917 and 1938, the laws governing agrarian reform, banking, communications, electrical generation and transmission, the national university, tariffs on foreign trade, and some tax laws were all enacted by presidential decree.[57]

The use of the Permanent Commission of Congress went beyond the right to legislate by decree. The Permanent Commission was regularly used by the president to depose state governors. Presidents de la Huerta, 1920, Obregón, 1920–24, and Calles, 1924–28, employed the permanent commission extensively for this purpose. De la Huerta and Obregón deposed 15 governors, Calles 11. There were only 28 governors at any one time, indicating that de la Huerta and Obregón deposed more than one-half of the sitting governors and Calles more than one-third.[58] In a similar vein, the president could use the Inauguration Commission of Congress (which was not, in fact, specified in the Constitution) to handpick members of the legislature. It officially ratified the results of congressional elections, and without its approval no deputy or senator could assume his seat.[59]

The president even sidestepped Congress on issues that were clearly specified by the constitution as requiring congressional approval. Article 76 of the constitution stated that diplomatic officers, military officers above the rank of colonel, and senior officials of the Ministry of the Treasury had to be approved by the Senate. In reality, treasury

---

[55] Weldon (1997), p. 240.
[56] Weldon (1997), p. 231.
[57] Weldon (1997), p. 240.
[58] Weldon (1997), p. 253.
[59] Weldon (1997), p. 230.

officials routinely informed Congress *after* they had taken office, not even bothering with the pretense of confirmation.[60]

The autocratic provisions of the Constitution of 1917, and the expansion of the power of the president in the early 1920s, were no accident. The formation of rent-seeking coalitions is difficult when policy making is constrained by democratic institutions. If policies that vest select asset holders with special privileges need to be ratified by an open and elected parliament, then the groups with which the government integrates will be constrained, reducing the rewards from integration. In short, freeing the president from congressional or judicial checks meant that decisions could be made in smoke-filled rooms without worrying about how they would play in the legislature.

Even with a constitution that provided him with an extraordinary amount of power, President Venustiano Carranza (1917–20) could not reestablish political stability. He faced multiple competitors for power, including Zapata and Villa. He also faced opposition from his own generals – who had political ambitions of their own.

The divisions within the Carrancista camp all came to the surface in the presidential "election" of 1920. Carranza sought to elect Ignacio Bonillas, an obscure politician whom Carranza had earlier picked as his ambassador to the United States. Bonillas had no constituency of his own, so it was clear to everyone that he would be entirely dependent upon Carranza, who would therefore maintain de facto control of the government. Álvaro Obregón, Carranza's most brilliant general, also had presidential aspirations. His campaign for the presidency in early 1920 met with attempts by Carranza to intimidate his supporters through violent means. When that strategy failed to achieve the desired results, Carranza summoned Obregón to Mexico City to answer charges of treason and conspiracy.

Threatening people who command armies is rarely a good idea, and this case does not violate that general principle. Obregón and his supporters, General Plutarco Elias Calles and General Adolfo de la Huerta, declared themselves in revolt in April 1920.[61] Most of Mexico's military leaders quickly joined them. Within a matter of weeks, these generals had driven Carranza from the capital. Carranza was captured and executed.

---

[60] Weldon (1997), pp. 240–41.

[61] Adolfo de la Huerta should not be confused with General Victoriano Huerta, the counterrevolutionary president of 1913–14. Victoriano Huerta went into exile in France in 1914, never to return to Mexico.

De la Huerta became provisional president until Obregón officially assumed office on December 1, 1920. President Obregón then named de la Huerta to be secretary of the treasury. Calles became secretary of the interior (Gobernación), in charge of internal security.

Politics during the Obregón presidency were not appreciably more stable than under Carranza. For starters, Obregón had to contend with a number of powerful state governors who had gained a great deal of de facto political autonomy from Mexico City. Four governors in particular (Adalberto Tejeda in Veracruz, José María Sánchez in Puebla, Francisco Múgica in Michoacán, and Felipe Carrillo Puerto in Yucatán) proved particularly difficult to rein in. Known in the conservative press as the "Four Horsemen of the Apocalypse," these governors had cultivated local working-class and peasant constituencies by promulgating their own labor laws and by carrying out de facto agrarian reforms, completely ignoring Obregón's requests for restraint. Given their popular support, Obregón could not remove these governors. The best he could do was to deploy conservative generals to be local army zone commanders, who often worked with conservative elements in the state to frustrate the populist reforms of the governors. Obregón also leaned on the federal judiciary (which was not independent) to grant injunctions that suspended many of the governors' state level reforms.[62]

The state governors themselves faced violent political opposition. Local political and military bosses fought over power, sometimes establishing authoritarian fiefdoms of long duration, sometimes managing to remain in power for but a few weeks. In the state of Puebla, to cite one example, there were 14 governors between 1920 and 1930, only 3 of whom were elected.[63] Other states with multiple annual changes in governorship include Aguascalientes, Chihuahua, Coahuila, Guanajuato, Morelos, Nayarit, Querétaro, Sonora, and Zacatecas.[64]

As was the case with the federal executive, the formal selection mechanisms for state executives were often ignored: violence or the threat

---

[62] To cite one example, Governor Adalberto Tejeda of Veracruz created a profit-sharing law in 1921 that required owners to share up to 50 percent of their profits with their workers. Factory owners in Veracruz filed injunctions against the law. The requests for injunctions were openly supported by Obregón, who used his influence to obtain a favorable ruling from a federal judge. See Collado Herrera (1996), pp. 138, 250–52, 254, 289.

[63] Camp (1991), appendix F.

[64] For information on the number of governors who ruled in each state, see Camp (1991), appendix F.

of violence replaced balloting.[65] One contemporary observer, after cataloging the violent and unconstitutional nature of politics in every Mexican state, summed it up as follows: "If life insurance existed in Mexico as in the United States one may presume that no político would be accepted as a risk."[66]

President Obregón also faced violent political opposition. The first violent rebellion occurred before he even had a chance to be formally installed in office. In July 1920 Esteban Cantú, a local strongman in Baja California (Cantú had been, at one point, the state governor) led a military uprising against Obregón. Cantú's ostensible goal was to prevent the distribution of lands in the state among "the friends and relatives of Mr. Álvaro Obregón."[67] The reality of the rebellion had far more to do with Cantú's aspirations to run the state as an independent fief. There is, in fact, abundant evidence that Cantú was financed by American oil companies and was encouraged by Secretary of the Interior Albert Fall. Fall was not particularly interested in Baja California, but he was interested in the Veracruz-Tamaulipas oil zone. He hoped to use a widespread military rebellion as a vehicle to cleave the oil region off from Mexico. In any event, Cantú was handily defeated and barely escaped across the border to the United States.[68]

Cantú continued to conspire against Obregón while in exile and appears to have become involved in a second plot, this one involving Manuel Peláez, a caudillo from Veracruz who had fought against the Carrancistas. The rebellion broke out in January 1921 and was led by one of Peláez's allies, General Daniel Martínez Herrera. This revolt, too, was quickly put down.[69]

A third rebellion, this one led by General Francisco Murguía, occurred the following year. Murguía was one of the few generals who had not sided with Obregón when he overthrew Carranza. He was punished with imprisonment for that political miscalculation. Once freed, he fled to the United States and organized a military campaign to overthrow Obregón.

---

[65] For detailed descriptions of state politics, see Benjamin and Wasserman (1990); Wasserman (1993); Falcón (1977, 1984); Ankerson (1984). For a summary of the political events in each Mexican state, see Gruening (1928), pp. 393–473.

[66] Gruening (1928), p. 474. For a discussion of political violence, imposition of governors by the federal government, and unconstitutional rule on a state-by-state basis, see ibid., pp. 393–473.

[67] Hall (1995), p. 55.

[68] Hall (1995), pp. 55–57.

[69] Brown (1993), p. 304; Hall (1995), pp. 56–58.

Unfortunately for Murguía, his political instincts had not improved with either imprisonment or exile. Convinced that he could get thousands of followers to rally to his cause, he crossed into Chihuahua with a small force in October 1922. Most of his troops defected as soon as they hit resistance. No mass following materialized. Murguía was easily captured and executed.[70]

More serious than any of these revolts was the one led by Obregón's own secretary of the treasury, Adolfo de la Huerta, in 1923–24. The de la Huerta revolt should, in fact, be understood not as a military rebellion but as a full-scale civil war in which a substantial portion of the army defected from the Obregón regime. The issue igniting the revolt was the presidential succession of 1924. Obregón had chosen Interior Minister Plutarco Elias Calles to succeed him as president instead of de la Huerta. De la Huerta and his military backers (each one aspiring to become president) therefore declared against the government in December 1923.

The leadership of the de la Huerta rebellion included a significant portion of Mexico's senior military leaders, including 8 of Mexico's 35 military zone commanders. The most prominent of the conspirators included Guadalupe Sánchez, the military zone commander whom Obregón had deployed to the strategically vital state of Veracruz to thwart the populist politics of Governor Adalberto Tejeda. Joining Sánchez were the zone commanders of Jalisco and Oaxaca: Enrique Estrada and Fortunato Maycotte. Maycotte's treachery provides a good sense of the way that alliances shifted continually throughout the rebellion. On hearing of the revolt, Maycotte rushed to Mexico City where he pledged his allegiance to Obregón and asked for 200,000 pesos and war material in order to go out into the field and crush the rebels. Safely outside of Mexico City with the cash and the arms, Maycotte then declared for de la Huerta.[71]

The de la Huerta rebellion came very close to success. Forty percent of the army, more than 23,000 troops, ultimately joined the rebellion against the government.[72] Moreover, those elements of the army that did not declare against Obregón were of questionable loyalty.[73] Obregón was saved by three factors. First, the rebels were internally divided. As one contemporary observer put it: "The rebels could have won had they been capable of loyalty to each other for even a few weeks. But hardly in the

[70] Hall (1995), pp. 124, 138; Katz (1998), pp. 738–39.
[71] Gruening (1928), p. 320.
[72] The official statistics mention 102 generals, as well as more than 2,000 officers of various ranks. Plasencia de la Parra (1998), p. 9.
[73] Gruening (1928), p. 322.

field each general began knifing the next, fearful that a victory might give a rival the pole in the presidential scramble."[74] In fact, internal squabbling kept them from capturing Mexico City after they had captured Puebla. Had they taken Mexico City, the rest of the army almost certainly would have recognized the de la Huerta government and the rebellion would have ended in victory.

Second, Obregón was helped by the U.S. government, which refused to permit the sale of arms to the insurgents. At the same time, the United States sold Obregón's government $1.3 million worth of arms.[75]

Third, Obregón was able to mobilize worker and peasant militias. The worker militias were organized by the country's largest labor federation, the Confederación Regional Obrera Mexicana (CROM). CROM battalions proved particularly effective at cutting enemy rail lines and communications, intimidating and executing civilian supporters of the rebels, and freeing up loyal regular troops for action.[76] Marjorie Clark, writing in the 1930s, flatly stated, "Without the support of this labor group [the CROM] it is doubtful if Obregón and Calles would have triumphed – and it is certain that they would not have done so as rapidly and effectively as they did."[77] Peasant militias, led by agrarian warlords and motivated by promises of land played a similar role.[78]

As the chances for a quick victory began to dissipate, the officers who had declared for de la Huerta began to rethink their loyalty. De la Huerta, realizing that the situation was deteriorating, escaped to exile in the United States. The officers who supported him were not so lucky. Obregón ordered the execution of all captured rebel leaders above the rank of major.[79]

The de la Huerta rebellion drove home to Obregón and Calles just how fragile their government was. They now faced three options. The first option was to do nothing. This meant facing the inevitable violent attempts to seize the presidential palace. Their expected payoff from following this strategy was highly negative – a bullet in the back of the head. The second option was to destroy all potential sources of opposition within the country. This was completely infeasible. Obregón and Calles

---

[74] Gruening (1928), p. 321.
[75] The $1.3 million was over the two-month period, January 7, 1924, to March 12, 1924. Hall (1995), pp. 168–69.
[76] Gómez Galvarriato (1999), pp. 309–10.
[77] As cited in Gómez Galvarriato (1999), p. 309.
[78] Ankerson (1984), pp. 108–9.
[79] Hall (1995), pp. 157–58, 166–67; Gruening (1928), p. 328.

simply lacked the financial and military resources to break the power of the state governors or bring the "generals" and their armed retinues to heel. Only one option remained: find a source of political support that would provide Obregón and Calles with the ability to survive future rebellions by their generals or ambitious regional strongmen. There existed two plausible candidates to play this role: the peasantry and organized labor.

Forming a national coalition with the peasants was not politically feasible. Obregón had formed ad hoc and local alliances with peasants in order to defeat the de la Huerta rebellion. These alliances, however, had been forged in regions where the landlords had declared their support for de la Huerta. In those regions, Obregón's alliances with radical state governors (such as Tejeda of Veracruz) or agrarian warlords (such as Saturnino Cedillo in San Luis Potosí) allowed him to deploy armed peasants around telegraph lines, railroad stations, and other strategic locations within pacified areas. This freed up regular troops for use against the rebels.[80] Institutionalizing this role for armed peasant militias on a national level, however, would have ignited a rebellion by those revolutionary generals who were still loyal. Gaining the support of the peasants would have meant giving the peasants land. The problem was, however, that Obregón and Calles relied on generals who received protection rents from landlords, or had become landlords themselves. They were therefore opposed to land redistribution. In fact, President Obregón was himself a general-turned-landlord. (We return to this issue in detail in Chapter 8.)

Organized labor was the only viable candidate to provide political support for Obregón and Calles. There had been, since 1919, a growing alliance between Obregón and the CROM – an alliance that had at times been broken by Obregón. In August 1919 Obregón struck a secret agreement with the CROM.[81] The CROM agreed to create a political party, the Partido Laborista Mexicano (PLM), which would mobilize support for Obregón's 1920 election. In exchange, Obregón promised to create enabling legislation for Article 123 and found a labor ministry that would be controlled by the CROM. Until the labor ministry was

---

[80] The peasants resisted being incorporated into the regular army, which they viewed as their enemy because it was often the army, in the pay of large landowners, that blocked agrarian reform. Plasencia de la Parra (1998), pp. 14, 28, 83–84.

[81] The details of this secret agreement were published in 1930, after Luis Morones (the leader of the CROM) decided to make it public following accusations that he had played a role in the assassination of Obregón in 1928. Hall (1981), p. 218.

founded, a person identified with the CROM would serve as secretary of industry, commerce, and labor, an already existing ministry that had authority over labor matters. The heads of these ministries would have to be approved by the leadership of the PLM. In addition, the agreement stated that the CROM was to be consulted on all matters having to do with labor. Indeed, the pact even specified that one day per week was to be set aside for meetings between the labor ministry and the central committee of the CROM.[82] As things turned out, the CROM's electoral support of Obregón in 1920 proved irrelevant: Obregón took the presidency by armed force. The CROM's support was moot. The CROM's leader, Luis Morones, became head of federally owned military factories – with all the concomitant opportunities for graft – but Obregón reneged on his promise to pass a federal labor law. In fact, Obregón leaned on federal judges to grant injunctions against state labor laws. He also got the Supreme Court to rule in 1922 that the decisions of the state labor boards were not binding because the federal government *had not created any enabling legislation for Article 123.*[83]

By 1923 it was becoming clear to Obregón that the CROM was a valuable ally. CROM agents proved especially useful in insuring that the Mexican Senate would not cause any unnecessary inconveniences. For instance, American recognition of the Obregón government was contingent upon the approval of the Bucareli Agreement of 1923, which settled private American claims against the Mexican government. The United States required ratification of this agreement (it was technically not a treaty) by the full Mexican Senate rather than permit the use by Obregón of one of the Constitution's emergency clauses. When the Mexican Senate balked at ratifying the agreement, Obregón had Senator Francisco Field Jurado, one of the leaders of the opposition, assassinated. When this assassination proved insufficient, the president arranged for the kidnapping of opposition senators (allegedly using PLM agents for the job). He then convened the Senate with the missing senators' alternates voting in their stead, so that he could get the agreement ratified.[84]

The de la Huerta rebellion increased the CROM's leverage over Obregón and Calles. After 1924 the CROM was no longer a marginal player in supporting Obregón's coalition – it now played a key role.

[82] Hall (1981), pp. 217–18; Middlebrook (1995), p. 77.
[83] Collado Herrera (1996), pp. 266, 314–15, 323, 325–26.
[84] Weldon (1997), p. 231.

Obregón's government therefore became an active supporter of organized labor's demands. In January 1924, right in the middle of the de la Huerta rebellion, Obregón convinced the Supreme Court to reverse its previous rulings regarding the power of the state labor boards. The court now upheld the CROM's favored interpretation of Article 123: the decisions of the Juntas de Conciliación y Arbitraje would be binding on all parties. The government also threw its active support behind CROM labor actions. A contemporary observer provides us with the following account. "When a strike is declared the strikers plant labor's red and black flag in the doorway of the shop or factory. The flag acts not as merely an announcement but as an effective padlock. None may come or go, striker or non-striker. Federal troops enforce this labor fiat. That these forces are to preserve order and prevent sabotage or other damages to the owner's property incidental to the strike is the allegation. Their truer purpose is to support the strike."[85]

In exchange, the CROM-PLM promised to help the Obregón-Calles faction steal elections. Stealing elections was important because Mexico was nominally a democracy. Openly abrogating the Constitution would provide a lightning rod for political opposition. It could also allow factions in the U.S. government to legitimize armed intervention. Particularly crucial to stealing elections was the fact that Mexico did not have secret ballots. Ballots generally differed for each candidate or party: voters asked for a ballot of some candidate or party, and they then made an X inside the color mark that denominated that party. The polls were supervised by government authorities and also by representatives of each candidate or party competing.[86] In short, the CROM-PLM could be used to ensure that citizens voted the way that the government wanted them to.

The CROM-PLM played key roles in the endless cases of electoral fraud and intimidation that characterized Mexican elections. Electoral fraud via political violence was so common that it even had a name: a *porra*. A *porra* was an armed organized mob that attacked polls, stealing the documents and ballots or intimidating citizens into casting ballots a particular way or not voting at all.[87] As one contemporary dryly noted, "The election itself is a formal affair, for once it is clear who is to be elected, it is not customary to vote against him, because the polling stations are in

[85] Gruening (1928), pp. 357–58.
[86] Gruening (1928), p. 395.
[87] Gruening (1928), p. 396.

the hands of his friends and any recalcitrancy is deemed unseemly, if not positively dangerous."[88]

The American consul in San Luis Potosí noted just how effective CROM thugs could be during the gubernatorial elections of 1923. "[The outgoing] Governor Nieto tried to identify himself with the election at an early hour of the day, but at the first election booth he was met by a volley of shots which killed the man next to him. After this the governor stayed at home. The chief activity of the election seems to have consisted in sending several automobiles loaded with club bearers and gunmen to each election booth, running the election judges away, and capturing the ballot box. It is claimed that so successful was this method as worked by opposing parties that long before the hour for closing the polls not a single voting place was open."[89]

Not all elections were characterized by *porras*, but many were. As one contemporary observer noted: "It is not possible, given existing conditions in Mexico, to elect an honest and conscientious state government without dishonesty and lack of conscience."[90] In fact, when Calles came to power in 1924 he contemplated withholding recognition from any candidate on whose behalf electoral fraud had been committed. As one contemporary observer noted, however, there was a fundamental problem with this noble idea: "Such a program would have disqualified nearly all of the candidates in nearly all of the states."[91]

Not surprisingly, the CROM supported Calles's presidential election bid in 1924. In return, CROM leader Luis Morones became secretary of industry, commerce and labor during Calles's term.[92] The CROM-PLM also built a powerful delegation in Congress. In 1926, at the height of the CROM's power, the PLM held 11 of 58 positions in the Senate, 40 of 272 seats in the federal Chamber of Deputies, and

---

[88] Rickard (1924), p. 173.
[89] As quoted in Ankerson (1984), p. 105.
[90] Gruening (1928), p. 489.
[91] Gruening (1928), p. 490.
[92] Radical state governors with large working-class constituencies, particularly Adalberto Tejeda, also gained political leverage from their alliance with Obregón and Calles. Tejeda was on his last legs politically and was about to be forced from power when the de la Huerta rebellion broke out. In exchange for organizing ad hoc peasant and worker militias to support Obregón – despite their earlier political antagonism – Tejeda was allowed to keep his governorship. Calles later rewarded him with a federal cabinet position as secretary of the interior (gobernación). After his stint in the cabinet, Tejeda resumed his position as governor. Gruening (1928), p. 629; Camp (1991), p. 443.

2 governorships (out of 28). It also controlled Mexico City's municipal government.[93]

These political connections, in turn, strengthened the CROM's organizational strength. The federal government deducted CROM dues directly from federal employees' salaries. The CROM's control over appointments to the constitutionally mandated state labor boards, coupled with the influence of its elected officials, meant that it could force employers to recognize CROM-affiliated unions and undermine rival non-CROM unions. The fact that the secretary of industry, commerce, and labor could rule a strike illegal (which in turn allowed employers to fire striking workers and hire replacements) gave Morones a very powerful tool against rival labor unions or federations.[94]

From the point of view of Obregón and Calles, and from the point of view of Mexico's employers, the CROM was the best available option in the new world of Mexican labor relations. The revolution had brought to the fore a number of labor organizations, many of them far more militantly anticapitalist than Morones and the CROM. Indeed, the CROM had a fundamentally reformist ideology. It did not so much want to overthrow capitalism as it wanted to win for its members their share of the economic growth that Morones believed was in Mexico's immediate future.[95] Morones, it should be pointed out, also wanted to win for himself a share of payments from unions and employers that the CROM extracted through various corrupt schemes. In 1925, for example, the El Águila oil company ended a strike by paying the CROM 400,000 pesos in "compensation," little of which ended up with the rank and file.[96]

The CROM produced labor peace. In part, this peace was accomplished through Morones's ability to declare strikes illegal. The CROM also accomplished this by supplying strikebreakers to firms during labor disputes and using its own armed squads to attack its enemies.[97] In 1922 there were 197 strikes in Mexico. They involved 71,736 workers, with a loss of 692,339 man-days of labor. By 1924 the number of

---

[93] Gruening (1928), p. 360.
[94] See Middlebrook (1995), pp. 79–80. The CROM did not hesitate to use its influence to support Obregón's and Calles's governments. In 1926, for example, the CROM used its power to get all suspected supporters of the Cristero rebels fired from the Buen Tono cigarette factory. See Carr (1976), p. 224.
[95] For discussions of the CROM's ideology, see Krauze, Meyer, et al. (1977), pp. 183–91.
[96] Carr (1976), p. 171. For other stories of Morones's corruption, see ibid., pp. 160–61.
[97] Hall and Spalding (1986), p. 353.

strikes fell to 138. Only 33,985 workers participated, and they produced a loss of 395,491 man-days of labor. By 1926 the CROM had effectively ended strikes. There were only 24 strikes, which involved 2,977 workers and 41,222 man-days of labor.[98] The CROM's ability to protect companies against strikes became so well known that a Royal Dutch–Shell subsidiary (La Corona) fired the entire labor force at its Tampico refinery in February 1925 – the workers were *not* on strike at the time – and hired only CROM workers as replacements.[99]

It should be clearly understood that Obregón and Calles allied with the CROM for pragmatic, not ideological reasons. One product of this alliance was that the CROM was able to use its privileged position to drive up the wages of its rank and file. This meant, however, that it was in the CROM's interest to support the special entitlements of the industries that were populated by CROM workers. Employers may not have liked the CROM, and they did not enjoy the fact that they had to pay for the CROM's services with higher wages, shorter working hours, and payoffs to CROM leaders. They did, however, know that the CROM made it impossible for the federal government to undo the special arrangements that allowed them to earn rents above the competitive level.

In fact, at the same time that Obregón and Calles were solidifying their alliance with the CROM, they were also forging a coalition with Mexico's bankers and industrialists. As was the case with the CROM, the impetus behind the government's desire to form a stable coalition was the de la Huerta revolt. The Obregón government feared that the country's bankers, in particular, would defect to de la Huerta. (The nation's bankers and industrialists were often one and the same.) In order to forestall this possibility, Obregón convened a national banking convention just 13 days after the rebellion broke out.[100] The purpose of the banking convention was nothing less than to write a series of laws that would establish the institutional rules under which the banking system would function. As was the case with a great deal of the legislation affecting property rights during the 1920s, the banking law that emerged from this commission was not put before the Mexican Congress. Instead, the special commission named by Obregón debated and drafted laws that Obregón then enacted by executive decree. What they essentially did was

---

[98] Gruening (1928), p. 377.
[99] Carr (1976), p. 171.
[100] Collado Herrera (1996), pp. 92–93, 330.

to recreate the arrangements that had created barriers to entry during the Porfiriato.

A similar process of special committees and executive decrees was used to provide benefits to the nation's industrialists and integrate them into the Obregón-Calles coalition. The industrialists had openly rejected an attempt by Carranza to bring them into his coalition in 1914. In 1917 Carranza again tried to integrate the country's manufacturers. In order to bring to an end conflict over the tariff, Carranza organized a congress of industrialists under federal government sponsorship. While this congress failed to create a stable coalition with the nation's manufacturers, it did give rise to a national manufacturer's association and an advisory commission on the tariff. In 1925 Calles formalized that advisory commission.[101] That commission allowed the industrialists to drive up tariff rates throughout the late 1920s. As was the case with the recommendations of the banking committee, the recommendations of the tariff commission were enacted without congressional debate or approval. Calles enacted them by executive decree.

The formation of this rather curious coalition of revolutionary generals turned landlords, Porfirian bankers and industrialists, and gangster-led unions was particularly crucial in light of the fact that there continued to be very real threats to the government until 1929. Mexican political instability did not end with the defeat of de la Huerta. Indeed, there were two additional, and not unrelated, sources of instability in the mid-1920s: church-state conflict and the political ambitions of Mexican generals.

From 1926 to 1929 the Calles government fought a vicious war with Catholic rebels angered by the anticlerical provisions of the Constitution of 1917 and Calles's strenuous opposition to the church. The Cristero rebels had a formal military structure of 25,000 men, at least an additional 25,000 irregular guerrillas, and operated over 13 states. The federal army responded with a scorched earth policy but could not produce a military victory.[102]

One of the reasons why the defeat of the Cristeros remained elusive was that Calles had to worry about the loyalty of his own generals. Toward the end of his term, Calles worked with Obregón in order to alter the constitutional provision prohibiting reelection of the president, the purpose being to engineer Obregón's return to power in 1928. They also engineered a constitutional reform extending the presidency from four to

---

[101] Márquez (2001).
[102] For a detailed history of the Cristero War, see Meyer (1973).

six years. This maneuver was motivated, in no small part, by the desire of Calles to head off a presidential bid by Luis Morones, the leader of the CROM. Calles feared that a Morones presidency would incite the army to rebel. In the midst of a civil war with the Cristeros, a military revolt could easily bring down the government – and Calles with it.

The Calles-Obregón reelection gambit ignited a rebellion by politically ambitious generals in October 1927. Calles nipped this rebellion in the bud by arresting and executing 25 of his generals and 150 other officers. These executions included the two leaders of the revolt, General Francisco Serrano, the former secretary of war and governor of the Distrito Federal, and General Arnulfo Gómez, military chief of the state of Veracruz.[103] Obregón then ran unopposed for the presidency. The day after he was reelected, however, he was assassinated by a Cristero fanatic.

Morones and other CROM leaders were alleged to have played a role in the assassination of Obregón and were forced to resign their positions in the Calles administration. Over the next several years, Morones would make a series of strategic blunders, including refusing to cooperate with Calles in his efforts to build the Partido Nacional Revolucionario (PNR). Morones preferred to preserve the PLM as an independent party. The result was that the first of the three puppet presidents controlled by Calles (Emilio Portes Gil, interim president from 1928 to 1930) worked to undermine the CROM by removing its members from federal jobs and the state labor boards, and using the army against CROM unions in worker-employer conflicts.[104]

With Morones out of the way, and with Obregón dead, Mexico was still being ruled by Calles, who pulled the strings of interim president Portes Gil. Many of the generals who had been loyal to Obregón now feared that Calles would install another handpicked puppet in the presidency in the upcoming 1930 election – thereby continuing his de facto rule. Mexico's military commanders were also unhappy with Calles's refusal to compromise with the Cristeros. Finally, many of Mexico's generals harbored political ambitions of their own.[105] Thus, right in the middle of the convention that named General Pascual Ortiz Rubio as the PNR presidential candidate for the 1930 election, nearly one-third of the army declared against Calles. They were led by General José Gonzalo Escobar,

---

[103] Markiewicz (1993), p. 52; Krauze, Meyer, et al. (1977), pp. 131–42.
[104] Middlebrook (1995), p. 81.
[105] For a full description of Mexico's political history from 1928 to 1934, see Meyer, Segovia, et al. (1978).

chief of military operations in the border state of Coahuila. It took several weeks of fighting to defeat the rebels, at a cost of 2,000 lives. Moreover, Calles's success was far from a foregone conclusion. He could not deploy all of his troops against Escobar because he was simultaneously fighting the Cristeros. This meant that the support of peasant militias was, once again, crucial – as it had been in 1923–24.[106]

The close result of the Escobar revolt finally convinced Calles to make peace with the Cristeros. In a deal brokered by the United States, the Mexican government agreed not to enforce the anticlerical provisions of the Constitution (although those provisions would remain on the books). The Cristeros, in return, would lay down their arms. In short, by 1929 the last credible threats to the government had been defeated.

Mexico finally achieved political stability after 1929. After Calles's formal presidency (1924–28), there followed a six-year period (1928–34), known as the Maximato, in which Calles installed three different puppets in the Presidential Palace, none of whom managed to serve a full term. In fact, one of them awoke one morning to read in the newspaper that he had resigned the day before. One key element of this newly stable dictatorship was the creation by Calles in 1929 of the PNR, a talking shop among the surviving generals and regional potentates designed to broker further political conflicts without resorting to violence.

In 1930 Calles appointed General Lázaro Cárdenas, who also served as governor of the state of Michoacán from 1928 to 1932, to be party president. Cárdenas succeeded the third Calles puppet (Abelardo Rodriguez) as president in 1934. It was Cárdenas who finally succeeded in formalizing the coalition of generals, industrialists, bankers, and organized labor to transform the PNR from a talking shop designed to distribute spoils among a few leaders into a genuine corporatist party and, in many ways, a branch of the federal government.[107] The result of Cárdenas's efforts was the Partido de la Revolución Mexicana (PRM). In the 1940s, President Miguel Alemán reorganized Cárdenas's PRM (by removing the army as a corporate branch of the party) into the Partido Revolucionario Institucional (PRI). The structure that emerged remained stable until the 1980s, and the distinction between party and government remained vague in Mexico until the 2000 presidential election.

---

[106] Meyer, Segovia, et al. (1978), chap. 12; Ankerson (1984), p. 128.

[107] This required Cárdenas to arm leagues of workers and peasants, carry out a sweeping agrarian reform, encourage the growth of unions, and deport Calles to Los Angeles.

There were a number of differences between the post-Cárdenas equilibrium and the Porfiriato. First, in the post-Cárdenas period, the mechanisms sustaining the government's ability to commit credibly were not based on the transfer of rents to powerful individuals (as had been the case under Díaz), but on the transfer of rents to organized labor. That is, while the CROM gradually lost organizational strength and eventually disappeared, many of its militants founded another labor federation – the Confederación de Trabajadores Mexicanos – which served the same function as had the CROM. Second, the movement of politicians into lucrative private activities was even more prevalent in the post-Cárdenas period, because of the existence of numerous state-owned enterprises. Third, and perhaps most important, there existed a credible selection mechanism by which a president appointed his successor and then permanently and completely retired from the political arena.[108]

While we do not discount the importance of these changes, the basic Porfirian game remained intact. In both the Porfirian and postrevolutionary periods, governments came to power amid political instability. In both periods the government was unable to commit to the global protection of property rights. In both periods, therefore, the nation's political and economic actors formed coalitions that produced VPI-like arrangements. The end result was that in both periods property rights were selectively enforced.

---

[108] It is a commonplace in the literature on Mexico under the PRI to note that the president named his successor and then retired from public life. What has not been explored by the literature is why this arrangement is credible: why would a president with quasi-dictatorial powers voluntarily abdicate every six years? For an interesting analysis of the mechanisms that make this succession mechanism credible, see Careaga (1998).

4

Finance

Financial systems are especially vulnerable to political instability. Under instability, governments and factions aspiring to be governments have strong incentives to steal bank reserves, force financial institutions to make them loans, engage in the unrestrained printing of currency (thereby setting off an inflationary tax on holding cash), and change the rules that regulate banking and the securities markets to maximize the government's access to funds.

The Mexican financial system was indeed negatively affected by political instability but only in the short run. The fight against Huerta in 1913–14 and the ensuing civil war among the victors from 1914 to 1917 brought about a near total collapse of the banking system. The governments that came to power after 1917, however, regardless of their stated ideologies, all recognized the need to accommodate the bankers. These governments understood that they needed a source of credit in order to restore political order. They also understood that without a functioning financial system there could be no economic growth, and without economic growth there would be no tax revenues. In short, the post-1917 governments realized that restoring the financial system was crucial to their own political survival.

The Obregón and Calles governments therefore recreated the vertical political integration (VPI) arrangements that underpinned banking during the Porfiriato. Just as Díaz had done, they selectively enforced property rights and allowed the bankers themselves to write the laws regarding entry into banking. In addition, the government created a hostage as a commitment device: a government-owned commercial bank (the Banco de México, or Banxico). As a result, the domestic banking system grew rapidly during the 1920s. One implication of the selective enforcement of property rights, however, is that there must have been some group of losers – in this case, Mexico's foreign creditors. In order to create a credible commitment to the country's domestic bankers, the government essentially abrogated the foreign debt from the Díaz and Huerta regimes.

In this chapter we explain how banks and securities markets form a financial system, and how the structure of the financial system is determined by government regulation. Next we describe Mexico's prerevolutionary financial system, briefly discussing the political economy of financial regulation during the Porfiriato and analyzing how the resulting regulatory structure affected competition; describe the experience of the banking system during the revolution and the 1920s; and, employing quantitative tools and historical evidence, explain the impact of political instability and institutional change on the financial system.

FINANCIAL SYSTEMS

A financial system is a network of banks, brokers, and exchanges that securitizes, distributes, trades, and values assets. This network turns illiquid physical assets into liquid contracts. At the simplest level, these contracts are bank notes, which are nothing more than a promise by a bank to redeem a piece of paper for gold or silver. At a more complex level, these contracts can be shares in corporations, which entitle the holder to a percentage of the profits of that corporation for the duration of the corporation's existence. Regardless of the complexity of the contract, the underlying function of the financial system is twofold: it eliminates the need for parties to a financial contract to have direct knowledge of one another; and it makes the contract liquid – easy to value and exchange.

Financial systems perform these tasks through two types of intermediaries: banks and securities markets. Banks take in funds from depositors, offering interest in return for the use of the funds. Banks also raise capital by selling equity in themselves (shares of stock) or by long-term borrowing (bonds). These funds, regardless of their source, are then lent at interest. Thus, banks serve to connect savers and borrowers – without the need for these individuals to actually know one another. In addition, the underlying set of contracts that allows banks to take in and lend out funds makes the wealth represented by those contracts highly liquid. For example, savers can transfer bank deposits in order to make payments – this is what happens when bills are paid by a check.

Securities markets, and the brokers who underwrite and trade on those markets, allow firms to sell claims on their future earnings for immediate cash. Most securities are based on two basic types of contracts first developed in the seventeenth century: equity participation in a firm (i.e., shares of stock) and long-term loans (i.e., bonds). What is crucial about both sets of contracts is that they are liquid. Stocks and bonds can be sold without liquidating the underlying investment; and buyers and sellers do not need to have direct knowledge of one another.

In theory, banks and securities markets can exist without one another. As a practical matter, however, banks and securities markets are closely interconnected and their activities are interwoven. To cite an obvious example, banks might raise their own capital by selling stock. Without the existence of a market that makes the bank shares liquid, however, there may be few investors who would purchase them. Similarly, banks may underwrite new share issues by other companies, purchasing the shares from the firm and then reselling them on a secondary market. Banks might also discount commercial paper (essentially a promissory note of short duration issued by a firm) that can then be traded on a market. Indeed, one of the primary functions of banks in the nineteenth century was precisely this kind of discounting. A firm would write a promissory note to a supplier that it would pay a debt in a specified number of days. The holder of the note would then sell the contract to a bank, who would give him or her immediate cash but at a discount off of the note's face value. These notes could also be traded on a securities market, where they might be bought and sold by banks as well as by private individuals.

The functioning of the organizations and markets that make up the financial system are crucial to private individuals, firms, and governments. The financial system allows private individuals to smooth their consumption and make purchases that would require them to save for an inordinately long time from their current income. Similarly, the financial system allows firms to expand at a rate faster than would be possible than if they had to rely solely on their own reinvested profits. The financial system also allows firms to borrow their way through downturns in the business cycle, thereby allowing them to hold more of their assets in productive investments (machines, buildings, and the like) and less as unproductive cash hoarded to protect the firm through hard times. Finally, financial systems allow governments to raise funds in excess of those they can obtain through taxation by borrowing against claims on future tax revenues.

Without an efficient financial system, the cost of capital faced by firms, governments, and individuals will rise. Inefficient financial intermediation will hamper new investment because investments will be less liquid. The time horizons of investors will shorten. Without a stable payments system, transactions costs will rise dramatically, shortening both time horizons and the ability to sell goods and services at a distance. In short, the functioning of modern economies is intimately tied to the functioning of their financial systems.

Governments have a special role in the formation and evolution of financial systems. The government not only influences the development of financial intermediaries and markets through its own demand for credit but also establishes the rules that govern the functioning of financial intermediaries. Financial systems allow claims on real – and often relatively immobile and illiquid – assets to be represented by relatively liquid contracts. Rules laid down by the government determine the security of these claims and how easily they may be traded or transferred. In fact, the government determines not only the security of financial contracts but also who can create them and the circumstances under which they can be created. The government, not the market, determines which group of financiers will receive a bank charter, the level of reserves that the bank must hold, and the composition of those reserves. In short, the government, while a participant in the financial system, simultaneously governs the financial system.

The critical issue between governments and the actors in the financial system is one of commitment. Governments need access to credit from the financial system. The financial system needs the government to enforce property rights. Otherwise, economic agents cannot write and enforce financial contracts. The privileged role of the government, however, means that it can behave opportunistically. Unless the government can tie its own hands, the financial system will not develop and the government will be denied the very resources it needs for its own survival.

SOLVING THE COMMITMENT PROBLEM
IN PORFIRIAN MEXICO

The government of Porfirio Díaz solved the commitment problem with Mexico's financial capitalists through a set of VPI arrangements. It allowed the country's major financiers to write the rules governing their own activities. These financiers responded by erecting extraordinarily high barriers to entry into banking, essentially granting themselves a series of segmented monopolies. In return, the government received a standing line of credit from the largest bank in the system. This gave the government the ability to restore political order and to reestablish its creditworthiness with international lenders, who had shunned Mexico because of its frequent defaults.[1] The VPI contract was enforced by powerful political actors – particularly state governors – who received a share of the rents earned by the banks.

Negotiated Agreement

How, exactly, did this system develop? Porfirio Díaz faced a dilemma when he came to power. Peace was necessary to promote economic activity. Imposing order, however, was costly. Armies had to be paid, a bureaucracy had to be created, and regional transport barriers had to be overcome by subsidizing the construction of a national railroad network. Díaz could not accomplish any of these goals by raising taxes because the federal government's ability to collect taxes was severely limited. In fact, the strongmen who ruled the provinces had every incentive to derail any attempt by the federal government to reform the tax system, because their de facto fiefdoms would have been eroded by centralized tax collection.[2] Foreign credit was not an option. Mexico had been locked out of international capital markets since the repudiation of the Maximilian regime's debts in 1867.

Díaz had only one option: use domestic sources of credit to finance the establishment of political order and then gamble that political order would produce economic progress that could be taxed. The problem was, however, that Mexican governments of the 19th century had regularly defaulted on their debts to domestic as well as foreign lenders.[3] The government could not rely on either the money markets or banks because both existed in a primitive state. As late as 1884 there were only eight banks in the entire country, five of which were minuscule operations in the northern frontier state of Chihuahua.

---

[1] For a discussion of how other Latin American countries followed similar strategies during the late 19th century, see Marichal (1998), pp. 112–41. For a discussion of how the newly formed Banco Nacional de México aided the Porfirian government in weathering a financial crisis in the early 1880s, see Ludlow (1998). For an excellent discussion of how Mexico's Porfirian rulers used Banamex to reestablish their credibility in foreign debt markets, see Marichal (1995).

[2] In point of fact, they scuttled an attempt by the federal government to reform the tax system in 1883. See Carmagnani (1994), pp. 268–69.

[3] Tennenbaum (1986); Walker (1986).

What Díaz therefore needed to do was to establish a bank large enough to provide his government with credit *and* make a credible commitment to that bank's owners that his government would repay its debts. To that effect, in 1884 the government engineered the merger of two preexisting banks into a semiofficial super bank, the Banco Nacional de México (Banamex). The charter that created this super bank and the accompanying legislation (the Commercial Code of 1884) had three crucial features: the merged bank was allowed to increase its uncalled capital by 8 million pesos, the government received a credit line from the bank in the exact same amount (at a below-market interest rate of 6 percent), and the bank was granted a monopoly on all federal lending and was to serve as the treasury's financial agent.[4] Because all loans to the government now had to go through a single intermediary, the government could no longer default on some creditors while receiving new credits from others. In short, creating Banamex solved the coordination problem among lenders and insured that the government would face a credible credit boycott should it default.[5] Solving the coordination problem was particularly important in reestablishing the government's credibility with foreign creditors.[6]

The logic of VPI agreements requires that the asset holders be able to earn rents as compensation for the risk they take by entering the coalition. The merchant-financiers and foreign bankers who held stock in Banamex were no exception. In return for providing a credit line to the government, they received a set of lucrative privileges. First, Banamex's monopoly on government lending meant that all foreign loans had to pass through its hands. The bank could then levy commissions and fees on foreign borrowing. Second, Banamex was granted a lower reserve ratio than other banks. Because Banamex was allowed to issue notes up to three times the amount of its specie holdings, whereas other banks could only issue notes up to twice the amount of specie in their vaults, it held a tremendous competitive advantage. Third, the federal government established a tax on banknotes of 5 percent and then exempted Banamex from this tax. Fourth, the government made it very difficult for new competitors to enter the market, because the Commerce Code of 1884 required

---

[4] México, Secretaría de Hacienda y Crédito Público (1951), p. 194; Marichal (2002).
[5] The Díaz government was therefore following a similar strategy to the English government in the 17th century. For a discussion of that case, and the logic of how a single monopolist increases the commitment by the government to repay its debts, see Weingast (1997a).
[6] Marichal (1997, 2002); Maurer (2002a).

that banks obtain the permission of the secretary of the treasury and the federal Congress in order to obtain a bank charter or to increase their capital.[7]

A fundamental problem with this agreement, however, was the absence of any politically crucial group to enforce it. In fact, some politically powerful groups stood to lose a great deal from the Banamex deal. One of these groups was made up of stockholders in competing banks, particularly stockholders in the Banco de Londres y México (BLM), among whom sat powerful financiers. A second group was made up of strongmen turned state governors, who ruled Mexico's provinces as quasi-independent fiefdoms and who wanted to award their cronies with lucrative bank charters. Not surprisingly, the BLM filed suit in federal court and obtained an injunction against the 1884 Commerce Code.[8]

Díaz therefore had to find a way to satisfy all of the parties to the dispute created by the Banamex charter and the 1884 Commerce Code. In the short run, the solution was that the secretary of the treasury granted charters to state banks on an ad hoc basis while Banamex acted as the treasury's sole financial agent. This was not, however, a viable long-run solution because it provided no commitments to any of the interested parties. The long-run solution required that a deal be brokered among the stockholders of Banamex, the stockholders of the BLM, the stockholders of the smaller state-level banks, and the state governors. In addition, after 1891 the secretary of the treasury was José Limantour – and he was not a disinterested party. His brother (Julio Limantour) was a major stockholder in the BLM and a member of the board of directors of Banamex.[9] Not surprisingly, when Limantour appointed the committee to formulate the new banking law, he made sure Banamex and the BLM were well represented. Of the committee's eight members, three were associated with Banamex and one with the BLM.[10]

The resulting arrangement, codified in the General Banking Act of 1897, could easily be predicted from knowledge of the players in the

---

[7] For a detailed discussion of the original Banamex charter and the Commercial Code of 1884, see Maurer (2000b), chap. 1; Marichal (2002a).

[8] Conant (1910). In the early 1880s the state governors could have credibly overthrown Díaz. They controlled state militias that outnumbered the federal army.

[9] Díaz Dufoo (1922), p. 108.

[10] The committee included Hugo Scherer and Miguel Macedo, major stockholders and board members of Banamex, as well as Carlos Varona, Banamex's general manager. The general manager of BLM, H. S. Waters, also sat on the committee.

negotiations. Banamex and the BLM were granted a duopoly in the Mexico City market. In addition, only Banamex and the BLM were permitted to branch nationally. They were also permitted to issue higher ratios of bank notes to reserves than the state-level banks – three-to-one as opposed to two-to-one. Banamex retained its position as the federal government's financial agent, although it agreed to reduce the fees it charged the government and open the government an additional credit line worth 4 million pesos. Banamex also retained its tax exemptions.[11] In short, the compromise allowed Banamex to retain the special privileges granted in 1884 and extended some of these privileges to the BLM.[12]

The local state-level banks were also protected from competition. The General Banking Act was written in such a way that, as a practical matter, only one bank could be established in each state, although existing banks were grandfathered in. The law specified that states could not grant banking charters; only the federal government could. In addition, the law stated that bank charters (and additions to capital) had to be approved by the secretary of the treasury *and* the federal Congress. The law also created three additional barriers to entry: the law created very high minimum capital requirements, U.S.$125,000 (later raised to U.S.$250,000); the law established a 2 percent annual tax on paid-in capital, from which the first bank chartered in each state was exempted, giving the first banks into each market a near-insuperable advantage;[13] and the state banks were not allowed to branch outside of their concession territories, preventing banks from challenging the monopolies of federally chartered banks in

[11] México, Secretaría de Hacienda y Crédito Público (1897), pp. 241–43. Unlike most commercial credit lines, Banamex would collect no interest on the unused portion of the credit line. Normally a bank would charge interest on any unused portion of a commercial credit line, albeit at a lower rate than on the amounts withdrawn by the borrower.

[12] Limantour justified these privileges by claiming that the national banks would "develop into banks of rediscount and, by that very fact, become true protectors of the local banks." This did not happen. Neither Banamex nor BLM ever acted as a lender of last resort, or provided any other type of special support to the banking system. Rather, they were wholly commercial operations, propaganda notwithstanding. Conant (1910), p. 24; Maurer (2002).

[13] The law contained numerous other privileges for the first banks of issue in any state. The law exempted them from any and all state and federal levies except local property taxes and the federal stamp tax, and reduced the burden of the stamp tax by exempting documents relating to the internal management of the banks or contracts with any level of government, marking down notarial fees by 33 percent, and reducing the stamp tax on banknotes, drafts, and checks to five centavos. McCaleb (1920), p. 107.

other states. In short, the only threat to the state banks could come from a branch of Banamex or the BLM.[14]

Enforcing the Agreement

The credibility of the arrangement defined by the General Banking Act of 1897 was not due simply to Congress passing a law but depended crucially on influential political actors including state governors and federal politicians, who helped craft an incentive compatible arrangement with three basic characteristics: the arrangement aligned the interests of powerful politicians and bankers; the politicians had direct access to Díaz, so they could monitor and signal the government on behalf of the banks; and these crucial political actors enforced the deal between asset holders and the Díaz government. The political actors, who had vested interests in the well-being of bankers, could respond accordingly to enforce compliance should the government renege.

At the federal level, the major banks clearly depended on crucial political actors to prevent opportunistic behavior by Díaz. These actors, often members of the federal cabinet, occupied board positions in the major banks.[15] For example, Banamex's board of directors was populated by members of Díaz's coterie, including Pablo Macedo (the president of Congress and long-serving congressman from the Distrito Federal), Roberto Núñez (the undersecretary of the treasury), Sebastián Camacho (senator for the Distrito Federal), Pablo Escandón (congressman from Guanajuato, governor of Morelos, and Porfirio Díaz's chief of staff), and Julio Limantour (the brother of the secretary of the treasury). The chairman of the board of the BLM was none other than the secretary of war (and former mayor of Mexico City, former secretary of the interior, and former secretary of development), Manuel González Cosío. Joining him on the board was Rafael Dondé (senator from the state of Sonora). In addition, Julio Limantour was a major stockholder in the bank. The Banco Internacional Hipotecario, a mortgage bank, was similarly populated with political notables, including Julio Limantour, Porfirio Díaz Jr. (the dictator's son), and Emilio Pardo (federal deputy from the states of Hidalgo, México, and the Distrito Federal, senator from Tlaxcala, and

[14] For discussions of the 1897 law, see Marichal (1986, 1998); Haber (1991); Maurer (2002b), chap. 2; Maurer and Haber (2002).
[15] As board members, federal cabinet members were entitled to director's fees. It is also very likely that the board position entitled them to a distribution of shares in the banks.

ambassador to Belgium and the Netherlands). The board of the Banco Mexicano de Comercio e Industria also contained insiders. Its chairman was Banamex board member and federal deputy Pablo Macedo. Joining Macedo was Guillermo de Landa y Escandón (a senator from the State of Chihuahua and governor of the Federal District).[16]

What was true for the banks based in Mexico City was also true for state banks with federal charters. The only difference was that state governors, not cabinet members, provided the necessary enforcement. Governors had the de facto ability to determine which group of financiers would receive the federal banking charter for their state. Given the barriers to entry in Mexico's banking laws, a state governor could effectively determine which group of financiers received a local monopoly. In return, the state governor – oftentimes along with politically powerful former governors – was then rewarded with a seat on the bank's board of directors. This would have entitled him to director's fees as well as stock transfers from the bank as payment for his services. In some cases, the governor himself received the bank concession.

The banks of the southern states of Chiapas and Oaxaca illustrate the influence of state governors. Emilio Rabasa served as governor of Chiapas in 1891–94. Rafael Pimentel succeeded him in 1895–99. The Rabasa family owned a large stake in the Banco de Chiapas, and a member of the Pimentel family sat on the bank's board of directors. Another member of the Pimentel family, Emilio Pimentel, governed Oaxaca from 1902 to 1911, and it should come as no surprise that the Pimentel family was represented on the board of the Banco de Oaxaca as well. The president of the Banco de Oaxaca, Luis Mier y Terán, had himself served as governor of the state between 1884 and 1887.

Northern state governors played as prominent a role in the banking system as their southern counterparts. In Durango, the founders of the Banco de Durango placed Governor Juan Manuel Flores on their board of directors.[17] In San Luis Potosí, two members of the Díez Gutiérrez family governed the state between 1881 and 1898 – both sat on the board of the Banco de San Luis Potosí. In the state of Sinaloa, Governor Mariano Martínez de Castro (governor from 1881 to 1884 and again in 1888–92) sat on the board of directors of the Banco Occidental. In the state of

---

[16] Board members from *Mexican Year Book*, 1908, pp. 269–78; political careers from Camp (1991). For more detail about the social and political bankgrounds and connections of Banamex's founders, see Ludlow (1986).

[17] Rodríguez López (1995), p. 22.

Zacatecas, Governor Génaro García Valdez (1900–4) served as president of the Banco de Zacatecas and sat on the board of the Banco Occidental in Sinaloa. In Chihuahua, Luis Terrazas and relatives sat on the boards of all the state's major banks. In fact, Enrique Creel, who had married into the Terrazas clan, received the concession for the Banco Minero de Chihuahua. Creel himself would later serve as governor of the state. In the central state of Mexico, the founders of the Banco del Estado de México reserved a board position for the former governor: José Zubieta, who governed from 1881 to 1889.[18]

In other cases, the connection to the state governor was less direct than a seat on the board but strong nonetheless. In Puebla, for example, Governor Mucio Martínez received neither stock in the Banco Oriental nor a seat on the board. The Banco Oriental did, however, lend over 264,000 pesos to Martínez. This debt, along with an additional 400,000 pesos held by individual creditors, was never repaid. Instead, the major financiers of Puebla, among whom were the principal shareholders of the Banco Oriental, bailed Martínez out by forming a partnership with him and effectively assumed his liabilities.[19]

In sum, at both the national and state levels, influential political actors provided third-party enforcement and information sharing through integration. These arrangements enabled the Díaz government to solve its commitment problem but in a limited way. The nature of third-party enforcement was personal and temporary. If any of these crucial politicians were to lose influence or were no longer available, the VPI arrangement would no longer be feasible. In fact, some individuals who had effectively enforced VPI arrangements during the Porfiriato were no longer able to sustain similar arrangements during or after the revolutionary years.

Implications for Financial Development

Díaz's solution created an extraordinarily concentrated and inefficient financial system. Mexico's banks used their legal privileges to behave like monopolists. These banks lent their funds only to those entrepreneurs who were tied to banks, which is to say to the bank directors, their families, and their business associates. Everyone else was locked out of bank credit. One upshot of this was that the securities markets could not serve as

---

[18] Board members from the *Boletín Financiero y Minero*, February 28 and June 18, 1907; June 10 and April 14, 1908. Political careers from Camp (1991), appendix F.
[19] Gutiérrez Alvarez (2000), pp. 125–26.

a substitute for Mexico's small and concentrated banking system. Only those firms that could obtain working capital from the banks *or* that had extraordinarily wealthy principals to begin with had much hope of selling equity. The reason was that only those firms could weather downturns in the business cycle and preserve their reputations as reliable entrepreneurs. Securities markets therefore remained small and illiquid, accessible only to those economic actors politically integrated with the government.

The Díaz government was well aware that the VPI arrangement it produced would have serious implications for the structure and efficiency of the financial system. Finance Secretary Limantour himself wrote, "In following this plan the new law will no doubt give birth, at least in the early years of its operation, to a sort of banking oligarchy."[20] The "early years" were to be the rest of the Porfiriato. In 1910, even if we include mortgage banks, there were only 42 banks in the entire country compared with 25,151 banks and trust companies in the United States in that year.[21] The capital available to this banking system was also small: total assets in 1911 totaled approximately U.S.\$400 million,[22] compared with total assets of \$22.9 billion in the U.S. banking system.[23] Finally, not only were Mexico's banks few in number and of small size, but the level of concentration was extremely high: Banamex and BLM accounted for more than 60 percent of all assets.[24] Estimates of the Herfindahl Index put it at 0.2, which is to say that even had there been interstate competition, the competitive structure of the industry would have been identical to that of an industry with only five, equally sized banks.[25]

The efficiency losses are quite clear from the monopolistic behavior of the banks in the system. The two largest banks in this system (Banamex and the BLM) rationed credit in order to drive up their rates of return. They did so by maintaining "excess liquidity," holding more of their assets in cash than was actually necessary. As a result, their stockholders earned substantial rents (measures of Tobin's q for both of these banks were substantially higher than one, or the measures for the other banks)

---

[20] Conant (1910), p. 26.
[21] Carter and United States Bureau of the Census (1997), Series X 580–87.
[22] México, Secretaría de Hacienda y Crédito Público (1912), p. 255.
[23] Carter and United States Bureau of the Census (1997), Series X 580–87.
[24] Calculated from data in México, Secretaría de Hacienda y Crédito Público (1912), pp. 236, 255.
[25] Maurer and Haber (2002). The Herfindahl Index is calculated as the sum of the squares of the market shares of all of the firms in an industry. The reciprocal of the Herfindahl is the number of equal-sized firms that it would take to produce the same competitive structure.

while they incurred very little risk (the yields on their common stock were roughly equal to those on government bonds). Although these strategies made a great deal of sense from the point of view of the stockholders in the banks, they were inefficient from the point of view of economic efficiency.[26]

The problems posed by a small, concentrated, and inefficient banking sector were compounded by informational asymmetries: banks could not assess the creditworthiness of potential borrowers. The result was that most lending went to insiders: bank directors, members of their families, or close friends.[27] This practice was common just about everywhere in the world in the nineteenth century – even in the United States.[28] There was a difference, however, between Mexico and the United States: Mexico had a few dozen banks, whereas the United States had tens of thousands. Thus, the potential number of entrepreneurs who could tap the banking system in Mexico was very small.

Essentially, banks in Mexico worked as investment clubs. Politically connected entrepreneurs banded together to obtain a bank charter under the General Banking Act. The club members would then cross-finance each other's activities and sell shares in the resulting bank to outside investors in Mexico City. The capital from the sales would then be used to finance the club members' enterprises further. In practice, investors knew full well that all bank lending was "insider lending." Investors thus bought shares in order to invest, indirectly, in the economic enterprises of the financiers who controlled the banks.[29] Investors preferred bank stocks over direct investments because the banks were lower risk. Bank directors had strong incentives to monitor one another carefully to guard their joint reputation. The federal government required the banks to issue monthly balances and placed highly paid inspectors in their offices. In addition, the banks had a ready mechanism to foreclose on bad loans. Bank loans (even those made to the bank's own directors) were made to entrepreneurs as individuals, who pledged shares in their firms as collateral. If the individual did not repay the loan, the bank could simply keep the shares that it held in its vault.

Financial markets did not serve as a substitute for this poorly developed banking system because it was very difficult for outside investors to

---

[26] Maurer (2002b), chap. 4.
[27] Maurer (1999) and (2002b), chap. 5.
[28] Lamoreaux (1994).
[29] Maurer (1999).

monitor the activities of firm directors and managers. Financial reporting requirements were not enforced. Despite legal requirements, publicly traded manufacturing companies often failed to publish balance sheets in public documents. Consequently, individuals tended to invest only in enterprises controlled by important financial capitalists with proven track records, which meant that they bought stock only in firms that were already tied to a bank or had reputable principals.[30]

Thus, to the degree that the securities markets were important, they mattered as a source of capital for the banking system. A few manufacturing firms were publicly traded, but these were either protected monopolies that were closely tied to banks or that were huge from the day of their first listing because their founders were extraordinarily wealthy financial capitalists. In short, brokers and financial markets did not play a particularly important role in the Porfirian financial system.[31] As a practical matter, the banks *were* the financial system.

In short, VPI solved the commitment problem in Porfirian Mexico. The government obtained a source of credit by allowing a group of financiers to fashion the laws regulating the banking industry. The set of laws they devised produced rents that were divided among the bankers, the federal government (which took its share of the rents via below-market-interest-rate loans), and the state governors and federal cabinet members, who monitored and enforced the contract between the Díaz dictatorship and the bankers. This solution to the commitment problem had a high cost: the resulting financial structure was inefficient and prevented the rest of the economy from attaining potentially higher rates of growth.

REVOLUTION, PREDATION, AND INSTITUTIONAL CHANGE

Predation under Huerta and Carranza

The revolution's initial effect on the banking system came through large-scale borrowing by Francisco Madero's government in order to finance military campaigns against the insurgents in Morelos and northern Mexico. In addition, 36 out of the nation's 42 banks suffered robberies or sackings as a result of revolutionary violence.[32]

---

[30] Haber (1997).
[31] This stands in stark contrast to Brazil, where financial markets were an important part of the financial system. See Haber (1997, 1998).
[32] Maurer (2002b), chap. 7.

This initial effect paled in comparison, however, to the activities of subsequent governments. The fundamental problem was that third-party enforcement of the coalition between governments and bankers had broken down. Governments or factions aspiring to be governments had little reason not to prey on the bankers. Indeed, the incentives ran the other way: the banks were a source of ready cash, and any faction that did not grab that cash would be defeated by a faction with fewer scruples.

Government predation began as early as 1913, under President Huerta. At first, Huerta tried to maintain the coalition with the bankers that had existed under Díaz. He soon, however, exhausted the government's credit lines at Banamex. He therefore turned to extortion by threatening taxes on bank deposits – unless the banks would grant him loans.[33] When extortion failed to produce sufficient revenues, Huerta seized the Banco de Morelos's specie reserves in order to support military efforts against the Zapatistas.[34]

Huerta's tactics triggered capital flight. As specie flowed out of the country, Huerta imposed a 10 percent tax on the export of gold coins.[35] The value of the peso rapidly began to fall. Between May and August the peso collapsed from 47¢ (U.S.) to 39¢.[36] The banks lost much of their specie and hard currency reserves.[37]

In response to these losses, Huerta decreed a ban on specie exports, followed by a declaration that private bank notes were now legal tender.[38] Previously, bank notes had circulated voluntarily, with no legal requirement that they be accepted in payment of all debts. Now refusing to accept paper money was a crime. Huerta then forced the banks into lending ever increasing amounts to the government, financed, of course, by note issues.[39] Huerta's predatory behavior led to bank runs.[40]

Other revolutionary factions also engaged in predation. In 1913 Villa's troops sacked Banamex's Torreón offices in the northern state of

---

[33] AHBNM, *Correspondencia con la SHCP*, vol. 7, 2nd table, no. 9899, Letter of May 30, 1913.

[34] *Boletín Financiero y Minero*, January 22, 1916.

[35] Decree of May 1, 1913, imposing a 10 percent value tax on gold exports, reproduced in Manero (1958), pp. 161–62.

[36] Kemmerer (1940), p. 14.

[37] AHBNM, *Correspondencia de la Dirección*, vol. 21, Letter of October 7, 1913, p. 672.

[38] Decree of 26 October 1913, prohibiting the export of gold and silver coins, reproduced in Manero (1958), pp. 162–63.

[39] AHBNM, *Actas de Consejo*, vol. 7, Ordinary session, December 30, 1913, and July 21, 1914; McCaleb (1920), p. 216.

[40] Kemmerer (1940), p. 16.

Coahuila, seized its specie reserves, and drew up drafts for U.S.$30,000 on New York, FFr30,000 on Paris, and £2,000 on London.[41] Carranza was no better. In 1914 he confiscated banks and bank branches in Sonora, liquidating their assets to finance his military efforts.[42] Armed movements affiliated with Carranza seized over half a million pesos from the Durango branch of the BLM.[43] Álvaro Obregón also plundered the banks, if slightly less crudely: his first action when he occupied Mexico City in 1915 was to impose a special bank tax.[44]

The worst predation occurred *after* Carranza secured Mexico City. On September 29, 1915, Carranza reinstated the provisions of the General Banking Act of 1897. He also declared that the government would liquidate those banks that had issued more bank notes than allowed under the 1897 act. Carranza knew full well that many banks had been forced by Huerta to issue bank notes beyond the old legal threshold. Three weeks later, he sent commissions to investigate which banks had complied with the law. Those failing to do so within 45 days were declared bankrupt, their specie reserves seized, and their other assets liquidated.[45] When banks protested, the government lodged criminal charges and arrested their managers.[46] As a result, only 9 of the 27 banks operating in 1916 survived this thinly veiled maneuver to capture their specie reserves.[47]

Carranza also engaged in the wild and promiscuous printing of paper currency. This triggered a hyperinflation, which destroyed the public's willingness to hold any kind of paper money.[48]

Hyperinflation and the disappearance of specie exacerbated tense relations between labor and government. A wave of strikes broke out in late

---

[41] AHBNM, *Actas de Consejo*, vol. 8, Ordinary session, January 5, 1914.

[42] The affected banks were the Nogales branches of the Banco Nacional and the Banco de Sonora, the Hermosillo branches of the Banco Nacional and Banco Minero de Chihuahua, the Hermosillo headquarters of the Banco de Sonora, and the local agency of the Banco Occidental de México. Circular no. 8 of February 18, 1914, reproduced in Manero (1958), pp. 170–71.

[43] McCaleb (1920), p. 217. The seizure consisted of Mx$400,000 in specie and Mx$100,000 in banknotes.

[44] *Mexican Herald*, February 11, 1915; AHBNM, *Actas de Consejo*, vol. 8, Extraordinary session, February 26, 1915. The banks protested that this action violated the law, because Obregón acted without legislative approval.

[45] *Boletín Financiero y Minero*, May 20, 1921.

[46] *Boletín Financiero y Minero*, January 22, 1916.

[47] *Boletín Financiero y Minero*, May 20, 1921, and August 23, 1922. An additional bank, the Banco de Morelos, reopened later (*Boletín Financiero y Minero*, October 31, 1921).

[48] For a discussion of Mexico's hyperinflation, see Cárdenas and Manns (1989); Kemmerer (1940).

1915: a goal of virtually all of them was that salaries be paid in specie or dollars. Miners in Hidalgo, México, and Michoacán all walked out over this issue. So did printers in Mexico City, machine shop operatives in Aguascalientes, and smelter personnel in Monterrey. In 1916 inflation provoked even more serious labor unrest: general strikes hit Veracruz in February and May, and railroad traffic in Chihuahua ground to a halt as engineers refused to work until they were paid in silver. In November riots broke out in Mexico City when the government tried to pay striking police and tram workers in paper money.[49]

As hyperinflation continued, the Carrancistas began threatening companies and workers. General Manuel Diéguez, in Sonora, called both workers and management at the Cananea mines "agitators" for the company's policy of paying its employees in silver and said they would have to be "disciplined."[50] The hyperinflation turned organized labor against the Carrancistas, causing a breach that would not be repaired until the Obregón presidency.[51] Carranza also cracked down on those who "shamelessly speculate on the fluctuation of national securities." Federal authorities took control of the licensing of all exchange operations in the country, requiring them to deposit 10,000 gold pesos on penalty of fines.[52]

By 1916 the public would no longer accept money backed by nothing more than the government's bluster. The government therefore lost its ability to finance its war effort through seignorage. The Carranza government could not force the population to work for worthless paper and prosecute a costly civil war at that same time, so it needed a new source of revenue.

The Carrancistas found new revenues inside the vaults of the remaining banks. On September 15, 1916, the Carrancistas effectively assumed control of the banks and appointed "Juntas de Incautación" (Intervention Boards) to supervise the banks' operations. In order to preserve a veneer of legality, Carranza did not simply have the Intervention Boards sack the banks' vaults. Rather, he amended the General Banking Act to increase the banks' legally required ratio of specie reserves to bank notes from 50 to 100 percent. On December 14, 1916, the Carrancistas declared the remaining state banks bankrupt, seized their specie reserves,

---

[49] Knight (1986b), p. 427.
[50] Knight (1986b), p. 432.
[51] See *El Demócrata*, September 12, 1916, for an example of the official line against organized labor.
[52] *Boletín Financiero y Minero*, January 7, 1916.

and began liquidating what assets they could.[53] The government extorted further loans from Banamex, authorizing the Intervention Boards to seize the funds if the bank refused.[54] On June 23, 1917, the government confiscated Banamex's remaining gold reserves at the stroke of a pen. This left the bank with silver reserves valued at approximately 500,000 pesos. By the end of the year, these reserves too had disappeared, as the government withdrew all deposits in Banamex claimed by the state banks. By October 1917, Banamex was effectively bankrupt.[55]

By the middle of 1917, the government had squeezed the banks for all they were worth. We estimate that Huerta and Carranza expropriated at least $92 million silver pesos from the banks (see Table 4.1). These are lower-bound estimates because they do not include losses from hyperinflation or expropriations by other revolutionary factions.

The Absence of Credible Commitments

Carranza was now trapped on the horns of a dilemma. He needed to reconcile with the private sector in order to insure his government's *future* access to credit. At the same time, his (desperate) need for current revenue remained, and he faced political opposition from without and within his government. Thus he could not make a credible commitment that he would not engage in predatory behavior should the need arise. This was more than an abstract problem.[56] In fact, in 1919 the Carranza government managed to persuade Banamex's directors to guarantee the payment of a money order for the importation of 4,000 tons of wheat from the United States in return for which the government agreed to repeal the decree placing the banks under the supervision of the Intervention Boards. The government then reneged both on the removal of the Intervention Boards and the payment of the money order.[57]

---

[53] *Boletín Financiero y Minero*, August 23, 1922.
[54] AHBNM, *Actas de Consejo*, vol. 8, Extraordinary session, February 17, 1917.
[55] AHBNM, *Actas de Consejo*, vol. 8, Ordinary session, October 9, 1917.
[56] Carranza was so desperate for income that he had already taken the dramatic step of increasing the so-called *contribución federal* (or federal contribution, the percentage of state and municipal tax receipts that had to be transferred to the federal government in order to cover the costs of sustaining the federation) from 20 to 60 percent – even though this undermined Carranza's delicate alliance with many of Mexico's politically powerful (and ambitious) state governors. Uhthoff Lopez (2001). For a detailed discussion of the problem of public finance in the Carranza government, see Uhthoff Lopez (1998).
[57] AHBNM, *Actas de Consejo*, vol. 8, Ordinary session, January 14, 28, and March 4, 1919.

Table 4.1. *Forced Loans from Revolutionary Governments*

	Huerta	Constitutionalist
Banamex[a]	$11,995,400	$14,934,000
Londres y México	$11,705,752	$17,526,376
Coahuila	$1,852,752	$100,000
Durango	$1,550,000	—
Estado de México	$1,470,194	$1,023,949
Guanajuato	$1,630,378	$690,920
Guerrero	$215,989	$1,212
Hidalgo	$985,157	$492,358
Jalisco	$2,100,531	$12,056
Minero de Chihuahua	—	$590,000
Morelos	$300,000	—
Oriental	$3,949,000	$6,477,997
Peninsular	$4,249,996	$1,940,209
Querétaro	$555,147	—
San Luis Potosí	$655,105	$851,000
Tabasco	$400,070	$396,506
Tamaulipas	$2,080,000	$925,520
Zacatecas	$190,046	$549,274
TOTAL	$45,885,517	$46,511,377

[a] The estimates for Banamex come from a different sources than the rest of the table. They were derived by adding up the forced loans listed in Banamex's *Actas de Consejo* (in AHBNM) between 1911 and 1921. They do not include the final confiscation of Banamex's specie reserves on June 23, 1917. The *Boletín Financiero y Minero* estimated Banamex's losses from forced loans to the federal government to be $19,471,377. The Boletín did not, however, distinguish between Huerta and the Constitutionalists for Banamex's debt. Because Banamex's internal records of forced loans were available, and did distinguish between the two regimes, those data were used instead.

Sources: *Boletín Financiero y Minero*, November 10, 1920.

After Carranza's assassination in 1920, President Obregón began meeting with bank representatives in order to reconcile with the bankers. Several private banks, without official charters, opened their doors, and the Mexico City clearinghouse restarted operations. The revival proved short-lived. It was killed by a banking panic in December 1920 provoked by extensive flooding in the northern cotton regions and the collapse of international copper prices.[58] The clearinghouse refused to grant the troubled banks any support.[59] Two of the new banks slid into

[58] *Boletín Financiero y Minero*, November 25 and December 9, 1920.
[59] *Boletín Financiero y Minero*, January 10, 1921.

bankruptcy, and daily clearances on the clearinghouse fell by half.[60] The Obregón government therefore tried to revive the banking system. On January 31, 1921, it announced that 12 banks would be returned to their owners.[61] Unfortunately, only 5 were healthy enough to reopen.[62]

By late 1922, more of the new banks had failed, and the credit revival, such as it was, was grinding to a halt. The *Boletín Financiero y Minero* described the situation. "In an atmosphere in which property is continually assaulted and threatened, under social and political conditions under which no one can offer an absolute guarantee which is theirs in order to obtain credit, the functions of this particular factor ... are impossible to carry out. So we are living a precarious and anguished life, practically vegetative. ... We do not believe this can be easily changed. ... It is not possible to reestablish credit in Mexico while there persists a lack of confidence and insecurity about property."[63]

The Obregón government attempted to use the parastatal Caja de Préstamos para Obras de Irrigación (Bank for Irrigation Works, or CPOI) to reestablish credibility. This bank had been created in 1908 in order to inject liquidity into the banking system after the Panic of 1907. By 1920 it was moribund but still existed as a legal entity. The government's idea was to issue bonds in order to purchase CPOI stock from the banks and then use revenues from CPOI operations to begin repaying those domestic bonds.[64] As a parastatal institution, the CPOI would not be subject to the constitutional restrictions on land ownership. In this way, the government would promote economic activity and at the same time make a commitment to Mexico's landowners by giving itself a stake in the maintenance of private property rights.[65]

---

[60] *Boletín Financiero y Minero*, January 10 and 31, 1921.

[61] *Boletín Financiero y Minero*, February 4, 1921. The government added BLM to the list of reopened banks soon afterward. *Boletín Financiero y Minero*, February 23, 1921.

[62] *Boletín Financiero y Minero*, February 26, 1921. The financial press attributed the reopening of the Banco Mercantil de Monterrey and Banco de Nuevo León to the fact that both banks had been able to spirit away some resources to the United States in the early stages of the revolution. As a result, the banks were not as badly affected by the specie seizures. *Boletín Financiero y Minero*, March 10, 1921.

[63] *Boletín Financiero y Minero*, April 28, 1922.

[64] *Boletín Financiero y Minero*, March 15, 1921.

[65] *Boletín Financiero y Minero*, March 31, 1921. The idea was not new. In 1919 the Comisión Refaccionaria de la Laguna (Reparations Commission for the Laguna Region) had been empowered to take deposits and make loans to landowners in the Laguna region states of Coahuila and Durango.

The commitment was not credible because there was no third-party enforcement. The federal government therefore never paid interest on the CPOI bonds. By June 1921 outstanding interest had risen to Mx$21.2 million, and bondholders in New York began judicial proceedings.[66] In point of fact, not only did the CPOI not repay its creditors; it did not try to maximize income from its assets either. The CPOI collected few outstanding loans from the pre-1913 period. When it did repossess a mortgaged property, it did not sell it. Instead, it transferred that property to the government so that it could be redistributed to the politically powerful.[67] The CPOI also distributed new loans in much the same manner as it collected the old ones: loans were made as political favors with little thought to their eventual repayment. Most went to politically favored clients for far more than the value of the collateral presented in guarantee and were never collected.[68] One particularly notorious case involved General Arnulfo González, who received a CPOI loan in 1921. When an attempt was made to collect González's debts, he replied, "As you see, my debts have a political origin. When the general management [financed me], it did so under a personal agreement with the President of the Republic, from whom I had directly requested the loan in order to finance a political campaign [in Coahuila]. . . . In my opinion it is only the most natural thing in the world that since this institution is a direct dependency of the government, it would serve the government's political interests and extend its benefits . . . with the equity and justice of which I consider myself a provider."[69] In 1922 the CPOI experiment ended in scandal and collapse, and the federal attorney general began criminal proceedings against its management.[70]

The government's need for credit continued to be desperate. On the income side of its ledger, it could not generate sufficient tax revenues. The government was so short of cash, in fact, that it required support from private moneylenders to carry out the day-to-day operations of the national railway company. On the expenditure side of its ledger, the very weakness of the government required it to distribute "loans" to powerful generals to purchase their loyalty; in addition, of course, the government had to pay for all of its regular operations. During the period 1922–24, President Obregón ordered that 12,600 pesos be lent to Manlio Fabio

[66] *Boletín Financiero y Minero*, June 17 and July 6, 1921.
[67] *Boletín Financiero y Minero*, June 17, 1921.
[68] *Boletín Financiero y Minero*, September 11, 1922.
[69] Méndez Reyes (2001), p. 25.
[70] *Boletín Financiero y Minero*, October 3, 1922.

Altamirano, a "socialist" from Veracruz and prominent political opponent. General Francisco Múgica, the radical governor of Michoacán, received 3,400 pesos. The president ordered 5,150 pesos to be loaned to the secretary of war, General Francisco Serrano. Francisco Tapia, a warlord in the state of Michoacán, received 21,200 pesos. Pancho Villa received over 100,000 *dollars* in 1922. In the most egregious case, Adolfo de la Huerta, in his capacity as the secretary of the treasury, ordered the federal government to loan *himself* 246,361 pesos in his capacity as the governor of Sonora.[71]

The de la Huerta revolt of 1923–24 exacerbated the government's need for cash. On the same day that the revolt began, Banamex transferred U.S.$13.5 million to the International Bankers Committee to restart payments on Mexico's foreign debt.[72] The government then borrowed 10 million pesos from the Huasteca Petroleum Company against future oil tax liabilities, with the intention of using the funds to make additional payments on the foreign debt.[73] Instead, the funds went to suppress the revolt.[74] That diversion of funds meant that the government had to borrow from Banamex to pay foreign creditors.[75] With memories of the revolutionary confiscations still fresh in their minds, prominent bankers contemplated sending their gold reserves overseas.[76] The revolt's defeat did not increase the government's ability to pay its foreign debt, and it officially suspended foreign debt payments on July 2, 1924.[77] The government continued short-term borrowing from Banamex and the Huasteca Petroleum Company – at exorbitant rates.[78]

---

[71] Méndez Reyes (2001), p. 24. If these "loans" were attempts to buy loyalty, the government did not receive good value for money. De la Huerta launched a revolt against the government that triggered a short civil war in 1923–24. Francisco Serrano remained loyal in 1923 but rebelled in 1927.

[72] AHBNM, *Actas de Consejo*, vol. 9, Ordinary session, December 5, 1923.

[73] AHBNM, *Correspondencia con la SHCP*, vol. 10, Letter from the Finance Secretary and General Treasury of the Nation, November 29, 1923; AHBNM, *Actas de Consejo*, vol. 9, Ordinary session, November 28, 1923.

[74] Ironically enough, de la Huerta himself had arranged the loan during his tenure as finance secretary. AHBNM, *Correspondencia de la Dirección*, vol. 22, Letter to de la Huerta, December 3, 1923, p. 395.

[75] AHBNM, *Correspondencia con la SHCP*, the Department of Special Taxes, vol. 10, Letter from Alberto J. Pani, January 12, 1924, and note.

[76] AHBNM, *Correspondencia del la Dirección*, vol. 23, Letter to Salvador Cancino, May 27, 1924.

[77] AHBNM, *Correspondencia con la SHCP*, vol. 11, July 9, 1924.

[78] AHBNM, *Correspondencia con la SHCP*, vol. 11, Letters from Alberto J. Pani, August 27 and December 16, 1924; AHBNM, *Actas de Consejo*, vol. 10, Ordinary session, November 19, 1924.

The lack of a functioning financial system not only jeopardized the government's short-run survival, but it also undermined any hope of creating a sustainable coalition with asset holders in other sectors. The Confederación de Cámaras Industriales (CONCAMIN, the national manufacturer's association), called for the establishment of new banks of issue. The Confederación de Cámaras de Comercio (COCACO, the Federation of Chambers of Commerce) called for intervention to ease the circumstances of otherwise solvent borrowers who failed to pay because they lacked liquidity. The secretary of industry, commerce, and labor published a report in 1923 on the economy of Puebla, one of Mexico's most important textile centers, blaming an output decline on extremely tight credit.[79]

Establishing a Credible Commitment

President Obregón left his handpicked successor, Plutarco Elias Calles, in a quandary, facing dissatisfaction on all fronts. Because there was no payments system, domestic manufacturers could not get credit. Foreign bondholders were suffering losses because the government was not making payments on its prerevolutionary and revolutionary debts. The government had already abrogated the property rights of domestic bankers and had made no commitment that it would not do so again. Last but not least, the government needed cash, and needed it badly, to restore political order.

The Calles government could not simultaneously satisfy all of these groups and still provide itself with adequate resources to defend itself against potential rivals. Tax increases were not an option. The most likely source of such an increase would have been the oil sector. Obregón tried, in fact, to raise oil taxes. The oil companies rebuked him, however, by essentially shutting down production until he compromised on a lower tax rate. Moreover, even if the government had obtained a higher tax rate, total oil tax revenues were falling because Mexico's easily tapped deposits were running out for purely geological reasons (see Chapter 6).

The only way out, therefore, was to make a credible commitment to some of the domestic bankers, while simultaneously preying on foreign bondholders for immediate resources. Calles's political calculus was straightforward. Given the problem he faced, a de facto default on the foreign debt was a logical move. Picture a sovereign borrower, like Mexico, which promises to repay a loan over a period of years at a certain interest

---

[79] Collado Herrera (1996), pp. 70–72.

rate. Each year, when the interest and principal payments come due, the sovereign must decide whether to repay or renege. If the sovereign reneges, the lenders must then decide whether to impose a penalty. The key insight is that lenders will not lend more than the present value of the penalty they can credibly impose. As Weingast has pointed out, there is a *maximum amount* that they will lend, regardless of the sovereign borrower's financial prospects or the interest rate offered on the loan. Therefore, if sovereign governments want to increase their debt limit, they must increase the ability of lenders to impose penalties upon them.[80] In 1924 Mexico was subject to few penalties by foreign lenders short of sending in the Marines to dislodge the government, something the United States was in no way prepared to do. The bottom line was that even if Mexico repaid its outstanding loans, it was extremely unlikely that foreigners would extend more credit. Calles therefore defaulted on the government's international debts.

The government then tried substantially and credibly to raise the penalties for reneging on its *domestic* debt. It did so by creating a VPI agreement with Mexico's bankers. The agreement delegated policy making to the bankers, provided the bankers with a forum through which they could coordinate their actions, created a single bank of issue that acted as the treasury's financial agent, and provided a mechanism by which politically crucial individuals received a stream of rents from that bank.

Calles took advantage of Obregón's previous move to allow the bankers to write a new and favorable banking law. Finance Minister Alberto Pani called a national banker's convention in late 1923, inviting representatives of both the old Porfirian banks and their newer competitors.[81] Pani was by this time an old hand at organizing "conventions" such as this one in order to form informal coalitions with asset holders. In fact, Pani had run a similar convention of industrialists in the fall of 1918, while Carranza was still in power (see Chapter 5). One of Pani's crucial moves was to signal the bankers that they were being invited to steer legislation back to the status quo ante by inviting two of Porfirian Mexico's most visible and, in some senses notorious, bankers to "advise" the convention. The first, Miguel Macedo, was a highly placed Banamex board member who had served as a federal senator from the state of Puebla and headed Mexico City's city council. The second, Enrique Creel, was one of Porfirian Mexico's most brutal (and greedy) governors. Creel and his father-in-law, Luis Terrazas,

---

[80] For a discussion of this problem, and a formal proof, see Weingast (1997a).
[81] Lobato López (1945), p. 280.

had run the state of Chihuahua almost as a private business enterprise. His holdings included, among a wide variety of other things, Chihuahua's most important bank.[82] (See Chapter 8 for a discussion of the Terrazas-Creel dynasty in Chihuahua.)

The legislation that emerged from the banking convention was tailor-made to protect the interests of the existing banks. The new law, enacted in 1925, established very high barriers to entry. Banks operating outside the Federal District required a minimum capital investment of 500,000 pesos, whereas those that wished to operate a branch or office in the capital had to invest at least 1 million pesos before they could open their doors. In addition, no banks could operate without the specific approval of the finance secretary and the president.[83] This last clause allowed the finance secretary to permit the new small institutions that had sprung up during and after the revolution to remain in operation despite the fact that most of them did not meet the minimum capital requirement.[84] The resulting system was therefore more competitive than the Porfirian banking system in the short run but protected existing banks from new competition over the long term.

One requirement for a successful VPI coalition is that the asset holders be able to monitor the government and coordinate their actions. The banking convention created a forum that allowed the bankers to do this easily: the Comisión Nacional Bancaria (National Banking Commission, or CNB). Prominent bankers were named to the commission, which became a "legislature" responsible for all banking and credit policy. The CNB regulated the banks, and reported to the president, not Congress.[85] Of course, the CNB's decisions could be overturned or ignored by President Calles. What the CNB did, however, was give the bankers an officially sanctioned way to coordinate their actions and pressure the government.

The Calles government understood that its good word alone would not be a credible commitment to the bankers. The actions of every Mexican government since 1913 provided abundant evidence that the country's rulers would behave opportunistically toward the bankers if given the chance. The government therefore created a hostage – the Banco de México (Banxico). Banxico was given a monopoly over government lending and the issuance of paper money. This bank was also capitalized

[82] México, Secretaría de Hacienda y Crédito Público (1924), pp. 264–72.
[83] Lobato López (1945), pp. 281–83.
[84] Sterret and Davis (1928), pp. 130–31.
[85] Collado Herrera (1996), p. 102.

at 50 million pesos by the federal government, most of which Banxico *lent to the private banks*. Banxico also lent a good portion of its portfolio to crucial political actors. In short, the system was set up in such a way that if the government reneged on its deal with the private bankers, it would be punished in two ways. First, it would lose all of the money it had lent to the private banks, which they had stashed overseas. Second, the government would immediately face sanctions from prominent politicians who received a direct stream of benefits (in the form of Banxico loans) from the banking system. This required, of course, that Banxico (and not Banamex) would be the linchpin of the banking system and would serve as a quasi-central bank.

Let us explore, exactly, how this worked. On December 24, 1924, Calles ordered that the receipts from the 10 percent railroad tax and the petroleum tax would henceforth go directly into federal coffers rather than through Banamex. He then reorganized the agency that collected the revenues, the monetary commission, into a state-owned corporation. This gave the government both a source of finance (the tax receipts) and an organization that could serve as the basis for a bank. Banamex's president, Agustín Legorreta, pointed out that Calles's actions violated Mexico's agreements with the International Bankers Committee. He also argued that the money freed up by the suppression of the de la Huerta rebellion should go to paying the international debt. These arguments went unheeded.[86]

Calles's next move (on January 1, 1925) was to incorporate the monetary commission as a bank.[87] Three weeks later, the government promulgated a new banking act.[88] Finance Secretary Pani then appointed a committee to manage the new bank.[89] The committee managed the Comisión Monetaria until it accumulated sufficient resources to open its doors as the Banco de México (Banxico) on September 1, 1925. The government immediately ordered Banamex to transfer all funds and securities held as deposits for contracts with the federal government to Banxico.[90] Four months later, the government officially transferred the revenues from

---

[86] AHBNM, *Correspondencia con la SHCP*, vol. 11, Letter from the Finance Subsecretary, January 15, 1925; AHBNM *Actas de Consejo*, vol. 10, Ordinary session, January 21, 1925.
[87] Sterret and Davis (1928), p. 134.
[88] AHBNM, *Correspondencia con la SHCP*, vol. 11, Circular no. 3 from the Comisión Nacional Bancaria (CNB).
[89] Krauze, Meyer, et al. (1977), pp. 37–38.
[90] AHBNM, *Actas de Consejo*, vol. 10, Ordinary session, September 17, 1925.

the oil and railroad taxes from Banamex to Banxico, ending the last of Banamex's Porfirian-era special privileges.[91]

Banxico was chartered as a commercial bank. Some Banxico stock was held by the federal government. Other stock was held by private banks, which had an incentive to buy Banxico stock to take advantage of its rediscount facilities. Even Banamex ultimately associated itself with Banxico. In late 1926 it affiliated on the condition that the 10 percent deposit the law required it to place in Banxico be compensated by an equal deposit from Banxico to its coffers.[92]

There were two key pieces to this arrangement. First, Banxico held a monopoly on lending to the government, which meant that the government could not default on loans to some groups of bankers while honoring its commitments to others. If it abrogated one bank's property rights, it abrogated all banks' property rights, because they all held stock in Banxico.[93] Second, Banxico was a commercial bank and therefore had the right, unlike the typical central bank, to make commercial loans to private parties. Banxico used this right to lend heavily to crucial political actors. President Calles's sugar refinery, the Compañía Azucarera El Mante, for example, received massive infusions of credit.[94] Other politicians, as well as Calles's relatives, also received credit. These included one of Calles's sons-in-law, Fernando Torreblanca, as well as Torreblanca's two brothers, Edmundo and Rodolfo. A sugar producer owned by another of the president's sons-in-law, Jorge Almada, the Compañía Azucarera Almada, also took out several long-term loans. Additional Banxico credits went to Foreign Secretary Aaron Sáenz (who was also a business partner of President Calles), Education Secretary Moisés Sáenz (the brother of Aaron Sáenz), Secretary of Industry, Commerce, and Labor Luis M. Morones, Finance Secretary Alberto J. Pani, ex–finance secretary Luis Cabrera, and, of course, ex-president Álvaro Obregón.[95] Banxico, in fact, took over 2.4 million pesos of Obregón's outstanding debts, not including 1.4 million pesos in unpaid interest. An additional government bank, also created in 1925, the Banco

---

[91] AHBM, *Correspondencia con la SHCP*, vol. 12, Circular 12–10, January 21, 1926.
[92] AHBNM, *Actas de Consejo*, vol. 10, Ordinary session, November 30, 1926.
[93] The Calles government therefore followed a similar strategy as the Díaz government when it created Banamex. Both governments were following a strategy that had been pursued by European governments since the 17th century. For a discussion of the English case, and a discussion of the economic logic of creating a monopoly on the public debt, see Weingast (1997a).
[94] Krauze, Meyer, et al. (1977), p. 50.
[95] Turrent Díaz (1982), p. 162.

Table 4.2. *Bank Assets Held Abroad, 1925–1930*

	Deposits in Foreign Banks (in current pesos)	% of Bank Assets
1925	24,438	5.9
1926	28,793	5.6
1927	37,319	7.2
1928	50,122	8.7
1929	48,988	8.2
1930	48,892	7.7

Sources: México, Departamento de Estadística Nacional, 1925–27, and México, Comisión Nacional Bancaria (1930).

Nacional de Crédito Agrícola, took over an additional 1 million *dollars* of the ex-president's obligations.[96] (We return to a discussion of this bank in Chapter 8.)

Banxico was, in short, a punishment coordination mechanism. It served this function in three ways. First, it coordinated private lending to the federal government. Its monopoly on lending meant that domestic lenders could easily cut off future credit should the government renege on any new debts. Second, by making Banxico's rediscount facilities available to the private banks, the government reinforced its promise to protect bankers' property rights in the future. In essence, the government put up a hostage to guarantee its good behavior. When the banks borrowed from Banxico, they received gold in exchange, which they could and did spirit out of the country (see Table 4.2). This gold would be lost if the government seized the banks' domestic assets. In short, the government would have to weigh the gains from predation against the almost certain loss of most of Banxico's capital. Third, Banxico's profits served to guarantee that the government would not unilaterally liberalize banking law. Its profits from commercial lending would be dissipated if the government allowed greater competition in banking. Because Banxico passed on many of these profits to important politicians in the form of cheap (or free) capital, anything that reduced these profits would directly damage the interests of powerful political actors.

By founding Banxico, the government created more financial stability than it could by the alternate strategy of maintaining payments on the foreign debt. Foreigners were unlikely to lend more to Mexico in the future under any circumstances. Nor were foreigners likely to provide the

[96] Calculated from data in Méndez Reyes (2001), p. 25.

private credit facilities demanded by Mexico's domestic merchants and industrialists. Calles, Obregón, and Pani realized this, and sacrificed foreign credibility in favor of domestic credibility. The only exceptions were the branches of foreign banks operating in Mexico, which would become part of the VPI coalition by buying stock in Banxico.

THE SUCCESS OF VERTICAL POLITICAL INTEGRATION IN THE FINANCIAL SECTOR

We address three questions in this section. What impact did revolutionary predation have on Mexico's banking system? How quickly did the banking system recover, and were there any long-term effects on the banking system? How well did the strategies of Obregón and Calles succeed in recreating Porfirian Mexico's VPI commitment devices to bankers?

Surviving the Revolution

A number of banks survived even the depredations of Huerta and Carranza. Indeed, it is surprising that circa 1921, after eight years of forced loans and legalized theft, there was any banking system left at all. Only 9 of Mexico's 42 previously existing banks reopened in 1921. Those 9 banks had lost all of their liquid assets during the revolution, and a large chunk of their less-liquid assets was now valueless.

But how far did total assets shrink under the depredations of Huerta and Carranza and how quickly did they recover afterward? Our analysis, using total real (inflation adjusted) assets as a measure of size, is complicated by the fact that the government stopped gathering data in a systematic fashion during the years when it engaged in predatory behavior. As a result, we do not have access to data on total assets for the period 1913 to 1924. We can, however, estimate total assets from 1921 to 1924. We have estimated total assets for the banking system in 1921 based on balance sheet data. (We assume that the 1921 estimate of total assets from balance sheets represents the universe of banks in Mexico.) From 1922 onward, we can estimate total assets using available data gathered by the government on the value of cash, loans, and discounts in the banking system. These items represented the largest part of bank assets (70 percent on average between 1925 and 1930) and allow us to estimate total assets by assuming that from 1922 to 1924 the ratio of cash, loans, and discounts to total assets was the same as it was from 1925 to 1930.

What do the data indicate? (See Table 4.3 and Figure 4.1.) Our estimates clearly show that there must have been a substantial drop in the

Table 4.3. *Real and Nominal Banking Assets,*
1894–1929

	Current Pesos	1900 Pesos
1894	61,216	63,858
1895	85,220	88,899
1896	96,317	91,281
1897	115,430	108,684
1899	162,748	188,788
1901	224,742	183,076
1902	255,621	202,541
1903	308,743	245,977
1904	366,406	296,809
1905	415,109	303,994
1906	526,105	389,210
1907	605,627	452,659
1908	680,396	490,833
1909	569,752	386,047
1910	606,422	350,323
1911	774,214	471,685
1912	686,599	418,306
1921	284,752	84,117
1922	148,916	53,714
1923	140,526	60,464
1924	205,509	82,317
1925	224,576	94,114
1926	416,981	166,105
1927	515,477	209,367
1928	521,205	221,427
1929	577,039	249,763

Sources: Estimates for 1894–1912 from data in annual reports published in Economista Mexicano. The estimate for 1921 was derived by taking the 1912 value of the assets of those banks which reopened in 1921, subtracting the estimated value of losses from Table 4.1, and adding in the value of the assets of new banking entrants taken from various 1921 issues of the *Boletín Financiero y Minero*. Estimates for 1925–27 from México, Departamento de Estadística Nacional, 1925–1927. Estimates for 1928–29 from the quarterly reports of México, Comisión Nacional Bancaria, 1928–29. Constant values derived using the wholesale price index in México, INEGI (1994).

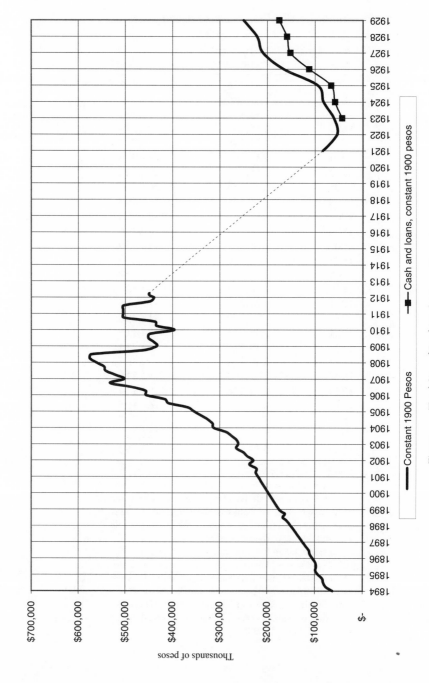

Figure 4.1. Total Size of Banking System, 1894–1929.

size of the banking system between 1912 and 1921. Total assets in March 1912 were 418 million pesos (in 1900 pesos). In 1921, we estimate total assets to have been 84 million pesos, roughly 20 percent of their 1912 level. The banking system then shrank an additional 31 million pesos in 1922.[97]

After 1922 the banking system began to recover. In 1925, after the creation of Banxico, the banking system's rate of growth accelerated dramatically. By 1929 the total real assets of the banking system stood at 250 million pesos, a *threefold* increase in eight years. In short, Mexico's VPI arrangements in banking succeeded in mobilizing a great deal of capital through the formal financial system during the 1920s.[98] Would the banking system have been appreciably larger had there not been a period of instability and predation at all? The answer clearly is yes. The banking system in 1929 was 37 percent smaller than it had been in 1912.

Whether the banking system, absent instability and predation, would have been much larger in 1929 than it was in 1912 is another matter. We can draw some inferences about the probable size and rate of growth of the banking system based on its performance in the years just before the polity became unstable. The data sets we have put together on total bank assets indicate that the growth of the Porfirian banking system was largely over by 1908. In fact, total assets in 1909, 1910, and 1911 were lower in absolute terms than in 1908. One reason for this was the financial panic of 1907–8. But that was not the only factor involved. Mexico's peculiar regulatory structure also prevented the banking system from growing. In order to increase their capital, banks had to obtain the permission of the secretary of the treasury – and he almost always responded in the negative. He allowed only Banamex to increase its capital. In addition, Mexico's banking law meant that few new banks were going to enter the market. Thus, there is very strong reason to believe that absent instability the Porfirian banking system would have grown at a very modest pace. This modest rate of growth would have meant that the size of the banking sector would have been larger than that observed circa 1929 but not

---

[97] It is conceivable that bankers may have engaged in systematic underreporting of their assets to avoid attracting predatory governments. We have no means of evaluating this possibility, but it does suggest that our estimates represent a lower bound on the amount of total banking assets.

[98] The gross growth in the real value of banking assets provides a minimum estimate of the amount of new capital mobilized by the banking system, because some existing debts had to have been amortized and replaced with fresh capital.

Table 4.4. *Herfindahl Concentration Index, Mexico's Banking Sector, 1897–1929*

1897	0.380
1898	0.341
1900	0.224
1901	0.198
1902	0.178
1903	0.184
1904	0.204
1905	0.199
1906	0.201
1907	0.223
1908	0.182
1909	0.156
1910	0.199
1928	0.115
1929	0.116

Sources: Calculated from data published in *Economista Mexicano*, 1897–1910; and México, Comisión Nacional Bancaria (1928–29).

much larger than in 1912. The weight of Mexico's political and regulatory institutions would have held it back.

Market Structure and Competition

What effect did the revolution and the reconstruction of VPI in banking have on competition? We estimate the Herfindahl concentration index for the banking sector in Table 4.4.[99] The data indicate that Mexican banking was highly concentrated both before and after the revolution. During the last five years of the Porfiriato, the average concentration index was 0.19. In 1928 and 1929 the average was 0.12. This implies a slight increase in the competitive structure of the market. Both index values, however, are quite high. For instance, the index value of 0.12 for 1928–29 implies a market structure of nine equally sized banks.[100]

The major difference in the competitive structure of the banking system in the 1920s was that Banamex lost its market dominance. In 1910

[99] Calculated from data in México, Comisión Nacional Bancaria (1928).
[100] Calculated from data in México, Comisión Nacional Bancaria (1932).

Banamex controlled 39 percent of all banking assets, 23 points more than the BLM, the second largest bank. In 1928 Banxico was now the largest bank, with 25 percent of the market. Banamex was second, with 19 percent, and the Bank of Montreal was third, with 10 percent. The BLM had fallen to fourth place with 5 percent of all banking assets.[101]

The revolution also altered the geographic distribution of banks. By design, Porfirian banks were widely distributed across the country. Northern banks, however, disproportionately survived the revolution and new entrants concentrated in Mexico City or the Tamaulipas oil zone.[102] The far south – Chiapas, Oaxaca, Guerrero, Tabasco, and Morelos – lost *all* its banks. Banking became far more geographically restricted.

New Market Entrants

A large number of new banking institutions entered the market between 1920 and 1925. The number of banks in the system exceeded Porfirian levels by almost 40 percent by 1928, despite the wave of bank failures in 1921 and 1922.[103] Many of the new entrants were Porfirian bankers starting under another name. For example, José Castelló, a former Banamex board member, took over many of Banamex's former clients in Mazatlán, Sinaloa. Another former Banamex member, Bernardo Zorrilla, did likewise in Ciudad Victoria, Tamaulipas, near Mexico's primary petroleum zones.[104]

Figures on the amount of paid-in capital in the banking system indicate a wave of new entry upon the passage of the Banking Act of 1925 and the establishment of Banxico. Unsurprisingly, most of the growth in the banking system after 1925 came through new deposits in existing banks or retained earnings.

The growth in the number of banks was not solely due to new domestic start-ups. Several foreign banks entered the market. Porfirian law had banned foreign banks from domestic operations. The 1925 banking law removed these restrictions. Foreign banks entered Mexico, including the Canadian Bank of Commerce, the Bank of Montreal, the German Bank of South America, and the Anglo-South American Bank.[105] These banks

---

[101] Calculated from data in México, Comisión Nacional Bancaria (1928).
[102] *Boletín Financiero y Minero,* January 18, 1922.
[103] Collado Herrera (1996), p. 70.
[104] México, Comisión Nacional Bancaria (1932).
[105] México, Comisión Nacional Bancaria (1928).

were later joined by the National City Bank in 1929 and the Chase Bank in 1930.[106]

Risks and Returns

While the banking system grew rapidly, it did not achieve anything like its prerevolutionary size. In addition, the government had to offer a hostage, in the form of Banxico, in order to solidify its commitment, something the Porfirian government had never had to do. President Calles had to proffer a hostage because he was unable to offer the bankers high enough returns to compensate them for their risk in joining the coalition. Finally, postrevolutionary governments integrated with a broader range of bankers, so rents had to be divided among more players. All of the above imply that banking profits, while positive (or the system would not have recovered at all), were lower than they had been before 1911.

We are able to measure rates of return for Porfirian banks from corporate balance sheets and profit and loss statements. This provides us with a comprehensive picture of rates of return on equity and rates of return on assets during the period 1901–10. Measuring rates of return in the 1920s is considerably more difficult, because we do not have profit and loss statements or balance sheets from 1911 to 1927. This means that we have to use 1928–29 as the basis for comparison with the Porfiriato. This almost certainly biases our postrevolutionary estimates downward, because of the effects of the Great Depression, which hit Mexico well before Wall Street's crash in October 1929.

We begin our analysis of profits by looking at the rate of return on equity. Conceptually, this measures the profits earned by stockholders in the firm. It is calculated as income minus costs, including interest payments to bondholders and depositors, divided by the par value of paid-in capital plus reserves and retained earnings.[107] As Table 4.5 shows, our estimates indicate that real returns on equity in banking were extraordinarily high during the Porfiriato. As one would expect in an industry characterized by high barriers to entry, real returns on equity averaged 25 percent per year during the period 1901–10. Real returns during 1928 were still remarkably high (13 percent), but they were substantially lower

---

[106] México, Comisión Nacional Bancaria (1929), (1930).
[107] We transformed nominal pesos to real (1900) pesos using the Gómez-Galvarriato and Musacchio price index. The price index can be found in Gómez Galvarriato and Musacchio (1998).

Table 4.5. *Rate of Return on Equity, 1901–1929*

| Year | Average Real Returns on Equity (%) | | |
	Weighted Average	Unweighted Average	Standard Deviation
1901	10	1	33
1902	27	26	61
1903	34	42	41
1904	1	5	23
1905	66	49	56
1906	31	18	16
1907	13	17	36
1908	22	76	154
1909	43	54	191
1910	1	−3	10
1928	13	21	112
1929	−1	0	121
1901–10	25	29	62
1907–10	20	36	98
1928–29	6	11	117

Sources: Calculated from annual reports published in *Economista Mexicano*, 1901–10, and the quarterly volumes of México, Comisión Nacional Bancaria (1928–30), available at the Hemeroteca Nacional, Mexico City.

than those observed for the Porfirian period. In addition, the standard deviation of returns on equity rose dramatically across the two periods. In other words, risk-adjusted returns fell by more than the absolute drop in profit rates.

The years 1928–29 coincide, of course, with the onset of the Great Depression. In order to adjust for business cycle effects, we have also compared average returns in these years with those in the period 1907–10. During those four years, Mexico passed through a prolonged recession called the Panic of 1907. This admittedly crude adjustment does not effect our conclusion that banking profits were lower after the revolution. Average real returns during 1907–10 were substantially higher than in 1928–29 (20 versus 6 percent).

One might believe that the decline in average rates of return (coupled with lower levels of concentration) would imply that there was more competition in the Mexican banking system during the late 1920s than there had been during the Porfiriato. This would imply, in turn, that the banking system was more efficient. One testable implication of this hypothesis is that Mexico's banks would have held less excess liquidity than they had before 1910. Surprisingly, this is not the case. During the 1920s, banks

Table 4.6. *Bank Liquidity Ratios,*
1895–1929

Year	Liquidity Ratio
1895	41
1896	40
1898	25
1901	21
1902	18
1903	17
1904	16
1905	14
1906	10
1907	10
1908	13
1909	14
1910	12
1911	12
1912[a]	12
1921	23
1922	24
1923	18
1924	22
1925	26
1926	19
1927	17
1928	16
1929	17

[a] 1912 data are based on second-quarter, not
end-of-year data.

Sources: Calculated from bank balance
sheets published in *Economista Mexicano*,
1895–1912; México, Departamento de Estadística Nacional (1925–27), and México,
Comisión Nacional Bancaria (1928–32).

held even more of their assets in cash than they did before 1911. During
the decade 1901–10, the average liquidity ratio was 15 percent. During
the last five years of the Porfiriato (1906–10), the average ratio was lower
still (12 percent). In the five years before the creation of Banxico (1921–
25), the average liquidity ratio nearly doubled, to 23 percent. Even the
creation of Banxico did not drive liquidity ratios back down to their late
Porfirian level. In 1926–29, the average liquidity ratio was 17 percent –
lower than in 1921–25 but well above its Porfirian level (see Table 4.6).

Liquidity ratios did not return to their Porfirian levels because the public remained skittish. Banks had to hold sufficient liquidity to cover potential runs. In 1926, for example, President Calles announced the definitive repudiation of all federal debts contracted under Huerta.[108] This provoked a short-lived American boycott of all financial dealings with Mexico and prompted bank runs.[109] Later came rumors that the government intended to shut down and seize the reserves of three Chihuahuan banks for illegally exporting gold to the United States. The rumor caused more runs and forced the Finance Secretariat to declare a bank holiday in Mexico City.[110] The Cristero Rebellion prompted rumors that Calles had nationalized Banamex.[111] In short, depositors had reason to be worried.

These worries present us with a paradox: bank stockholders were making quite considerable real rates of return (9 percent per year), but a good part of bank resources were tied up in unproductive cash. The implication is that banks must have had very high spreads (the ratio of the interest rate they charged for loans to the interest rate they paid depositors). We are unable to estimate spreads directly. Two pieces of evidence, however, support the hypothesis that banks in the 1920s enjoyed very large spreads.

First, we can estimate the rate of return on assets. This provides us with a measure of the profitability of banks as enterprises, instead of the profitability of banks to their shareholders (the rate of return on equity). This measure of profitability includes additional liabilities in the denominator (owner's equity, plus the value of deposits, bonds, and notes) and treats the bank's interest payments to bondholders as part of profits.[112] As Table 4.7 shows, returns on earning assets *net* of payments to depositors and other creditors remained at Porfirian levels.

The second piece of evidence that suggests that spreads were very large includes the observations of contemporaries about the high level of retail

---

[108] AHBNM, *Actas de Consejo*, vol. 10, Ordinary session, January 13, 1926.

[109] Banxico helped several banks weather this particular crisis. *Banker's Magazine*, October 1926, pp. 512–13.

[110] *El Universal*, April 14, 1926.

[111] AHBNM, *Correspondencia de la Dirección*, vol. 24, Letter to Robert Riveroll, Banamex representative in New York, January 31, 1927, p. 592.

[112] Conceptually, the value of these interest payments are profits that are shared with owners of nonequity capital. The bond- and noteholders are, in this conception of profits, providing investment capital to the firm – just as stockholders do. The returns they earn from this capital are therefore part of profits, not costs. Note that interest payments to depositors are not treated in this conception of bank rates of return as profits. They are still treated as costs.

Table 4.7. *Rate of Return on Assets, 1901–1929*

Year	Weighted Average	Unweighted Average	Standard Deviation
	Average Real Returns on Equity (%)		
1901	2	−2	16
1902	5	6	11
1903	10	13	15
1904	−1	1	8
1905	18	13	15
1906	7	5	3
1907	3	4	6
1908	6	5	6
1909	0	−3	13
1910	0	−1	3
1928	7	6	29
1929	6	6	35
1901–10	5	4	10
1907–10	2	1	7
1928-29	4	3	9

Source: Calculated from annual reports published in *Economista Mexicano*, 1901–10, and the quarterly volumes of México, Comisión Nacional Bancaria (1928–30), available at the Hemeroteca Nacional, México City.

lending rates. Nominal commercial loan rates oscillated between 24 and 36 percent through 1925.[113] The *Boletín Financiero y Minero* complained in 1922 that interest rates were so high that no conceivable business venture could support them.[114] Nominal rates began to fall in 1925, reaching 12 percent by the end of 1928,[115] where they remained through 1931.[116] In contrast, the nominal Porfirian interest rate never surpassed 12 percent. The difference in real (inflation-adjusted) rates between the Porfiriato and the 1920s is even greater. Porfirian real rates averaged 8.7 percent between

[113] *Boletín Financiero y Minero*, August 26, 1920.
[114] *Boletín Financiero y Minero*, January 19, 1922.
[115] Sterret and Davis (1928), pp. 137–39. Sterrett and Davis's estimates of retail interest rates before 1925 agree with the sporadic quotes available in the *Boletín Financiero y Minero*. Banxico rediscounted at 7 percent. They attribute the decline in rates to the opening of Banxico, which made over 31.3 million pesos of loans and discounts to private borrowers between late 1925 and 1928.
[116] Rates briefly fell to 9 percent during the beginning of 1929. However, by October rates on unsecured commercial paper had risen again to 12 percent. Banamex (1929), p. 7. They remained at that level until Mexico left the gold standard in late 1931. Banamex (1931), p. 12.

1900 and 1910, whereas postrevolutionary real rates averaged 34.4 percent in 1920–24 and 12.5 percent in 1925–29.[117]

If banks increased their net returns on earning assets, what explained the substantial decline in the return on equity compared with that during the Porfiriato? The answer is that more of the banks' resources came from capital investment by shareholders, instead of deposits, bonds, or bank note issues. This is consistent with the perception of the public that holding bank deposits was risky. In addition, bank notes disappeared as a source of bank liabilities in the 1920s. The public simply would not hold them. The result is that bank equity ratios (the ratio of the value of paid-in capital plus retained earnings and reserves to all liabilities) increased from 29 percent of liabilities in 1901–12 to 47 percent in 1921–29 (see Table 4.8).

Where did the new capital come from? The stock market dried up as a source of funds. Few of the new banks listed their shares. Rather, their initial capital came from their founders, not impersonal investors. Later growth was financed almost entirely from retained earnings. (The system's total paid-in capital did not budge between 1925 and 1930, when it began to shrink slightly.) In addition, no new industrial conglomerates bothered to turn to the market as a source of funds, although a secondary market in surviving Porfirian issues remained active.

Investor Expectations

If the banking system was growing, one would expect asset prices to reflect rising investor expectations about future profits. In order to test the hypothesis that investor expectations were improving, we constructed a weighted index of the stock prices of all banks and financial companies traded in Mexico City (Figure 4.2). We used buy prices except when transactions were made.[118]

---

[117] Rates for the Porfiriato taken from start-of-month issues of the *Economista Mexicano* between 1900 and 1910. Rates for the 1920s taken from Banamex annual reports and the start-of-month issues of *Boletín Financiero y Minero*. Prices adjusted by the index calculated by Aurora Gómez-Galvarriato and Aldo Musacchio. The price index can be found in Gómez Galvarriato and Musacchio (1998). Real interest rates briefly turned negative in 1925, due to an unexpected burst of double-digit inflation in a decade during which prices *fell* at an average annual rate of 4 percent.

[118] Bank stocks did trade after 1919, although not often: most stocks changed hands about once per year. Trading volume only rose again after 1925, although it remained low by international standards. The indices were constructed as a weighted

Table 4.8. *Bank Equity Ratios,*
1895–1929

Year	Equity Ratios[a] (%)
1895	25
1896	27
1898	25
1901	32
1902	28
1903	27
1904	26
1905	29
1906	28
1907	27
1908	34
1909	34
1910	26
1911	29
1912[b]	29
1921	35
1922	34
1923	64
1924	63
1925	51
1926	52
1927	52
1928	38
1929	36

[a] The equity ratio is calculated as paid-in capital plus retained earnings and reserves divided by the total value of all bank liabilities.
[b] 1912 data are based on second-quarter, not end-of-year data.
Sources: Calculated from bank balance sheets published in *Economista Mexicano*, 1895–1912; México, Departamento de Estadística Nacional (1925–29), and México, Comisión Nacional Bancaria (1928–32).

average of the prices of all banking stocks traded on the market. As existing banks issued new stock or new banks entered the market, shares of the index were reweighted to insure that changes in the index were not driven by the entry of new stocks trading at higher or lower levels than the index average. The composition of the stocks making up the indices for the periods before and after the revolution is therefore different.

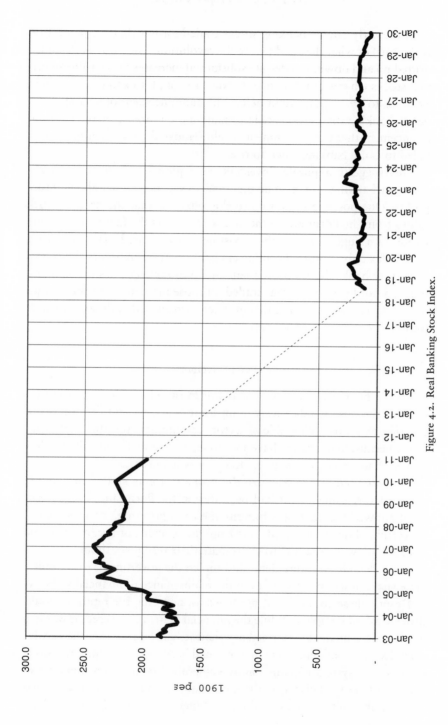

Figure 4.2. Real Banking Stock Index.

In the early 1920s, banking stocks traded for less than 10 percent (in real terms) of what they had before the revolution. The value of the index drifted up and down, but despite substantial increases in the value of certain stocks (shares in the Banco de Nuevo León, for example, rose from 15 pesos to 57.50 pesos right before the announcement of its 1922 dividend), banking shares stagnated throughout the 1920s. Even the 1921 announcement that the government would remove the Intervention Boards failed to cause banking stock to rise.

This suggests a puzzle: investors were plowing resources into the Mexican banking system, but they had low expectations about future profits. One possible resolution to this puzzle is that the drop in stock values from the Porfiriato to the 1920s represents the fact that investors wrote off a huge chunk of their existing investments. In fact, our stock price index only captures Porfirian era banks that survived into the 1920s. Most new banks did not raise their capital in the securities markets and thus did not have shares that traded on those markets and cannot enter the index. The implication is that investors perceived that these new banks were going to be remarkably profitable.

CONCLUSIONS

In theory, finance is the economic sector most vulnerable to political instability, because it relies heavily on legal contracts and definitions. In practice, this most vulnerable of sectors can mitigate the effects of instability, because most rulers have incentives to negotiate with the holders of wealth in order to gain access to credit when necessary.

In postrevolutionary Mexico, the property rights system in banking was structured much as it had been during the Porfiriato. The government allowed the financiers to write the rules governing their activities. Powerful politicians received rents from the bankers, or became bankers. Banxico allowed creditors to coordinate their responses should the government default on future debts and forced the government to commit a large share of its own resources to the maintenance of financial stability.

Despite these commitment mechanisms, however, the return of confidence was not complete. While the financial system recovered, it was less efficient as a financial intermediary than it had been before the revolution. Because confidence in bank notes had been lost, and faith in deposits reduced, the system remained more vulnerable to bank runs than it had been before 1910. This meant that more liquid resources had to be left tied up in bank vaults, earning nothing and financing nothing. The banking system had not reached its former size as late as 1929, while the securities markets, which was small and thin before 1910, essentially ceased to function as a means of capital mobilization in the 1920s.

Nevertheless, the selective specification and enforcement of property rights, coupled to the integration of bankers into the governing coalition, mitigated the effects of political instability in this key economic sector. The banks maintained their net real return on assets, recovered substantially from the civil war, reinvested, and continued to extend credit despite a highly unstable polity. The ability to mitigate the effects of instability on the banking system, however, depended crucially upon the fact that instability was equally (if not more) mitigated in other economic sectors. If manufacturers, farmers, and miners failed to produce and invest due to continuing uncertainty, then there would be no private demand for credit regardless of the credibility of the government's commitments to the bankers. Therefore, we now turn our analysis to the manufacturing sector.

5

Industry

What impact did Mexico's long period of instability have on its manufacturing industries? What strategies did manufacturers and political factions employ to mitigate the impact of adverse institutional change on their businesses? How successful were those strategies?

Our analysis indicates that political instability had only a short-run impact on investment and economic performance. Firm- and industry-level data indicate that the size, ownership structure, and productivity growth of the manufacturing sector was little affected by political turbulence, except for the period 1914–17. In the medium term, however, Mexico's manufacturers were able to mitigate the effects of instability by recreating the vertical political integration (VPI) coalitions that had sustained investment under Díaz. The one major difference was the third party that enforced the coalition. During the Porfiriato, the third-party enforcers of VPI were politically crucial individuals. After 1918 the third-party enforcer was the labor movement, acting as an institutionalized entity embedded into the country's governance structure.

In our argument we discuss first the development of large-scale industry in Mexico during the two decades prior to 1910 and then the direct impact of violence and the indirect impact of institutional change on Mexican manufacturers during and after the revolution. We then employ firm- and industry-level data and econometric techniques to assess the effects of these institutional changes before advancing an argument to explain why extreme political instability and dramatic institutional change had little impact on the performance of industry over the medium term.

Industry

MANUFACTURING BEFORE THE REVOLUTION

Mexico grew rapidly in the two decades from 1890 to 1910. Driving this growth was foreign direct investment in railroads and export activities, such as petroleum, industrial and precious metals, and agricultural commodities (discussed in Chapters 6, 7, and 8.) The expansion of these sectors gave rise to a wage-earning population of roughnecks, ranch hands, stevedores, railway men, and miners – a work force of close to 2 million. Assuming that each wage earner supported 1.5 dependents, the population with the wherewithal to consume manufactured goods was roughly 5 million.[1] Linked together via the railroad network, this population constituted an important market for manufactured goods, such as cloth, beer, soap, cigarettes, and shoes.[2] At the same time, the growth of Mexico's cities, and the public works projects that urban growth entailed, gave rise to demand for construction goods such as structural steel and cement. The production of these final goods, in turn, produced demand for manufactured intermediate inputs. This gave rise to industries that produced products such as glass bottles (whose primary customer was the beer industry), paper (whose primary customer was the nation's growing number of newspapers), and basic chemicals (which were required for the production of goods such as soap, ammunition, and dynamite).

During this period, Mexico's small and backward manufacturing sector was transformed. Previously, Mexican manufacturing had been characterized by small, family-run firms that produced for local markets using nonmechanized production techniques. Between 1890 and 1910, they were supplanted by large-scale, capital-intensive firms. The adoption of mechanized production methods, which permitted firms to realize scale economies in production, was accompanied by a rapid increase in industrial concentration. Monopolies and oligopolies dominated many product lines. By the outbreak of the Mexican Revolution, many of Mexico's present-day industrial giants had been founded.[3]

A description of the rapid growth and transformation of the cotton textile industry gives a sense of the process. Mexico's first mechanized textile mills were founded in the 1830s with the assistance of a government-run industrial development bank. The growth of this industry, however, was

[1] Haber (1989), p. 27.
[2] For a discussion of the role of the railroads in the creation of the national market, see Kuntz Ficker (1995).
[3] For a detailed discussion, see Haber (1989, 1992); Cerutti (1992); Keremetsis (1973).

hampered by Mexico's limited market size and the scarcity of capital. From 1830 to 1850 the industry appears to have grown little, and then grew at a modest pace until 1890. In 1850 the entire industry comprised 59 firms running 135,000 spindles.[4] Nearly four decades later, the industry had barely doubled in size, reaching 250,000 spindles in 1888. Productivity growth was no more impressive. Estimates of total factor productivity (TFP – output per worker holding captial constant) for this period indicate a lower-bound rate of productivity growth of 0 percent and an upper-bound rate of 2.6 percent per year.[5]

Beginning in the latter part of the Porfiriato, growth accelerated dramatically. From 1888 to 1900 the industry more than doubled to 588,000 spindles. By 1911 it had grown another 50 percent, to 725,000 spindles. Estimates of TFP indicate growth on the order of 1.5 percent (lower bound) and 3.3 percent (upper bound) per year. Labor productivity grew even faster: the estimates indicate that output per worker grew between 3.0 and 4.7 percent per year.[6]

The quantitative expansion of the cotton textile industry was accompanied by a qualitative change in the methods of production and in the industry's competitive structure. Until the 1880s most Mexican cotton mills were small and ran with water power. Indeed, as late as 1895 there were still 41,000 artisan cloth producers in Mexico, producing cotton goods on manually operated looms.[7] In the decades after 1890 production technology changed considerably. The larger, newer mills now employed high-velocity, electric-powered looms and spindles. Mexico's leading firms were not simply large relative to the small Mexican market; they were enormous even by U.S. standards. The largest firm in the industry, for example, the Compañía Industrial de Orizaba (CIDOSA) consisted of four mills employing 4,284 workers running 92,708 spindles and 3,899 looms. Had it been located in the United States, it would have ranked among the 25 largest cotton textile enterprises.[8]

Equally dramatic transformations took place in the industrial organization of other manufacturing industries. Mexico's first integrated steel mill (Fundidora Monterrey) was founded in 1900. Its American-designed

---

[4] Spindles constitute the most important capital input for the production of cotton textile goods, and thus the literature tends to use spindlage as the measure of capital or capacity. See, for example, Kane (1988).
[5] Razo and Haber (1998).
[6] Razo and Haber (1998).
[7] Anderson (1976), p. 47.
[8] AGN, Ramo de Trabajo, box 5, file 4. See also Haber (1997).

blast furnace, Bessemer converters, and rolling mills allowed it to establish rapidly a domestic monopoly in the production of structural shapes, rails, and other products. In the paper industry, one giant, vertically integrated firm brought in high speed, Swiss-made machinery with a capacity three times that of all its competitors combined, bought out its actual *and* potential rivals, and established a national monopoly in the market for newsprint and other low-value-to-bulk paper products.[9] In the cigarette industry, two giant firms, employing automated cigarette rolling machines and thousands of workers, pushed out the hundreds of artisanal shops that had characterized the tobacco industry. These two firms, El Buen Tono and La Tabacalera Mexicana, controlled over 60 percent of the market by 1910.[10]

In beer brewing, a domestic industry was created almost overnight, with local monopolies established in virtually every major city by the turn of the century. One of the industry's leading firms (the Cervecería Cuauhtémoc) soon came to control 28 percent of the national market. It went on to spin off a glass-bottle-making company (Vidriera Monterrey) that quickly established itself as a domestic glass monopoly that persisted until the 1990s.[11] A similar situation developed in the cement industry. Until the turn of the century, Mexico produced no cement at all. By 1911 three firms were in operation with a combined capacity of 150,000 metric tons per year.[12] In soap and glycerin, Mexico's hundreds of artisan producers were forced out of business by the mammoth Compañía Industrial Jabonera de la Laguna – one of the four largest soap factories in the world. La Laguna not only created a near monopoly in the production of soap and glycerin (taking 80 percent of the market); it also tried (unsuccessfully) to establish a monopsony on one of the crucial inputs for soap production.[13] La Laguna later turned its expertise in basic chemicals

[9] Lenz and Gómez de Orozco (1940); *Mexican Yearbook*, 1908, p. 539; 1909–10, pp. 416–17; 1911, p. 287; 1912, pp. 113, 126; 1913, p. 93; 1914, p. 103; *La Semana Mercantil*, November 29, 1898, and February 8, 1904; *El Economista Mexicano*, April 23, 1904; México, Secretaría de Hacienda (1936), p. 8.

[10] México, Secretaría de Hacienda (various years); *Mexican Yearbook*, 1908, p. 531; 1911, p. 281; 1914, p. 102; *La Semana Mercantil*, December 4, 1893; *El Economista Mexicano*, March 12, 1904; March 4, 1905; and August 18, 1906.

[11] Haber (1989), pp. 52–54, 90–91. Vidriera's absolute dominance was only broken by Mexico's entry into NAFTA in 1994.

[12] Unpublished data from Cámara Nacional de Cemento (n.d.). Rojas Alonso (1967); Patiño Rodríguez (1964); and *Mexican Yearbook*, 1914, p. 104.

[13] Barragán (1993), pp. 1–13; *La Semana Mercantil*, August 8, 1898, p. 444; Graham-Clark (1909), p. 37; *Journal of the American Chamber of Commerce of Mexico*, October 1925, p. 16; *Mexican Yearbook*, 1911, p. 289; 1914, p. 101.

toward the establishment of a spin-off firm that produced dynamite and other explosives, which controlled the entire national market for dynamite through a lucrative concession from the federal government.[14]

Virtually none of these industries could have existed without government support in the form of high tariffs. Mexican industry was large scale and technologically modern, but with few exceptions none of it could have competed head to head against U.S. or British imports. The higher cost of capital, the expenses associated with importing intermediate inputs and capital equipment, and the lower productivity of labor in Mexico swamped the benefits Mexican manufacturers obtained from lower wage rates than those that prevailed elsewhere.[15]

Protectionism was not a new phenomenon in Mexico; Mexican governments had imposed both tariff and nontariff barriers to imports throughout the 19th century. The problem was that import tariffs were high across the board – on raw materials, on intermediate goods, and on final manufactures. Manufacturers may have had a tariff on the goods they produced, but they had to pay the cost of the tariff on the goods they employed in production. The result was that Mexico imported very little (and hence the government received little tariff revenue) and that manufacturers had very low *effective* rates of protection.

Beginning in 1891, the government quite consciously honed the existing system with an eye toward protecting domestic manufacturers *and* maximizing government revenues. On the one hand, the government drove down the tariffs on manufactured goods that Mexico did not produce, the goal being to reduce the costs facing the users of those goods and to increase the government's revenues from import taxes. On the other hand, the government drove up the tariffs on goods produced by Mexico's new and rapidly growing industries, the goal being to protect firms from international competition. Thus, tariff rates *on a select group of products* were extraordinarily high: 76 percent for bottled beer, 72 percent for common cloth, 88 percent for fine cloth, 198 percent for printing paper, 225 percent for candles, and 234 percent for soap, to cite a few examples. Over the course of the 1890s the level of tariff protection declined because the tariff was specific, not ad valorem. Declines in nominal tariffs, however, were more than mitigated by the fact that the peso was depreciating

---

[14] México, Banco Central Mexicano (1908), pp. 288–89; *El Economista Mexicano*, January 1, 1902, p. 217; February 1, 1902, p. 284; Wasserman (1984), p. 18; *Mexican Yearbook*, 1909–10, pp. 414–15.

[15] For an analysis of costs in the cotton textile industry, see Clark (1987).

in real terms – which provided implicit protection. Given the government's commitment to protecting specific industries, when Mexico finally switched to the gold standard in 1905, it revised its tariff schedules upward to insure that favored industries would continue to receive protection.[16]

In addition, the government created a "cascading" tariff structure: duties on final manufactured goods were high whereas duties on the inputs to produce those final goods were low or zero. Trade protection in steel illustrates the case clearly. In 1909 the tariff on steel products produced by Fundidora Monterrey (the nation's sole integrated steel producer) was 43.7 percent. The tariff on products that the firm did not produce was roughly half that: 22.9 percent. The tariff on the imported inputs that Fundidora Monterrey consumed was 3.4 percent.[17] This was true in the textile industry as well. The tariff on imported cloth tended to be twice that of the tariff on imported raw cotton. The result was an effective rate of protection that varied from 39 to 78 percent (the variance driven by movements in the real exchange rate, which affected the peso price of imports).[18] The effects of the tariff structure were, in some cases, magnified by charging imported goods a higher excise tax than their domestic substitutes. In the case of cigarettes, for example, imported products paid an excise tax that was 70 percent higher than their domestic competitors.[19]

The mechanism by which some industries obtained protective tariffs (while others did not) was entirely consistent with the logic of VPI systems. As Graciela Márquez has demonstrated, from 1887 to 1905 Congress delegated the authority to legislate on tariffs to the executive branch. Beginning with the 1905 tariff reform, Congress once again voted on the tariff, but it could only accept or reject proposals made by the executive branch; it could not initiate tariff legislation. This meant that for all intents and purposes the power to raise (or lower) tariffs resided in a single person – José Y. Limantour, Mexico's secretary of the treasury from 1893 to 1911. Limantour essentially made decisions based on the following principle: those industrialists who were parts of small, well-organized groups that were politically connected to the Díaz regime obtained a property right to trade protection. Everyone else was left out in the cold.[20]

---

[16] Beatty (2001), chaps. 3 and 4; Kuntz Ficker (2002); Beatty (2002); Márquez (2001).
[17] Gómez Galvarriato (1997), p. 216.
[18] Gómez Galvarriato (1999), p. 604.
[19] Domestic producers paid 50 centavos for 100 stamps. Every 25 grams (or fraction thereof) of cigarettes required one stamp. Foreign cigarettes paid 85 centavos for 100 stamps. *Mexican Yearbook*, 1908, p. 958.
[20] Márquez (2001).

Trade protection is not, of course, an excludable property right. The rents generated by protective tariffs should have encouraged market entry, and those new domestic competitors should have dissipated the rents earned by the privileged group that surrounded the Díaz government. This did not happen for three reasons. First, many of Mexico's new industries were characterized by extremely large economies of scale. There was simply not room for more than one or two producers in the small Mexican market. Thus, the firms that obtained trade protection and erected production facilities obtained substantial first-mover advantages. Second, Mexico's peculiar banking laws created financial barriers to entry. Third, a similarly peculiar set of patent laws created technological barriers to entry. When these three reasons proved insufficient, and when it was in the interest of the government to do so, the government created barriers to entry by erecting high excise taxes, to which it then selectively granted exemptions.

The paper industry provides an example of how financial market imperfections created barriers to entry in manufacturing. A single firm, the San Rafael paper company, dominated the market because its principal investors could mobilize capital through the financial markets and the banking system, whereas its actual and potential competitors could not. Its basic business strategy was to buy out any operation whose principals had the knowledge required to run a competing paper mill. Thus, within a decade of its founding, it had purchased five of its seven competitors. For most of the Porfiriato, the only competition San Rafael faced came from two small factories that had been founded, ironically, by German technicians that San Rafael brought to Mexico to supervise its own operations. These competitors, however, lacked access to the banks or the financial markets, and therefore remained very small in scale. They competed with San Rafael on the basis of their ability to produce high-quality paper products that could compete with imported goods. San Rafael, on the other hand, monopolized the market in low-value products, particularly newsprint. The only serious threat to its control of the market occurred in 1902, when the El Progreso paper mill opened its doors in the Mexico City suburb of Tlalnepantla. Within two years, San Rafael used its privileged access to the capital markets to buy out its new competitor. San Rafael then used the Tlalnepantla factory's modern machinery to produce high-quality book, envelope, waxed, coated, and linen paper.[21]

---

[21] Haber (1989), pp. 96–99.

One might argue that paper manufacturing was a special case. Financial market imperfections could create a barrier to entry in this industry because there are very sizable scale economies in papermaking and because the knowledge required to run a modern paper mill is not easy to acquire. How significant were financial barriers to entry in industries that were characterized by modest scale economies, in which the knowledge of the specific technologies of production were broadly distributed?

The cotton textile industry provides us with a perfect test case of the relationship between the development of the financial markets and banks that provide capital to an industry, and the development of the industry itself. In textile manufacturing the capital equipment was easily divisible, the minimum efficient scale of production was small, and the technology was easy to acquire and operate. In fact, most companies around the world used the same machines, easily acquired from the United States and United Kingdom. In addition, unlike industries that make use of heat or chemical reactions (such as beer brewing, steelmaking, cement making, or paper milling), textile production does not require the careful coordination of inputs and outputs across different departments. Specific (and costly) technical knowledge is less crucial.[22]

What effects did privileged access to capital have in textile manufacturing? The evidence is unambiguous. An industry that should have been characterized by near perfect competition instead had a market structure that was surprisingly concentrated. Moreover, the industry was characterized by increasing levels of concentration over time – exactly the opposite of what one would expect from an expanding industry with modest scale economies. These features of the industry are captured in Table 5.1, which presents estimates of four-firm concentration ratios (the percent of the market controlled by the four largest firms) and the Herfindahl Index. For purposes of international comparison, we also present data on the United States, Brazil, and India.[23]

---

[22] This does not mean that scale economies were insignificant in cotton textile production. Indeed, had economies of scale been negligible, access to capital could not have served as a barrier to entry. It does mean, however, that scale economies were exhausted in textiles at relatively small firm sizes compared with such industries as steel, paper, cement, and chemicals.

[23] The Herfindahl Index is calculated as the sum of the squares of the market shares of all firms in an industry. These estimates of concentration are calculated at the firm level. This involved combining the market shares of all mills held by a single corporation, partnership, or sole proprietor. Market shares for Mexico and Brazil were calculated from estimates of the actual sales or value of output of mills. Market shares for India and the United States were calculated from data on installed capacity. For

Table 5.1. *Indices of Concentration in the Cotton Textile Industries of Brazil, Mexico, India, and the United States, 1840–1934[a]*

Year	Four-Firm Ratio				Herfindahl Index		
	Brazil	Mexico	India	United States	Brazil	Mexico	India
1840		0.579				0.114	
1850		0.270		0.100		0.040	
1860–62		0.273		0.126		0.041	
1870				0.107			
1880–82	0.509			0.087	0.115		
1891		0.188				0.023	
1900		0.316	0.190	0.070		0.036	0.018
1905	0.215	0.315			0.027	0.041	
1910		0.255		0.075		0.028	
1915	0.157	0.348			0.016	0.043	
1920		0.286	0.206	0.066		0.036	
1925	0.237	0.297			0.027	0.038	
1929–30		0.281	0.189	0.095		0.034	
1932–34	0.176	0.256			0.017	0.029	

[a] Concentration by estimated capacity, measured at the firm level. A detailed discussion of the estimation procedures is available from the authors.

Sources: Maurer and Haber (2002); Haber (1997, 1998).

There are at least two striking features of the data. The first is that Mexico's financial market reforms of the 1880s and 1890s actually produced an *increase* in concentration in the textile industry. The trend in Mexico from the 1840s to the early 1880s was a gradual decrease in concentration: exactly the trend that one would expect in an expanding industry characterized by constant returns to scale technology. Beginning in the 1880s, the trend reversed, even though the industry was witnessing rapid growth. By 1902 both the four-firm ratio and the Herfindahl had surpassed their 1843 levels, standing at 0.381 and 0.063, respectively. Second, by international standards, Mexico's textile industry was extremely concentrated. To provide some comparisons, in the United States circa 1900 the four-firm ratio was 0.07 (one-sixth of the Mexican level), in India it was 0.19 (one-half the Mexican level), and in Brazil it was 0.22 (two-thirds of the Mexican level).

In addition to the barriers to entry created by Mexico's peculiar banking laws, the government created barriers to entry through the patent system.

a detailed discussion of the data used to calculate industrial concentration, see Razo and Haber (1998); Haber (1997, 1998); Maurer and Haber (2002).

In the 1890s the Díaz government completely reformed the patent laws. One of the features of the resulting law was that foreigners who had already developed and patented a technology or process elsewhere could receive a patent for that invention in Mexico as well.[24] Offering domestic patent rights to foreign inventors was not, in and of itself, unusual. The patent laws of most countries allowed for this. What was highly unusual about Mexican law was that it did not impose limits on those rights, most importantly compulsory working or licensing clauses. In most countries, the patent laws specified that a foreign patentee who was granted domestic rights had to productively employ the patent within three years; otherwise the patent would be void and the technology would be in the public domain. In Mexico, there was no time limit (other than that granted to domestic patentees). The upshot was that a Mexican manufacturing firm could purchase the sole rights to use a particular invention in Mexico, thereby creating a monopoly through the control of the requisite technology.[25] Two industries provide us with relevant examples. In cigarette manufacturing, for example, one firm, El Buen Tono, dominated the market because it was the only firm that had the right to use the Bonsack cigarette rolling machine.[26] Glass-bottle making provides another relevant example. In this case, one firm, Vidriera Monterrey, purchased the sole rights to use the Owen's automatic glass-blowing machine. It therefore monopolized the manufacture of glass bottles, an essential input into the country's growing beer industry.[27]

Finally, the federal government could create barriers to entry via the tax code. We have already mentioned that the government sometimes created different excise tax rates depending on whether a product was produced domestically or abroad. In at least one case that has been

---

[24] For a complete discussion of Mexico's patent laws, see Beatty (2001), chap. 5. For a discussion of how those laws compared with those of other countries, see Khan and Sokoloff (2002).

[25] Had the foreign inventor not been able to repatent the technology in Mexico, he could not have guaranteed that the Mexican purchaser would have had the sole rights to use it. Other Mexican firms could have copied the invention without paying royalties. The result would have been that technologies developed in the United States would have been diffused more quickly to Mexico because they could have been appropriated without cost.

[26] For the history of this firm and the Bonsack machine, see Haber (1989), pp. 99–100; Beatty (2001), pp. 121–22.

[27] Haber (1989), pp. 89–91. Vidriera's owners also owned the Cervecería Cuauhtémoc, and their glass-bottle monopoly probably gave their brewery a competitive advantage. Competing firms would have either had to blow bottles by hand, import them from the United States, or buy them from Vidriera Monterrey.

extensively studied, the Compañía Nacional Mexicana de Dinamita y Explosivos (the Mexican National Dynamite and Explosives Company), the Díaz government used the excise tax to create a domestic monopoly. The tax concession that the firm received from the Díaz government was a masterpiece of rent-producing legislation. In 1897 the Díaz government granted a concession to August Genin, a French expatriate who represented a group of French investment syndicates, to build an explosives factory. Three years later, Díaz granted a second concession to a competing group of Mexican and U.S. investors. Although neither had as yet produced any dynamite, or even begun to build a factory, they merged their firms the following year (1901) to form the Compañía Nacional Mexicana de Dinamita y Explosivos. In order to avoid the possibility that they would have to buy out other potential competitors, the new company obtained a new concession with a 14-year duration from the Díaz government.

First, the company got the government to establish both an import tax and an excise tax on dynamite. Then it got the government to grant it an exemption from both of these taxes.[28] The excise tax was set at 210 pesos per ton, the import tax at 30 pesos. The average price of imported dynamite was 301 pesos per ton, exclusive of taxes and transport costs. The combined taxes, then, of 240 pesos would have levied an 80 percent tariff on imports, clearly giving the company a high degree of protection. If we assume that a hypothetical domestic competitor could have produced dynamite at the pretax cost of imports, the 210 peso excise tax would have added 70 percent to the final price of its products. The government further agreed that if it should ever lower either of these taxes, it would pay the company the equivalent amount per ton of explosives produced, in order to compensate it for the drop in the rate of protection. Finally, in a seeming concession by the company, Dinamita y Explosivos "agreed" that if dynamite prices rose beyond the "normal price," it would import the amount necessary in order to restore equilibrium to the market. The imported dynamite would enter the country "as if it were the product of the firm's own operations," *that is, without payment of either the import or the excise tax.* What this effectively meant was that what the company could not produce it was allowed to import duty free. The concessionaires

---

[28] There is some disagreement in the literature as to whether the exemption was total (the firm paying zero in excise taxes) or was partial (the firm paying 14 percent of the excise tax rate facing everybody else). Regardless, the point is still clear: the firm had obtained for itself an insuperable barrier to entry. See *Engineering and Mining Journal*, January 3, 1905, p. 575.

had, in effect, gotten the government to award them a monopoly on dynamite production and distribution. The purpose of this monopoly, as Mexico's miners pointed out, was to transfer rents from miners to the stockholders of the dynamite company.[29]

Enforcing the Porfirian VPI Coalition

Who provided third-party enforcement of the coalition between the Díaz government and Mexico's manufacturers? The answer depended on what the asset holders needed protection from. The Porfirian government could alter their property rights or the rents from property rights in three ways: it could encourage new entry, reduce trade protection, or raise taxes. The government's incentive to carry out any one of these three actions was that it would increase the government's total tax revenues.

The threat of new, domestic competition was, in part, mitigated by economies of scale. Many of the monopolies that did exist ran well under capacity.[30] In addition, financial barriers further limited entry – and those barriers were maintained by the Porfiriato's VPI coalitions in banking. Manufacturers with privileged access to the capital markets did not need much third-party protection to insure that the government would maintain barriers to entry in their industries. As a practical matter, if the government had wanted to encourage new entry in their industries, it would have also had to undo the financial laws that restricted entry into banking.

The Porfirian government was also constrained by the fact that much (although not all) of Mexican industry was not, as yet, particularly profitable. Many of Porfirian Mexico's manufacturing industries should be understood in the same terms as the oil industry. Manufacturers were investing ahead of demand, with the view that they would make low returns (or lose money) in the short run but be in a position to earn high returns in the long run. The steel industry, for example, consistently lost money throughout the Porfiriato. The textile industry, Mexico's largest, was also

---

[29] One contemporary estimate indicates that the monopoly raised miners' total costs of production by 3 percent. This is considerable in light of the fact that it was close to the value of total state and federal taxes (4.3 percent) and in light of the fact that a 3 percent increase in total costs would have been an even larger percentage of profits (the percentage depending on the profit margins of the particular mining company). See *Engineering and Mining Journal*, March 9, 1905, p. 475. Also see Haber (1989), pp. 91–93; *Engineering and Mining Journal*, December 17, 1903, p. 918; March 9, 1905, p. 475; April 23, 1905, p. 575; December 9, 1905, pp. 1074, 1077–78; March 31, 1906, p. 429–30; April 23, 1905, p. 575.

[30] Haber (1989), chap. 3.

not particularly profitable. We calculate that average pretax profit margins in 1893, the year the federal government imposed a 5 percent excise tax, were only 13 percent.[31] Profits in textile manufacturing varied greatly between firms. Had the government imposed a higher excise tax (or reduced the level of trade protection), our estimates indicate that it would have driven a substantial percentage of the industry out of business. In short, low-margin industries had little to fear in terms of higher taxes (or lower tariffs), because the government well knew that a significantly higher tax burden might cause them to shut down. That is not to say that companies would not pay for political protection to insure lower taxes or high tariffs – just that they would not choose to pay very much for protection, because they did not have very much to protect.[32]

The implication is that highly profitable industries would be willing to pay a lot for political protection, because they had a lot to protect. The available evidence supports this view. The Buen Tono cigarette company, whose market dominance was the product of its control of a foreign patent is a classic case in point. The firm was extraordinarily profitable: its rate of return on assets from 1902 to 1910 averaged 13 percent; it traded for several multiples of its par value; and it paid a consistent stream of dividends.[33] Not surprisingly, the firm's board of directors was made up of a group of Porfirian insiders. Some of these individuals, such as Roberto Núñez (the undersecretary of the treasury), Julio Limantour (brother of the secretary of the treasury), Pablo Macedo (the president of Congress), and Porfirio Díaz Jr. (the dictator's son) could monitor the government on behalf of the firm. Others, such as Manuel González Cosío (the secretary of war), could credibly threaten to punish the government.[34] As one would expect, given this line-up, Porfirian cigarette taxes were very low. The taxes on a one-ounce pack of cigarettes were barely more than half a centavo.[35]

---

[31] These pretax margins are calculated from data on sales and operating costs from the 1893 cotton textile census, published in México, Dirección General de Estadística (1894).

[32] In 1908, the federal government raised 2 million pesos from the textile excise tax. This came to around 2 percent of all federal revenues. Taxes on alcoholic beverages raised 864,000 pesos, less than 1 percent of all federal revenues. *Mexican Yearbook*, 1908, p. 105.

[33] Haber (1989), chap. 7.

[34] Haber (1989), p. 100; *Mexican Yearbook*, 1908, p. 531; 1909–10, p. 420;

[35] *Mexican Yearbook*, 1908, p. 958. Total revenues from the tobacco stamp tax in 1908 came to 2.8 million pesos. This came to slightly less than 3 percent of all federal revenues.

The board of the highly profitable Compañía Nacional Mexicana de Dinamita y Explosivos tells a similar story. Its board of directors included a set of Porfirian insiders, including Enrique Creel (the governor of Chihuahua and, later, secretary of foreign relations), Julio Limantour, Roberto Núñez, and Porfirio Díaz Jr.[36] This group of monitors and enforcers was particularly crucial in light of the fact that it was years before the firm produced a single stick of dynamite. Most of its business consisted of importing dynamite from the United States and then reselling it at inflated prices. Moreover, the monopoly that Díaz and Limantour had granted the firm was clearly in violation of the Constitution of 1857, Article 28 of which specifically stated that "there shall be no monopolies nor privileged places of any kind; nor prohibitions with titles of protection to industry."[37] This was of little consequence in Porfirian Mexico. Third-party enforcement allowed the firm not only to retain its initial concession (1903–17) but to extend it, as of 1908, for an additional 25 years, until 1933.[38] As one contemporary observer put it: "[T]his is a country where it is claimed the Government will not allow a monopoly; but it is different when the Government is interested, and when the head officials are shareholders."[39]

THE IMPACT OF THE REVOLUTION

The revolution that overthrew Díaz had little effect on Mexican manufacturing. Markets continued to operate under Madero pretty much as they had under Díaz. In addition, Madero raised taxes but only marginally.[40] Once Madero was overthrown by Huerta, Mexico entered

---

[36] Haber (1989), pp. 92–93; *Mexican Yearbook*, 1909–10, p. 421; 1912, p. 418; *Engineering and Mining Journal*, December 17, 1903, p. 918.

[37] Mexico's miners pointed this out, with no effect. See *Engineering and Mining Journal*, December 9, 1905, p. 1074.

[38] During this time, the government guaranteed that it would not grant a similar concession to other individuals or set aside the special excise tax on dynamite for any other producer, manufacturer, or importer, whether domestic or foreign, of any dynamite or other explosive made of nitroglycerine. *Engineering and Mining Journal*, November 14, 1908, p. 950.

[39] *Engineering and Mining Journal*, December 9, 1905, p. 1077.

[40] Taxes on domestic cigarettes, to cite one example, tripled, but from a very low base. Taxes on imported cigarettes quadrupled. Taxes on domestic cigarettes went from 0.5 centavos per 25-gram package, to 1.5 centavos per 25-gram package. Taxes on imported cigarettes (in addition to import duties) rose from 0.85 centavos per 25-gram package to 3.5 centavos per 25-gram package. *Mexican Yearbook*, 1914, p. 236.

into a prolonged period of coups and civil wars. The upshot was that markets were interdicted and governments (and factions) behaved in a predatory manner.

Violence and Civil War

The campaign against Huerta, and the civil war that followed, led to the collapse of the national railway and monetary systems. By July 1913 the national railroad system had already begun to collapse. Of the 1,000 miles of track in Mexico owned by the Southern Pacific Railroad, for example, only 200 miles of line were actually in operation. A similar state of affairs affected the National Railways of Mexico. In mid-1913 only 47 percent of its mileage was under operation.[41] As one contemporary account put it in early 1916, "The rolling stock of all the railroads has practically ceased to exist.... While rolling stock may be imported promptly provided there is money to pay for it, it will not be so easy to put the roadbed in such condition that trains may be operated over it."[42]

As early as August 1913, 86 cotton textile factory owners – virtually the entire industry – had written to the government saying that the transport situation was forcing them to cease operations. They could not obtain necessary inputs, notably raw cotton, from either the cotton fields of the north or the port of Veracruz, the rail lines having been cut in both directions. The situation only deteriorated thereafter. Mexico's manufacturers therefore continually petitioned the federal government for assistance in obtaining the raw materials and spare parts that they needed in order to continue production.[43] Neither the Huerta nor the Carranza governments were able to offer much help. They needed the railroads to move soldiers and war matériel. Nor could they insure that rail freight could freely move between their territory and areas controlled by their opponents.

The problems of distribution arising from the breakdown in communications and transport were further complicated by the breakdown of the national system of currency and exchange. During the revolution silver and gold coin disappeared from circulation and were replaced by paper

[41] *Engineering and Mining Journal*, July 26, 1913, p. 171.
[42] *Engineering and Mining Journal*, January 8, 1916, p. 94.
[43] AGN, Ramo de Trabajo, box 46, file 3, pp. 1–5; box 52, file 12, pp. 1–3; box 90, file 9, p. 45; box 107, file 16, p. 1; box 107, file 22, p. 2; box 110, file 28, p. 1; box 173, file 23, p. 1. Also see Ramirez Rancaño (1987), p. 138.

currencies issued by each of the warring factions. Because each army printed bills as it saw fit, and because bills were not backed by anything except the belief that the army in question was going to continue to control a particular area, this money was constantly being discounted and devalued. Inflation was rampant, and the different currencies of different areas were not interchangeable (see Chapter 4).

Revolutionary violence not only interdicted factor and product markets, it posed direct threats to the property rights of Mexico's manufacturers because of armies' pressing financial needs. Armed factions viewed factories much the same way as they viewed banks: factories were strategic assets that could be used to generate income for the army. What typically occurred in occupied areas was that a faction would seize the factories and run them for its own benefit, or it would threaten to do so unless a forced loan was paid. To cite one example, in April 1914 the forces of Pablo González took control of Monterrey. For most of the year González occupied and ran the Cervecería Cuauhtémoc, where he continued to employ the brewery's work force. By November the company's stocks of raw materials had been used up. At that point, having extracted what he could from the operation, González returned the factory, apparently undamaged, to its owners.[44]

Factory owners could avoid occupation if they agreed to pay forced loans to revolutionary armies. For example, in 1915 Pancho Villa threatened to occupy and run for his army's benefit the massive soap and glycerin works of the Compañía Industrial Jabonera de la Laguna, unless its owners provided him with two loans totaling U.S.$350,000. The owners of the factory knew that Villa's threat was credible. He had already occupied the cotton plantations of the region (many of which were owned by the major shareholders of the soap works) and was running them in order to finance his military campaigns (We return to this issue in detail in Chapter 8.) Needless to say, the management of the Compañía Industrial Jabonera de la Laguna paid the protection money, in exchange for which Villa left the factory alone.[45]

---

[44] Fuentes Mares (1976), p. 123; and, García Naranjo (1955), pp. 48–52.
[45] In fact, the owners of the La Laguna soap works had served as intermediaries when Villa sold his cotton crop in the United States. The president and general manager of La Laguna, John Brittingham, bought Villa's cotton crop for a steeply discounted cash price at the U.S. border. Brittingham, in turn, sold the cotton in Liverpool at inflated World War I prices, turning a sizable profit for the company. See Haber (1989), p. 133.

Property Rights to Trade Protection

The Carrancista victory over the Villistas and Zapatistas restored the national market. It brought with it, however, institutional changes that directly threatened the interests of Mexico's manufacturers. Complicating matters further were state governors, who sought to curry favor with local constituencies by enacting state-level reforms or by enforcing federal laws in arbitrary ways.

Mexico's manufacturers faced a government that had the ability and incentive to reduce their property rights. Article 27 of the Constitution of 1917 declared that private property was a privilege, not an inherent right. The government therefore had the authority to terminate private property in the public interest. The implications of Article 27 were not lost on the country's industrialists, who feared that the government would expropriate their factories. From their point of view, this threat was very real. The government had already carried out a de facto nationalization of the banking system from 1915 to 1917. Many of the country's largest industrialists were, in fact, bankers. The industrialists had also already seen the confiscation of part of the railroads in 1914, the seizure the Compañía de Tranvías (a streetcar company) in order to resolve a labor dispute that same year, and the expropriation of the telephone company in 1915.[46]

Reducing the property rights of Mexico's manufacturers did not require the government actually to expropriate factories. Mexico's presidents could reduce the property rights of Mexico's industrialists because they had the ability to set import tariffs by decree. Moreover, the Carranza government had a strong incentive to reduce tariffs: it was desperate for tax revenues.[47] Protective tariffs, by design, generate no tax revenues – the effect of the tariff is to drive imports to zero. Thus, the government wanted to set the tariff at a level that would maximize its revenues, but this would come at the expense of the nation's manufacturers, who would no longer be protected. In addition, Carranza wished to quell urban unrest

[46] Ramirez Rancaño (1987), p. 177.
[47] Indeed, Carranza was so desperate for income that he had already taken the dramatic step of increasing the so-called *contribución federal* (or federal contribution, the percentage of state and municipal tax receipts that had to be transferred to the federal government in order to cover the costs of sustaining the federation) from 20 to 60 percent – even though this undermined Carranza's delicate alliance with many of Mexico's politically powerful (and ambitious) state governors. See Uhthoff Lopez (2001).

produced by Mexico's hyperinflation. Pushing down tariffs on cloth would drive down prices.

The conflict over the tariff escalated to the point that Carranza threatened to expropriate the industry. In July 1917 Carranza declared that common cloth with less than 40 threads per square centimeter (which characterized the vast majority of Mexico's output) would be made exempt from all import tariffs. One month later, Carranza amplified this exemption, completely removing the tariff on common cloth with less than 70 threads per square centimeter and lowering the tariff on fine weave, printed cloth to only 25 percent of its former value.[48] Without protective tariffs, Mexico's textile industry had no hope of competing against foreign manufacturers. The industrialists of Mexico City responded by declaring a lockout, throwing 4,000 mill hands out of work. Carranza upped the ante, sending a telegram to every state governor asking for a list of the paralyzed factories and drafting a law, based on Articles 27 and 123 of the Constitution, that would allow the government to seize control of factories and place them under the administrative direction of the secretary of the treasury, much in the same manner as it had earlier done with the banks. The Chamber of Deputies approved the law that same day. The Senate followed two months later.[49]

Ultimately, the seizure of the factories was headed off by a coordinated response from the country's manufacturers. A delegation of 112 industrialists met with the secretary of industry, commerce, and labor throughout the month of November 1917. The industrialists hoped to open the Congress of Industrialists with the issue of the tariff and then to move on to attack Articles 27 and 123. This strategy was only partially successful. The government made it clear that Articles 27 and 123 were nonnegotiable.[50] Mexico's industrialists were simply going to have to live with the labor and property laws that came out of the revolution. Carranza also stated that as a general principle his government was going to hew to a free trade policy. Yet, although he might in principal be in favor of free trade, Carranza could on an ad hoc basis depart from this policy.

---

[48] Ramirez Rancaño (1987), pp. 208–10.

[49] Ramirez Rancaño (1987), pp. 213–17.

[50] The government took the position that amendments to the Constitution could only be enacted by a vote of two-thirds of the lower house of Congress and a majority of the state legislatures. Neither the government's representative at the Congress, Alberto J. Pani, the minister of industry, commerce, and labor, nor the industrialists had the authority to amend the Constitution.

President Carranza therefore backed down on the tariff. Aurora Gómez's research on textile tariffs indicates that the specific tariff on coarse unbleached cloth increased from 4 centavos per kilo to 5 centavos per kilo in 1918. At the same time, the tariff on raw cotton imports was set at only 1.6 percent. The result was an effective rate of protection of 28 percent. For fine unbleached cloth, the effective rate of protection was double that of coarse cloth, 56 percent. The end result was a compromise. Effective rates were significantly higher than they had been in any year since 1912, but rates were still lower than they had been under Porfirio Díaz.[51]

Mexico's industrialists had won a battle over the tariff against Carranza, but they knew that the tariff could be revised downward at any time. In fact, the coefficient of protection (total tariff revenues divided by the value of all dutiable goods) dropped from 27 to 14 percent, nearly 50 percent, from 1919 to 1920.[52] This general decline does not appear to have been the product of changes in the composition of imports. Aurora Gómez's estimates of nominal and effective rates of protection for cotton textiles indicate a similar drop: the nominal tariff on coarse cloth fell to 7 percent in 1920 (from 13 percent in 1918), while the effective rate of protection dropped to 14 percent (from 28 percent).[53]

As soon as Álvaro Obregón took office in 1920, Mexico's major textile manufacturers appealed to him to raise tariffs. They were assured that the government would revise import tariffs industry by industry with the goal of protecting domestic manufacturers against foreign competition. The industrialists had asked for tariff increases in certain classes of goods by as much as 100 percent and thought that they had been promised revisions in the area of 50 percent. When the government published the new tariff schedules, however, the increase was only 10 percent.[54] Thus, the 1921 coefficient of protection (total tariffs divided by total dutiable imports) was only slightly higher than it had been in 1920 – roughly half of its 1910 value.[55]

The industrialists therefore lobbied the Obregón government. During the early 1920s, however, their ability to force the government to recreate the Porfirian tariff system was constrained. By the mid-1920s,

---

[51] Gómez Galvarriato (1999), pp. 604, 608.
[52] Cosío Villegas (1989), p. 58.
[53] A similar drop occurred to nominal and effective rates of protection for fine cloth. The nominal rate fell from 26 percent to 14 percent, and the effective rate fell from 56 percent to 29 percent. Gómez Galvarriato (1999), pp. 604, 608.
[54] Collado Herrera (1996), p. 208.
[55] Cosío Villegas (1989), p. 58.

however, they had not only recreated the Porfirian tariff regime; they had pushed tariffs well beyond Porfirian levels. In order to understand how that happened, however, we must leave aside the tariff for a moment and focus our attention instead on the labor movement.

Organized Labor as a Third-Party Enforcer

Prior to the revolution, unions were small and persecuted, and the only laws that protected industrial workers, as members of the Díaz government often boasted, were the laws of supply and demand.[56] Mexico's factory owners could count on federal troops and the rural police to safeguard strikebreakers, protect their property, and, if need be, open fire on striking workers. They could also rely on the local judicial and political authorities to discipline their work forces – at times with imprisonment – because the salaried employees of the mills tended to serve as the municipal presidents in the mill towns.[57]

This situation changed dramatically with the fall of Díaz. As Jeffrey Bortz has summed it up: "The revolution did not arrive as a distant theoretical abstraction. For textile workers, the revolution was a fleeing president and cabinet, the savagery of rival armies, the mill owner's inability to call in the forces of repression, and most importantly, the work of labor agitators, radicals, militants, propagandists, articulate ideologues, and other undesirables who flourish in revolutionary environments."[58] The results were not only waves of strikes that lasted from 1911 to the early 1920s, but a level of worker militancy that had never before been seen in Mexico. The authority that factory owners had in 1910 had largely vanished by 1920.[59]

During the revolution, the various governments in power attempted to manage the increasing militancy of labor. Madero, for example, attempted to negotiate an increase in wages and a reduction in work hours for textile workers. These initial attempts at meeting labor demands were unsuccessful, however, because labor was not an active participant in these negotiations.[60] Later, during the 1914–17 civil war, Carranza allowed radical labor movements to organize unions in those areas of Mexico

[56] Anderson (1976), p. 36; Bortz (2002), pp. 257–59.
[57] Gómez Galvarriato (2002).
[58] Bortz (1997), p. 271.
[59] Bortz (1997), pp. 253–88; Ramirez Rancaño (1987), pp. 39, 96–97.
[60] Ramirez Rancaño (1987), pp. 69–70.

under his control.[61] The military governors of regions controlled by the Carrancistas also carried out reforms designed to appease labor. As we discussed in Chapter 3, these reforms often went far beyond what Carranza himself envisioned.

Many of the labor reforms carried out by military governors at the state level found their way into the Constitution of 1917. Article 123 brought about the eight-hour day, the six-day week, equal pay for equal work, profit sharing, minimum wages, the right to organize and strike, protection for workers from arbitrary dismissal, mandatory labor arbitration by state boards, and other dramatic reforms.

One of the most dramatic provisions of Article 123 was that manufacturers could not close down their plants without permission. Lockouts were now banned by the Constitution, unless they could be demonstrated to be necessary because of overproduction and were approved by the Junta de Conciliación y Arbitraje (state labor board). Lockouts declared illegal by the state labor board could result first in the requirement that all lost wages be paid to the workers and ultimately in the confiscation of the factory by the government.[62] This principle was subsequently written into the enabling legislation to Article 123 passed by state governments. In the states of Guanajuato, Veracruz, Puebla, and Michoacán, the governor had the right to take over any factory, ranch, or mine in the event that the owners tried to close it down.[63] In fact, even though there was not yet enabling legislation to Article 123, President Obregón confiscated factories that had been shut down by their owners. In February 1921 the Compañiá Industrial Veracruzana (CIVSA) textile conglomerate staged a lockout over a labor dispute. In August 1924 the owners of the La Abeja textile mill declared a lockout for similar reasons. In both cases, Obregón seized the factories until employers granted concessions to the workers. Once they had agreed to do so, he returned their properties.[64]

In states where the governor was courting the labor movement, the labor boards were very likely to side with workers and declare lockouts illegal because the constitution specified that workers and employers were to have equal numbers of representatives on the state labor board, with

---

[61] Hall and Spalding (1986), p. 351.
[62] Collado Herrera (1996), p. 144.
[63] *Engineering and Mining Journal,* June 10, 1922, p. 1017. For a discussion of the state labor codes and their relationship to the Constitution of 1917, see Bortz (2002), pp. 263–73.
[64] Collado Herrera (1996), p. 145.

the state government having one representative – effectively giving that representative veto power over the outcome of each case. Industrialists tried to argue that the rulings of the state labor boards could not be binding because of the lack of adequate enabling legislation. Initially, the Supreme Court agreed with them, but in 1924, in light of the de la Huerta revolt, Obregón pressured the Supreme Court into reversing its decision. The reason Obregón did this was that he was now indebted to the CROM and the radical governors who had come to his aid against de la Huerta. The labor boards' rulings were now declared obligatory. (See Chapter 3 for a full discussion.)

Under Calles, the CROM was so powerful that it was the federal government, and not the constitutionally specified state labor boards, that decided whether firms could temporarily shut down their operations. By 1926 cotton textile firms had to seek the permission of Luis Morones, secretary of industry, commerce, and labor *and* head of the CROM, to shut down. When they did so, Morones responded that if the firms shut down, they would have to pay three months' severance pay to the workers. Factory owners in the states of Puebla and Tlaxcala, who were in the most difficult financial position, appealed directly to Calles. Instead of granting their request to close down their operations, Calles ordered the mill owners to operate their mills by turn, each mill to run 24 hours per week for four months, thereby protecting the jobs of the workers. The end result was that by March 1928 Mexico's cotton textile mills had nine months of output stockpiled in their warehouses, forcing many factories to sell off stock below their costs of production.[65]

These labor reforms amounted to a dramatic reduction in the property rights of factory owners. The government had the power to force factories to operate even if they were unable to cover their variable costs. If they refused to continue operating, factory owners could have all of their fixed assets confiscated. The net effect was that the fixed assets of factory owners were now less valuable, because any purchaser of a factory was buying it with the knowledge that he could be forced to operate it at a complete loss.

Profit Sharing

Article 123 of the Constitution further reduced property rights by giving workers the right to share in the profits of the enterprises that employed them. The exact arrangement by which profits would be shared was left

[65] Haber (1989), p. 157.

up to individual state labor boards. In states dominated by governors who had to appeal to militant labor constituencies, such enabling legislation followed on the heels of Carranza's assassination. On July 3, 1921, the legislature of the state of Veracruz approved a law initiated by Governor Adalberto Tejeda that required the owners of enterprises to share up to 50 percent of their profits with their workers, with each worker receiving a portion proportional to his salary. In November 1921 the state legislature of Puebla approved a similar law initiated by its populist governor, José María Sánchez.[66]

The fact that Mexico's presidents faced an unstable polity meant that manufacturers were able to mitigate the impact of the profit-sharing laws. Obregón, as did Carranza before him, realized that he needed to bring the country's industrialists into his coalition – or risk having them support some other faction. Mexico's industrialists therefore knew that the Obregón government would pressure federal courts. The industrialists therefore obtained injunctions from federal judges that suspended the state profit-sharing laws. Indeed, filing such injunctions became such a common strategy that the Confederation of Chambers of Commerce even published a template for what a successful writ should look like so as to simplify the process for employers.[67]

The strategy of drawing on the federal courts to block state-level reforms could work only so long as Obregón did not need organized labor, and the state governors who had allied themselves with labor, to assure his survival – in both the political and literal senses of the word. The de la Huerta rebellion changed the calculus. Radical state governors and the CROM came to Obregón and Calles's rescue in 1924. Thus, Obregón and Calles could no longer afford to use federal courts to block state-level labor laws.

Obregón and Calles now had either of two options. One was to simply let the state governors pass whatever legislation they pleased. This would satisfy their labor allies but would come at the cost of completely alienating the country's industrialists. The other was to wrest control of labor legislation from the states by federalizing labor law. This option was attractive to industrialists, because they believed that they could more easily negotiate with the federal government than with state governors who were completely beholden to local labor constituencies. Indeed, Mexico's industrialists had realized as early as 1917 that they would be better off

[66] Collado Herrera (1996), pp. 250, 253.
[67] Collado Herrera (1996), p. 195.

negotiating with the federal government than with the states. [68] The federalization of labor law was also an attractive option for the CROM. It essentially gave the CROM a monopoly on labor representation in Mexico.

Trade Protection, Organized Labor, and the VPI Coalition in Manufacturing

It is not a requirement of VPI coalitions that their members need to be in ideological agreement. They can be ideologically opposed. They can even actively loathe each other. The only necessary requirement is that there be incentive compatibility among the three groups that compose the coalition: the government, the asset holder, and a politically crucial third group that receives a stream of rents from the asset holder. All three must receive greater benefits from staying in the coalition than from breaking it.

The creation of a VPI coalition in manufacturing conformed closely to the abstract concept of three potentially antagonistic groups who create a scheme to create and distribute rents among themselves. The government had to lay down policies that generated rents. The group that served as the coalition's third-party enforcer – in this case organized labor, particularly the CROM – had to be able to punish the government should it alter this policy. The manufacturers had to be sufficiently confident about their property rights to invest and to produce.

The process of forming a VPI coalition in manufacturing began shortly after the Obregón-Calles victory over de la Huerta. Although it would take until 1931 for there to be a national labor law, the outlines of the government's and asset holders' arrangements with the CROM were laid down in the 1925–27 cotton textile agreements. After pursuing the question of how federal, industry-wide labor agreements in the textile industry allowed the formation of a stable coalition among factory owners, government, and organized labor, we will address the formation of such agreements in other manufacturing industries.

---

[68] The problem was that Carranza resisted the federalization of labor law, which he viewed as a potential source of endless political problems. At one point in 1917 he even proposed closing the Federal Department of Labor (which was part of the Ministry of Industry, Commerce, and Labor) on the basis that labor relations should be handled at the state level by the labor boards. See Collado Herrera (1996), pp. 237–38; Ramirez Rancaño (1987), pp. 200–1.

The cotton textile industry was perhaps the most logical place for the building of a VPI coalition to begin. It was Mexico's largest manufacturing industry. It employed more workers than any other industrial sector. It had been a hotbed of labor unrest since the late Porfiriato. Indeed, Mexico's earliest – and most violent – strikes had taken place in the textile mills of Veracruz. Finally, it was an industry spread across a multitude of states. Different state laws regarding wages and hours had created large disparities in labor costs, and the threat of expropriation – or changes in taxes, labor laws, and regulations tantamount to expropriation – by state governments hung continually over the heads of the factory owners.

In 1925 the textile manufacturers in the high-wage states of Puebla and Veracruz, which accounted for 53 percent of Mexico's cotton textile production in 1925, called for a national convention to end disparities in wage rates between states. Participating in the convention were the CROM-controlled textile worker's union, the industrialists, and the federal government. Representatives from state governments were not invited. The reason was simple. The federal government was the government that could generate rents for the manufacturers through trade protection and subsidized inputs. Some of those rents could be transferred to the CROM, which the federal government depended on for vital political support. State governments also had incentives to buy off the CROM – and many, in fact, did just that through radical labor laws – but their only source of rents involved extraction directly from the industrialists with no corresponding benefit. The state governments' ability to create benefits for the factory owners and the CROM was therefore ultimately limited. All three participants had incentives to federalize labor law and cut the state governments out of the picture as much as possible.

The 1925–27 agreements in cotton textiles were nothing less than a VPI coalition among the manufacturers, the government, and the CROM. Manufacturers obtained two things: a credible commitment to high levels of trade protection and subsidized raw materials. Textile tariffs climbed in the mid-1920s, back up to their Porfirian levels. Gómez-Galvarriato's estimates of nominal and effective rates of protection indicate that the specific tariff on coarse, unbleached cloth was raised in 1923, 1927, and 1930. This produced nominal tariff rates of 24 percent in 1923, 32 percent in 1927, and *183 percent* in 1930. The effective rate of protection moved just as dramatically. Gómez-Galvarriato's lower-bound estimates indicate effective rates of 38 percent in 1923, 46 percent in 1927, and *345 percent* in 1930. Tariffs on fine-weave goods rose even faster. The nominal tariff was 31 percent in 1923, 41 percent in 1927, and 206 percent in 1930. The effective rate of protection was 53 percent in 1923, 65 percent in 1927, and 397 percent in 1930.[69]

In addition to protective tariffs, Mexico's textile manufacturers also received subsidized cotton. This subsidy was accomplished by a prohibition on exports of raw cotton until domestic demand had been satisfied. Because Mexico was now a net cotton exporter, this implied that the cotton textile factories could buy cotton at less than the world market price. Manufacturers could simply hold up cotton exports until producers sold them what they wanted at the price they were willing to pay. In fact, many manufacturers used this to transfer rents from cotton growers to themselves by buying more cotton than they needed at the domestic price and then reselling it at the international price. Thus, many of Mexico's exports were reexports by domestic purchasers.[70]

What did the government get from this arrangement? The payoffs for the government were not financial. It did receive a stream of tax revenues from the excise on cotton cloth, equal to 5 percent of the value of production. The benefits from the excise tax, however, were almost certainly overwhelmed by the costs imposed by high tariffs and subsidized cotton. The revenues from the excise were considerably less than the taxes the government could have received had it imposed the revenue-maximizing import tariff. Also, the government earned the enmity of the cotton growers. Essentially, the government forced cotton growers to accept lower prices from domestic purchasers of cotton than those the growers could have obtained in the world market. This effectively reduced the value of their assets (because the stream of revenues those assets could produce was reduced). The payoff for the government was therefore political. It obtained the CROM's support in rigging and stealing elections, as well as the CROM's support in the event of military uprisings (see Chapter 3 for details).

What did the CROM receive in exchange for providing the muscle to enforce the agreement between the government and the manufacturers? The evidence is overwhelming that the CROM received a tremendous stream of rents from the textile mill owners. First, CROM workers obtained substantial wage increases. Our estimates, based on state-by-state manufacturing surveys, indicate a rise in real wages of 35 percent from

---

[69] Gómez Galvarriato (1999), pp. 604, 608.

[70] To further discourage exports and depress the domestic price of cotton, the government imposed a 15 ¢ export tax per kilogram of cotton. See Vargas-Lobsinger (1999), p. 77.

1923 to 1929 in the cotton textile industry.[71] These estimates are clearly lower-bound approximations. Aurora Gómez-Galvarriato's estimates for the CIVSA textile conglomerate indicate that the combination of price deflation in the late 1920s coupled with increases in nominal wage rates drove up the purchasing power of wages by 131 percent from 1920 to 1929.[72]

CROM workers also received job security. Union agreements gave unions, not employers, the right to hire and fire. In addition, as Aurora Gómez-Galvarriato has shown, the CROM effectively blocked the introduction of labor-saving technologies. In the early 1920s this was accomplished through the kind of thuggery that the CROM used in winning elections. In the textile industry, for example, the CROM intimidated firms and workers from running automatic machinery. The first attempt to employ automatic looms was by the CIVSA textile conglomerate in 1920. The 100 automatic looms it purchased, however, never went into operation. The union refused to allow the machines to be run. CIVSA eventually sold the looms to other factories, but the unions blocked their use in those factories as well. A second attempt to import automatic looms was made by the Compañía Atoyac Textil in 1923, when it bought 24 automatic looms from the Stafford Loom Company. In order to bring them into the country, however, the president of the loom company had to travel to Mexico to obtain the permission of President Obregón and Interior Secretary Calles. Obregón and Calles allowed the automatic looms into the country only on the condition that they were considered an exhibition. Once they were mounted, however, the CROM blocked their operation. The worker who ran the looms was stabbed to death. His successor soon started receiving death threats and promptly resigned. No one else dared tend the looms.[73]

These kind of "informal" arrangements blocking technological change were institutionalized in the 1925–27 cotton textile agreements. The agreements produced wage lists that specified the maximum number of machines that could be assigned to each worker and the specific, uniform pay rates per unit of output. This meant that industrialists had no incentive to introduce labor-saving machinery: the piece rate and the number of machines per worker could not vary. This did not completely forestall

---

[71] México, Secretaría de Hacienda (1924–29); México, Dirección General de Estadística (1926). Wages deflated using the Gómez-Galvarriato and Musacchio price index (see Gómez Galvarriato and Musacchio 1998).

[72] Gómez Galvarriato (2002).

[73] Gómez Galvarriato (1999), pp. 584–85.

productivity growth: workers had incentives to maximize their individual efforts because of the piece-rate pay schedule. It did, however, place a limit on the rate at which productivity could grow because it strongly discouraged technological innovation. This by-product of the cotton textile convention was not, it should be pointed out, inadvertent. The Saco-Lowell Shops had written to the cotton textile convention in 1926 explaining that the regulations that were being adopted would discourage the adoption of new technologies. From the point of view of both Mexican workers and Mexican industrialists, however, there were strong incentives to block the introduction of new technology. It protected the workers' jobs and it protected industrialists against the threat of new, more efficient rivals.[74]

VPI Coalitions in Manufacturing

The exact details of the VPI arrangements in other industries are not, as yet, as well established as they are in the case of cotton textiles. Nevertheless, the evidence strongly indicates that what took place in textiles – a coalition of manufacturers, unions, and the government – occurred in other manufacturing industries.

First, based on the work of Graciela Márquez, we know that the mechanism by which tariffs were set changed.[75] Under Calles (as under Díaz), the president took back from Congress the right to set tariffs. The difference was the mechanism by which industrialists made their demands. Under Díaz the mechanism was informal – the ability to get an audience with Secretary of the Treasury Limantour. Under Calles the mechanism was institutionalized – a formal tariff commission on which industrialists sat. This tariff commission had existed as an informal body since 1919, and had been established as part of the negotiations that took place between the industrialists and Secretary of Industry, Commerce, and Labor Alberto Pani at the First Congress of Industrialists of 1917. This commission, however, had no direct authority. It was a purely consultative body that existed to coordinate the demands of industrialists and to signal the government.[76] Under pressure from industrialists (and perhaps to curry their favor as he moved to form an anti-Calles coalition) in 1923, Secretary of the Treasury Adolfo de la Huerta extended an invitation to the various

[74] Gómez Galvarriato (1999), pp. 585–88.
[75] Márquez (2001).
[76] Márquez (2001), pp. 9, 24.

industrialist and merchant associations to form technical commissions on the tariff. Unfortunately, the intrigues of Mexican politics undid their work. Four days after the commission submitted its report in September 1923, de la Huerta resigned. Within a few months, he would be leading a military revolt against the government.[77]

The wisdom of giving industrialists a powerful voice in tariff setting was not lost on the victors of the de la Huerta rebellion. In 1925 newly installed President Calles established a Tariff Reform Commission (Comisión de Reformas de la Ordenanza General de Aduanas). This commission would make recommendations to the president, who would then, acting by decree, determine the tariff. What had been an informal commission of industrialists and merchants that had made suggestions regarding tariff rates on individual products was now being institutionalized and placed in charge of reforming the entire tariff system. The commission was made up of two representatives of the Secretariat of Industry, Commerce, and Labor (which was controlled by the CROM), two representatives from the Secretariat of the Treasury, one representative from the Secretariat of Agriculture, one representative from the Federation of Chambers of Commerce (Confederación de Cámaras de Comercio), and one representative from the Federation of Industrial Chambers (Confederación de Cámaras Industriales). The representative of the industrialists was allowed to express his opinions, but was not given a formal vote. The lack of a vote did not, in the final analysis, matter much.[78] The industrialists had a mechanism to coordinate and signal their demands, and consumers had no representatives.

Second, we know that tariffs climbed dramatically in the 1920s. Cosío Villegas's estimates of the coefficient of protection (tariff revenues divided by the value of dutiable goods) indicates that in 1920 protection stood at only 14 percent, roughly half of its 1910 level. By 1923 the coefficient of protection had nearly doubled, to 24 percent. It then continued to rise, reaching 27 percent in 1927 and 31 percent in 1928.[79]

Cosio Villegas's gross estimates are consistent with the more fine-grained estimates obtained by Márquez. Her careful estimates, based on samples of products drawn across different years, indicate that for consumer goods as a whole (not including foodstuffs) the average tariff in 1924 was 38 percent. In 1930 the average tariff on that same group of

---

[77] Collado Herrera (1996), pp. 218–19, 233.
[78] Márquez (2001), pp. 9, 24–25.
[79] Cosío Villegas (1989), p. 58.

products had increased to 47 percent. In some individual product lines the average tariff had increased even more dramatically. In textiles, for example, the tariff increased from 45 to 59 percent, and in manufactured clothing, from 43 to 69 percent. Moreover, in intermediate goods, the average tariff (36 percent in 1930) was lower than in nonagricultural consumer goods (47 percent in 1930), suggesting a cascading tariff structure.[80] Márquez's estimates of intermediate goods tariffs, it should be pointed out, are most likely upward biased, because they are strongly driven by chemicals and iron and steel products – industries that existed in Mexico and that demanded protection from foreign competition. A sample drawn on intermediate goods that were not manufactured domestically would probably indicate even lower tariffs on intermediate goods. In short, the evidence indicates that the same trend that we saw in textiles – of increasing rates of effective protection – almost certainly held across manufacturing as a whole.

The evidence also indicates that some of the rents that were generated by trade protection were being shared with organized labor. We have been able to estimate real wages in the steel industry based on detailed reports of wages paid by the Fundidora Monterrey steel monopoly. These estimates indicate that real wages were rising at the same rate as in cotton textiles: 35 percent from 1923 to 1929.[81]

Third, we know that the number of CROM workers rose at a rapid rate during the 1920s, growing from 50,000 in 1920 to 2 million in 1928. The 1928 figure is clearly an overestimate. Even if it is off by a factor of four, however, we would still be talking about levels of organization – in a single labor federation – higher than the percentage of all unionized workers in the contemporary United States.[82] In short, the CROM obviously had organized industries well beyond the 30,000 or so workers in cotton textiles.

[80] Márquez (2001), p. 15.
[81] Calculated from department-by-department wage data in Compañía Fundidora de Fierro y Acero de Monterrey (1923–30).
[82] The annual estimates are as follows: 1920 – 50,000; 1921 – 150,000; 1922 – 400,000; 1923 – 800,000; 1924 – 1.2 million; 1925 – 1.5 million; 1927 – 1,862,000; 1928 – 2,000,000. Carr (1976), p. 158; Brown (1927), p. 36. These estimates are somewhat incredible, considering that the entire Mexican work force in 1930 came to 5.2 million people, 70 percent of whom worked in agriculture. For these estimates to be credible, one would have to believe that the CROM organized *every* worker in manufacturing, mining, transport, urban services, government, and commerce – in addition to one out of every seven agricultural workers. Figures on work force from México, INEGI (1994), p. 347.

Fourth, we know that at the same time that the CROM gained organizational strength the number of strikes was declining dramatically. In 1922 there were 197 strikes in Mexico, involving 71,736 workers, with a loss of 692,339 man-days of labor. By 1924 this fell to 138 strikes, involving 33,985 strikers, and a loss of 395,491 man-days of labor. By 1926 the CROM had effectively ended strikes. There were only 24 strikes, involving 2,977 workers, with a loss of only 41,222 man-days of labor.[83]

Finally, there is evidence from the sugar milling industry that some manufacturers actively solicited the CROM to form a coalition that would provide the manufacturers with protection from any government attempt to lower tariffs. The incentives were much the same as in textiles: Mexico's sugar millers could not have survived against Cuban imports in the 1920s without high tariffs, and high tariffs could only be maintained if the government could be punished by the CROM. Thus, the sugar millers of Veracruz actively sought the help of the CROM. The manager of the San Cristóbal mill, in fact, went so far as to invite a representative of the CROM to attend the company's board meetings. As in textiles, informal arrangements soon became formalized. In 1926, the Comisión Mixta de Obreros, Campesinos y Empresarios Azucareros (Mixed Commission of Workers, Peasants, and Sugar Industry Entrepreneurs) met in Jalapa, Veracruz, to discuss the industry's problems. A few months later the Comisión Nacional Azucarera (National Sugar Commission) met in Mexico City, providing a national forum for discussions between the sugar growers, the unions, and government. [84]

DATA ANALYSIS

The recreation of a VPI coalition after the revolution suggests that the political events of the 1910s and 1920s did not have had powerful effects over the medium term on industrial ownership, investment, output, investor expectations, and productivity growth. What, then, does the quantitative evidence indicate about the performance of industry?

Surviving the Revolution

The data we have retrieved on manufacturing indicate that the vast majority of firms survived the revolution. Nor did the revolution appear to

---

[83] Gruening (1928), p. 377.
[84] Aurrecoechea and Paz Paredes (1993), p. 107.

significantly affect the rate at which firms failed. In the steel, cement, paper, glass, woolen textile, beer, soap and glycerin, tobacco products, and dynamite and explosives industries, monopolies or oligopolies dominated their product lines in the decades prior to and following the revolution. Of all of these large firms, only one, Cementos Cruz Azul, went out of business. Moreover, Cruz Azul was not destroyed by military action. Cruz Azul was taken over by its creditors and was later merged with another cement manufacturer after the revolution.[85]

Detailed annual data on the cotton textile industry allow us to examine the relationship between survival and firm size systematically. The results indicate that most firms survived the fighting intact. Firms that failed were small enterprises. Prior to the revolution, typically 6 to 8 percent of firms failed in each five-year period. The failure rate temporarily rose in 1910–15, when 16.5 percent of firms closed their doors permanently. These were very small firms, collectively accounting for only 7 percent of total industry output. In the period 1915–20 the percentage of firms failing fell to 5.7 percent, *lower* than the rate that prevailed before the revolution. These firms accounted for only 2.7 percent of output (see Table 5.2). Even more striking than the low failure rate was the fact that these firms were replaced by new entrants of roughly comparable size.

Are there any systematic patterns to the data on the cotton textile industry that explain firm survival? We estimate probit and logit regressions to estimate the probability of survival from 1910 to 1920 as a function of several firm characteristics. We test for the effects of size (measured by market share), location (by geographic region), age of firm, total factor productivity, and the capital-labor ratio. To determine whether these regression results have historical verisimilitude, we analyze the characteristics of those firms that actually failed during the revolution.

Our probit regression results, reported in Table 5.3, indicate that size was the only statistically significant factor in determining firm survival during the revolution. Our samples are unbalanced (four to five survivors for every firm that exited the market) so we used an alternate logit model to cross-check our probit results. The logit regressions in Table 5.3 show similar results: size is the only statistically significant variable.

Our regression results for 1910–20 are corroborated by examining the characteristics of textile firms that did not survive the revolutionary years. The median size of firms that went out of business during the

[85] Haber (1989), pp. 91–92, 143, 188.

Table 5.2. Exit and Entry in the Mexican Cotton Textile Industry, 1895–1929

	Number of Firms		Exit			Entry		
Years	In First Year	End of Period[a]	Number of Firms That Exit the Market Permanently	Percentage of Firms That Exit the Industry[b]	Combined Market Share	New Firms Entering the Market within the Period	Percentage of New Firms That Enter the Market[c]	Combined Market Share
1895–1900	109	132	7	6.4	1.3	28	21.2	25.7
1900–05	132	130	11	8.3	5.1	13	10.0	9.9
1905–10	130	121	9	6.9	2.7	11	9.1	4.2
1910–15	121	87	20	16.5	7.0	10	11.5	4.7
1915–20	87	131	5	5.7	2.7	14	10.7	4.4
1920–25	131	118	15	11.5	2.0	7	5.9	2.2
1925–29	118	142	15	12.7	6.7	25	17.6	5.0

[a] In order to be counted as an exiting firm, a firm must meet the following condition: the factory owned by that firm must cease to be listed on tax records or censuses. Factories that change ownership are not considered to be exiting firms.
[b] As a percentage of total number of firms in the beginning year of the period.
[c] As a percentage of total number of firms by the end of the period.
Source: Haber and Razo (1998), p. 115, n. 43.

Table 5.3. Probit and Logit Survival Regressions, 1910–1920

Variables[a]	Probit			Logit		
	Spec 1	Spec 2	Spec 3	Spec 4	Spec 5	Spec 6
Intercept	−0.451	−0.640	−0.349	−0.875	−1.163	−0.905
	(−1.108)	(−0.767)	(−0.550)	(−1.260)	(−0.824)	(−0.770)
Size – as Share of Industry Output	213.923	168.614	156.368	393.578	312.066	297.495
	(2.890)	(2.117)	(2.046)	(2.800)	(2.135)	(2.086)
Region – Dummy for Firms in States of DF, México, Puebla, Veracruz, and Tlaxcala	0.445	0.704	0.869	0.743	1.253	1.592
	(1.247)	(1.632)	(1.860)	(1.165)	(1.590)	(1.840)
Joint Stock – Dummy for Public, Limited Liability Firms	0.578	0.749	0.808	1.082	1.547	1.755
	(1.292)	(1.257)	(1.363)	(1.264)	(1.287)	(1.412)
Vintage – Dummy for Age of Firm	−0.543	−0.931	−1.213	−0.939	−1.641	−2.103
	(−1.101)	(−1.595)	(−1.553)	(−1.104)	(−1.625)	(−1.592)
TFP (Production Proxied by Real Value of Output)		0.004			0.006	
		(0.958)			(0.899)	
TFP (Production Proxied by Meters of Output)			0.000			0.001
			(0.496)			(0.682)
Capital-Labor Ratio (Spindles-Workers)		−0.004	−0.006		−0.007	−0.012
		(−0.272)	(−0.730)		(−0.307)	(−0.787)
N	108	90	87	108	90	87
Adjusted R2	0.29	0.30	0.29	0.30	0.31	0.31

Notes: t statistics in parentheses. TFP and K/L data were taken from the 1912 census. We assumed that the input mix and productivity of firms remained constant in the short run.

[a] Dependent variable: Survival (1 if firm survives entire period; 0 if firm disappears from the industry).

Source: See source note for Table 5.2.

revolution corresponded to a market share of only 0.3 percent. There were, in fact, only two firms that failed with market shares greater than 1 percent.

Several hypotheses explain why larger firms had a greater probability of surviving the revolution than their smaller competitors. One possible explanation is that very small firms were more likely to go out of business because they were technically inefficient (they were of a size below the minimum efficiency scale). The revolution merely hastened their demise. There are two problems with this interpretation. First, we would expect that firm survival would always be correlated with firm size. We therefore estimated similar regressions for the period 1900–10. The results are shown in Table 5.4. The coefficient on firm size has the right sign, but it is not statistically significant. Second, one would expect that survivorship would be correlated with technical efficiency. As specifications 2 and 3 make clear, that is not the case. Differences in total factor productivity are extremely poor predictors of firm survival.

A more likely explanation for the correlation of firm size with firm survival during the revolution is that larger firms had the financial resources to weather the severe economic crisis of 1913–17. Owners of smaller firms likely had less liquid wealth to buttress their enterprises during hard times (their more modest wealth explains, in fact, the small size of their firms), and thus were less likely to be able to purchase stocks of raw materials to get them through prolonged periods when inputs were unavailable, less likely to be able to go for long periods when they could not earn revenues from production, and less likely to be able to pay ransoms or forced loans to passing armies.

This interpretation is buttressed by the documentary evidence we have from company histories and the correspondence of factory owners with Mexico's Department of Labor, both of which indicate that revolutionary armies rarely destroyed the mills they occupied. It was in the interests of armies to run the mills themselves and appropriate the sales revenues (minus the wages paid to the work force) in order to finance their military operations. Once the stock of raw materials had been exhausted, armies typically returned factories to their owners, often for a ransom.[86]

More serious than the threat of occupation by revolutionary armies was the fact that it was difficult to obtain raw materials or move product to market because of the collapse of the railroad system and the

---

[86] Haber (1989), pp. 132–34.

Table 5.4. *Probit and Logit Survival Regressions, 1900–1910*

Variables[a]	Probit			Logit		
	Spec 1	Spec 2	Spec 3	Spec 4	Spec 5	Spec 6
Intercept	1.023	3.499	1.651	1.717	7.371	3.139
	(3.349)	(2.799)	(1.569)	(3.023)	(2.630)	(1.437)
Size – as Share of Industry Output	31.113	31.548	12.185	59.675	67.914	28.135
	(0.719)	(1.155)	(0.371)	(0.692)	(1.192)	(0.377)
Region – Dummy for Firms in States of DF, México, Puebla, Veracruz, and Tlaxcala	0.082	−0.046	−0.196	0.132	−0.110	−0.353
	(0.250)	(−0.083)	(−0.335)	(0.204)	(−0.093)	(−0.293)
Joint Stock – Dummy for Public, Limited Liability Firms	0.402	−0.653	−0.383	0.820	−1.252	−0.828
	(1.039)	(−1.138)	(−0.757)	(1.001)	(−1.061)	(−0.768)
TFP (Production Proxied by Real Value of Output)		−0.013			−0.029	
		(−1.881)			(−1.976)	
TFP (Production Proxied by Meters of Output)			0.000			0.000
			(0.088)			(−0.009)
Capital-Labor Ratio (Spindles-Workers)		−0.018	0.002		−0.051	0.000
		(−0.627)	(0.053)		(−0.873)	(−0.002)
N	125	76	72	125	76	72
Adjusted R2	0.02	0.14	0.01	0.02	0.18	0.01

Notes: t statistics in parentheses. TFP and K/L data were taken from the 1896 census. We assumed that the input mix and productivity of firms remained constant in the short-run.

[a] Dependent variable: Survival (1 if firm survives entire period; 0 if firm disappears from the industry).

Source: See source note for Table 5.2.

disappearance of a national currency. In fact, the archives are full of appeals from manufacturers to the federal government requesting that it reopen the rail lines so as to permit the movement of necessary raw materials. The archival evidence makes little reference, however, to cases of factory destruction.[87]

Recovery of Production

One implication of the result that few firms were destroyed or forced into bankruptcy by the revolution is that production should have quickly regained its Porfirian levels once the transportation and monetary systems began again to function. Two bodies of evidence support this hypothesis. We have retrieved evidence on output in the steel, cement, cigarette, beer, and cotton textile industries. The data for all five industries indicate that there were dramatic declines in production during 1913–17, followed by a rapid recovery after 1917 (see Tables 5.5, 5.6, 5.7, 5.8, and 5.9). By the early 1920s production in most industries had surpassed Porfirian levels and continued to grow. Data we have retrieved on the dynamite industry, where we have production figures beginning only in 1918, indicate that output grew at a spectacular rate in this industry as well throughout the 1920s: output doubled every two years from 1918 to 1929 (see Table 5.10). As with beer, textiles, cigarettes, paper, and cement, the national dynamite industry satisfied all of Mexican demand by the early 1920s.

We have no direct data on small-scale industries such as apparel or leather goods. We do, however, have data on electric power consumption for commercial uses in Mexico City (the data exclude power generated for the water, tramway, or public lighting systems). We know that the majority of small-scale manufacturing establishments used electric-powered machinery by the 1920s. Thus commercial power consumption is a reasonable proxy for industrial activity. Table 5.11 shows a steady rise in commercial power usage from 1907 through 1912. Power usage declined from 1912 to 1915, falling by roughly 40 percent, and then recovered rapidly. By 1917 commercial power consumption in Mexico City was 17 percent higher than in 1910. It rose continuously thereafter. By 1927

---

[87] Mexico's factory owners regularly communicated their problems to the government. See AGN, Ramo del Departamento de Trabajo, box 45, file 3, pp. 1–5; box 52, file 12, pp. 1–3; box 90, file 17, p. 1; box 91: file 21, pp. 1–2; box 96, file 5, pp. 49–53; box 96, file 9, p. 45; box 107, file 22, p. 2; box 107, file 22, p. 2; box 110, file 28, p. 1; box 173, file 23, p. 1.

Table 5.5. *Capacity, Output, and Value of Physical Plant in*
Fundidora Monterrey (Mexico's Steel Monopolist), 1903–1929

Year	Capacity[a]	Output[b]	Capacity Utilization (%)	Value of Physical Plant[c]
1903	110	22	20	8,388
1904	110	36	33	9,236
1905	110	4	4	9,833
1906	110	25	23	10,032
1907	110	16	15	9,526
1908	110	17	15	9,082
1909	110	59	54	9,317
1910	110	45	41	9,365
1911	110	71	65	9,087
1912	110	33	30	9,337
1913	110	12	11	9,226
1914	110	0	0	8,989
1915	110	0	0	8,509
1916	110	0	0	8,161
1917	110	12	11	7,819
1918	110	21	19	7,830
1919	110	21	19	7,374
1920	110	15	14	9,133
1921	110	42	38	10,421
1922	110	24	22	10,217
1923	110	44	40	10,238
1924	110	19	17	10,340
1925	110	49	45	9,872
1926	110	62	56	9,700
1927	110	41	37	9,436
1928	110	51	46	9,173
1929	110	60	55	8,679

[a] Capacity of the blast furnace, in thousands of metric tons.
[b] Output of the blast furnace, in thousands of metric tons.
[c] Book value of the physical plant (land, equipment, buildings), net of
depreciation in thousands of pesos. Physical plant depreciated at flat
rate of 5 percent per annum.
Source: Calculated from Compañía Fundidora de Fierro y Acero de
Monterrey (1900–30).

commercial power consumption in Mexico City was three times what it
had been in 1910.

There are two implications of the dramatic rise in power consumption.
First, output in small-scale industries was increasing. Second, one of two

Table 5.6. *Capacity and Output in Mexico's Cement Industry, 1906–1929 (in thousands of metric tons)*

Year	Capacity	Output	Capacity Utilization (%)
1906	66	20	30
1907	66	30	45
1908	66	40	61
1909	86	50	58
1910	151	60	40
1911	152	50	33
1912	177	40	23
1913	177	30	17
1914	177	25	14
1915	177	10	6
1916	177	20	11
1917	177	30	17
1918	177	40	23
1919	177	40	23
1920	222	45	20
1921	222	50	23
1922	222	70	32
1923	222	90	41
1924	222	107	48
1925	222	110	50
1926	222	151	68
1927	222	158	71
1928	246	204	83
1929	291	158	54

Source: Haber (1989), n. 29, and pp. 41, 127, 165, 177.

developments (or both) was taking place: either firms were running their existing capital stock more intensively (e.g., by using electric lights to allow night shifts), or they were investing in additional machinery and equipment. That is, there might have been capital deepening.

Investor Confidence and Expectations

One implication of the rapid recovery and growth of output is that investors should have regained the confidence they had before 1911. We measure investor expectations by looking at the price of assets, which reflects the expectations of investors about the future ability of those assets to produce profits. Reduced expectations about the ability of assets

Table 5.7. *Mexican Beer Production, National and Cervecería Cuauhtémoc, 1900–1929 (in thousands of liters)*

Year	Cervecería Cuauhtemoc	National Output	Cuauhtémoc Market Share (%)
1900	4,866		
1901	4,685		
1902	5,581		
1903	5,925		
1904	6,865		
1905	8,884		
1906	13,344		
1907	14,005		
1908	11,183		
1909	11,582		
1910	13,275		
1911	14,172		
1912	16,519		
1913	11,732		
1914–15[a]	3,359		
1916	2,758		
1917	4,640		
1918	4,977		
1919	7,735		
1920	14,929		
1921	16,689		
1922	13,156		
1923	12,335		
1924	11,564	52,003	22
1925	15,736	53,673	29
1926	21,521	67,925	32
1927	23,201	71,613	32
1928	22,229	67,911	33
1929	23,174	71,973	32

[a] Combined year.

Source: Haber (1989), pp. 53, 127, 163.

to earn positive returns should result in a decline in the market value of those assets.

We are unable to look at the price of all industrial assets in Mexico. We can, however, look at the price of common stock in Mexico's publicly traded manufacturing companies. We have therefore retrieved year-end stock prices from the Mexico City financial press for publicly traded manufacturing firms and produced a real (inflation adjusted) stock price

Table 5.8. *Mexican Cotton Textile Industry, 1883–1929*

Year	Estimated Nominal Value Output[a]	Estimated Real Value Output[a]	Estimated Meters of Output[a]	Estimated Spindles	Estimated Worker Equivalents[b]
1878[c]	950	1,135	73,597	249,294	11,922
1883	11,484	8,538	76,331		
1888[c]	264	216	60,842	249,561	15,083
1889	10,909	8,942	83,827		
1891	12,066	9,891	93,527	277,784	14,051
1893	19,064	15,628	122,550	370,570	21,963
1895	23,554	21,222	170,929	411,090	18,208
1896	23,658	23,658	206,412	430,868	19,771
1899	29,753	29,753	231,686	491,443	23,731
1900	35,459	35,459	261,397	588,474	27,767
1901	33,877	33,877	262,044	591,506	26,709
1902	28,780	28,780	235,956	595,728	24,964
1903	36,907	36,907	262,170	632,601	26,149
1904	42,511	42,511	280,710	635,940	27,456
1905	51,214	51,214	310,692	678,058	30,162
1906	51,171	51,171	349,712	688,217	31,673
1907	51,686	51,686	428,284	613,548	33,132
1908	54,934	54,934	368,370	732,876	35,816
1909	43,370	43,370	314,228	726,278	32,229
1910	50,651	50,651	315,322	702,874	31,963
1911	51,348	51,348	341,441	725,297	32,147
1912	63,802	72,834	319,668	762,149	32,209
1913	54,002	33,978	298,897	752,804	32,641
1917[d]	25,125	12,226		573,092	22,187
1918	48,567	15,111	180,453	689,173	23,067
1919	80,781	23,333	305,509	735,308	21,877
1920	120,492	27,840	298,829	753,837	24,691
1922	85,023	53,040	330,601	803,230	26,451
1923	97,563	44,214	303,090	802,363	26,419
1924	96,435	44,155	285,594	812,165	25,155
1925	102,527	56,839	380,041	840,890	33,262
1926	88,766	60,562	327,487	832,193	27,476
1927	73,179	51,156	308,940	821,211	27,492
1928	89,630	52,529	300,425	823,862	25,348
1929	105,055	67,861	389,147	839,100	27,598

[a] Output reported in thousands.

[b] Number of workers adjusted for changes in the length of the workday: 12 hours from 1850 to 1913, 10 hours from 1914 to 1917, 8 hours from 1918 to 1933.

[c] For these years, the majority of firms only reported output in meters.

[d] Spindles and workers data for 1917 was taken from Mexico, INEGI (1999), 616, n. 27.

Source: See source note for Table 5.2.

Table 5.9. *The Mexican Cigarette Industry, Output and Investment, 1899–1928*

Year	Factories	Production: Thousands of Kilos	Production: Millions of Packages of Cigarettes	Capital Invested: Nominal Pesos	Value of Output: Nominal Pesos	Number of Workers
1899	766	4,916	329			
1900	766	5,907	376			
1901	740	5,974	365			
1902	701	6,203	372			
1903	670	7,305	406			
1904	605	7,724	468			
1905	469	8,174	483			
1906	491	8,456	505			
1907	479	8,856	524			
1908	469	8,904	515			
1909	437	8,661	505			
1910	451	8,451	512			
1911	341	8,380	493			
1923	169	10,202	411	19,457,999	26,174,851	4990
1924	207	7,830	380	19,668,424	24,062,005	4766
1925	197	9,020	385	19,948,643	28,536,637	5905
1926	163	9,546	452	22,435,177	29,124,007	5201
1927	143	10,649	542	23,123,888	31,174,424	5051
1928	127		543	26,639,540	30,551,504	4685

Sources: Haber (1989), p. 49; México, Departamento de Estadística Nacional, September 1928; and February 1930.

index.[88] Our data set includes the four largest cotton textile producers (the Compañía Industrial de Orizaba, the Compañía Industrial Veracruzana, the Compañía Industrial de Atlixco, and the Compañía Industrial de San Antonio Abad, which jointly accounted for roughly one-third of national output), the country's steel monopoly (Fundidora Monterrey), the single largest wool textile manufacturer (the Compañía Industrial de San Ildefonso), two of the country's most important beer brewers (the Cervecería Moctezuma and the Compañía Cervecera de Toluca y México), the country's only large-scale producer of soap and glycerin products (the Compañía Industrial Jabonera de la Laguna), the largest producer of paper products (the Compañía Industrial de San Rafael y Anexas, which

[88] Data were gathered from *El Economista Mexicano* and *La Semana Mercantil* from 1896 to 1914. Data from 1914 to 1929 were gathered from the *Boletín Financiero y Minero*. In cases where no shares were traded, the average of the bid and ask prices was taken.

Table 5.10. *Output and Consumption of Dynamite, 1918–1929*
(in thousands of kilograms)

Year	Output	Consumption	Production as % of Consumption
1918	301,644	285,519	106
1919	776,223	585,711	133
1920	646,698	741,114	87
1921	706,709	565,004	125
1922	571,604	647,242	88
1923	586,573	633,362	93
1924	535,747	721,428	74
1925	1,221,870	1,202,653	102
1926	1,424,524	1,463,975	97
1927	3,182,704	3,072,732	104
1928	4,766,470	4,671,643	102
1929	5,759,625	5,620,138	102

Source: Mexico, Secretaría de Industria, Comercio y Trabajo (1932), p. 358.

monopolized the lucrative newsprint market), and two of the three firms that dominated the production of tobacco products (El Buen Tono and La Cigarrera Mexicana). We estimate the index using both real (inflation-adjusted) pesos and real dollars, and compare it with the performance of the Dow Jones Industrials in the United States. The use of both real pesos and real dollars allows us to cross-check our results, in order to be certain that they are not driven by the choice of price index. The data are presented in Table 5.12 and graphed in Figure 5.1.

Regardless of whether stock prices are deflated by a Mexican price index or converted to U.S. dollars, they indicate that share prices fell from 1910 to 1918. Calculated in real pesos, the value of share prices fell 80 percent from 1910 to 1918. Calculated in real dollars, the index fell 77 percent. During the same period, the Dow Jones Industrials fell 46 percent in real terms. The implication is that share prices in Mexico would have fallen anyway – even had there been no revolution. The sharper drop of the Mexican index indicates, however, that the revolution exerted an additional negative effect on share prices.

The stock indices indicate a recovery of Mexican share prices after 1918. By the end of the 1923, share prices in real pesos rose 133 percent (growing from an index value of 20 in 1918 to 47 in 1923). Calculated in real dollars, share prices grew 45 percent during the same period (from an index value of 33 to 48). In comparison, The Dow Jones Industrials rose by 52 percent during the same period. The 1918–23 data suggest that

Table 5.11. *Power Generated by the Mexican Light and Power Company for Commercial Purposes, 1907–1927 (in thousands of kilowatt hours)*

Year	Power	Index (1910 = 100)
1907	45,779	80
1908	44,061	77
1909	47,074	82
1910	57,112	100
1911	59,244	104
1912	67,565	118
1913	62,117	109
1914	56,274	99
1915	39,096	68
1916	42,888	75
1917	67,062	117
1918	72,901	128
1919	82,212	144
1920	91,145	160
1921	88,379	155
1922	103,111	181
1923	113,704	199
1924	125,424	220
1925	144,230	253
1926	166,483	292
1927	178,089	312

Note: Does not include municipal lighting.
Source: Sterret and Davis (1928), p. 213.

investors were not terribly concerned about political stability. Neither the overthrow of Carranza by Obregón in 1920 nor the de la Huerta rebellion of 1923–24 appears to have exerted a negative effect on share prices.

There was, of course, a very big difference between the performance of the Dow Jones Industrials and Mexican industrial stocks over the course of the late 1920s. A stock market bubble grew in the United States, taking the Dow Jones (in real dollars) to nearly three times its 1910 value by 1928. Whether Mexico would have had a stock bubble in the absence of the political events of 1910–29 is a hypothesis that cannot be tested. What is clear, however, is that Mexican share prices never regained their 1910 values, implying that investors discounted the value of their Porfirian era investments heavily.

Table 5.12. *Stock Price Indices of Mexican Manufacturing Compared with U.S. Manufacturing, 1900–1930 (base year 1910 = 100)*

Year	Mexico		United States:
	Mexican Industrial (real pesos)	Mexican Industrial (real U.S.$)	Dow Jones Industrial (real U.S.$)
1900			109
1901	126	99	101
1902	96	74	95
1903	98	76	72
1904	99	90	101
1905	141	121	139
1906	155	130	132
1907	145	120	78
1908	120	104	119
1909	104	92	127
1910	100	100	100
1911	92	99	109
1912	80	85	110
1913	72	74	98
1914	61	46	69
1915			124
1916			96
1917			55
1918	20	33	54
1919	30	39	67
1920	26	37	40
1921	27	43	72
1922	38	47	89
1923	47	48	82
1924	43	47	107
1925	39	50	131
1926	35	44	136
1927	34	38	184
1928	32	33	268
1929	30	30	226
1930	25	30	165

Sources: Mexican data estimated from *Economista Mexicano*, 1900–14; *Boletín Financiero y Minero*, 1914–38.

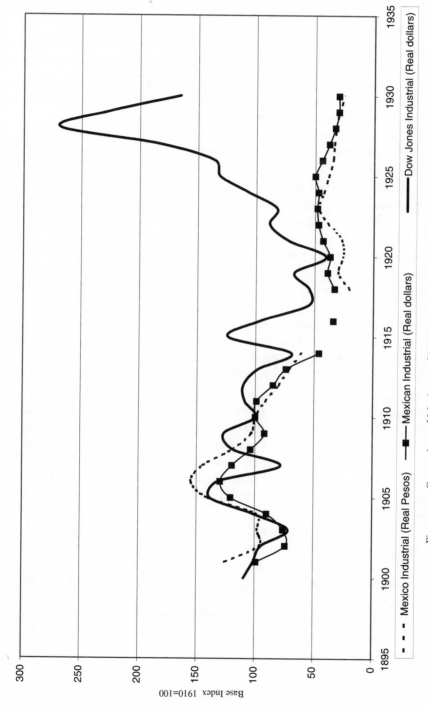

Figure 5.1. Comparison of Mexican and U.S. Stock Indices. *Source:* See Table 5.12.

- - - Mexico Industrial (Real Pesos)   ━■━ Mexican Industrial (Real dollars)   ━━ Dow Jones Industrial (Real dollars)

Base Index 1910=100

New Investment

The fact that stock prices were depressed does not mean that there would be no new investment. Investors may have written off a large chunk of the value of their existing investments, but they would continue to purchase new plant and equipment as long as the expected return on new investments exceeded their cost of capital.

How can we know firms' cost of capital? We already know that nominal retail interest rates were on the order of 12 percent. Most firms, however, did not raise their capital by borrowing from banks. Instead they raised capital from retained earnings. Their cost of capital can be thought of as the implicit price charged by investors to hold their stock – which can be captured by the dividend yield (dividends per share divided by the market price per share) on their common stock. If future investments in plant and equipment cannot earn *at least* the yield available on common stock, then investors would be better off purchasing stock in existing companies than purchasing new plant and equipment. What happened to yields in the 1920s? Were they prohibitively high?

We calculated average yields on common stock for the same set of companies for which we tracked share prices. We restricted our analysis, however, only to those firms that paid dividends (non-dividend-paying firms have a yield of zero, which clearly is not their cost of capital). Our analysis indicates that the average yield rate on industrial common stocks from 1918 to 1925 was 11 percent. The comparable yield rate during the last decade of the Porfiriato (1901–10) was 7 percent. In addition, the trend in yields after 1921 is strongly downward, reflecting a decline in firms' cost of capital. By 1925 yields had returned to Porfirian levels. The reason for the decline is most likely lower uncertainty. That is, investors perceived less systemic risk in the Mexican economy as the 1920s went on.[89]

Data that we have retrieved on new investment are consistent with the hypothesis that firms invested substantially in new capital equipment in the 1920s. We have been able to retrieve data on new capacity or investment in the cement, steel, cigarette, and cotton textile industries; and on exports of industrial machinery from the United States and United Kingdom to Mexico, which is an excellent measure of the flow of new investment because virtually all of Mexico's capital goods had to be imported.

[89] Yields estimated from data in Haber (1989), pp. 115, 129.

Productive capacity in the cement industry continued to expand both during and after the revolution, growing from 66,000 metric tons per year in 1906 to 151,000 in 1910, 177,000 in 1912, 222,000 in 1920, and 246,000 in 1928. This rate of growth in capacity is especially impressive in light of the fact that capacity utilization was almost always less than 60 percent, implying that the owners of firms were confident enough about the future to invest well ahead of demand (see Table 5.6).[90] Data on the nation's integrated steel-producing monopolist, Fundidora Monterrey, tell a similar story. During the years of civil war, when the plant was cut off from its input and product markets, Fundidora Monterrey closed its doors and spent no funds on plant and equipment. As soon as normalcy returned, however, the firm invested in a dramatic fashion: the value of its physical plant grew 41 percent from 1919 to 1921, even in the face of capacity utilization of less than 40 percent (see Table 5.5).

One might argue that the recovery of the steel and cement industries should not be surprising. The physical destruction of the years of revolutionary violence might have stimulated demand for construction goods in the 1920s. These two industries might therefore not be representative of the manufacturing sector as a whole. This hypothesis is not sustained by an analysis of data on the country's most important consumer goods industry: cotton textiles. As Table 5.8 indicates, the textile industry, measured in spindlage, declined in size by 25 percent from 1913 to 1917.[91] Much of this loss clearly represented firms temporarily closing their doors during the worst phases of the fighting. Indeed, the only way to explain a 28 percent jump in capacity from 1917 to 1919 is that firms that had closed their doors during the years of civil war reopened them as soon as the railroads started running again. The recovery went well beyond the reopening of old capacity, however. In fact, in 1921 the cotton textile industry was 10 percent larger than it had been in 1910 (and roughly equal to its 1913 level), and in the four years from 1921 to 1925 the industry grew an additional 9 percent, making it 20 percent larger than it had

---

[90] The fact that firms invested ahead of demand is explained by the fact that cement production throughout the world is characterized by local monopolies. The high bulk-to-price ratio of cement means that it is economical to ship it only over short distances. In order to expand, therefore, firms must erect new production facilities in new areas of the country. Firms also tend to erect more productive capacity than they need in these new markets in order to keep out potential rivals. See Johnson and Parkman (1983).

[91] Spindles constitute the most important capital input for the production of cotton textile goods, and thus the literature tends to use spindlage as the measure of capital or capacity. See, for example, Kane (1988).

been in 1910. Significantly, this increase in capacity cannot be explained as the result of population growth, because the Mexican population was 5 percent smaller in 1921 than it had been in 1910.[92] The rate of growth of industry capacity then slowed in the late 1920s. This should not be surprising in light of the fact that by this point domestic production had virtually eliminated imports. The industry could now only grow as fast as incomes or population growth would allow.

Data we have retrieved on the cigarette industry tell much the same story (see Table 5.9). The total nominal capital invested in the industry was 19.5 million pesos in 1923. By 1928 total capital invested had grown 37 percent, to 26.6 million pesos. These estimates almost certainly understate the amounts spent by firms on new plant and equipment. The number of firms in the industry declined from 169 in 1923 to 127 in 1928, continuing a trend toward increasing concentration that began in the 1890s. The capital equipment of the failing firms was almost certainly being taken out of production, meaning that net new investment by surviving firms was significantly higher than the 37 percent we have measured.[93]

The patterns displayed by the cotton textile, cigarette, steel, and cement industries are corroborated by data on U.S. and British exports of industrial machinery to Mexico. In Table 5.13 we present estimates of the real value of exports of industrial machinery from these two countries to Mexico. We break down industrial machines into three categories: textile machinery, manufacturing machinery other than textiles, and total. All of the series indicate the same pattern. The data for 1911, 1912, and 1913 indicate that investment rates were not, on average, much different than they had been during the period 1900–10. By 1915, when the railroads effectively closed for civilian use, new investment was in aggregate one-sixth of what it had been just three years before. Imports of industrial machines climbed rapidly, however, just as soon as the civil war of 1914–17 wound down. By 1920 every category of industrial machinery exported from the United States and Great Britain to Mexico had surpassed its Porfirian levels. In fact, during the 1920s industrial machinery exports to Mexico were anywhere from twice (in the case of textile machines) to six times

---

[92] Mexican population data are from México, INEGI (1994), p. 44.

[93] Ideally, we would deflate these nominal capital values to produce a series on real capital invested in the industry. This would require, however, that we know the vintage of the capital employed in 1923, that we know the depreciation rates applied by firms to their capital equipment, and that we know the breakdown of capital spending by type of asset. Unfortunately, these data are not available.

Table 5.13. *Combined United States–United Kingdom Industrial Machinery Exports to Mexico, 1900–1929 (in thousands of 1929 U.S. dollars)*

Year	Textile Machinery	Other Manufacturing Machinery	Total Manufacturing Machinery	Index (1910 = 100)
1900	468	267	735	72
1901	184	219	402	40
1902	248	139	387	38
1903	147	374	521	51
1904	396	393	789	78
1905	266	625	891	88
1906	355	804	1,158	114
1907	472	1,003	1,475	145
1908	473	968	1,441	142
1909	525	629	1,154	113
1910	350	668	1,017	100
1911	331	1,041	1,373	135
1912	391	720	1,111	109
1913	26	1,417	1,443	142
1914	6	294	300	30
1915	3	112	116	11
1916	9	420	428	42
1917	36	860	895	88
1918	86	1,458	1,544	152
1919	164	2,727	2,892	284
1920	457	4,503	4,960	488
1921	139	3,917	4,056	399
1922	1,113	1,667	2,780	273
1923	596	1,454	2,050	202
1924	634	1,377	2,012	198
1925	917	1,783	2,700	265
1926	1,111	6,187	7,299	718
1927	1,066	5,538	6,604	649
1928	1,124	5,140	6,264	616
1929	681	7,935	8,616	847

Note: Price deflator is wholesale price index found in Carter and United States Bureau of the Census (1997), Series E40–51.

Sources: United States: United States, Department of Commerce (1902–30). United Kingdom: United Kingdom, Customs and Excise Dept. Statistical Office (1900–34).

(manufacturing machines other than textiles) what they had been during the decade before the revolution.

One might argue that it should not come as a surprise that industrialists reopened their mills after the civil war ended. The capacity that existed prior to the revolution represented sunk costs. As long as industrialists could cover their variable costs, it paid to put capacity back into production. One might also argue that incremental investments by industrialists should not come as a surprise either: if investments in small increases in productive capacity could, at the margin, allow for the efficient use of already existing capacity, then it would be in the interest of industrialists to undertake those investments, even if the general business environment was uncertain.

There are two problems with these arguments. First, the data on exports of industrial machinery to Mexico indicate that firms were doing much more than undertaking incremental increases in productive capacity: the flow of new machinery to Mexico after 1920 exceeded the levels attained before 1910. Second, this argument cannot account for the fact that new firms entered the market for manufactures both during the revolution and afterward, even in the face of the failure of older, more established firms. As Table 5.2 indicates, in the cotton textile industry, for example, from 1910 to 1915 10 new firms entered the industry (8 of these during the turbulent years 1913, 1914, and 1915), adding 4.7 percent to the industry's capacity. From 1915 to 1920 more firms actually entered the industry than exited: 5 firms closed their doors, but 14 new firms entered, accounting for 4.4 percent of output. From 1920 to 1925 7 new firms entered the industry, accounting for 2.2 percent of output. Between 1925 and 1929 the number of new entrants rose to 25, accounting for 5 percent of output. In fact, these rates of entry during and after the revolution are indistinguishable from the rates of entry that prevailed in the five years before the revolution broke out.

We do not have the kinds of systematic data on entry and exit for other industries that we have for cotton textiles. The partial data we have, however, indicates entry in a number of industries by new, large, capital intensive firms in the early 1920s. In the tobacco industry, for example, the British-American Tobacco Company established two subsidiary manufacturing plants in Mexico that dwarfed their Mexican competitors and quickly drove them out of business. The International Match Company opened a subsidiary in Mexico. In the dynamite industry, the Dupont de Nemours Company acquired the plant of the Compañía Industrial Nacional Mexicana de Dinamita y Explosivos. In the cement industry, Cementos Monterrey was founded, soon fusing with Cementos Hidalgo to form the mammoth Cementos Mexicanos, and in the beer industry the huge Cervecería Modelo was established in Mexico City, quickly establishing itself as one of the largest brewers in the country. Lastly, Ford Motors opened an assembly plant in Mexico City in 1925.[94]

Ownership Continuity

One implication of our analysis is that there was continuity of ownership of Mexico's manufacturing sector. Indeed, our analysis suggests that the post-1917 governments formed VPI coalitions with the same asset holders as had Díaz.

Systematic evidence that we and others have assembled on the membership of corporate boards indicates that there was a striking degree of continuity in the ownership of manufacturing companies. Our sample includes 11 large manufacturing firms for circa 1910 and 1921. In some cases, we have data for the 1930s as well. These 11 firms include the Fundidora Monterrey steel monopoly, the El Buen Tono and La Tabacalera Mexicana cigarette companies, the Compañía Industrial Jabonera de la Laguna soap and glycerin company, the Compañía Industrial de Orizaba (CIDOSA), Compañía Industrial Veracruzana (CIVSA), and Compañía Industrial de Atlixco (CIASA) textile conglomerates, the Toluca y México beer brewery, the Cuauhtémoc beer brewery, the Vidriera Monterrey glassworks, and the San Rafael y Anexas paper monopoly.

We note that all of these industries were extremely concentrated both before and after the revolution. Thus, an analysis of these companies is comprehensive for that product line. The paper, steel, glass, and soap industries were monopolies or near monopolies, while the cigarette industries and beer industries were dominated by two or three producers.[95] To cite a few examples, circa 1923, the Compañía Industrial Jabonera de la Laguna was still the only large-scale soap manufacturer in Mexico, employing 59 percent of all the workers in the industry. Given the sizable scale economies in soap manufacturing, its market share was almost certainly much higher.[96] In the paper industry the San Rafael y Anexas company controlled 83 percent of the market circa 1929.[97] In the steel industry, Fundidora Monterrey

---

[94] Haber (1989), pp. 143–44; Sterret and Davis (1928), p. 208.

[95] Haber (1989), chap. 4.

[96] Even measuring by number of workers, the four-firm ratio was 0.72 and the Herfindahl Index was 0.36. Calculated from data in *Boletín Financiero y Minero*, September 26, 1923.

[97] México, Secretaría de Hacienda (1936), p. 191.

continued to be the sole integrated steel producer in the country until the 1940s.[98]

What do the ownership data show? Let us look at two typical examples. Tabacalera Mexicana, a major tobacco products manufacturer, had been formed out of the amalgamation of the various tobacco manufactories of the Basagoiti and Zaldo families. The 1911 board of directors therefore included Antonio Basagoiti (as company president), Dionisio Ramón Zaldo, A. R. Zaldo, and Basagoiti's right-hand man, Adolfo Prieto. Luis Barroso Arias (a partner of Prieto), Eugenio Alvarez, and William Mitchell served on the board as well. In 1921 Basagoiti was still serving as company president and board member. Dionisio Ramón Zaldo and Adolfo Prieto were also both still on the board. The board now included family relations (likely nephews) of Basagoiti: Juan Castano Basagoiti and Ramón Castano Basagoiti. In fact, as late as 1938 members of the Basagoiti-Zaldo clans still dominated the board, with Dionisio Ramón Zaldo still appearing and what appears to be the son of Antonio Basagoiti, J. Antonio Basagoiti Ruíz.[99]

The Compañía Industrial de Orizaba textile conglomerate, our second example, was founded and run by a group of French expatriate dry goods merchants and financiers in the 1890s. In 1911 its board of directors included Henri (Enrique) Tron (as president) as well as three other French merchant-financiers: Eugenio Roux, David Adrian, and Mauricio Honnorat. In 1920 the company was still being run by French expatriates. In fact, the president of the board in 1920, Justino Tron, was almost certainly a relative of the 1911 president, Henri Tron, who now headed the Paris Consultative Committee of the firm. Mauricio Honnorat was no longer on the board, but León Honnorat was, along with his long-term business partner León Signoret. In fact, as late as 1937 the board had not dramatically changed: French surnames predominated, including Tron, Honnorat, and Signoret.[100]

The other firms in our sample show similar results. The surnames of board members barely change from the decade 1900–10 to the decade 1920–30.[101]

---

[98] Haber (1989), p. 46.

[99] *Mexican Yearbook*, 1912, p. 126; *Boletín Financiero y Minero*, April 17, 1922; April 16, 1930; October 29, 1938.

[100] *Boletín Financiero y Minero*, January 30, 1920; April 28, 1937; *Mexican Yearbook*, 1912, p. 123.

[101] For data on the other companies in our sample, see as follows. For Fundidora Monterrey. Compañía Fundidora de Fierro y Acero de Monterrey), 1910 and 1921.

Our conclusions are consistent with the observations of contemporary observers. When Joseph Sterrett and Joseph Davis wrote their 1927 report on Mexico's economic situation for the International Committee of Bankers, they noted: "The industries were in almost all cases started by foreigners and are still largely controlled by the same groups; but the companies are generally Mexican corporations, and in some cases the present active leaders, descendants of the earlier operators, are Mexican citizens who still, as a rule, retain close connection with their country of national origin."[102]

Our analysis also squares with the detailed histories of elite families studied by social historians. Research by Mark Wasserman on the Terrazas-Creel clan of Chihuahua, by Alex Saragoza on the Garza-Sadas of Monterrey, by Mario Cerutti on the business enterprises of John F. Brittingham, by Leticia Gamboa Ojeda on the textile magnates of Puebla, and by María del Carmen Collado Herrera on the Braniff family all point to the same conclusion: these family business empires weathered the revolution and the political instability of the 1920s intact.[103]

These results are also consistent with an analysis we have carried out of ownership in the Mexican cotton textile industry.[104] Table 5.14 indicates that there was, in fact, remarkable ownership stability. Of the 10 largest companies (by which we mean the individuals, partnerships, or corporations that owned mills, not the mills themselves) in the industry in 1920, 8 had been industry leaders in 1910. All 10 companies had been founded before 1910, half of them before 1900. Similarly, of the 20 largest textile companies in 1929, 15 had been founded during the Porfiriato (see Table 5.15). This is a lower-bound estimate. The other 5 were joint-stock companies that had obtained limited liability status in the 1920s, although the mills they owned were of Porfirian origin. It is likely

---

For CIASA, *Boletín Financiero y Minero*, April 7, 1919, *Mexican Yearbook*, 1911, p. 280; for CIVSA, *Boletín Financiero y Minero*, May 3, 1937; June 11, 1924; *Mexican Yearbook*, 1911, p. 289; 1912, p. 123; for El Buen Tono, *Boletín Financiero y Minero*, May 28, 1919; April 21, 1924; October 26, 1926; April 30, 1938; *Mexican Yearbook*, 1911, p. 281; for San Rafael, *Boletín Financiero y Minero*, April 27, 1921; April 13, 1928; *Mexican Yearbook*, 1912, p. 126; for Vidriera Monterrey, Saragoza (1988), pp. 64, 126, 146; for Cervecería Cuauhtémoc, Saragoza (1988), pp. 2, 64, 146; for the Compañía Cervecera de Toluca y México, Barrera Pages (1999).

[102] Sterret and Davis (1928), p. 207.

[103] Barrera Pages (1999); Wasserman (1993); Marichal and Cerutti (1997); Cerutti and Flores (1997); Gamboa Ojeda (1985); Collado Herrera (1987).

[104] By company ownership we refer either to a corporation or a person with distinct ownership rights over a given mill (or group of mills). This may be a corporation, partnership, or sole proprietorship.

Table 5.14. *Top Ten Companies in the Mexican Cotton Textile Industry, 1910–1929*

Owner	Started Business	Market Share(%)	Rank in 1910	1915	1920	1925	1929
Cia. Ind. de Orizaba, S.A.	1888	9.1	1	1	1	1	1
Cia. Ind. Veracruzana, S.A.	1900	6.8	2	3	2	2	2
Cia. Ind. de Atlixco, S.A.	1904	5.5	3	–	4	5	8
Cia. Ind. Antonio Abad, S.A.	1895	4.1	4	9	7	10	–
Cia. Indl manufacturera S.A.	1888	3.2	5	8	3	4	3
Hijos de Angel Diaz Rubin	1895	3.2	6	–	–	–	13
Veyan Jean y Cia., Sucesores	1906	3.2	7	10	6	6	–
Eusebio Gonzalez, S en C	1878	2.9	8	19	–	–	19
Cia. La Hormiga S.A.	1909	2.7	9	–	9	9	6
C. Noriega y Cia. Sucrs	1895	2.7	10	11	5	3	4

Source: See source note for Table 5.2.

Table 5.15. *Ownership and Share of Output of Top Twenty Cotton Textile Companies, 1929*

Rank	Owner	Started Business	Market Share(%)
1	Cia. Ind. de Orizaba, S.A.[a]	1888	12
2	Cia. Ind. Veracruzana, S.A.[a]	1900	8
3	Cia. Ind. Manufacturera, S.A.[a]	1888	5
4	C. Noriega y Cia. Sucrs[a]	1895	4
5	Cia. Atoyac Textil S.A.	1924[b]	3
6	Cia. La Hormiga S.A.[a]	1909	3
7	Cia. Ind. de Parras, S.A.[a]	1900	3
8	Cia. Ind. de Atlixco, S.A.[a]	1904	3
9	Viuda e Hijos de Leopoldo Gavito[a]	1895	3
10	Barron y la Colmena S.A.	1929	2
11	Cia. Ind. de Guadalajara, S.A.[a]	1900	2
12	La Magdalena, S.A.	1929	2
13	Schmelz Hnos.	1919	2
14	E. Artasanchez y Cia.[a]	1909	2
15	Cia. Fab. San Martin, S.A.	1929	2
16	Manuel M. Conde[a]	1888	1
17	V Rivero Sucrs[a]	1893	1
18	Negociacion Fabril La Aurora, S.A.	1929	1
19	Eusebio Gonzalez, Sucesores[a]	1878	1
20	Zaldo Hnos y Cia.[a]	1900	1

[a] Porfirian companies.
[b] The mills composing this new company had previously belonged to Quijano, Rivero y Cia., who started business in 1878.

Source: See source note for Table 5.2.

Table 5.16. *Rates of Ownership Change in the Mexican Cotton Textile Industry,*
1895–1929

Period	Firms Appearing in Both Years	Firms That Change Ownership	Percentage of Firms That Change Ownership	Output Affected by Ownership Turnover(%)
1895–1900	94	27	29	23
1900–1905	112	30	27	15
1905–1910	102	18	18	13
1910–1915	66	7	11	4
1915–1920	77	12	16	7
1920–1925	103	22	21	19
1925–1929	100	20	20	12

Source: See source note for Table 5.2.

the case that some of these companies were in fact sole proprietorships or partnerships that decided to obtain limited liability, corporate status.[105] In short, with few exceptions, the very same mill owners that dominated the industry in 1910 dominated it in 1920 and beyond.

Even among midsized companies there was very little turnover of assets. In Table 5.16 we present estimates of the rate at which companies changed hands in five-year intervals from 1895 to 1929. During the years 1910–15, 11 percent of companies changed owners, and during the period 1915–20, 16 percent of companies changed owners. These rates of ownership turnover were little different than the rates that prevailed under political stability. From 1895 to 1900, 29 percent of companies changed hands. In the next five-year period, from 1900 to 1905, 27 percent changed hands. From 1905 to 1910, roughly 18 percent of companies changed hands.

Moreover, the changes in ownership during the period 1910–20 occurred primarily among very small companies. The percentage of industry output affected by changes in ownership was only 4.2 percent from 1910 to 1915 and 7.0 percent from 1915 to 1920. This was less than half of the average industry output affected by ownership change before 1910. The rate of ownership change in the 1920s was also not dramatically different from that prevailing before 1910. Regardless of whether we estimate ownership turnover by the percentage of companies in the industry or

---

[105] Doing so would have made it easier for them to obtain credit, as the shares in the firm could then be pledged as collateral.

the percentage of output they controlled, the period 1920–30 is virtually indistinguishable from the period 1895–1910.[106]

Productivity

One might imagine that the dramatic changes in institutions that came out of the Constitution of 1917 should have had adverse consequences for industrial productivity. The rise of unions, the increase in wages, the shortening of the workday, and the increase in worker militancy on the shop floor all should have raised the unit costs of labor. Similarly, the disappearance of a major portion of the banking sector in the 1910s, the subsequent rise in interest rates, and the increase in risk premia associated with new investments in the 1920s should have increased the unit cost of capital. The result might have been a decline in the productivity of labor (output per worker) and the productivity of capital (output per machine). The net result would have been a decline in total factor productivity (TFP – output per worker, holding the amount of capital per worker constant).

The detailed data we have retrieved on the cotton textile industry allow us to estimate all three measures of productivity: output per worker, output per machine, and TFP. We measure output in two different ways: the real (inflation-adjusted) value of production, and the volume of production (meters of cloth).[107] Following Kane, we employed spindlage as a proxy for capital.[108] Following the work of Atack and Sokoloff on the United States and Bernard and Jones on international productivity comparisons, we employed the number of workers as a proxy for the labor input.[109] We adjusted, however, for changes in the length of the

---

[106] The decade 1910–20 showed a difference in one dimension from the decades that preceded and followed it. There was a sizable decline (on the order of 50 percent) in the average *size* of firms that were sold during this period. This result is consistent with the finding that small firms had less chance of surviving the civil war of 1914–17 intact. Because small firms had lower probabilities of survival, the relative price of small firms should have fallen. This would explain the propensity of small firms to change hands with greater frequency than larger firms.

[107] Both proxies of output have advantages and disadvantages. Real output is sensitive to the textile price index we have developed. The volume of production gets around the price index problem, but it understates productivity growth because it cannot capture changes in the quality of cloth over time. We therefore employ both measures in order to provide a cross-check on our results.

[108] Kane (1988).

[109] See Atack (1985); Sokoloff (1984); Bernard and Jones (1996).

workday.[110] Estimating labor productivity was straightforward: it is simply the real value of output or the physical volume of output divided by the (workday-adjusted) number of workers.[111] Estimating capital productivity was equally straightforward: we divided output by the number of spindles. Estimating TFP required us to estimate capital and labor weights from a panel data set of firm-level observations that we built covering the years 1850–1913. We then used these weights to estimate TFP for all census years.[112]

Our results, presented in Table 5.17, indicate that TFP was adversely affected during 1914–17, when manufacturers could not obtain necessary inputs and could not ship their output to market. It then recovered at a rapid pace. TFP continued to grow through the 1920s at a *rate* comparable with that of the 1901–10 decade. This does not mean that the 1914–17 disruption had no effect on TFP trends. TFP regained its absolute level of 1910 by 1926 but did not reach the level it *would have obtained* had TFP continued to grow at the pre-1910 rate with no interruptions.

---

[110] For a discussion of these adjustments, see Razo and Haber (1998).

[111] Workday-adjusted figures are the number of workers adjusted for differences in the length of the workday before and after the revolution.

[112] Ideally, we would have had censuses enumerated at the firm level covering both the pre- and postrevolutionary years allowing us to employ panel-data techniques to estimate time trends for TFP growth across different subperiods. Unfortunately, after 1913 the censuses no longer enumerate at the firm level. We therefore had to proceed in two stages. First, we used the 1850–1913 firm-level censuses to estimate a Cobb-Douglas production function of the form $Y = A \cdot K^\gamma \cdot L^{1-\gamma}$ with constant returns to scale, where K and L represent the capital and labor inputs and A is a function that captures improvements in technology over time. In order to use linear estimation procedures, we took natural logarithms of a normalized production function of the form $y = k^\alpha$ where $y = {Y}/{L}$ and $k = {K}/{L}$ and added explanatory variables to arrive at the following model.

$$\ln y = \alpha + \beta_1 \ln k + \beta_2 \ln L + \beta_3 \text{Time Trend} \qquad (1)$$

We then estimated TFP directly from output and input data for all years for which we have cross-sectional census data using the weights for capital and labor estimated from the 1850–1913 production function. For any given time t, where we had data on output, spindles, and workers, we estimated TFP employing the following formula:

$$TFP_t = \frac{\sum_i \text{Output}_{t,i}}{\left(\sum_i \text{Spindles}_{t,i}\right)^\alpha \cdot \left(\sum_i \text{Workers}_{t,i}\right)^\beta} \qquad (2)$$

where α and β are the (normalized) shares of capital and labor as estimated in the panel regression procedure described above and the subscript i identifies the inputs and output of reporting unit i.

Table 5.17. *Indices of TFP in the Mexican Cotton Textile Industry, 1850–1929*

Year	TFP Real Value	TFP Meters	Exponential Trend, 1900–10 Real Value[a]
1878		65	45
1888		66	58
1891	45	68	63
1893	55	64	67
1895	69	91	70
1896	75	107	72
1899	82	102	78
1900	82	97	80
1901	80	99	82
1902	69	92	84
1903	84	97	87
1904	95	101	89
1905	106	103	91
1906	103	113	94
1907	109	142	96
1908	101	108	99
1909	84	98	101
1910	100	100	104
1911	99	106	107
1912	112	94	110
1913	115	102	113
1918	30	68	128
1919	52	115	132
1920	59	105	135
1922	105	109	143
1923	87	100	146
1924	88	96	150
1925	99	108	154
1926	115	104	158
1927	98	98	163
1928	104	100	167
1929	128	122	171

Note: Base year 1910 = 100.

[a] Predicted growth based on 1900–10 performance.

Source: See source note for Table 5.2.

TFP growth after 1917 is quite surprising in light of what we know about the institutional history of Mexico in the 1920s. First, the CROM had blocked the adoption of labor-saving technologies. Second, employers could not easily substitute high-efficiency for low-efficiency workers because unions hired and fired.

In order to understand TFP growth amid these adverse institutional changes, we looked at the productivity of capital and the productivity of labor individually. The productivity of capital behaved as one would expect (see Table 5.18). Capital productivity dropped during the years of civil war (1914–17) and remained flat during the 1920s. In fact, output per spindle never regained its 1910 absolute value (see Figure 5.2).

If the productivity of capital was flat and if TFP grew, then it must have been the case that labor productivity was rising. Our estimates of labor productivity, presented in Table 5.19, indicate, in fact, that labor productivity grew *faster* during the 1920s than it had during 1900–10. Growth in output per (workday-adjusted) worker was so fast that whatever losses in labor productivity growth were incurred during the civil war of 1914–17 had been compensated for by 1929. That is to say, absolute levels of labor productivity were *higher* in the 1920s than they had been in 1910.

Rising labor productivity presents an interesting puzzle. We know that firms could not adopt more-efficient labor-saving technologies. We also know that the CROM industry-wide wage agreements prevented firms from forcing workers to run more of the existing kind of spindles or looms. If workers could not run more machines or employ better machines, how then did this impressive increase in labor productivity occur?

The answer to the puzzle is that workers worked more intensively. This was accomplished by substituting piece rates for hourly wages. The new piece rates were set at a level much higher than the implicit piece rates that had prevailed under the Porfirian wage system. Workers' real pay rose substantially, but so did their incentives to produce more. Shirking would be expected to drop substantially, and the data indicate that that is precisely what occurred during the 1920s.

Estimates we have made of labor productivity, in which output is measured by meters of cloth rather than real value, corroborate the hypothesis that workers worked harder during the 1920s. In 1900–10 meters of cloth produced per man-hour scarcely rose at all. Almost all productivity growth was due to firms moving into higher-quality lines of cloth, using better machines and more skilled workers. Growth in meters of cloth per man-hour was also very low during the 1920s, but the data indicate a onetime jump in the early part of the decade. Meters of cloth produced

Table 5.18. *Indices of Capital Productivity, Mexican Cotton Textile Industry*

Year	Real Value	Meters	Exponential Trend, 1900–10 Real Value
1888		54	
1889			
1891	49	75	59
1893	59	74	62
1895	72	93	66
1896	76	107	68
1899	84	105	74
1900	84	99	77
1901	79	99	79
1902	67	88	81
1903	81	92	84
1904	93	98	86
1905	105	102	89
1906	103	113	91
1907	117	156	94
1908	104	112	97
1909	83	96	100
1910	100	100	103
1911	98	105	106
1912	133	93	109
1913	63	89	112
1917	30		126
1918	30	58	130
1919	44	93	133
1920	51	88	137
1922	92	92	146
1923	76	84	150
1924	75	78	155
1925	94	101	159
1926	101	88	164
1927	86	84	169
1928	88	81	174
1929	112	103	179

Note: Base year 1910 = 100.

Source: See source note for Table 5.2.

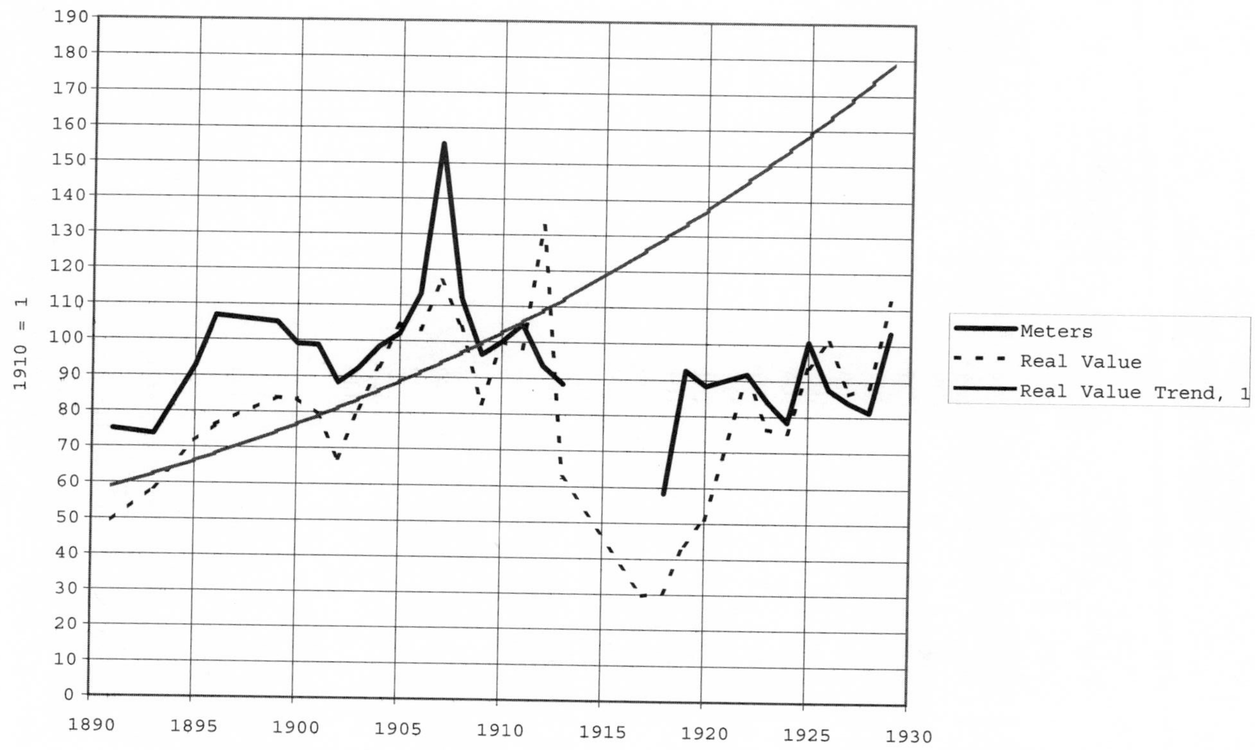
190
180
170
160
150
140
130
120
110
100
90
80
70
60
50
40
30
20
10
0
1910 = 1
1890
1895
1900
1905
1910
1915
1920
1925
1930
Meters
Real Value
Real Value Trend, 1

Figure 5.2. Productivity of Capital in the Mexican Cotton Textile Industry. *Source:* See Table 5.2.

Table 5.19. *Indices of Aggregate Labor Productivity,*
Mexican Cotton Texitle Industry

Year	Real Value	Meters	Real Value Exponential Trend, 1900–10
1891	44	67	66
1893	45	57	69
1895	74	95	72
1896	76	106	74
1899	79	99	79
1900	81	95	81
1901	80	99	83
1902	73	96	85
1903	89	102	87
1904	98	104	89
1905	107	104	91
1906	102	112	93
1907	98	131	96
1908	97	104	98
1909	85	99	100
1910	100	100	103
1911	101	108	105
1912	143	101	108
1913	66	93	110
1917	35		121
1918	41	79	124
1919	67	142	127
1920	71	123	130
1922	127	127	136
1923	106	116	139
1924	111	115	142
1925	108	116	146
1926	139	121	149
1927	117	114	153
1928	131	120	156
1929	155	143	160

Note: Base year 1910 = 100.
Source: See source note for Table 5.2.

per man-hour averaged more than 20 percent higher during the 1920s than in 1900–10.

The implication is that intensive growth in the textile industry took a substantially different form after 1920. Before 1910, growth was due to better machines. After 1920, growth was due almost entirely to an increase in work effort per hour. The industry-wide evidence we have presented here is consistent with Aurora Gómez Galvarriato's detailed study of the Compañía Industrial Veracruzana textile conglomerate. The firm adopted no new labor-saving technology during the 1920s, because the combination of piece rates and explicit restrictions gave it no incentive to do so. Workers, however, produced more per man-hour despite the fact that they were employing the same machinery as they had during the Porfiriato. According to Gómez Galvarriato, workers under piece rates "tried to get as much done as their strength allowed," despite the fact that managerial authority on the shop floor was replaced almost entirely by the unions.[113]

CONCLUSIONS

If we think about our quantitative results in terms of the three hypotheses we framed at the beginning of this book, the outcome is clear-cut for at least two of them. We can reject the hypothesis that political instability produced the collapse of the manufacturing sector. We can also reject the hypothesis that political instability produced stagnation. The data on investment, output, ownership structure, and TFP all indicate growth over the long run from 1911 to 1929. The most that one could argue in support of either the economic collapse or economic stagnation hypotheses is that during the three year period 1914–17 there was a strong downturn in investment, output, and TFP. The cause of that temporary downturn was the interdiction of factor and product markets. Once the railroads were once again available for civilian use, output and investment recovered rapidly.

Evaluating our third hypothesis, that Mexican industry could have grown even faster had the polity been stable, is much less straightforward. The problem is the specification of the appropriate counterfactual. One potential counterfactual is Mexico before 1911. Testing the slow-growth hypothesis would therefore involve comparing the growth rates of Mexican industries after 1911 with the growth rates of those same industries before 1911. The problem with this approach is that most industries were new circa 1895–1900 and thus were able to grow extremely rapidly during the period in which they were capturing the domestic market from foreign imports. By 1911 this process was largely over. In order to argue that Mexico's industries would have continued to grow at

---

[113] Gómez Galvarriato (1999), pp. 579–80.

their pre-1911 pace, it is necessary to make some very strong assumptions with regard to productivity growth (it would have to increase rapidly) and with regard to consumer demand (it would have to be highly elastic with respect to price and/or income). In short, the counterfactual is inappropriate.

Specifying the counterfactual as another country that looked just like Mexico in every way, except that it was politically stable from 1911 to 1929, is theoretically appealing. As a practical matter, however, it is far from straightforward. There were other Latin American countries that had industrialized by 1911 (Brazil, Chile, and Argentina), but they tended not to have the same range of consumer and construction goods industries as Mexico. None, for example, had steel and cement industries of any size before the 1920s. Circa 1911, Mexico was also well ahead of other Latin American countries in terms of the development of its paper, cigarette, glass bottle, and basic chemical industries. In addition, there were tremendous differences between some of these cases (most particularly Brazil) and Mexico in terms of the development of the financial systems that provided capital to industry, and these exerted a powerful influence on their relative industrial performance.[114]

What we can say with certainty is that the sharp downturn in output and investment that occurred from 1914 to 1917 in Mexico also occurred in Brazil, Argentina, and Chile as a consequence of World War I. The war had two negative effects on industry in these three South American cases: foreign capital inflows (which had financed their railroad, mining, and export agricultural sectors, and hence the growth of their consumer markets) dried up; and imports of machinery and intermediate inputs were no longer available. In fact, Wilson Suzigan's detailed data on machinery imports to Brazil look much like our data on machinery imports to Mexico during 1914 to 1918: complete collapse followed by a strong and rapid recovery.[115] Thus, on both the demand side and the supply side, industry was squeezed. There was some variance from industry to industry and from country to country, but the basic pattern was a sharp contraction in new investment, a fall in corporate profits, and a decline in output during the war years.[116] The implication is that even without the 1913–17 civil war, Mexican industry would have undergone a sharp, and temporary,

---

[114] Haber (1991, 1997, 1998, forthcoming).
[115] For a discussion of the effects of World War I, see Albert (1988), pp. 202–22; Haber (forthcoming).
[116] Suzigan (1986), pp. 360–64.

contraction because of the shortage of raw materials, machines, and spare parts.

Beyond this, we cannot falsify the third hypothesis because of the problem of specifying the correct counterfactual. We do know that Mexican industry continued to grow throughout the turbulent 1920s. We also know that industry in other Latin American countries grew in the 1920s. Beyond that, the comparisons are far from straightforward because there was a great deal of variance across different country cases and across specific industries in the 1920s. To cite one example, Mexico had better-developed steel and cement industries than did Brazil in the 1920s, but the Brazilian textile industry outperformed that of Mexico in the 1920s. Without more research into the performance of manufacturing, both in the aggregate and in terms of specific industries, in other Latin American cases during the 1920s, we hesitate to draw any strong conclusions.

6

Petroleum

No sector of the Mexican economy was as immune to political instability as petroleum. In fact, crude oil production increased every single year from 1910 to 1921. By the time the upward rally in output began to reverse in the early 1920s, Mexico was the world's second most important producer (behind the United States), controlling 25 percent of world output. Even with the decline in output from its 1921 peak, oil output for the decade 1921–30 was more than 2 times what it had been during the decade 1911–20, and more than 87 times what it had been in the decade 1901–10.

This feat of production was remarkable because it took place under two major threats to property rights. First, petroleum, like other industries with high sunk costs, was particularly vulnerable to predation.[1] The very nature of the industry rested on the ability of asset holders to claim and enforce a politically created property right, specifically the rights to wealth in the subsoil. Governments could abrogate those rights, allocate them to a third party, tax the rents they produced, or diminish them by permitting offset drilling on an adjoining property.[2] Second, the oil industry was a ready source of revenue for revolutionary factions. Large infusions of cash were needed – and were needed badly. Moreover, the oil companies were an ideal target for predation. They could easily be taxed, because it was easy to monitor the value and volume of production.[3] Not surprisingly, every government that came to power after 1911 tried to increase tax rates or create new taxes.

---

[1] See Levy and Spiller (1996) for theory and evidence in the case of telecommunications.
[2] Because petroleum deposits are found thousands of feet beneath the surface in vast deposits, it is possible to tap into those deposits by drilling on a property adjoining the established claim, hence the term offset drilling.
[3] Exports had to move through easily monitored pipelines to tankers. The price could be determined by looking at the New York spot market.

Mexico's governments and political factions could not, however, limitlessly prey on the oil companies. Four features of the relationship between the oil companies and the government were particularly crucial. First, the oil industry was owned by powerful constituents of powerful countries. These constituents could appeal to their home governments, particularly the U.S. government, to apply diplomatic pressure or threaten military intervention when their property rights or rents from property rights were threatened.

Second, the oil companies were the government's single most important source of tax revenue until the late 1920s. In the context of an unstable polity, this meant the government needed the tax revenues generated by the oil companies more than the oil companies needed the government. The oil companies could therefore hold back production in the short run, in order to deprive the government of crucial tax revenues. If timed correctly, such production cutbacks could undermine the government's ability to defend itself against opposing factions. Cutting production would also throw tens of thousands of workers out of their jobs. Mexican presidents feared the political consequences of an empty treasury and of widespread unemployment among an easily mobilized constituency.

Holding back production required that the oil companies be able to work in concert. A third crucial feature of the industry made this possible: a small number of firms accounted for the vast majority of output and those firms were members of a producer's association. In essence, they acted like a cartel.

The fourth crucial feature was that the government did not have the ability to run the petroleum industry itself. It lacked the know-how to find, extract, and market the oil. Any attempt to take over the industry would have caused a substantial, if temporary, disruption in output and taxes. No Mexican government during 1914–29 could have survived such a disruption. In the time horizon that mattered to Mexican armed factions and governments, the payoffs from expropriation were far less than the payoff from levying taxes.

The oil companies therefore exploited new discoveries of oil in Mexico as if the polity was stable. They also were unconcerned about changes in institutions that attempted to respecify their de jure property rights. The oil companies knew that any government that came to power would face the same constraints as its predecessor. In fact, the period of strongest instability and largest de jure reforms coincided with the period of highest investment and output.

Ultimately, Mexican petroleum production declined for geological reasons. As we demonstrate in the data analysis section of this chapter, this was due neither to institutional changes nor to tax increases nor to political instability.[4] The history of Mexico's oil in the period 1900–30 is analogous to the history of Pennsylvania oil in the late 19th century. At one time, Pennsylvania was the largest producer of oil in the United States. Pennsylvania has not been a consequential producer of petroleum for decades, but no one thinks that this is the result of political instability, high taxes, or Pennsylvania's institutions. Pennsylvania simply ran out of oil deposits that could be extracted at a competitive cost given the available technology.[5]

Much the same was true of Mexico's oil. When Mexico had its second great oil boom in the 1970s, it tapped sources of petroleum that were located at depths well beyond those accessible with 1920s technology. In fact, most of Mexico's current oil wells are offshore, several hundred miles away from the region of the original boom. Even had the petroleum companies known about these oil deposits, it would not have been technologically possible to actually exploit them.

DEVELOPMENT OF THE INDUSTRY UNDER DÍAZ

Mexico's oil industry developed initially as a source of *domestic* energy. At the time that the first oil companies began to explore Mexico's lagoons,

---

[4] Our analysis therefore sharply diverges from interpretations offered in much of the extant historical literature. Most accounts by historians stress the negative impact that uncertainty over property rights and taxes had on exploration and new investment by the industry. As Linda Hall put it, "The intransigence of both sides to the controversy over Article 27 [the article of the Mexican Constitution that vested petroleum rights in the nation] would lead to the gradual and finally abrupt withdrawal of U.S. firms from Mexico." Hall (1995), p. 35. Jonathan Brown concurs: "For eleven years, from the promulgation of the 1917 constitution to the 1928 Calles-Morrow agreement, the government sought to enforce public dominion over a resisting industry. The conflict retarded exploration and drilling programs. By the time that the companies and the government had settled the issue of public dominion sufficiently to permit new exploration in Mexico, cheaper production from Venezuela had captured world markets while prices reached a nadir." Brown (1985), p. 362. Some authors, such as Meyer, do argue that there were factors other than property rights and taxes that explain the decline of the industry. They tend, however, to focus their attention almost exclusively on the diplomatic maneuvering about property rights and taxes. Meyer, for example, concedes that "one can say that the factors mainly responsible for the situation were technical and economic rather than political." Meyer (1977), p. 9. Nevertheless, the evidence he brings to bear is overwhelmingly concerned with the diplomatic conflicts.

[5] For a discussion of the economics of oil production, see Adelman (1995), chap. 2.

swamps, and coastal plains for petroleum, their vision – and that of the Mexican government – was to produce for the national market. It was not until 1911, when the so-called Golden Lane in Veracruz was discovered and a veritable bonanza began, that companies began to export.[6]

High costs in the energy sector had been a major impediment to growth during the nineteenth century. Previously, Mexico had relied on imported coal and oil to satisfy the demand of its growing railroads, mining, manufacturing, and electric power industries.[7] A single firm, the Waters-Pierce Oil Company of St. Louis, held a monopoly on oil imports from the United States through two mechanisms: Waters-Pierce had an agreement with Standard Oil that specified that no other Standard affiliate was allowed to enter the Mexican market; and Waters-Pierce erected refineries in Mexico ahead of demand, threatening to drive the price down below variable costs in the event that anyone should try to enter the market.[8]

Solving the bottleneck created by high energy costs was thus a vital issue facing the Díaz government. At the same time, however, the costs of developing the oil industry were huge and the time horizon uncertain. Thus, national entrepreneurial groups, constrained by their lack of both knowledge of the necessary technologies and access to capital markets that could finance the risky business of petroleum exploration, did not enter the industry.

The Díaz government therefore needed foreign firms to invest in Mexican oil exploration and exploitation. It employed two policies for this purpose, one of which was designed to guarantee the property rights of the foreign companies and the other of which was designed to guarantee the rents from those property rights. The legal reform process guaranteeing subsoil property rights was already underway well before anyone recognized the extent of Mexico's oil reserves. Mexico's 1884 mining code granted ownership of subsurface coal, water, and oil to the surface owner, a dramatic departure from the preexisting law that had specified that all subsoil wealth was national patrimony. A further law in 1892 stipulated that the owners of the surface could freely exploit petroleum in the subsoil without any special concession from the government. Foreigners only needed to make contracts with local landowners to commence drilling. A third law in 1901 gave the Mexican president, without the consent of Congress, the right to award concessions on national lands for oil drilling.

[6] Brown (1993), pp. 44–45; Meyer (1977), pp. 3–4.
[7] Meyer (1977), p. 4.
[8] Brown (1993), pp. 14–21.

A final reform in 1909 put an end to any ambiguities that existed in earlier laws, declaring that the fields or deposits of mineral fuels were the "exclusive property" of the surface landowner.[9]

The second policy of the Díaz government was to award temporary tax concessions that guaranteed the stream of rents produced by the oil companies' property rights. Two firms in particular took advantage of these tax incentives and quickly established dominant positions by leasing or buying millions of acres of Mexico's potential oil-bearing lands. Edward L. Doheny, a California oil man who arrived in Mexico at the invitation of the Mexican Central Railway to prospect for oil, received the first major concession. This concession granted Doheny a 10-year tax exemption covering both the import tariffs on the necessary machinery and export and production taxes on the resulting output. Doheny's Mexican Petroleum Company and its numerous subsidiaries ultimately came to control 1.5 million acres of land, either through fee simple ownership or leasehold.[10] The Mexican Petroleum Company soon found itself competing for properties against a second, even larger firm, the El Águila oil company (also called the Mexican Eagle Oil Company), headed by the British civil engineer turned oil magnate, Sir Weetman Pearson.[11] Pearson, in fact, obtained an even better deal than Doheny: he received a 50-year exemption from taxes.[12]

Post-hoc it is easy to view these concessions as giveaways to foreign interests, and they are often portrayed as such in the historical literature. Ex ante, however, it was not clear that the concessionaires were engaging in profitable operations. In fact, Doheny's backers lost faith within a year

---

[9] For the most thorough history of the Porfirian oil laws, see Rippy (1972), pp. 15–28. Also see Meyer (1977), pp. 24–25; Brown (1993), p. 93.

[10] The Mexican Petroleum Company of Delaware, Ltd. was a holding company for a network of firms that included the Mexican Petroleum Company of California, the Huasteca Petroleum Company, the Tuxpan Company, and the Tamihua Petroleum Company. In 1917 these firms were all brought together by Doheny under the aegis of another holding company, the Pan-American Petroleum and Transport Company.

[11] Pearson was one of the late 19th century's master civil engineers and entrepreneurs. He built the Blackwall Tunnel under the River Thames, as well as four tunnels under New York's East River. His financial empire eventually came to include the *Financial Times*, the *Economist*, and Penguin Books. Yergin (1991), p. 230. A detailed analysis of Pearson's history as Mexico's major public works contractor can be found in Connolly (1997).

[12] Meyer (1977), pp. 23–24; Brown (1993), p. 28. In addition to these tax breaks, the companies also received protection from external competition by a tariff of three centavos (cents) per kilo of imported crude oil and eight centavos per kilo on imports of refined oil. Brown (1993), pp. 63–64.

(1902), and Doheny and one of his partners had to buy back much of the stock, raising their share of the Mexican Petroleum Company from 8 to 40 percent. Pearson also lost vast amounts of money in the early years, and, like Doheny, he had to invest his own funds (in this case £5 million sterling) to keep the enterprise afloat.[13]

Moreover, the Díaz government behaved toward the oil companies precisely the way we would expect from a revenue-maximizing state. As soon as the 10-year tax exemptions began to expire in 1911, which also coincided with the first big oil strikes, Díaz began to raise taxes on the industry, erecting "bar duties" in order to pay, putatively, for the dredging of the harbor at Tampico. In effect, this was a tax on exports, as well as a tax on crude oil brought by barge from Tuxpan to the refineries in Tampico.[14]

How did the Díaz government make its concessions to the oil companies credible? Ex ante, the Mexican government had every incentive to give generous concessions to the foreign firms in order to get them to invest. Ex post, however, the government would have every incentive to abrogate those concessions – and the oil companies knew it. Oil industries everywhere are characterized by large, appropriable quasi rents. These quasi rents are generated by the fact that once a well is sunk and a pipeline laid, those assets cannot be easily redeployed. Even if investors cannot recoup their sunk costs, they will have every incentive to keep producing (the payoff from staying put and recouping variable costs plus some small fraction of sunk costs exceeds the payoff from redeploying fixed assets to an alternative use). All governments have strong incentives to expropriate these quasi rents (via taxation) or divert them to politically favored domestic entrepreneurial groups (by permitting them to offset-drill).[15]

The problem was, in short, similar to that of bilateral monopoly between firms in which there are asset specificity considerations. The Mexican government needed foreign firms to find, extract, and market the country's oil. The oil companies needed the Mexican government to guarantee their property rights and the stream of rents produced by those property rights. Either side could hold the other up.

Díaz and the oil industry resorted to vertical political integration (VPI) to mitigate opportunism. Pearson, the founder of El Águila, was

---

[13] On the losses incurred by Pearson and Doheny, see Meyer (1977), pp. 23–24; Yergin (1991), p. 231.

[14] Brown (1993), p. 40. It is not clear from the historical literature if the bar taxes applied to El Águila, or if its concessions applied only to excise and import taxes.

[15] Monaldi (2002), chap. 2. Also see Klein, Crawford, et al. (1978).

particularly well positioned to carry this off. Pearson was one of the great civil engineers of the late nineteenth century and had worked on a number of high-profile projects for the Díaz government. He built the Great Canal that drained Mexico City's swamps. He had also built the Veracruz Harbor and had finished the construction of the government-owned Tehuantepec Railway, which connected the Atlantic and Pacific Oceans. His interest in Mexican petroleum, in fact, grew out of the railroad project, as his engineers noticed pools of oil that had seeped up through fissures in the ground as they cut a path through the jungles and swamps of southern Mexico.[16] As Jonathan Brown has shown, Pearson built upon these experiences to integrate himself into the Porfirian elite. Some of his tactics were subtle. For example, he provided objets d'art for Secretary of the Treasury Limantour's home. In addition, Díaz's in-laws (the Rubio Romero's) and other notables stayed at the home of El Águila's general manager when they visited the city of Veracruz. Pearson also saw to it that Porfirio Díaz Jr. was appropriately "entertained" when he traveled through Europe. Then there were the not so subtle tactics. Pearson's firm leased lands from important elite families, including Díaz's in-laws. Doña Carmen Rubio de Díaz (Porfirio's wife) was a lessor to Pearson on contracts that provided royalties of two to five centavos per barrel of crude oil produced. Pearson also had an option on an hacienda belonging to José Yves Limantour, Mexico's secretary of the treasury. So deeply embedded was Pearson into the dictatorship that when Díaz stepped down in 1911 Pearson offered him an English estate for his retirement. While Díaz declined the offer, preferring the comforts of Paris, he did stay at the home of Pearson's general manager in Veracruz before boarding a German liner for exile.[17]

Given these kinds of ties, it is not surprising that Pearson obtained policies tailor-made to his interests. He received a 50-year concession to all national land, lakes, and lagoons in the states of Veracruz, San Luis Potosí, Tamaulipas, Tabasco, Chiapas, and Campeche.[18] Pearson also obtained an exemption from all import tariffs on the necessary equipment, and the tax-free export of all oil found on those federal lands. Finally, the concession granted his company a zone of three kilometers surrounding each producing well, in which no other party would be allowed to drill.[19]

---

[16] Brown (1993), pp. 47–48; Yergin (1991), pp. 230–31.
[17] Brown (1993), pp. 48, 51, 54, 63, 96, 99, 120.
[18] *Moody's Manual of Investments*, 1913, p. 1536.
[19] The purpose was to protect Pearson against offset drilling. Lewis (1959), p. 41.

In return, the national government and state governments received royalties of 7 and 3 percent, respectively, on the value of production from the federal lands. At the last minute, Pearson managed to get the concession amended to give El Águila tax exemptions on both the federal leased lands *and on his privately owned lands.* Pearson never worked the federal lands at all (avoiding the 10 percent royalties). Instead, he concentrated his efforts on his private lands, whose inputs and outputs were now free of all taxes until 1956.[20]

Who provided third-party enforcement for this agreement? The third group was other members of the dictator's coterie, people whose support was crucial to Díaz. Pearson incorporated his company in Mexico, and distributed stock to prominent members of the Porfirian political elite, who sat on the company's board.[21] In this way, Pearson directly transferred a share of the rents from his special concession to a group with the ability to make President Díaz's political life miserable should the advantages granted the firm be unilaterally altered. Any reduction in El Águila's property rights would negatively affect them, which meant that they had a strong incentive to check opportunistic behavior. Thus, the president of El Águila's board of directors was the Porfirian insider Guillermo de Landa y Escandón. Landa y Escandón had joined Díaz's inner circle in 1886 when he joined the effort to amend the constitution in order to permit Díaz's reelection. He served periodically as Mexico City's municipal president, governor of the Federal District (Mexico's equivalent of Washington, D.C.), and senator from Chihuahua. Other board members included Enrique Creel (governor of Chihuahua, secretary of foreign relations, and former ambassador to the United States), Pablo Macedo (president of Congress and board chairman of the National Railways of Mexico), Fernando Pimental y Fagoaga (the president of the Banco Nacional de México), and Porfirio Díaz Jr. (Díaz's son).[22]

Edward Doheny, Pearson's main rival, followed a similar strategy. He hired politically influential Mexican lawyers to represent the various oil companies under his control. The purpose of these lawyers was not to protect property rights via the court system, but to take advantage of their considerable political connections. Doheny's principal legal counsel was

[20] Meyer (1977), p. 244, n. 21.
[21] It is alleged that Porfirio Díaz Jr. received 200 El Águila preferential shares, with a par value of $1,000 each. These paid a guaranteed 8 percent rate of return (in addition to other dividend distributions), providing a guaranteed $16,000 per year regardless of whether the firm actually made any money. Rippy (1972), p. 136.
[22] Brown (1993), p. 63.

Joaquín de Casasús, who had served in the lower house of the Porfirian Congress and had been Mexico's ambassador to the United States.[23]

Vertical political integration paid off for Pearson and Doheny. They operated in an environment in which their property rights were unambiguous and the taxes on their activities were low. By the end of the Porfiriato, Mexico had emerged as the world's fourth most important oil producer, and Pearson and Doheny clearly dominated the industry, jointly controlling more than 90 percent of output.[24]

THE IMPACT OF REVOLUTIONARY INSTABILITY

The overthrow of Díaz undid the comfortable relationship that the foreign oil companies had with the Mexican government. Under Díaz, the dictator's own coterie provided third-party enforcement, but once Díaz was overthrown, this group no longer had to be at the center of ruling coalitions. Thus, as of 1911 there was no longer domestic third-party enforcement of the contract that existed between the Mexican government and the oil companies. This meant that there were forced loans from local warlords, new taxes levied by every revolutionary government, and institutional reforms that sought to reduce the oil companies' de jure property rights.

Yet, throughout the revolution and the political turmoil of the 1920s, the oil companies continued working. As Table 6.1 demonstrates, petroleum production during the 1910s and 1920s was *several orders of magnitude* greater than it had been in the decade before the revolution. In fact, during the years of greatest uncertainty (1917–28) the industry set production records that would not be matched again until 1974.[25] This surge in activity was not the result of overexploitation of current capacity in anticipation of expropriation. This increase in output actually required tremendous investments in new plant and equipment – an issue that we will return to in considerable detail. Not only did existing firms expand, but new firms entered the industry. By the early 1920s, hundreds of companies were prospecting for oil in Mexico.[26] These included

---

[23] Brown (1993), pp. 39, 95.

[24] *Mexican Yearbook*, 1914, p. 79. Even as late as 1918, after dozens of other companies had entered the market, El Águila and the Mexican Petroleum Company still controlled 61 percent of Mexican crude production. Calculated from data in *Engineering and Mining Journal*, May 1, 1920, p. 1030.

[25] México, INEGI (1994), 1:559.

[26] Brown (1993), p. 101.

Table 6.1. *Estimates of Mexican Petroleum Output (in thousands of barrels)*

Year	Crude Production	Export of Crude and Derivatives
1901	10	
1902	40	
1903	75	
1904	126	
1905	251	
1906	503	
1907	1005	
1908	3933	
1908	2714	
1910	3634	
1911	12,553	902
1912	16,558	7,729
1913	25,696	21,331
1914	26,235	23,366
1915	32,893	24,769
1916	40,545	27,269
1917	55,293	46,024
1918	63,828	51,767
1919	87,073	75,550
1920	156,539	145,509
1921	194,756	172,268
1922	185,057	180,866
1923	149,341	135,607
1924	139,105	129,700
1925	115,588	96,516
1926	90,610	80,719
1927	64,121	48,344
1928	50,151	10,532
1929	44,688	
1930	39,530	
1931	33,039	9,912
1932	32,805	12,302
1933	31,101	
1934	38,172	
1935	40,241	
1936	41,026	
1937	46,803	18,253
1938	38,482	

Sources: México, INEGI (1994), 1:559; Meyer (1977), p. 16; México, Dirección General de Estadística (1930), pp. 395, 517–21; Sterrett and Davis (1928), p. 197.

big international firms such as Royal Dutch–Shell, Sinclair, the Texas Company, Standard Oil of New Jersey, and Cities Service.

Surviving the Revolution

Why would companies invest in oil facilities that could be devastated by revolution? One might easily imagine a scenario in which pitched battles in the oil zone would have destroyed pipelines, storage tanks, port facilities, and other installations. Another possibility was that retreating armies would have had every incentive to set fire to the oil wells in order to deprive competing factions of the opportunity to finance their military activities with rents from the oil companies.

Devastation did not occur for two reasons. First, the two most important factions in the oil zone, the Carrancistas and the Pelaecistas, did not engage in pitched battles with each other. Rather, they devoted most of their energies to extracting rents from the oil companies and dedicated very little effort to finding and fighting one another. Why take the risk of a fire fight with another armed faction when it was easier to get rich by levying protection rents or stealing payrolls from the oil companies?

Second, revolutionary factions faced a standoff with the United States. After the sinking of a tanker belonging to the Waters-Pierce oil company in 1914, Secretary of State Bryan demanded that the oil region be declared a "neutral zone" and made it clear that the United States would enforce this demand. None of Mexico's warring factions gave any formal recognition to the U.S. State Department's notion of a "neutral zone," but no one doubted that had the oil fields been physically attacked U.S. forces would have landed.[27] In short, all factions in the revolution understood that if they seized or destroyed the oil fields they would force a conflict with the United States, which in turn would have deprived them of their most important source of tax revenues. As Navy Secretary Josephus Daniels was fond of saying, there was no point in killing "the goose that laid the golden egg."[28]

Why did the United States not land Marines and occupy the oil zone as a preemptive measure? There were certainly those who favored this strategy, Secretary of State Lansing being the most prominent. In fact, the original plan for the invasion and occupation of the port city of Veracruz in April 1914 (to head off arms destined for Huerta) called for the

[27] Meyer (1977), pp. 39–40; Brown (1993), pp. 190–91.
[28] Quoted in Brown (1993), p. 198.

simultaneous occupation of the oil port of Tampico. The Marines destined for Tampico had to be diverted, however, to support the invasion of Veracruz – which met considerably more resistance than anticipated.[29] The Wilson government never again raised the idea of the invasion of Tampico. Some historians have suggested that the reason was ideological: Woodrow Wilson was against intervention to protect some of America's wealthiest men.[30] Given the fact that there had been an earlier plan to invade Tampico, we highly discount this explanation. A more likely reason has to do with the fact that the resistance met by the Marines in the Veracruz invasion signaled the U.S. government that it would meet similar resistance in Tampico. Indeed, it would have been very hard to launch a quick and decisive strike against the oil zone, because the sand bar outside the harbor of Tampico would have slowed an amphibious landing and because most of the oil fields were 30 miles inland. This would have given the Mexicans plenty of time to destroy a significant portion of the wells.[31] An invasion would therefore almost certainly have assured the destruction of the very oil fields the U.S. wanted to protect. In fact, when the United States sent a punitive expedition after Pancho Villa in 1916, the Carrancista commander in Tampico explicitly threatened the American consul that any attempt by the United States to land the Marines in the oil zone would result in the burning of the oil fields.[32]

Rents from Taxes and Production

The fact that the oil zone was so valuable meant that every single faction in the revolution viewed it as a source of revenue. Some of these revenues were extracted as taxes by whichever government happened to be in power. Some of them were extracted directly at the well head, by whichever military faction happened to be passing by.

No sooner was Francisco Madero in power than he began to increase taxes on the oil companies. To put down the challenges to his government, he had to double the size of the army. Badly in need of funds, Madero increased the stamp tax (a specific excise duty) that had been a nominal amount under Díaz to 20 centavos per ton of oil. He also tried to triple the amount of the bar tax (from 10 to 30 centavos per ton). The companies

---

[29] Womack (1986), p. 102.
[30] Meyer (1977), pp. 45, 70–71; Hall (1995), p. 16.
[31] The deep draft of the American battleships would not have allowed them to get past the bar. Brown (1993), p. 202.
[32] Brown (1993), pp. 201–2.

launched a campaign against the bar tax increase, and ultimately negotiated a tax increase of 10 centavos instead 20.[33] In the process, they
formed a lobbying organization, the Association of Petroleum Producers
in Mexico (the APPM), that would, over time, allow them to coordinate
their responses to other tax and property rights initiatives that came out of
the Mexican government. Madero also demanded that the oil companies
register their holdings with the government, so that it could identify owners for the purpose of expropriation. The oil companies simply refused
to comply, and Madero, lacking the ability to win a showdown with the
companies, dropped the demand.[34]

The overthrow and assassination of Madero intensified the military
conflict, and increased the need to extract rents from the oil companies.
Huerta raised the taxes on the importation of oil equipment by 50 percent,
ignoring the companies' Porfirian-era exemptions. He further raised the
stamp tax, from 20 to 75 centavos per ton of oil. Several months later,
Huerta increased the bar duties to 1 peso per ton. His customs officials
insisted on collecting these in U.S. currency, rather than Mexican pesos.[35]
We estimate that the tax burden rose from 10 percent of the gross value
of output under Madero to more than 15 percent under Huerta.

Huerta's tax increases met with a mixed response from the oil companies. The American firms simply refused to pay. This was not hard
to do: the Carrancistas, not Huerta, controlled the oil port of Tampico.
The APPM complained to the U.S. State Department. Huerta held his
ground and now demanded a $400,000 peso fine from the Huasteca
Petroleum Company, one of the major entities of Doheny's interlocking
empire of oil production and transport companies. Huasteca refused to
pay.[36] Huasteca's general manager, Harold Walker, on a business trip to
Mexico City, was dragged before Huerta who threatened him with death if
he did not pay the company's back taxes. Walker wrote out a 100,000 peso
draft, to get away from Huerta, and then stopped payment on the check.[37]

Weetman Pearson, the master of VPI under Díaz, decided to pay
Huerta's new taxes, even though the concessions he had obtained from

---

[33] Brown (1993), p. 179; Meyer (1977), p. 37; Rippy (1972), p. 29; Davis (1932),
p. 406.
[34] In 1913 the Chamber of Deputies actually received a proposal to nationalize the
industry. Rippy (1972), p. 29. Also see Meyer (1977), pp. 31–32.
[35] Brown (1993), pp. 181, 184. There is some dispute in the historical literature about
exact tax rates. Davis puts the bar tax at 50 centavos per ton. Davis (1932), p. 406.
[36] Brown (1993), pp. 182–83.
[37] Brown (1993), pp. 186–87.

Díaz gave him a 50-year tax exemption. Ever thinking about the need to cut future political deals, Pearson simultaneously agreed to a demand from the Carrancistas not to sell fuel oil to the railroads controlled by Huerta.[38] Still desperately short of cash, Huerta turned to Pearson to help him obtain foreign loans. Pearson, always playing the angles, agreed to help Huerta and put up 6 million pesos of a 220-million-peso loan that was made by a syndicate headed by the Banque de Paris. [39]

Huerta's regime collapsed in 1914, but his fall from power did not bring relief to the oil companies. During the ensuing years of civil war, the oil companies were subject to two threats to the security of their property rights and the revenues generated by those property rights: predatory behavior by revolutionary factions and increases in taxes by governments.

The oil fields were an obvious target for extortion by passing armies. The best organized of these was the independent armed movement of Manuel Peláez. Peláez, a Veracruz landowner turned military chieftain, rose up against Carranza in 1914, declaring that he intended to keep the oil lands in the hands of its legitimate owners – the oil companies. He and Felix Díaz (Porfirio Díaz's nephew) issued a joint proclamation offering to protect Americans from a plot to give control of the oil industry over to the Germans. The U.S. government evidently agreed with Peláez and Díaz, because the U.S. State Department told Carranza's government that it was indispensable for Peláez to remain in the oil district to protect it against German saboteurs.[40]

The Pelaecistas should be understood not as an ideological faction with political goals, but as a mafia-like military force. Peláez lacked the troops, firepower, and will to oust the Carrancistas from Tampico or even to prevent the Carrancistas from entering the oil fields whenever they chose to do so. The only protection that the Pelaecistas could offer was

---

[38] Brown (1993), p. 187. Why did Pearson follow a different strategy from his American competitors? First, Pearson was *not* an American citizen, and therefore could not easily call on the U.S. government to protect his property rights. This meant that Huerta could have punished Pearson (had he refused to pay) by reallocating his assets to an American company. Pearson also had reason to believe that Huerta might win the revolution and be in a position to award him lucrative future concessions. (It was not until President Wilson lifted the arms embargo against Mexico in 1914 that Huerta's regime began to collapse.) In fact, Pearson would later cooperate with President Álvaro Obregón, who transferred *privately owned* lands to Pearson in return.

[39] Brown (1993), p. 181.

[40] Meyer (1977), pp. 45, 50–51.

from themselves. For this service, they extorted 2 million pesos from the oil companies over the period January 1915 to May 1920.[41] The only positive aspect of this predation was its predictability. As in all repeated games, rules quickly got established between the players. In the early stages of the game, Peláez's troops would cut the water lines to the oil camps and then demand money to allow the oil companies to reconnect them. The high drama (and bother) of cutting water lines then got replaced with a standard payment of 10,000 pesos per month. In later iterations of the game, this got upped to 20,000 pesos, and ultimately 30,000 pesos (about U.S. $15,000) per month from each producer. When military activities intensified, Peláez assessed additional charges or demanded the payments be made in advance.[42]

The Carrancistas, as Jonathan Brown has shown, also preyed on the oil companies. Carrancista officers commandeered company yachts to go fishing. They commandeered food and livestock from the oil camps. They stole oil company payrolls, often murdering paymasters in the process. They even stole the payrolls destined for their own soldiers.[43]

From the point of view of what really mattered to the oil companies, their revenues, neither Pelaecista extortions nor Carrancista looting was much more than an annoyance. We estimate that the gross revenues of the oil companies totaled $645 million pesos during the years 1915–20. Peláez's 2 million in protection rents did not equal even one-third of 1 percent of that figure.[44]

The oil companies' real problem was not predatory behavior by local militaries, but Carranza's ultimately unsuccessful attempt to increase oil

[41] Brown reports the figure at 1.5 million pesos, but this is almost certainly too low. He himself notes that Huasteca (Doheny's firm) alone paid Peláez 1.235 million pesos from 1916 to 1920. Brown (1993), pp. 271, 303. Also see Meyer (1977), p. 50. We therefore take the *Engineering and Mining Journal* estimate of "more than 2,000,000 pesos" as the more likely figure. *Engineering and Mining Journal*, October 23, 1920, p. 825.

[42] Brown (1993), pp. 262, 270.

[43] In the 12 months between August 15, 1917, and August 15, 1918, there were 83 robberies. At one point, representatives of the oil companies requested that the Tampico military commander send military escorts with paymasters. "I cannot do that," he informed the oilmen. "The officers and men might steal the payrolls." Quoted in Brown (1993), pp. 208–10. Also see Brown (1993), pp. 204, 207, 260–64; Yergin (1991), p. 231.

[44] Meyer (1977), p. 51; Brown (1993), pp. 299–300. In May 1920 Peláez joined Obregón's movement against Carranza and laid down his arms following Obregón's victory. Peláez's political ambitions did not end in 1920. He played a role in the anti-Obregón rebellions of Esteban Cantú in 1921 and de la Huerta in 1923. See Hall (1995), pp. 56–57, 166–67.

taxes in order to finance his fight against Zapata and Villa.[45] Within weeks of their retreat from Mexico City to Veracruz in 1914, the Carrancista government began to squeeze the oil companies. One of the first accomplishments of Candido Aguilar, the Carrancista military commander in Veracruz (and Carranza's son-in-law), was to extract forced loans of 10,000 pesos from the El Águila and Huasteca oil companies.[46] He also demanded that firms pay the bar duties in gold.[47] When the oil companies refused, Aguilar threatened to shut down their pipelines. He simultaneously declared null and void all of the oil concessions given by the Huerta regime. A short time later, he forbade the sale or leasing of lands to the oil companies without federal authorization. The U.S. State Department protested to Carranza, who reversed all of Aguilar's decrees, save the rise in the bar tax. Carranza also agreed that the tax could be paid in paper pesos, rather than gold or dollars. The companies paid under protest.[48]

Carranza was not satisfied with these small gains, but he needed to know how far he could push the oil companies if he was to extract the maximum amount of taxes from them. Therefore, in January 1915 he demanded that they turn over their financial data. He also levied an assessment for back taxes. With the support of the U.S. State Department, the oil companies refused to turn over the requested financial information and negotiated their way out of paying the back taxes.[49] In fact, the companies managed to obtain a reduction in the bar tax from 50 to 10 centavos per ton. Our estimates of the overall tax rate indicates that the tax burden fell from 16 to 14 percent between 1914 and 1916.

In 1917 Carranza managed to temporarily push taxes back to their 1914 level. On April 13 he changed the excise tax (the so-called stamp tax) on petroleum to an ad valorum production tax.[50] Crude petroleum

---

[45] Meyer (1977), p. 46.

[46] Brown (1993), p. 259.

[47] There is some confusion in the historical literature about the tax rate in the early years of the Carranza government. According to Davis (1932), Carranza lowered the stamp tax from 75 centavos per ton to 60 centavos per ton. The bar tax was also lowered: from 1 peso per ton to 50 centavos per ton. Davis (1932), p. 406. Brown, on the other hand, simply states that Carranza raised the bar duties.

[48] Carranza also agreed to recognize the validity of the tax payments made by the companies to Huerta. Meyer (1977), pp. 28, 47–48; Brown (1993), pp. 214–15.

[49] Carranza agreed to credit their tax bills with past shipments of oil they had made to the government-owned railroads. Meyer (1977), pp. 48–49.

[50] This was formally called a production tax, but only oil that was exported was actually taxed. The reason that the government engaged in this semantic game was because its export taxes were pledged to pay the government's bonded debt. Calling

and fuel oil were assessed at 10 percent of their value, based on the New York price. Specific duties were levied on refined products. Domestically consumed output was exempted.[51]

The next year, Carranza again tried to increase the tax rate. On February 19, 1918, he decreed a 5 percent royalty on all petroleum production and levied a tax of 10 to 50 percent on the value of royalties paid to lessors, the exact tax rate depending on the royalty rate per hectare. The decree also required that the oil companies register their properties with the government. If they failed to do so within three months, third parties could "denounce" or lay claim to the land.[52]

Carranza's attempts to increase oil taxes failed. All of the companies refused to pay the royalty. Virtually all of the companies refused to register their lands.[53] The government responded by giving out unregistered claims to Mexican citizens.[54] Carranza also ordered the army to occupy the oil fields and cap recently drilled wells. At this point, the U.S. State Department intervened, and Carranza backed down.[55] The mix of new taxes changed, and government revenues increased (because of a dramatic rise in output), but the tax rate actually *fell* from 16 percent of gross revenues in 1917 to 11 percent in 1919.[56]

In addition to tax increases, the Carranza government also reformed the institutions governing property rights. Article 27 of the Constitution of 1917 made oil and other subsoil wealth the property of the nation. The oil companies no longer had a property right to the oil beneath the ground.

---

it a production tax allowed Carranza to deploy the revenues for domestic needs, such as paying the army. Rippy (1972), p. 119; Davis (1932), pp. 408–9.

[51] Davis calculates that the conversion of the stamp tax to an ad valorum tax resulted in an increase in the tax rate on crude oil from 60 centavos to 1.16 to 1.40 pesos (the amount depending on the specific gravity) per barrel. Davis (1932), pp. 408–10.

[52] Rippy (1972), pp. 42–43; Meyer (1977), p. 62.

[53] El Águila and La Corona (a Royal Dutch–Shell subsidiary) agreed to register their lands. El Águila made it very difficult for the oil companies to maintain a united front against the government. In fact, in 1920 it negotiated a deal by which the company was no longer free of export, capital, or production taxes. It also gave up the right to a protected zone three kilometers around its open wells. It had to pay a royalty of 25 percent of production in specie or cash, at the option of the government. In return it received private lands in the states of Tabasco and Veracruz. Hall (1995), pp. 76–77.

[54] Meyer (1977), p. 62; Brown (1993), pp. 231–32; Rippy (1972), pp. 43–45.

[55] Carranza's decree, backing down on the ownership and tax issue, can be found in *Engineering and Mining Journal*, January 31, 1920, p. 354.

[56] Revisions of the production tax changed the method of valuing the crude, but also raised the nominal rates. Davis (1932), pp. 208–10; Meyer (1977), pp. 62–63; Rippy (1972), p. 46; Hall (1995), pp. 19, 67; Brown (1993), pp. 236–37.

Instead, they had a revocable concession from the federal government to exploit a national resource. Worse yet, the Constitution stated that only Mexican citizens and Mexican companies had the right to acquire concessions to develop the nation's subsoil wealth. It went on to say that the government might grant this right to foreigners, provided that they agreed to be considered Mexican in respect to such property and to therefore not invoke the protection of their governments. On top of this, the Constitution declared the banks and beds of rivers, streams, lagoons, lakes, and other bodies of water federal property. The oil fields, of course, sat along Mexico's Gulf Coast and were crisscrossed by innumerable bodies of water.[57] The government therefore had the right to award drilling rights to third parties on those lands, allowing them to tap into the common pool of oil that the oil companies had already identified.[58]

No one debated the right of the Mexican government to declare that the subsoil was national patrimony. In fact, the *only* country where the owner of the surface land was also the owner of the subsoil rights was the United States of America. Everywhere else, petroleum deposits were considered national patrimony.

The real bone of contention between the oil companies and Carranza's government was whether Article 27 affected the millions of acres of land already owned or leased by the oil companies, or whether it only pertained to new lands. The oil companies argued that Article 27 only affected properties acquired or leased after May 1, 1917 (the date the Constitution took effect), because Article 14 of the Constitution stated that laws cannot be retroactive. By extension, the companies did not have to obtain drilling permits to lands acquired prior to this date because they already had property rights to the oil. President Carranza, of course, did not agree with this analysis.[59]

The result of this contention was an increase in tax revenues, a fall in tax rates, and little genuine redefinition of property rights. When you consider the preferences of the parties involved, the ex post result seems

---

[57] Brown (1993), p. 226; Meyer (1977), p. 55.

[58] By 1922 the Mexican government had set up its own bureau to explore the 86 percent of the oil lands held as public lands. The company came to produce 1 percent of Mexican output, but according to Standard Oil of New Jersey it obtained its production primarily by drilling in the federal zones of creek beds, lagoons, and ponds within the boundaries of established private oil fields. See Rippy (1972), p. 164; Hall (1995), pp. 25–26; and Brown (1993), p. 227.

[59] Brown (1993), p. 227. For a discussion of these views, as well as the legal theories that underpinned them, see Rippy (1972), pp. 33–43.

obvious. The Carranza government, as well as its successors, was desperately in need of a source of revenue. This meant that the government was ultimately more interested in short-run tax revenues than in redefining usufruct property rights. The oil companies were concerned about maintaining their property rights. The U.S. government wanted to protect the oil companies, but for domestic political reasons it could only stage an invasion under extreme circumstances: expropriation or taxes so high as to amount to virtual expropriation.

When Alvaro Obregón came to power in 1920, he evidently believed that he enjoyed a stronger negotiating position against the oil companies than had Carranza. He therefore hiked oil taxes the following year.[60] On June 7, 1921, Obregón imposed a new oil export tax: a specific duty of from 1.55 to 2.50 pesos per cubic meter of petroleum (depending on the crude's specific gravity) that was assessed in addition to Carranza's export tax.[61] We calculate that by 1922 the combined incidence of these taxes reached 25 percent of the value of gross production.

Tax hikes of this magnitude provoked strong resistance by the oil companies. In protest against the tax increase, they curtailed output. Exports fell from 14 to 15 million barrels per month to less than 6 million barrels per month in the summer of 1921. The companies also stopped all construction. Employment in the oil fields fell from 50,000 to 20,000. The discharged workers were not permitted to use company transportation to reach Tampico. Swarms of workers crowded the roads toward the city. Discontent against the government fanned among the workers and ranch owners of the region.[62]

Obregón was taking a calculated risk. He knew that a prolonged shutdown of the oil industry could bring down his government. The gamble was that the oil companies would compromise on a tax rate somewhere between the 1919 tax rate and his 1921 demands.

---

[60] In 1920 Obregón decreed a tax on "infalsificables" (paper money printed during the revolution). This was levied as a surcharge on taxes paid by oil and mining companies at a rate of one peso in paper infalsificables for every peso paid in gold. Davis (1932), p. 412. It is not clear if this tax amounted to more than a small surcharge on existing petroleum taxes, because infalsificables only traded at 10 centavos to the peso in 1920. (Infalsificables were quoted as merchandise in the *Boletín Financiero y Minero*.) The government's apparent purpose was to enlist the oil and mining companies as its agents in collecting the outstanding emissions of paper money and removing them from circulation.

[61] There are approximately 6.5 barrels of petroleum per cubic meter. A barrel of petroleum is 42 gallons.

[62] Rippy (1972), p. 119; Meyer (1977), p. 82; Davis (1932), pp. 413–15.

Obregón's gamble paid off. In order to break the deadlock, the oil companies sent a delegation – the so-called Committee of Five – to a secret conference in Mexico City.[63] The agreement reached by the oil companies and Obregón was not made public, but its terms were made clear by the subsequent actions of each party. The oil companies agreed to pay Obregón's export tax, in addition to all taxes instituted before 1920. The government, for its part, agreed that the oil companies could pay the export tax in Mexican bonds, which could be purchased for 40 cents on the dollar. Shortly thereafter, the government declared that the export tax had to be paid in cash but simultaneously lowered the nominal tax rate to 40 percent of its former value.[64] In short, the oil companies managed to negotiate a 60 percent reduction in Obregón's new export tax. The overall tax rate therefore fell from 25 percent of the gross value of production in 1922, to 20 percent by 1924.[65]

The question of the retroactivity of Article 27, however, remained unresolved. In 1922 the Mexican Supreme Court, in a case brought by the Texas Company, ruled in favor of the oil companies: Article 27 could not be retroactive as long as the companies had undertaken "positive acts." The problem was that the definition of "positive acts" was ambiguous. Did it mean that the companies had to be extracting oil, that they had drilled for oil, that they had mapped the area, or just that they had purchased or leased the land? Depending on what definition was applied to "positive act" between 80 and 90 percent of the oil companies' lands could still be affected by the Constitution.[66]

The United States again intervened in order to resolve the dispute. The U.S. State Department wanted a treaty that explicitly recognized and protected American property rights. Obregón, however, refused to agree to a treaty that would limit Mexican sovereignty. The two sides therefore came to a gentlemen's agreement (the Bucareli Agreement, named for the street in Mexico City where the negotiations took place) in which the

[63] The "Committee of Five" included Walter Teagle of Standard Oil of New Jersey, E. L. Doheny of the Mexican Petroleum Company, J. W. Van Dyke of Atlantic Refining, Harry Sinclair of Sinclair Oil, and Amos Beaty of the Texas Company. Hall (1995), pp. 28–30.

[64] The government also dropped the infalsificables tax. Davis (1932), pp. 414–16; Rippy (1972), p. 120. The tax rates of different products, before and after the decree, can be found in *Engineering and Mining Journal*, September 2, 1922, p. 420.

[65] Due to the oil companies' resistance, taxes incurred in 1921 were not actually paid until 1922, after the negotiated agreement. This is why the tax rate spiked in 1922, despite the agreement.

[66] Meyer (1977), pp. 84–85; Hall (1995), pp. 115, 137; Rippy (1972), p. 80.

property titles of the oil companies would be turned into "confirmatory concessions" (a de facto recognition of the oil companies' property rights), provided that the oil companies had made "positive acts" to the property. Positive acts were defined in the broadest way imaginable. Thus, leasing land before May 1, 1917, even if the companies had not actively searched for oil, would be considered a positive act. Similarly, the purchase of land before May 1, 1917, for a price that reflected the potential oil-bearing nature of the subsoil also would be a positive act. In return, the United States agreed to recognize the Obregón government.[67]

No sooner did Obregón name his protégé Plutarco Elias Calles to the presidency in 1924 than Calles (unsuccessfully) attempted to abrogate the agreement reached just the year before with the United States. Calles handpicked a congressional committee charged with writing enabling legislation to Article 27. The committee drafted a law that defined positive acts only as actual drilling prior to May 1, 1917. In addition, property holders had to apply for confirmation of their rights.[68] In December 1925 the Mexican Congress approved the law. The oil companies filed injunctions against the law, citing the 1922 Supreme Court decisions. Calles responded that his government was bound neither by the agreement with the United States nor, astoundingly, by the decisions of the Mexican Supreme Court.[69]

Mexico's leading oil producers decided to defy the new law openly, refusing to obtain confirmation of their rights.[70] Calles responded by remanding the oil companies to the attorney general and began canceling drilling permits. The oil companies were not intimidated. They drilled without permits. Calles upped the ante, imposing heavy fines

---

[67] Meyer (1977), p. 102; Rippy (1972), pp. 89–91; Hall (1995), p. 149.

[68] The law also imposed a 50-year limit on those rights, counting from the time that operations began, and reaffirmed that subsoil rights held by foreigners were not recognized along coasts and national borders.

[69] Meyer (1977), pp. 110–12, 115; Hall (1995), p. 173; Rippy (1972), pp. 57–58.

[70] The companies who held out included Atlantic Refining Company and its Mexican subsidiary, La Atlantica Compañía Mexicana Productora y Refinadora de Petróleo, the Atlantic Gulf Company and its subsidiary Compañía Petrolera del Agwi, Humble Oil and Refining Company and its subsidiary Compañía Petrolera Tamaulipas S.A., Standard Oil of California and its subsidiary Richmond Petroleum Company of Mexico S.A., Standard Oil of New Jersey and its subsidiary Compañía Transcontinental de Petróleo S.A., Anglo Mexican Petroleum Company Ltd. and its subsidiary Compañía Mexicana de Petróleo S.A., El Águila S.A., Royal Dutch–Shell and its subsidiary Compañía Holandesa La Corona, S.A. These firms controlled 90 percent of the oil-producing lands in Mexico and 70 percent of output. Rippy (1972), p. 70.

and capping wells that lacked permits. The companies broke the seals on the wells. The government sent in troops and capped the wells once again.[71]

Once again, the United States stepped into the breach as third-party enforcer. President Coolidge announced that the United States was going to allow the sale and transport of arms across the U.S.-Mexico border. This was an obvious threat. Calles knew that his government was not secure. He had faced a rebellion over his own succession to the presidency in 1923–24. He now faced a civil war against lay elements of the Catholic Church who sought to overthrow him because of his anticlerical policies (the Cristero War of 1926–29). Under these circumstances, the United States could easily enforce the oil companies' property rights by the simple expedient of threatening to arm the rebels. In case the message was not already clear, Coolidge followed up his declaration that the rebels could freely purchase arms in the United States by issuing a corollary to the Monroe Doctrine in April 1927, which declared that the persons and property of American citizens, even abroad, enjoyed protection from the United States.[72]

U.S. Ambassador Dwight Morrow could now broker a deal with Calles to break the deadlock. In accordance with the Calles-Morrow agreement, on November 17, 1927, the Mexican Supreme Court, on Calles's instructions, granted an injunction against the 1925 oil law. Shortly thereafter, Congress formally amended the law. On March 27, 1928, the U.S. State Department announced that the controversy beginning in 1917 was at a practical conclusion. Further discussions concerning the oil companies' property rights would have to be handled through Mexico's executive departments, not through the Department of State.[73] The issue of the rights to the subsoil was settled. Properties acquired or leased prior to May 1, 1917, were not affected by Article 27 of the Mexican Constitution.

The issue of property rights to Mexico's petroleum would only reemerge in 1938, long after the instability of the revolutionary era had passed. In 1934 the Roosevelt administration announced the "Good Neighbor Policy," which essentially declared that the United States would no longer enforce American property rights in Latin America. Mexico's oil

---

[71] Meyer (1977), pp. 123–24; Rippy (1972), pp. 58–59, 167–68; Sterret and Davis (1928), pp. 205–6.
[72] Rippy (1972), p. 170.
[73] Rippy (1972), pp. 62–63; Meyer (1977), pp. 133–34; Sterret and Davis (1928), pp. 205–6.

unions, whose workers shared in the rents earned by the companies, tried to assume the role of protecting the oil companies' property rights, much as militant labor unions did in the manufacturing sector (see Chapters 3 and 5 for more detail). In 1935, they fused into a single union representing all workers in the industry and demanded that the oil companies increase the workers' share of revenues.

Nationalization eventually took place because all sides in this drama drastically miscalculated. The oil companies miscalculated how much they needed the union's protection to prevent them from being expropriated. The oil worker's union miscalculated how much the oil companies were willing to pay for its services as third-party enforcer. The government miscalculated the economic value of Mexico's remaining oil industry. The net result was that the oil companies refused to meet the union's demands and the union would not back down. The ensuing dispute wound its way to the Mexican Supreme Court, which sided with the workers. The oil companies refused to obey the Court's decision. They thereby set the stage for their confiscation by the government in 1938. Indeed, the open refusal of the companies to abide by a ruling of the Supreme Court gave President Cárdenas little choice but to nationalize the industry. When nationalization finally came, however, it came in the context of an industry made up of played-out wells and aging equipment. By 1938 output was less than 20 percent of its 1921 peak – and trending downwards.

Output and Investment

As Table 6.1 indicates, Mexican petroleum output increased regardless of political instability, the Constitution of 1917, or increases in the tax rate. In fact, even the period of civil war (1914–17) could not stop the upward surge in output. Every single year from 1910 to 1921 witnessed higher levels of crude production. Even with the decline in output from its 1921 peak, oil output for the decade 1921–30 was more than 2 times what it had been during the decade 1911–20, and more than 87 times what it had been in the decade 1901–10.

One might argue that the rapid increase in output to 1921, followed by a gradual decline thereafter, is consistent with an industry that feared that its property rights were being reduced. The oil companies were increasing output from already proven sources, pumping the oil out of the ground before the government could increase taxes or nationalize the oil.

If this hypothesis were true, we should not observe the oil companies undertaking new exploration or making new investments. We should, in fact, observe that investment peaked well in advance of output.[74] The data we have assembled on oil exploration and investment do not, however, reveal this pattern. In fact, the data reveal exactly the opposite: investment peaked well after output peaked. This evidence is not consistent with the hypothesis that the companies feared expropriation or tax increases that amounted to de facto confiscation. It is, however, consistent with the hypothesis that output contracted for geological reasons. It is also consistent with accounts of contemporary observers regarding the invasion of Mexico's oil pools by salt water.[75] The deposits that had been tapped were not particularly large. It took only a few years for the sheets of salt water that lay beneath them to invade the petroleum.[76] The oil companies kept searching for petroleum.[77] They simply could not find enough to maintain their 1918–21 levels of production.

Data on the drilling of new wells indicate that firms were continuing to search for new oil deposits, long after production peaked, but were simply not able to find much new oil. The data, reported in Table 6.2, show several striking features. The first is the strong upward trend in the number of new wells drilled. There were more wells drilled in 1921 than in the *combined* period 1917–20. In 1924, three years after production peaked, there were more than twice as many wells drilled as in 1921. By 1926, while production continued to decline, the number of wells drilled finally peaked at 2.5 times its 1921 level; and 20 times its 1919 level.

The second striking feature of the data is the decline in the percentage of these new wells that contained oil in commercial quantities. In 1919, 76 percent of new wells were productive. In 1921 the ratio was 64 percent. It then steadily declined to 28 percent in 1929. The falling ratio of productive to unproductive wells indicates that firms were trying hard to find new sources of oil but were not succeeding. Had they been attempting

---

[74] This is the result that Monaldi (2002) obtains, for example, regarding the contraction of the Venezuelan oil industry in the 1950s. Investment began to decline four years before output began to decline.

[75] See, for example, *Engineering and Mining Journal*, December 11, 1920, p. 1136; January 4, 1920, p. 1096; November 13, 1920, p. 956; January 22, 1921, p. 185; November 11, 1922, p. 860.

[76] See, for example, Hall (1995), pp. 105, 109, 111; Brown (1993), pp. 143, 164.

[77] In the early 1930s they found enough in the new Poza Rica field to cause a minor rise in total output. In short order, it too became played out.

Table 6.2. Wells Drilled and Capacity (in thousands of barrels)

Year	Total Number of Wells Drilled[a]	Number of Productive Wells	Percent Productive	Initial Daily Capacity per Well	Total Initial Daily Capacity[b]
1901–16	279	174	62	3.7	644
1917	79	43	54	6.3	271
1918	43	28	65	19.8	554
1919	41	31	76	15	465
1920	97	62	64	24.8	1,538
1921	317	203	64	16.7	3,390
1922	265	158	60	9.1	1,438
1923	467	259	55	3.4	881
1924	699	296	42	3.4	1,006
1925	801	298	37	3	894
1926	808	318	39	3.7	1,177
1927	570	204	36	1.9	388
1928	237	96	41		
1929	114	32	28	3.6	115

[a] 1901–16 lists the total number of wells in that 16-year period.
[b] Daily capacity per new productive well, times the number of new productive wells.
Sources: México, Dirección General de Estadística (1926), p. 141; Mexico, Departamento de la Estadística Nacional, February 1930, p. 49, and March 1930, p. 91. Sterret and Davis (1928), pp. 203–4; Brown (1985), pp. 381–82.

to increase output from established sites, we would expect the ratio of productive wells to increase, not decrease.

Third, even when the oil companies sank successful wells, the initial output per well (the capacity of the well, measured in barrels per day) continuously fell. At its peak in 1921, the average initial capacity per new well was 24,800 barrels per day. By 1924 the average initial capacity of new wells had collapsed to only 3,400 barrels per day. It remained at that level throughout the 1920s. The combination of lower ratios of productive to unproductive wells and lower initial capacities was deadly in two senses. First, it meant that *total new capacity* was declining rapidly. In 1921 the total capacity of new wells totaled 3.4 million barrels per day. By 1924 the total capacity of new wells had fallen to 1.0 million barrels per day. By 1927 total new capacity was only 384,000 barrels, and by 1929 it fell to 114,000 barrels. Thus, in the space of only eight years, new capacity collapsed by 97 percent. Second, the combination of falling ratios of productive to unproductive wells and lower initial capacities implied higher costs per unit of output. It meant, as two expert observers put it, "a very pronounced increase in the cost of obtaining a barrel of crude oil."[78] By 1927 the oil companies realized that their exploration efforts were generating only new expenses, not new gushers. They therefore began to cut back on new drilling – a full six years *after* production began to decline.

Data on the amount of land owned or leased by the oil companies also support the hypothesis that Mexico's oilmen continued to search for new petroleum in the 1920s. In 1920, according to the historian Merrill Rippy, the oil companies leased 2,012,604 hectares and owned an additional 677,553 hectares, for a total of 2,690,159 hectares. Five years later, the companies registered their claims under the 1925 petroleum law. Their total claims now covered 6,226,063 hectares, more than twice the amount claimed in 1920.[79] Data gathered by Lorenzo Meyer yields similar results. Meyer estimates that in 1917 the oil companies held rights to 2,151,025 hectares of oil lands.[80] When the government granted confirmatory titles, during the period 1928–37 (as a result of the 1925 oil law) it granted titles to 6,940,568 hectares.[81]

The quantitative evidence we have retrieved is also consistent with the observations of contemporaries regarding new exploration. As early as October 1920 – well before the resolution of the property rights question – firms were exploring for petroleum well beyond their original claims in Veracruz and the Isthmus of Tehuantepec. These new exploratory operations were taking place in a large number of sites spread across Durango, Colima, Chihuahua, Coahuila, Chiapas, San Luis Potosí, Jalisco, and Yucatán.[82] Contemporary observers also reported that these exploratory operations gave rise to a great many new leases. As the *Engineering and Mining Journal* noted: "Owing, possibly, to the fact that many wells in the older districts of Tamaulipas and northern Vera Cruz [*sic*] have run into salt water, there has been a tendency to increase exploration further south. During the last three months of 1920, a great deal of land changed ownership in the states of Tabasco and Chiapas and Southern Veracruz.

[78] Sterret and Davis (1928), p. 204.
[79] Rippy (1972), pp. 162, 172.
[80] Meyer (1977), p. 57.
[81] Meyer (1977), p. 135. Meyer's claim, that any new investment after 1917 was designed solely to exploit already proven reserves, is therefore not supported by his own evidence. See Meyer (1977), p. 57.
[82] *Engineering and Mining Journal*, October 9, 1920, pp. 725–26. Later accounts from contemporary sources discuss other exploration and wildcatting operations. See, for example, *Engineering and Mining Journal*, November 27, 1920, p. 1050; January 8, 1921, p. 69; January 29, 1921, p. 232; June 16, 1923, p. 1074.

Despite the government's insistence on its ownership of oil, leases for oil rights constantly are being entered into between land owners and representatives of important companies now on the ground."[83] It went on to state that "considerable development work has recently been started in the states of Sonora, Lower California, Sinaloa, Guerrero, Puebla, and Oaxaca. British capitalists recently began borings at Port Angel, on the Pacific coast, where seepages and other external evidence of oil are abundant, although the territory has been repeatedly rejected by geologists. Considerable activity has also been shown in the tier of Mexican states bordering on Texas and Arizona, though no wells have been actually brought in."[84]

The entry of new firms supports the hypothesis that the oil companies were actively searching for new sources of oil and not just intensively exploiting proven reserves. These new firms included many of the established international giants in the oil industry. The Texas Company (later Texaco), for example, entered the Mexican market in 1912 and established a subsidiary in 1917 with an initial capital of $5.3 million. Gulf Oil arrived in 1912, and established a wholly owned subsidiary. Union Oil, Sinclair, and Standard Oil of California all soon followed, establishing subsidiaries by 1917.[85] These were all new operations, rather than purchases of already established oil companies. The world's two largest petroleum companies, Shell and Standard Oil of New Jersey, also entered Mexico. Shell began production in Mexico in 1912, through a small subsidiary operation, La Corona, S.A. In 1919 Royal Dutch–Shell purchased a controlling interest in Mexico's second largest oil firm, El Águila.[86] Standard Oil entered the market in 1917 by purchasing the Transcontinental Petroleum Company for $2.5 million. It had earlier tried to purchase El Águila, making unsuccessful offers in 1913 and 1916. By 1919 it had 10 subsidiaries operating in Mexico. It is not clear how many of Standard's subsidiaries were entirely new ventures and how many were purchases of existing firms.[87] Nevertheless, Standard Oil believed that existing Mexican oil companies were a good bet – at least at the prices on offer – as late as 1932, when it acquired the Pan American Petroleum and Transport Corporation (the holding company that controlled Doheny's interlocking empire of Mexican oil companies, including Huasteca and

[83] *Engineering and Mining Journal*, January 22, 1921, p. 185.
[84] *Engineering and Mining Journal*, January 22, 1921, p. 185.
[85] Brown (1993), p. 141; Rippy (1972), p. 137.
[86] Rippy (1972), p. 154.
[87] Meyer (1977), p. 4; Rippy (1972), pp. 160–61; Brown (1993), pp. 152, 160–61.

the Mexican Petroleum Company) and became the largest producer of petroleum in Mexico.[88]

Data on the value of new investment by the oil companies follow the same pattern as the data on new wells and support the hypothesis that both new entrants and existing companies continued to invest long after production peaked. We have gathered the financial statements of major Mexican oil companies from *Moody's Manual of Investments*. Our sample includes the Mexican Petroleum Company, El Águila, Pan-American Petroleum and Transport, the Mexico-Pánuco Oil Company, the Mexican Seaboard Oil Company, and the Penn-Mex Fuel Company.[89] These firms accounted for 76 percent of total Mexican petroleum output in 1918, meaning that our sample captures the largest part of the industry.[90] We focus on the value of each firm's fixed assets, rather than total assets, which may include cash, securities, and other liquid investments. This allows us to know whether firms were investing in productive apparatus or were diverting profits into other activities.[91] We convert the raw data into index numbers, so as to permit easy comparison in investment growth trends across companies, and report the results in Table 6.3.[92]

Every company in the sample continued to invest in new plant and equipment well after output began to fall. The only variance was the year of peak investment. In the case of the Mexican Petroleum Company, investment levels peaked in 1924. For other firms it came later: 1925 in the case of Mexican Seaboard, 1930 in the cases of Mexico-Pánuco and Penn-Mex, and 1931 in the case of El Águila.

---

[88] Pan-American was first purchased by Standard Oil of Indiana in 1925, which then sold it to Standard Oil of New Jersey. Meyer (1977), p. 4; Brown (1993), p. 45.

[89] This is not a random sample of Mexican oil companies but is a sample of large, publicly traded firms that were followed by *Moody's Manual of Investments*.

[90] Market shares were calculated from data in *Engineering and Mining Journal*, May 1, 1920, p. 1030; July 1, 1922, p. 25.

[91] We look at fixed assets (land, equipment, and buildings), not total assets. The reason is that total assets can increase through the purchase of securities or increases in cash balances, without these assets being invested in productive apparatus. In fact, total assets can increase even if a firm is selling its productive assets and holding the proceeds as cash.

[92] Our figures are the book values of fixed assets, calculated at acquisition cost minus depreciation. Optimally, we would have converted these figures into replacement costs. This involves applying the same depreciation schedules across companies by asset type and adjusting the value of new acquisitions of productive apparatus for inflation. Unfortunately, many of our financial statements either lumped depreciation in with other expenses (making it difficult to back out) or failed to break down productive assets into sufficiently detailed subcategories.

Table 6.3. *Fixed Assets of Major Mexican Oil Companies*

Year	El Águila	Mexican Petroleum	Mexican Seaboard	Mexico Pánuco	Penn-Mex Fuel
1911	55	66			
1912					
1913	112	71			
1914	129	80			
1915	126	87			
1916	113	86			
1917	103	89			
1918	97	106			
1919	94	92			82
1920	94	100			92
1921	100	100	100	100	100
1922	163	127	121	101	100
1923	178	130	126	97	99
1924	159	137	137	97	101
1925	142	129	172	150	
1926	126	106	152	171	
1927	104	98	132	273	
1928	93	95	120	272	
1929	89	89	127	350	
1930	91	57	123	443	107
1931	318	51	91	266	98
1932	284	47	91		
1933	98	44	91		
1934	93		93		
1935	115		95		
1936	114		97		
1937	120		108		
1938			51		

Notes: Assets valued at acquisition cost minus depreciation (book value). Base year 1921 = 100. Full company names are: Mexican Eagle Oil Co. (El Águila); Mexican Petroleum Company of Delaware; Mexican-Seaboard Oil Company; Mexico-Pánuco Oil Company; Penn-Mex Fuel Company.

Source: Estimated from balance sheets in *Moody's Manual of Investments*, various years.

These results are consistent with estimates made by the Mexican government of total investment in the oil industry. We have taken these estimates and converted them to real dollars, using the U.S. wholesale price index, with the base year reconverted from 1967 to 1928. The results indicate a rapid run-up of investment from 1912 to 1924 – three years after production peaked – and then a gentle decline from 1924 to 1936. In 1912 the real (1928) dollar value of oil company investments in Mexico was $246 million.[93] Ten years later, in 1922, the real value of investments had more than doubled to $511 million. The total stock of investment grew an additional 11 percent by 1924, to $569 million. The data indicate a drop in investment to mid-1926, when it hit $393 million, followed by a slight recovery to 1928 when it rose to $425 million. By 1936, according to the Mexican government, total invested capital had fallen, in real terms, to $370 million.[94]

A final method of estimating investment in the Mexican oil industry is to look at the real value of capital goods imported into Mexico from the United States. This method allows us to measure flows rather than stocks. It is also an extremely accurate measure, because Mexico produced no oil drilling equipment, pipes, casings, or storage tanks. *All* of this machinery and equipment had to be imported from the United States. Our estimates, in 1929 U.S. dollars, are presented in Table 6.4. Prior to 1922 the U.S. Department of Commerce did not disaggregate petroleum machines from mining machines. Thus, the 1907–21 data are estimates based on the reasonable assumption that the ratio of oil equipment expenditures to oil and mining equipment expenditures during 1907–21 was the same as it was from 1922 to 1929 (55 percent of total mining and petroleum spending). We note that partial data on mining and oil well equipment imports into Mexico in 1919 are consistent with this ratio.[95] We also note that the results are not sensitive to the ratio chosen; even if 100 percent of mining and petroleum equipment imports during the 1907–21 period had been destined for the oil industry, it would not affect our qualitative results.

The data unambiguously support the hypothesis that investment was not affected by political instability or expectations about future institutional change. New investment dropped dramatically in 1914 and 1915, but then recovered rapidly. In 1920 gross investment in machinery was more than twice what it had been in 1910. The data also indicate that gross

---

[93] The nominal estimate, made by Carlos Díaz Dufoo, was 175 million. Díaz Dufoo (1921), p. 102.
[94] The nominal amounts, estimated by the Mexican government and reported by Rippy (1972) are as follows: 1922 equals $510 million, 1924 equals $575 million, 1926 equals $406 million, 1928 equals $425 million, 1936 equals $306 million. Data from Rippy (1972), pp. 164, 166, 173, 181.
[95] In the month of August 1919 oil equipment accounted for 67 percent of total oil and mining equipment. *Engineering and Mining Journal*, October 11, 1919, p. 623.

Table 6.4. *Estimates of Petroleum Equipment Exported to Mexico from the United States, 1907–1929 (in thousands of 1929 U.S. dollars)*

Year	Reported Mining and Petroleum Machinery	Reported Oil Line Pipe and Casings	Reported Petroleum Machinery	Estimated Total Petroleum Equipment[a]	Index of Total Petroleum Equipment (1921 = 100)
1907	2,136			1,175	90
1908	1,539			847	65
1909	1,166			641	49
1910	1,099			604	47
1911	1,172			644	50
1912	914			503	39
1913	1,166			641	49
1914	898			494	38
1915	133			73	6
1916	184			101	8
1917	255			141	11
1918	803			442	34
1919	875			481	37
1920	2,469			1,358	105
1921	2,362			1,299	100
1922		881	944	1,825	140
1923		1,751	864	2,616	201
1924		1,943	897	2,841	219
1925		1,451	1,141	2,592	200
1926		1,069	584	1,654	127
1927		749	628	1,377	106
1928		681	952	1,632	126
1929		683	606	1,289	99

[a] From 1907 to 1921 estimated total is 55 percent of reported mining and petroleum machinery. The 55 percent ratio is derived from the ratio of reported oil line pipe and casings plus reported petroleum machinery to the the total of those categories plus mining machinery from 1922 to 1929. From 1922 to 1929 the estimated total is the sum of reported oil line pipe and casings, plus reported petroleum machinery. We note that the final results of these calculations are not sensitive to the ratios chosen.

Source: United States, Department of Commerce (various years).

investment in the petroleum industry continued its high rates throughout the 1920s. The peak year of investment was 1924.[96] In the late 1920s,

[96] This is not the same thing as saying that the stock of investment declined after 1924. As long as new investment flows exceeded the depreciation of old equipment and the reexport of used equipment from Mexico to third countries, the stock of investment would have increased. Without estimates of reexports of petroleum equipment and

flows of new investment were, on average, considerably higher than they had been in 1921.

The various measures we have put together of exploration and investment, taken as a group, indicate that the oil companies continued to invest even after output began to decline. Output peaked in 1921, but investment did not peak until sometime between 1924 and 1928, depending on how it is measured. The implication is that firms were not dissuaded from investing by changes in institutions, increases in taxes, or political instability. Indeed, the data indicate that Mexican historians have been incorrect in arguing that the oil companies stopped exploring for new sources of oil after 1917 and stopped making new investments in fixed capital after 1921, in order to "concentrate on Venezuela."[97] The data suggest, instead, that the oil companies believed that they could mitigate threats to their property rights and rents from those property rights. They left Mexico because they could no longer find sources of petroleum that could be extracted at a reasonable price using existing technology.

Taxes

Our interpretation of the rise and decline of the Mexican oil industry implies that the oil companies should have been relatively immune to changes in the tax rate. Historians have noted, quite correctly, that the oil companies fought the Mexican government's attempts to introduce new taxes or raise existing ones and have surmised from this that the tax rate was a vital determinant of whether the oil companies continued to operate in Mexico. The problem with this interpretation is that all companies at all times in all places complain about taxes. Whether they complained and whether taxes really were a determinant of their level of operations are separate issues. What was germane to the oil companies was how badly taxes cut into profits.

In Table 6.5 we present estimates of Mexican government revenues, oil tax revenues, per barrel taxes, total oil industry revenues, and the tax rate (total taxes divided by total industry revenues). Our estimates of per barrel taxes indicate a steady increase from 3 centavos per barrel in 1912 to 47 centavos (gold pesos) per barrel in 1922. The tax then oscillated

---

the rate at which equipment depreciated, it is not possible to estimate the stock of investment from these data. It is unlikely, however, that reexports and depreciation would have exceeded the stock of new flows, at least through the late 1920s.

[97] See, for example, Meyer (1977), pp. 11, 57. Also see Brown (1985).

Table 6.5. *Estimates of Mexican Petroleum Taxes and Prices*

Year	Price per Barrel (gold pesos)	Value of Crude Produced (thousands gold pesos)	Total Petroleum Taxes[a] (thousands gold pesos)	Tax per Barrel (gold pesos)	Tax Rate (%)	Total Tax Revenues (millions of pesos)	Petroleum Taxes as % of Total Revenues
1911	0.2	2,512	14	0	1	111	0
1912	0.25	4,142	494	0.03	12	126	0
1913	0.3	7,713	767	0.03	10	121	1
1914	0.3	7,874	1,234	0.05	16		
1915	0.4	13,164	1,943	0.06	15		
1916	0.55	22,300	3,088	0.08	14		
1917	0.85	46,999	7,553	0.14	16	154	5
1918	1.4	89,656	12,008	0.19	13	157	8
1919	1.83	159,036	17,332	0.2	11	188	9
1920	2	313,076	51,314	0.33	16	260	20
1921	1.89	368,441	67,695	0.35	18	293	23
1922	1.93	357,034	87,779	0.47	25	280	31
1923	1.91	285,452	62,394	0.42	22	287	22
1924	1.95	270,966	54,467	0.39	20	284	19
1925	2.59	299,459	46,798	0.4	16	322	15
1926	2.49	225,892	41,438	0.46	18	309	13
1927	2.46	157,543	25,538	0.4	16	307	8
1928	2.03	101,946	18,349	0.37	18	311	6
1929	2.06	92,167	19,390	0.43	21	322	6

[a] Includes production, export, bar, excise, infalsificable, and income taxes.

Sources: Davis (1932), p. 419; Meyer (1977), p. 16; Sterrett and Davis (1928), p. 197; México, Dirección General de Estadística (1930), pp. 517–21.

without trend through the rest of the 1920s.[98] In short, the data for the 1910s and 1920s indicate that the Mexican government did not know, ex ante, the point at which the oil companies would begin to push back, so it experimented by gradually increasing per barrel taxes until finding a threshold level at which the oil companies began to shut down. The government then negotiated a slightly lower tax rate.

From the point of view of the Mexican government, finding the threshold tax rate was difficult for two reasons. First, the threshold was not a constant value but a moving target that changed with exogenous factors. These factors included the world price of oil (which could be

[98] The variation was driven by annual differences in the percentage of oil exported versus domestically consumed. The tax rate was considerably higher on exported oil.

easily observed) and the extraction costs faced by companies in Mexico (which were extremely difficult to observe). Second, the government had to anticipate the response of the oil companies. This meant that the government had to take into account the perception that the companies had of the government's vulnerability to a dramatic decline in oil tax revenues. This would have been a particularly difficult factor to measure. The government could guess, but it could only know whether it guessed correctly ex post.

If the government guessed incorrectly, and the oil companies shut down production in protest of a tax increase, the results could have been deadly. The basic fact of the matter was that petroleum taxes were a vital component of the Mexican federal budget. In 1912 oil tax receipts made up less than 1 percent of total government revenue. This ratio climbed rapidly, reaching 5 percent by 1917, 20 percent by 1920, and 31 percent by 1922. It declined after 1922, but as late as 1926 oil taxes still accounted for 13 percent of government revenue.

Profits

How high were Mexican taxes from the point of view of the oil companies? That is, did increases in taxes lower the net revenues per barrel to the point that the oil companies could have more profitably deployed their capital elsewhere? We answer this question in three ways.

The first method we employ is to calculate the after-tax price for a barrel of Mexican crude oil received by the oil companies. The calculation from the data in Table 6.6 is straightforward. We simply subtracted the per barrel tax payments made by the companies from the average pretax price of a barrel of Mexican oil in that year. We calculated the average pretax price of a barrel of oil by dividing the industry's total revenues by the total amount of production.

The result, presented graphically in Figure 6.1, is clear. The run-up in oil prices during and after the First World War was so pronounced that the after-tax price per barrel received by the Mexican oil companies increased fourfold, despite the increase in petroleum taxes. The data support the argument that any decline in the companies' profits, therefore, was not induced by increases in taxes.

Because the Mexican oil prices are imputed values, we performed the same exercise using the average U.S. price for crude oil. We then subtracted the average total tax per barrel paid by the Mexican oil producers. Because the average American price was consistently higher than our imputed

Table 6.6. *Estimates of Mexican Petroleum Pre- and Posttax Prices, U.S. Dollars*

Year	Price of U.S. Oil (per barrel)	U.S. Oil Price Net of Mexican Taxes	Price of Mexican Oil (per barrel)	Mexican Oil Price Net of Mexican Taxes
1914	0.81	0.80	0.09	0.08
1915	0.64	0.61	0.20	0.17
1916	1.10	1.06	0.28	0.24
1917	1.56	1.49	0.45	0.37
1918	1.98	1.88	0.78	0.67
1919	2.01	1.91	0.92	0.82
1920	3.07	2.91	1.00	0.83
1921	1.73	1.56	0.93	0.76
1922	1.61	1.38	0.94	0.71
1923	1.34	1.14	0.93	0.73
1924	1.43	1.24	0.94	0.75
1925	1.68	1.48	1.28	1.08
1926	1.88	1.66	1.20	0.98
1927	1.30	1.11	1.16	0.97
1928	1.17	0.99	0.98	0.80
1929	1.27	1.06	0.99	0.78

Sources: Mexico data from: Sterrett and Davis (1928), p. 197; Meyer (1977), 16; México, Dirección General de Estadística (1930), pp. 517–21; Davis (1932), p. 419; México, INEGI (1994), 1: 559.

Mexican price – most Mexican crude was of rather low quality – the results are even more dramatic. Tax payments did not substantially reduce the revenues per barrel received by the oil companies.

The second method we employ is to estimate rates of return on assets for six of Mexico's major oil companies from their financial statements.[99] We retrieved balance sheets and profit and loss statements from *Moody's Manual of Investments* for El Águila, the Mexican Petroleum Company,

[99] Returns on assets are the value of profits divided by the value of the investment that produced those profits. Returns on assets are calculated by dividing total profits (gross revenues minus expenditures) by the total value of all assets (both fixed and liquid) of the company. Interest payments made by the company to bondholders and other creditors are added back to profits, because the value of the debts are included in the value of total assets. An alternative measure is the rate of return on owner's equity, which divides profits by the value of paid-in capital, reserve accounts, and retained earnings. In this measure, the value of interest payments is subtracted from profits and the value of the debts is subtracted from assets. As a practical matter, the Mexican companies in our sample did not carry significant amounts of debt on their balance sheets. Thus, there would have been little difference in the rate of return on assets and the rate of return on owner's equity.

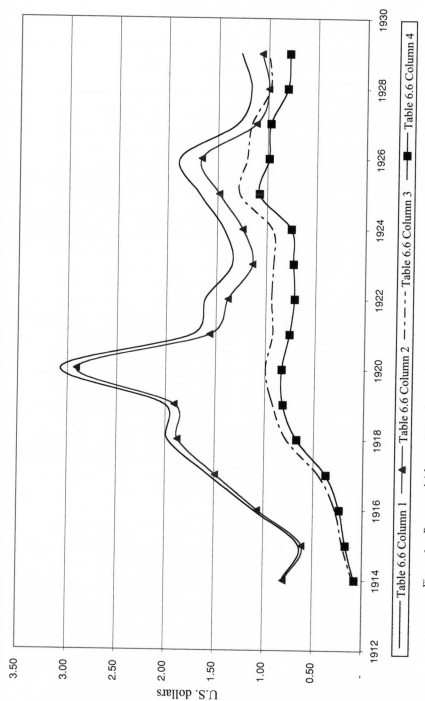

Figure 6.1. Pretax and Aftertax Prices for Crude Oil Faced by Mexican Producers. *Source:* Table 6.6.

Table 6.6 Column 1 ——— Table 6.6 Column 2 — — — Table 6.6 Column 3 ——■—— Table 6.6 Column 4

the Mexican Seaboard Oil Company, the Mexico Pánuco Oil Company, the Mexican Investment Company, and the Penn-Mex Fuel Company.[100] These firms accounted for 76 percent of total Mexican petroleum output in 1918, and 40 percent in 1922.[101] We then compare the financial performance of these Mexican firms with the performance of the major international oil companies. Our comparison set includes the Texas Company, Sinclair, Gulf Oil, and Standard Oil of New Jersey.[102]

Our estimates of returns on assets for Mexican and international oil companies are presented in Tables 6.7 and 6.8. There is some variance across companies, but the general pattern is for very strong rates of return in the period roughly 1916 to 1922 with some falloff thereafter, but the decline experienced after 1922 is highly variable. For some companies, such as El Águila, Penn-Mex, Mexico-Pánuco, and the Mexican Investment Company, the drop is quite pronounced. For others, such as the Mexican Seaboard Oil Company and the Mexican Petroleum Company, rates of return remained in the double digits until 1926 for the former and 1929 for the latter.

Did Mexican taxes cause rates of return to decline? The first way to answer this question is to compare Mexican oil company rates of return against those of the major international oil companies (see Tables 6.7 and 6.8). The pattern for Sinclair, Gulf, Standard Oil of New Jersey, and the Texas Company is strikingly similar to that of the Mexico-only firms. Rates of return were highest in 1916 to 1922 and declined thereafter. As was the case with the Mexican companies, there is a high degree of variance in the amount and timing of this decline. The implication is that whatever was driving declines in rates of return after 1922 was not

---

[100] These six companies were not chosen at random. Rather, we selected them because it was possible to retrieve their balance sheets and profit and loss statements from *Moody's Manual of Investments*.

[101] Market shares were calculated from data in *Engineering and Mining Journal*, May 1, 1920, p. 1030; July 1, 1922, p. 25.

[102] We note that these firms all had Mexican investments. The value of those investments, however, was trivial compared with the value of their worldwide assets. Thus, their Mexican operations could not have driven their overall levels of profitability. The Texas Company, Standard Oil of New Jersey, and Gulf Oil, for example, earned less than 1 percent of their gross revenues from their Mexican operations. Revenue shares calculated from data on output in *Engineering and Mining Journal*, May 1, 1920, p. 1030, prices per barrel of output in Table 6.5, and total revenues in the profit and loss statements of each company reported in *Moody's Manual of Investments*.

Table 6.7. *Estimated Rate of Return on Assets, Mexican Petroleum Companies (%)*

Year	El Águila	Mexican Petroleum	Mexican Seaboard	Mexico Panuco	Mexican Investment	Penn-Mex
1911	3	6				
1912	6	6				
1913	10	10				
1914	8	5				
1915	9	4				
1916	11	10				
1917	14	7				
1918	15	9				
1919	27	8			12	18
1920	33	9			40	34
1921	9	12	34	2		2
1922	8	21	53	0	−2	−7
1923	2	10	5	1	1	6
1924	2	3	33	1	−2	5
1925	2	22	22	1	2	
1926	2	34	16	−1	0	
1927	2	15	4	−1		
1928	0	14	0	−1		
1929	7	11	2	−1		
1930	3	4	7	0		4
1931	−1	2	1			0
1932	3		5			

Notes: Returns on assets are calculated by adding back interest payments to net profits and dividing these by the value of total assets. Interest payments are added back because the value of debts of the firm are included in assets. This allows the analysis of corporate profitability normalizing for difference in debt-equity ratios.

Full company names are: Mexican Eagle Oil Company (El Águila), Mexican Petroleum Company of Delaware, Mexican Seaboard Oil Company, Mexico-Pánuco Oil Company, Mexican Investment Company, Penn-Mex Fuel Company.

Source: Estimated from balance sheets and profit and loss statements in *Moody's Manual of Investments*, various years.

peculiar to Mexico.[103] Thus, Mexican taxes do not appear to be a likely candidate for explaining falling rates of return.

A third way to determine the impact of Mexican taxes on rates of return is to conduct a counterfactual exercise by estimating the rates of return

[103] The average American price of a barrel of crude oil declined rather precipitously from its peak in 1920. In 1920 a bench mark barrel of oil was valued at $3.07. By 1923, that price had fallen to $1.34. See Potter and Christy (1962), pp. 318–19.

Table 6.8. *Estimated Rate of Return on Assets, International Petroleum Companies (%)*

Year	Texas Company	Gulf Oil	Sinclair Consolidated Oil	Standard Oil of New Jersey
1911	6			
1912	5			
1913	11	22		
1914	8			
1915	8			
1916	12	15	45	
1917	14	7	61	
1918	15	6	27	13
1919	9	4	12	11
1920	11	10	4	17
1921	6	3	6	3
1922	10	5	9	4
1923	4	2	13	5
1924	8	3	9	7
1925	13	7	11	8
1926	15	6	11	8
1927	5	2	8	4
1928	9	8	4	9
1929	8	9	7	9
1930	3			4
1931	−1			2
1932	0			1

Notes: Returns on assets are calculated by adding back interest payments to net profits and dividing these by the value of total assets. Interest payments are added back because the value of debts of the firm are included in assets. This allows the analysis of corporate profitability normalizing for differences in debt-equity ratios.

Source: Estimated from balance sheets and profit and loss statements in *Moody's Manual of Investments*, various years.

for the same set of Mexican companies under the assumption that the Mexican tax rate was zero.[104] We backed out the value of Mexican taxes

[104] We took the estimated tax rate from our calculations in Table 6.5. We then estimated the absolute value of taxes for each year by multiplying the tax rate by the value of each firm's gross revenues. We then subtracted these estimated taxes from the value of expenditures, to calculate zero-tax profits. We then divided these zero-tax profits by the value of assets. This is essentially an exercise in comparative statics. The calculations assume that short-term output is entirely inelastic, holding fixed investment constant. Short-term inelasticity is a reasonable assumption given the high sunk costs in the petroleum industry. Once a well is drilled and a pipeline

by first estimating the value of those taxes, using the tax rate estimates in Table 6.5 and information in the firms' balance sheets about the value of gross revenues. Because we could not separate out income from Mexican oil sales from income from other sources, we assumed that all income was generated in Mexico and was therefore subject to Mexican taxes. This maximized the impact of the tax rate on rates of return. We note that we were able to measure taxes directly for the Mexican Petroleum Company during the period 1912–17.[105] The results indicate that the method we employed in our counterfactual exercise overstates Mexican taxes by a factor of two. We further note that all of the companies in our sample had income-earning assets outside of Mexico. In short, our assumptions create upper-bound estimates for the impact of the tax on rates of return and bias our results against the hypothesis that taxes did not substantially affect profitability.

The results of our tax analysis are presented in Table 6.9. Two features of the data are obvious. First, even with a zero tax rate, rates of return still decline in the mid-1920s. Second, for most companies, a zero tax rate only pushed up rates of return by a few percentage points. Thus, for example, El Águila's rates of return moved from 2 percent in 1923–27 (with positive taxes) to an average of 3 percent (with a zero tax rate). We obtain roughly similar results for the Mexican Investment Company, Penn-Mex, and Mexico-Pánuco. For the Mexican Petroleum Company and the Mexican Seaboard Oil Company, the impact of zero taxes would have been significant in the early 1920s, when these firms already had double-digit rates of return. Once income began to fall for these firms in the late 1920s, however, cutting taxes to zero would have raised rates of return by only 4 percentage points in any given year. Even had taxes been zero, other expenses – those associated with discovering reserves and developing wells – would have continued rising. The end result would not have been dramatically different. The bottom line was that Mexican petroleum pools were becoming more difficult to find and more expensive (per barrel) to develop.

---

built, it is almost impossible to redeploy them to other uses. As long as firms are covering their variable costs, they will continue to produce as much as their fixed investment will allow.

[105] The Mexican Petroleum Company paid taxes from 1912 to 1917 under protest. It therefore carried the value of the taxes on its balance sheets as an asset. We can therefore back out the yearly additions to this account, thereby imputing the actual amount of tax paid.

Table 6.9. *Counterfactual (No Tax) Analysis of Oil Company Rates of Return (%)*

Year	El Águila	Mexican Petroleum	Mexican Seaboard	Mexican Investment	Mexico-Pánuco	Penn-Mex
1911	3	6				
1912	7	7				
1913	11	11				
1914	10	6				
1915	12	6				
1916	14	11				
1917	18	10				
1918	19	14				
1919	31	10		14		
1920	39	11		47		
1921	11	15	45		2	
1922	10	29	82	−1	1	
1923	4	13	11	2	1	8
1924	3	5	44	−1	2	7
1925	3	28	28	3		
1926	3	43	23	0		
1927	2	19	8			
1928	1	18	2			
1929	10	15	7			

Notes: Returns on assets are calculated by adding back interest payments to net profits and dividing these by the value of total assets. Interest payments are added back because the value of debts of the firm are included in assets. This allows the analysis of corporate profitability normalizing for differences in debt-equity ratios.

For full company names see Table 6.7

Sources: See Tables 6.7 and 6.8.

Investor Perceptions

If the view that we have advanced – that the Mexican oil industry went into decline for geological, not institutional, reasons – is true, then it must also be true that investors were not perturbed by the political instability and institutional changes of the 1910s and early 1920s. One way to test this hypothesis is to look at the real price of common stocks in Mexican oil companies relative to the real price of common stocks in big international oil companies. If investors were not concerned about political developments inside Mexico, then the price of Mexican oil stocks would move with the price of stocks in the big international oil companies. The price of stocks might rise or fall, depending on the international price of oil, but we would not expect share prices in the two classes of firms to consistently move in different directions.

We therefore gathered data on two groups of petroleum companies: a set of six companies that operated within Mexico, and a set of three oil companies that had worldwide sources of petroleum. The group of Mexican oil companies includes the Mexican Petroleum Company, the Pan-American Petroleum and Transport Company, the Penn-Mex Fuel Company, the Mexican Seaboard Petroleum Company, the Mexican Investment Company, and the Mexican Eagle Oil Company (El Águila). We note that most of the stock of Mexican Petroleum was held by Pan-American Petroleum. Hence, we report the stock values of both companies. We also note that these six companies controlled roughly three-quarters of Mexican petroleum output circa 1918. The set of big international oil companies includes Standard Oil of New Jersey, Sinclair Consolidated Oil Company, and the Texas Company. Neither set of firms is a random sample. Rather, we chose them because it was possible to find price quotes of their common shares.[106] We adjusted the nominal stock prices for stock dividends and stock splits, converted nominal values to real values using the U.S. producer price index, and then converted the real values to index numbers (1921 = 100) in order to be able to compare the movement of prices across companies. The data are presented in Tables 6.10 and 6.11.

What do stock prices indicate? To judge by the Mexican Petroleum Company, which is the only Mexican firm for which we can construct a series back to 1912, the counterrevolution against Madero (1912), the overthrow of Huerta (1914), and the civil war between Carranza, Villa, and Zapata (1914–17) do not appear to have had a negative effect on investor confidence. The inflation-adjusted price of its stock more than doubled between 1912 to 1917. Investors in the Mexican Petroleum Company were so confident about the future of the firm, in fact, that its market value rose faster than the market values of the Texas Company and Standard Oil of New Jersey over the same period.

We have data for El Águila, Mexico's largest producer, starting in 1914. From 1915 onward we can add two additional companies: Pan-American Petroleum and Transport and Penn-Mex. The data show a sharp decline

---

[106] Price data for all companies save El Águila came from either the *Wall Street Journal* or *Moody's Manual of Investments*. In the case of El Águila, price data (in pounds sterling) came from de la Fuente Piñeirua (2001), p. 98, and was converted into dollars using the average dollar-pound exchange rate for the year.

Table 6.10. *Index of Real Stock Prices, Mexican Oil Companies (1921 = 100)*

Year	Mexican Petroleum	Pan-American	Penn-Mex	Mexican Seaboard	Mexican Investment	El Águila
1912	79					
1913	49					
1914	60					
1915	120	165	525			
1916	325		408			
1917	194	67	297			
1918	95	137	266			
1919	114	129	271		183	
1920	82	90	133		88	91
1921	100	100	100	100	100	100
1922	250	126	85	47	80	71
1923		180	224	42	37	31
1924	159	185	115	43	49	18
1925	188	175	89	41	47	20
1926		192	92	23	45	25
1927	214	141	177	189		18
1928	267	130	164	15		

Notes: Nominal stock prices deflated using U.S. producer price index from Carter and U.S. Bureau of the Census, *Historical Statistics of the United States*, 1926 base year. Real values then converted to an index with base year equal to 100 in order to have consistent base year for all firms. Note that prices have been adjusted to account for stock dividends and stock splits, as reported in *Moody's Manual of Investments*.
For full company names see Table 6.7.

Sources: Year-end stock prices, as quoted in the *Wall Street Journal*, except for the Mexican Investment Company (all years), Mexican Eagle Oil Company (all years), the Mexican Petroleum Company (1924 and 1925), and the Mexican Seaboard Petroleum Company (1921), which are average annual prices. Averages calculated as mean of the annual high and low prices as reported in *Moody's Manual of Investments*, various years.

in stock prices for three of the four firms for which we have data between 1915 or 1916 to 1921. The index moves from 358 to 100 for Mexican Petroleum, from 182 to 100 for Pan-American, and from 525 to 100 for Penn-Mex.

It is not possible to attribute this decline, however, to events in Mexico. First, stock prices of the three international giants in our sample also declined. The index for the Texas Company declined from 185 in 1915 to 100 in 1921. The index for Standard Oil declines from 106 to 100, and the index for Sinclair collapses from 217 to 100. The Mexican oil companies were not the only oil stocks making investors nervous during this period. Second, the stock price of one major Mexican producer, El Águila, which

Table 6.11. *Index of Real Stock Prices,*
International Oil Companies (1921 = 100)

Year	Texas Company	Standard Oil of New Jersey	Sinclair Consolidated Oil
1912	78	82	
1913	90	71	
1914	95	79	
1915	163	106	201
1916	132	79	278
1917	56	69	108
1918	67	70	134
1919	79	71	127
1920	55	55	61
1921	100	100	100
1922	101	9	101
1923	93	38	119
1924	95	20	77
1925	90	22	73
1926	126	21	84
1927	150	23	195
1928	150	30	96

Note: Nominal stock prices deflated using U.S. Producer Price Index from Carter and U.S. Bureau of the Census, *Historical Statistics of the United States,* 1926 base year. Real values then converted to an index with base year equal to 100 in order to have consistent base year for all firms. Note that prices have been adjusted to account for stock dividends and stock splits, as reported in *Moody's Manual of Investments.*

Sources: Year end stock prices, as quoted in the *Wall Street Journal.*

faced the same institutional environment as the other companies, rose from 44 to 100 between 1915 and 1921.[107]

Beginning in 1921 we have observations for six Mexican companies. The data about the 1920s are mixed. Mexican Petroleum's index rose through the 1920s, reaching a level of 267 in 1928. Pan-American's index rose through 1926 and then dropped. Penn-Mex's index showed no clear pattern. It peaked at 224 in 1923, dropped to 89 in 1925, and then rose

---

[107] The run-up in El Águila's price coincides with the purchase of a controlling share in the company by Royal Dutch–Shell. Evidently, Shell thought that Mexican oil was an excellent investment.

again to 177 in 1927. Conversely, stock indices for Mexican Seaboard, the Mexican Investment Company, and El Águila declined in a consistent manner throughout the 1920s.[108]

In short, the analysis of stock prices indicates that, until the oil companies themselves began to lose confidence in their ability to find oil in the late 1920s, investors in Mexican firms were, on average, neither more nor less confident about the ability of these firms to produce positive profits than investors in the big international oil companies.

CONCLUSIONS

The quantitative evidence we have retrieved and analyzed indicates that the three hypotheses specified in Chapter 1 regarding the impact of instability on growth do not hold in regard to the oil industry. First, instability did not cause output and investment to decline. Mexico produced more oil under instability than under stability. Second, output and investment did not grow more slowly because of instability. Output and investment grew fastest when the polity was the most unstable. Third, the evidence indicates that Mexico did not continue to grow on trend after 1921. But this does not mean that in a hypothetical, politically stable Mexico, output would have continued growing at its 1901–21 trend. The evidence is quite clear that this was not an empirically plausible counterfactual. For purely geological reasons, Mexico could not have sustained this rate of growth. With or without political instability, Mexico could not have sustained its 1921 level of output and world market share.

The implication is that Mexican oil companies perceived – correctly – that they could weather any threat to their property rights. American saber rattling, often taken by historians as evidence that the oil companies' property rights were genuinely threatened, should instead be understood as a signal by the U.S. government that it would provide third-party enforcement of American property rights. It did not indicate that the oil companies faced a credible threat from the Mexican government. The quantitative data we have amassed indicate that the firms responded accordingly.

The U.S. government could not, of course, threaten to intervene over each and every institutional change in Mexico. It could only intervene

---

[108] The series indicates a value of 189 for Mexican Seaboard in 1927, which is not consistent with the observations for 1926 and 1928. We suspect a misprint in the data source.

if property rights were completely abrogated or if tax rates reached the point at which they constituted a de facto expropriation. The oil companies were, however, able to parry most of the minor thrusts made by the Mexican government. The very fact that the Mexican government was so weak and the polity was so unstable gave the oil companies a very powerful weapon: they could withhold output in a coordinated manner and deny the Mexican government crucial tax revenues. The oil companies and the government both understood that an empty treasury and politically ambitious generals were (quite literally) a deadly combination.

Mexican political instability was not, therefore, a threat to the oil companies. Quite the opposite was the case. It was precisely because the Mexican governments of the 1910s and 1920s were so weak that they were unable to challenge the foreign oil companies effectively. Only when the Mexican government became stable in the mid-1930s and when the U.S. government signaled that it would not intervene was it possible for Mexico to abrogate the property rights of the petroleum companies. By the time that happened, however, the geologic conditions of Mexico had already undermined the industry.

7

Mining

The political instability of 1911–29 did not have a long-term impact on mining. There was a short-term decline in output during 1913–17. That downturn, however, was short-lived and was mostly caused by the interdiction of the railway system by warring factions, which made it extremely difficult to get ore and coal to smelters, or metals to the United States. In addition, during the early years of World War I, the markets for Mexico's major minerals were so depressed that, even had there not been a revolution, Mexico's mines could not have been run at a profit.

By 1918, when the railways returned to functioning and international prices recovered, Mexico's mining companies began to get back to work. They quickly resumed their pre-1911 growth path and Mexico ended the 1920s producing more copper, silver, and lead (its three most important mineral exports) than it had produced in any year before 1911. When Mexico's mining boom came to an end, it was the product not of the political instability of 1910–29 but of the Great Depression, which decimated metals prices.

Four reasons explain why the mining sector was able to weather political instability. First, the amount of technical knowledge required to run a modern mining and refining enterprise was extremely high, and Mexico's warring factions, as well as the governments of the 1920s, did not have the ability to run the mines and smelters themselves. Second, attempts to increase tax rates could be met with the threat of production cutbacks by the mining companies. In the short run, the government needed tax revenues more desperately than the companies needed income, and thus the government almost always backed down. Third, the Mexican government could not threaten to reallocate the property rights of recalcitrant miners to those who were more pliable (or those who were friends of the government). Large U.S. companies, particularly the American Smelting and Refining Company (ASARCO) overwhelmingly dominated the refining end of the industry, and ASARCO simply refused to process "stolen" ore. Fourth, American companies represented three-quarters of the capital invested in the Mexican mining and smelting industry. They could (and did) call on the U.S. government to enforce their property rights. The U.S. government could do this at very low cost, because virtually all of Mexico's industrial metals were exported to the United States. Unlike the petroleum industry, where enforcement required the U.S. Navy, the enforcement of mining companies' property rights could be done by the Customs Service, which could block the entry of "stolen" ores into the United States.

DEVELOPMENT OF THE INDUSTRY UNDER DÍAZ

Mining had been an important economic sector in Mexico since the early colonial period. At independence in 1821, it was common knowledge that Mexico possessed considerable mineral wealth. Moreover, the precise location of the major mineral-bearing areas was well known. Nevertheless, the mining industry went into severe decline in the 19th century. The exact causes of this collapse have not been systematically studied. Several issues, however, are clear. First, virtually all of the British companies that had invested in Mexican mining in the early nineteenth century failed by 1850.[1] Second, Mexico's capital markets were far too primitive to finance the kind of large-scale investment that was needed in order to exploit successfully Mexico's remaining silver ores, which tended to be of very low grade. Third, Mexico's governments, desperate to obtain the resources necessary to remain in power, appropriated most of the quasi rents generated by the existing mines. In 1868, for example, taxes on mining output were on the order of 24 to 26 percent *of revenues*. At this tax rate, existing mines would continue to operate (because they could cover their variable costs), but few would have been profitable.[2] The incentives to invest in new exploration and development would therefore have been extremely low. The government, out of short-term desperation, was killing the goose that laid the golden (and silver) eggs.

Changes in markets and technologies in the last decades of the nineteenth century changed the cost-benefit calculus of investing in Mexican mining. First, there now existed demand not just for Mexico's precious

[1] Cleland (1922), pp. 264–68.
[2] Cleland (1922), p. 269.

metals (silver and gold), but for its industrial metals as well. These included zinc, copper, lead, and antimony. Because many of these less valuable industrial minerals also existed in the same ores that held precious metals, their joint exploitation was potentially profitable. In addition, developments in refining technologies made many low-grade ores (which had not been worked in the past) profitable to mine, refine, and ship to foreign markets.

Three obstacles stood in the way of Mexico's ability to take advantage of these changes in markets and technologies. The first was the high cost of transport, particularly a problem in industrial metals production, where there was a low value-to-weight ratio of both the ore and the refined product. Mexico possessed few navigable rivers, and those that it did have were not located in the mining regions. Mexico's mines therefore had to be served by railroads, but the rail system existed in only the most primitive state. In 1877 there were only 640 kilometers of track in the entire country, of which 114 employed mules rather than steam engines as their source of motive power.[3]

Overcoming the absence of railroads required that the Díaz government subsidize foreign companies to build a railway system. Unlike the subsidy system in the United States, which took the form of land grants, or the subsidy systems in Brazil and Argentina, which took the form of profit guarantees, the Mexican subsidy system was based on monetary payments per kilometer constructed. This shifted much of the cost of constructing the railroads from foreign stockholders to Mexican taxpayers.[4] The cost of this subsidy program in the early 1880s nearly bankrupted

---

[3] Coastworth (1981), p. 35.

[4] The political economy of Mexico's railroad system has still not been fully explored by researchers. Several features of the railroads are, however, clear. First, the railroads dramatically lowered transport costs and thereby provided very large social savings to the Mexican economy (Coatsworth's upper-bound estimates are on the order of 39 percent of GDP in 1910; the lower-bound estimates are still huge, 8.1 percent of GDP in 1910). Second, the benefits of these social savings were mostly captured by shippers, not the railroads. In fact, most of the large trunk lines were perennial money losers. Mexico's railroads appear to have been built ahead of demand. Thus, freight densities were simply too low to support the high fixed costs of the industry. In addition, there is some evidence that the competing trunk lines between Mexico City and the U.S. border engaged in cut-throat competition (much as coast-to-coast trunk lines did in the United States until the formation of the Interstate Commerce Commission). The government's ability to set freight rates may have also played a role. It might have established tariffs in order to satisfy shippers (who were constituents of the government), not railway stockholders (who were foreign citizens). What is clear, however, is that in order to keep the big trunk lines from going bankrupt, the

the government and played a key role in the federal government's decision to create a semiofficial super bank that could provide it with credit (see Chapter 4).

The Díaz government essentially awarded concessions to foreign railroad companies on an ad hoc basis, but the ultimate effect was a fairly well developed railroad grid. By the turn of the century, most of the country's major cities, as well as the major mining zones, were connected to one another. Railroad track under federal concession grew from 640 kilometers in 1877, to more than 5,000 kilometers in 1883, to just over 10,000 kilometers in 1893, and to 16,000 kilometers by 1903. Circa 1910, there were 19,000 kilometers under federal concession and an additional 7,800 kilometers of feeder and commuter lines under state or municipal concessions.[5]

The second obstacle to the development of the mining industry was the lack of domestic capital markets that could finance the revival of the mines. Individual prospectors might be able to mine a particularly rich surface vein of gold or silver with only rudimentary tools. Those kinds of mines, however, were more the product of fantasy and legend than of Mexico's geology. Most of Mexico's mining sites were characterized by low-grade ores at substantial depths. Exploiting those ores required that mining companies sink deep shafts, and then continually battle the water that invaded the lower reaches of the mine. It also required that mining companies invest in smelters that could reduce the ore to metal. In short, if Mexico was going to revive its mining industry, it was going to have to do it with foreign capital.

The third obstacle was the lack of guarantees by the Díaz government to protect the property rights of foreign investors. Mining is characterized by large appropriable quasi rents. These quasi rents are generated by the fact that once a set of shafts has been drilled and blasted out of the side of a mountain, adits dug to drain the shafts, and railroads built over rough terrain to connect the mine to a reduction works or a railway trunk line, it is virtually impossible to redeploy those assets. This means that even if investors cannot recoup their sunk costs, they still have every incentive to keep producing. (The payoff from staying put and recouping variable costs plus some small fraction of sunk costs exceeds the payoff

government bought them out and operated them as a national industry as of 1908. See Kuntz Ficker (2000). Also see Kuntz Ficker and Riguzzi (1996); Kuntz Ficker (1995); Coastworth (1981); Summerhill (1997).
[5] Coastworth (1981), pp. 36, 40.

from redeploying those assets to an alternative use.) All governments have strong incentives to expropriate these quasi rents (via taxation) or divert them to politically favored groups. The existence of appropriable quasi rents meant that there was a problem of bilateral monopoly between the government and the mining companies. The Mexican government needed foreign firms to extract, refine, and market the country's mineral wealth. The mining and smelting companies needed the Mexican government to guarantee their property rights and the stream of rents produced by those property rights. For investment and production to take place under these conditions, there had to be a commitment mechanism that constrained the government from behaving opportunistically.

In order to create an implicit contract with the miners, Díaz delegated policy making to private interests. The government created a forum for miners to shape policy (the Sociedad Mexicana de Minería), essentially allowing the miners to lay down the property rights system that governed their activities. This forum was founded in 1883 by the Ministerio de Fomento (Ministry of Development) and was composed of government functionaries and private miners. It lost no time in crafting institutions beneficial to mining interests. The same year it was founded, it drafted a reform to the Constitution, which federalized the mining industry, taking away the authority that states previously had to create their own mining codes and tax systems. The following year (1884) it drafted a federal mining code, which laid down the property rights and taxation systems that would govern mining.[6]

The mining laws of Porfirian Mexico – contrary to the suggestions of the standard textbooks on Mexican history – did not award the miners fee simple ownership of the subsoil.[7] In point of fact, the Porfirian mining codes did not give the owners of the surface ownership of the subsoil, except for certain products (water, petroleum, and building materials).

---

[6] Velasco Avila, Flores Clair, et al. (1988), pp. 344–53. The constitutional reform had to be approved by Congress. The 1884 mining code, however, was put into effect by presidential decree. That is, the property rights system was not discussed or publicly debated.

[7] Many standard works in Mexican history strongly suggest that, because the 1884 mining code did not explicitly state that the subsoil was national patrimony, it somehow conveyed to the miners the impression that they had been awarded fee simple ownership of the subsoil. See, for example, Meyer, Sherman, et al. (1999), p. 431. In point of fact, the 1884 mining code explicitly stated that if a miner did not work his claim, the government could reallocate it to another miner, without compensation. By logical extension, the government was implicitly the owner of the subsoil: you cannot reallocate the usufruct rights to something you do not own.

All other wealth in the subsoil was either implicitly vested in the nation (in the 1884 and 1892 mining codes) or was explicitly vested in the nation (as spelled out in the 1909 mining code).

From the point of view of the mining companies and the Mexican federal government, this property rights system was actually superior to fee simple ownership of the subsoil by the surface owner. In a fee simple system, in which the surface owner also owns the subsoil, a landowner can appropriate most of the economic rent produced by a mine by charging the mining company a high rental rate or sales price for his land. In addition, in a fee simple system, neighboring property owners can appropriate much of the economic rent produced by the mine because they can charge high rental rates for the necessary rights of way. The mine is, in fact, worthless without these rights of way, because the miner needs to run power lines, tram- or cableways, railroads, and aqueducts to his mine. Mining output under a fee simple property rights system will therefore be lower, because the rents charged by landowners will lower the returns available to mining companies and therefore make many deposits unprofitable to work. Lower output will, in turn, decrease the tax revenues available to the government.

Mexico's mining code of 1884 therefore made the Mexican government the residual claimant on subsoil property rights (with the exceptions of water, petroleum, and building materials). This meant that miners, acting through the federal government, had the right to expropriate surface landowners in order to access the minerals beneath the surface. In the parlance of the time, they had the right of "denouncement." This right of denouncement included the right to prospect for ore, the right to mine an area, and rights of way on adjoining properties. Landowners were entitled to compensation, but the amount of compensation only had to reflect the value of the surface land and improvements thereon – not the value of the minerals underneath the surface. If the miner and the landowner could not agree on this level of compensation, the law stipulated that a federal mining agent would simply set the price.

The authors of Mexico's mining code also foresaw that state governments would have strong incentives to appropriate the quasi rents from mines in their jurisdiction. (Once asset holders had developed the mines, the states could levy high taxes that would expropriate most of the revenues.) Miners, of course, would anticipate that state governments would behave in this opportunistic fashion and would not, therefore, invest in the first place. The 1884 mining code therefore made the awarding and regulation of mining concessions a federal, not a state, affair.[8] The code also capped the amount of tax that a state could levy on a mining company at 2 percent of the gross value of production. The federal government, in addition to any assay and export taxes that it might later levy, was entitled to a surtax of 25 percent of the mining tax revenues earned by the states.[9]

The 1892 mining code made for a more advantageous property rights system for the miners. The 1884 law had specified that a mine that had been abandoned could be "denounced," the rights to the subsoil and preexisting works transferred, without compensation, to another owner. A mine could be declared abandoned if it had not been worked by at least six workers for a period of 26 weeks in the preceding year.[10] The 1892 mining code redefined abandonment as the failure to pay an annual parcel tax of 10 pesos per hectare.[11] This particular feature of the law had two important implications. First, mining claims now resembled, in many respects, a clear and secure property right: unless the miner failed to pay the parcel tax, his claim could not be reassigned.[12] Second, this feature of the law permitted companies to lay claim to vast tracts of ore-bearing lands, which they could effectively lock up simply by paying an annual tax. They no longer had to work their claims actively in order to retain their property rights.

The 1892 revisions to the mining code also established a unified federal tax code for mining.[13] In addition to the parcel tax of 10 pesos per hectare, the federal government also levied an assay tax on output (on a sliding scale, depending on the product), a special excise tax on gold and silver (equal to 3 percent of value), a coinage tax (equal to 2 percent on gold and

---

[8] These provisions did not dispense with the problem of opportunism by the federal government, but at least it created safeguards against state governments.

[9] México, Secretaría del Estado y del Despacho de Fomento (1885).

[10] México, Secretaría del Estado y del Despacho de Fomento (1885), p. 11.

[11] In order to register the parcel, an initial payment of 10 pesos per hectare was also required. México, Secretaría del Estado y del Despacho de Fomento (1893).

[12] This is not quite the same as saying that Mexico's system approximated a fee simple system of property rights. The possession of a mining claim gave the owner no rights to the surface ground. In theory, the mining claim owner held a "primary right" to the subsoil and the surface owner held a "secondary right" to the surface. The owner of the primary right had priority over the owner of the secondary right. In addition, the owner of the subsoil did not have absolute perpetual ownership. Technically, the residual claimant on the subsoil was the government. The miner had a lease on the underground, which would be automatically forfeited for failure to pay the parcel tax. *Engineering and Mining Journal,* November 15, 1902.

[13] México, Secretaría de Hacienda (1893); *Engineering and Mining Journal,* March 14, 1903.

silver), and a stamp tax on the documents necessary to transfer bullion or ore (equal to 0.6 percent of value). The law also retained both the maximum tax that could be levied by state governments at 2.0 percent of the gross value of production and the federal surtax of 25 percent. We estimate that in 1905 (before the 1905 tax reform went into effect) total federal and state taxes on mining output came to 7.7 percent of the gross value of production. The combined federal and state tax rate on gold and silver production was a good deal higher (10.4 percent), because of the special excise tax and the coinage tax on these two products.[14] We note that our estimates square with the calculations of contemporary observers, who placed the tax burden on gold and silver production at 9.5 to 11 percent of the gross value of output.[15]

In response to complaints by miners that these tax rates prevented them from profitable operation, particularly because of the declining

---

[14] We estimated these taxes in several steps. First, we estimated the value of production. For gold and silver, we took the value of output directly from *Mexican Yearbook*, 1908, p. 505. For zinc, copper, lead, and antimony, we took the volume of output figures from Bernstein (1964), pp. 128–29, and multiplied them by the average price per pound of those commodities as reported in Mexico, Secretaría de Industría, Comercio y Trabajo (1932), p. 365. To this result, we then added the 2 percent coinage tax and the 3 percent export tax on gold and silver (under the assumption that all silver and gold was coined and exported). We obtained these rates from the *Engineering and Mining Journal,* April 6, 1905, pp. 663–64. To this result, we then added the stamp tax revenues from the transfer of bullion or ores (0.6 percent) on the assumption that ore would be transferred only one time (rates from ibid.). We then computed the value of the parcel tax by multiplying the tax per hectare (as reported in ibid.) by the total number of hectares in mining claims (as reported in Bernstein 1964, pp. 28–29). In order to estimate the fees for the registration of new parcels, we took the number of active parcels in 1905, subtracted the number in 1892 (from ibid.), and then divided by the number of years between the two dates. This almost certainly underestimates new registrations for 1905, but our estimates are not sensitive to changes in the number of new claims registered, as this represented a very small percentage of total tax revenues. Finally, we computed the value of federal assay taxes by taking the rates published in México, Secretaría de Hacienda (1895). We estimated state taxes by assuming that all states taxed at the 2.0 percent rate, the maximum allowable under the law. We note that estimates of actual state tax rates for 1910–11 made by Velasco and coauthors indicate this to be a reasonable assumption. Of the 16 states they studied, 13 taxed at the maximum allowable rate (Velasco Avila, Flores Clair, et al. 1988, p. 332). We then estimated the federal surtax on state taxes by simply multiplying the state tax rate by the federal surtax rate, 25 percent. We summed all taxes, and then divided our estimates by the total value of output. In order to calculate the taxes on gold and silver mines separately, we assumed that they paid parcel registration fees and taxes in the same ratio as their value of production to the total value of mining production. All other estimates were made exactly as given here.

[15] *Engineering and Mining Journal,* April 6, 1905, pp. 663–64.

international price of silver, the federal government reformed the tax system in March 1905. The parcel tax was reduced to 3 pesos per hectare for claims exceeding 25 hectares, and 6 pesos per hectare for smaller claims; state taxes were capped at 1.5 percent of the gross value of production. The federal government eliminated the coinage tax completely, and the special excise on gold and silver was set on a sliding scale (from 1.5 to 3.5 percent) depending on the state of the metals prior to refinement.[16] We estimate that in 1907 total federal taxes on mining output, including assay fees, the parcel tax, gold and silver excise taxes, and the surtax on state taxes, came to 2.8 percent of the gross value of production. State taxes took another 1.5 percent, yielding an average tax rate across all mineral products of 4.3 percent.[17] The combined federal and state tax rate on gold and silver mines was somewhat higher (6.0 percent), because of the special excise on these two products. These estimates are in rough agreement with figures reported by gold and silver mines at the time. The Mexico Mines of El Oro, Ltd., according to its 1908–9 annual report, paid taxes worth 5.3 percent of its gross revenues.[18] The Santa Gertrudis

[16] *Engineering and Mining Journal*, January 27, 1906, p. 180; *Mexican Yearbook*, 1908, pp. 503–7.

[17] We estimated tax rates in several steps. First, we estimated the value of production. For gold and silver, we took the value of output directly from the *Mexican Yearbook*, 1908, p. 505. For zinc, copper, lead, and antimony, we took the volume of output figures from Bernstein (1964), pp. 128–29, and multiplied them by the average price per pound of those commodities as reported in Secretaría de Industria, Comercio y Trabajo (1932), p. 365. We then calculated assay tax revenues by applying the rates per kilogram reported in *Mexican Yearbook*, 1908, p. 504. To this result, we then added the stamp tax revenues on gold and silver (p. 503). We then computed the value of the parcel tax by multiplying the tax per hectare (p. 504) by the total number of hectares in mining claims (p. 507). We assumed that most mining claims were held in parcels of more than 25 hectares, and thus paid the lowest per hectare tax rate (three pesos). We make this assumption because contemporaries (and subsequent governments) noted that most claims were held by very large companies that did not actively work the entire claim. We estimated the number of new claims registered by subtracting the number of claims registered in 1905 (from Bernstein 1964, pp. 28–29) from those registered in 1907 (from the *Mexican Yearbook*, 1908, p. 507), and divided by two. To obtain the value of the registration tax, we then multiplied the result by five pesos per hectare (the registration tax rate). State tax rates were taken directly from Velasco Avila, Flores Clair, et al., (1988), p. 332. We calculated the federal surtax of 25 percent directly from information on state taxes. We summed all taxes and then divided our estimates by the total value of output. Some states levied an additional tax on refined ores that we were unable to compute. In order to calculate the taxes on gold and silver mines separately, we assumed that they paid parcel registration fees and taxes in the same ratio as their value of production to the total value of mining production. All other estimates were made exactly as given here.

[18] *Engineering and Mining Journal*, November 6, 1909, p. 911.

mine reported paying taxes worth 7 percent of its gross revenues in the same year.[19]

Mining in Porfirian Mexico was not, therefore, a low-tax industry. We have been able to estimate profit margins for five large, publicly traded gold and silver mining companies circa 1907. These firms accounted for 12.4 percent of gold and silver output in Mexico in that year. We estimate that the (weighted) average before-tax profit margin for these firms in 1907 was 49 percent and ranged from 29 percent (San Rafael y Anexas) to 59 percent (La Esperanza).[20] The weighted average, implicit tax rate was therefore 12.3 percent of profits. Had the 1905 tax reform not taken place, the implicit tax rate would have been 21.2 percent of profits.[21]

For most mines, the implicit tax on profits would have been even higher than the 12.3 percent (1907) or 21.2 percent (1905) we have estimated for these five firms. The reason is that mining taxes were assessed as specific fees or as a percentage of *revenues*. This means that the lower the profit margin of the mine, the higher the implicit profit tax. The five companies that we have looked at were almost certainly among the most profitable in the country. Our calculations indicate that unless a mine was able to earn a (before tax) double-digit profit margin, its after tax profits – *even after the 1905 tax reform* – would have been negative. These estimates match the observations of contemporaries. As the *Engineering and Mining Journal* put it: "Taxation of this type is very severe on mines, the ores of which carry only small margins of profit. Where the profit is not greater than 20 to 25 percent of the gross output, as is the case with many splendid mining properties,... a government tax of this character would take a

---

[19] *Engineering and Mining Journal*, February 5, 1910, p. 320.
[20] We calculated these profit margins from direct data on cost and revenue per ton in *Mexican Yearbook*, 1908, pp. 482–83, 485, 486, 491–92, and 1909–10, pp. 494, 498. The companies we included in this analysis were the El Oro Mining and Railway Company, Ltd., the Mexico Mines of El Oro Ltd., La Esperanza Ltd., San Rafael y Anexas, S.A., and Dolores S.A.
[21] We calculated these implicit profit tax rates in several steps. First, we calculated the total value of production of the firms from data in the *Mexican Yearbook*, 1908, pp. 482–83, 485, 486, 491–92, and 1909–10, pp. 494, 498. We then assumed that, on average, these firms paid the same percentage of their gross value of production as did the gold and silver industries as a whole in 1905 and 1907 (10.4 and 6.0 percent, respectively) in order to estimate the total state and federal tax paid by these firms. We then divided the total estimated taxes paid by the total before-tax profits of the firms, as calculated from data in their financial statements reprinted in *Mexican Yearbook*, 1908, pp. 482–83, 485, 486, 491–92, and 1909–10, pp. 494, 498.

big share of the profits; it tends inevitably to discourage that kind of mining which is based on low grade ores."[22] In short, the claim in the historical literature that the tax rate was "minimal" is without empirical foundation.[23] The mining industry in Porfirian Mexico was not like the oil industry, where virtually no taxes were collected. In mining, the Mexican government was extracting a significant share of the rents produced by the industry.[24]

The tax rate was, however, not set so high that it discouraged investment. The outcome was a mining boom that was driven by foreign direct investment.[25] Circa 1888 American miners were estimated to have invested only $20 million in Mexico. By 1897 this figure had more than trebled, to $68 million.[26] By 1911 the total capital invested in mining had grown roughly 16-fold since 1888, and now stood at $323.4 million. U.S. investment accounted for 77 percent of this figure, with British (13 percent), Mexican (5 percent), French (2 percent), and other countries (3 percent) accounting for the rest.[27]

This wave of investment was accompanied by a phenomenal increase in mining claims. In 1892, when the parcel tax was created, mining companies registered 34,999 hectares. By 1905 total mining claims covered 256,243 hectares, an eightfold increase in just 13 years.[28] Circa 1911 the

---

[22] *Engineering and Mining Journal*, March 14, 1903, p. 398.

[23] Meyers (1991), p. 342.

[24] The reason for the difference in tax treatment had to do with the fact that when foreign oil men began looking for petroleum in Mexico nobody knew whether they would find any. The Díaz government therefore granted them tax exemptions in order to encourage exploration, and these were still in effect at the time that the government fell (see Chapter 6). In mining, on the other hand, the presence of significant mineral wealth was common knowledge. Mexico had been a major mineral producer since the mid-16th century. Many of the Porfirian silver mines, in fact, were located on the sites of colonial mines that they had revived through the application of new mining and refining technologies. An 1887 law allowed Díaz to grant exemptions, if mining companies would invest at least 200,000 pesos within 5 years. Not every mining company received an exemption. Moreover, the exemptions from local, state, and federal taxes were restricted to 10 years. By the turn of the century, most of these exemptions had run out. See Cleland (1921), p. 641; Velasco Avila, Flores Clair, et al. (1988), pp. 336, 355. For an example of one such exemption, that of the Compagnie du Boleo, see *Mexican Yearbook*, 1909–10, p. 493.

[25] For a discussion of the growth of the foreign mining companies, and an analysis of the labor relations system in those firms, see Cárdenas García (1988), especially chaps. 2, 3.

[26] Bernstein (1964), p. 72.

[27] Calculated from data in Bernstein (1964), p. 75, table 4.

[28] Bernstein (1964), pp. 28–29.

total number of hectares under concession had most probably grown to an additional 75 percent, to approximately 450,000.[29]

Mexico's refining capacity grew as well, rivaling that of the United States. In 1913, of the 129 silver-lead blast furnaces in North America, 49 were in Mexico. These 49 smelters had a total annual capacity of 2,297,000 tons, which was 31 percent of total North American capacity.[30] Much the same was true in copper smelting. In 1913 there were 220 blast or reverberatory copper smelting furnaces in North America, 41 of which were in Mexico. These 41 furnaces had an annual capacity of 3.9 million tons, 14 percent of total North American capacity.[31]

This wave of investment produced a rapid rise in mining output. Between 1890 and 1911 the output of gold increased from 2,718 to 37,111 kilos, the output of silver increased from 1.07 million to 2.3 million kilos, and the output of lead increased from 30 million to 117 million kilos. The rate of growth of copper output dwarfed even these impressive leaps: copper output increased by an order of magnitude, growing from 5.6 to 56 million kilos.[32] By 1911 Mexico accounted for 32 percent of world silver production, 11 percent of world lead, and 7 percent of world copper production.

The industrial structure of the Mexican mining industry was characterized by a high degree of concentration. While there were literally hundreds of mines and mining companies spread across the republic, a small number of foreign-owned mining companies dominated the production of Mexico's most important products – silver, lead, and copper. The very largest of these mining companies had also vertically integrated into refining. Foremost among these was the Guggenheim's American Smelting and Refining Company (ASARCO). ASARCO owned or leased 10 mines

---

[29] In 1919 there were 446,549 hectares under concession. It is highly unlikely that the number of hectares under concession increased dramatically between 1911 and 1919.

[30] Canada had less than 2 percent of total North American capacity. Calculated from data in *Engineering and Mining Journal*, January 10, 1914, p. 67. Capacity for one firm, the Compañía Fundidora y Afinadora de Monterrey was not reported in the 1913 census. We therefore estimated it from 1919 data in *Engineering and Mining Journal*, January 17, 1920, p. 119, under the assumption that the firm did not increase its capacity during the period 1913–19. This assumption is supported by the fact that capacities for other firms (both in Mexico and the United States) did not vary much between 1913 and 1919. Thus, our reported total number of smelters and capacities is slightly different than that reported in the 1913 census.

[31] Calculated from data in *Engineering and Mining Journal*, January 10, 1914, p. 63.

[32] México, INEGI (1994), pp. 539, 540, 542, 544.

spread across the states of Aguascalientes and Chihuahua. The ore from these mines, some 165,000 tons per year, was smelted in ASARCO's own furnaces. In fact, ASARCO's smelting capacity was a multiple of its ore-producing capacity.[33] Most of its business came from the smelting of silver, lead, and copper ore that was produced by mining firms that did not have their own furnaces. ASARCO's 20 silver-lead furnaces and 14 copper smelters gave it control of 43 percent of Mexico's silver-lead blast furnace capacity and 27 percent of Mexico's copper smelting capacity in 1913.[34] ASARCO, in fact, had a virtual monopoly in the custom smelting business because most of its competitors' furnaces were dedicated to refining their own ores.

Even had these other firms actually been available for custom smelter work, however, the result would still have been an industry with a remarkably uncompetitive structure. In silver-lead refining there were only five major firms: ASARCO, the Compañía Metalúrgica Mexicana, the Compañía Metalúrgica de Torreón, the Compañía Minera de Peñoles, and the Compañía Fundidora y Afinadora de Monterrey. The four-firm ratio was 0.90 (the four largest firms controlled 90 percent of capacity).[35] Copper smelting was also extremely concentrated. In addition to ASARCO (and its subsidiary, the American Smelter's Security Corporation), there were only five other major firms: the Compagnie du Boleo, the Cananea Consolidated Copper Company, the Mazapil Copper Company Ltd., the Teziutlán Copper Mining and Smelting Company, and the Compañía Metalúrgica de Torreón. The four-firm ratio in copper smelting was 0.86.[36]

How did the Díaz government get foreign mining and smelting companies to invest hundreds of millions of dollars in an industry characterized by high sunk costs and, therefore, appropriable quasi rents? Ex ante, the Mexican government had every incentive to give generous concessions to firms in order to get them to invest. Ex post, however, the government had every incentive to abrogate those concessions or raise taxes – and the mining companies knew it.

---

[33] *Mexican Yearbook*, 1909–10, p. 492.
[34] Calculated from data in *Engineering and Mining Journal*, January 10, 1914, pp. 63, 67.
[35] Calculated from data in *Engineering and Mining Journal*, January 10, 1914, p. 67; Capacity for one firm, the Compañía Fundidora y Afinadora de Monterrey, was not reported in the 1913 census.
[36] Calculated from data on installed capacity of blast and reverberatory furnaces in *Engineering and Mining Journal*, January 10, 1914, p. 63.

The threat posed by the Mexican government was limited. The mining industry was characterized by specialized production knowledge. Running a modern, deep-shaft mine and its accompanying refining works required knowledge of engineering, geology, hydrology, chemistry, and metallurgy. This meant that the Mexican government could not credibly threaten to confiscate the industry, because the government could not run it.

The government also had little incentive to push taxes much higher than they already were, because the industry was growing very rapidly. That is, the marginal productivity of capital in mining was very high. Had the government raised the tax rate much further, it would have discouraged new investment because the producers that worked low-grade ores (the majority of the industry) would have become unprofitable. Thus, increases in *tax rates* might have produced increases in *tax revenues* but only over the short term. Over the medium term, increases in tax rates would have produced the same results as in the mid-nineteenth century: they would have served as a powerful disincentive to search for new sources of ore, and ultimately caused production (and tax revenues) to fall. The maximization of tax revenues probably explains why the Díaz government lowered taxes in 1905: lower tax rates produced higher output in the medium run, and therefore a larger stream of revenues than would have been possible at the earlier tax rate.

These features of the mining industry meant that the only credible threat to the property rights of mining companies came from the possibility that the government would reallocate their rights to other miners. The fact that most of the very large mining companies were foreign-owned gave the government strong incentives to carry out such a reallocation. What better way, after all, to reward domestic political supporters than to hand them mines that had been developed by foreigners?

To a limited extent – but only to a limited extent – miners mitigated this threat by transferring rents to prominent Porfirian politicians, who could punish Díaz if he changed the property rights system. One powerful Porfirian insider, Guillermo de Landa y Escandón, seems to have played a particularly crucial role. Landa y Escandón was a member of Díaz's inner circle, serving on different occasions as Mexico City's municipal president, governor of the Federal District, and senator from Chihuahua. He received seats on the boards of directors of three major mining companies: the Compañía Minera de Blanca y Anexas, the Mexican Mines of El Oro, Ltd., and the Compañía Minera de Dos Estrellas. Enrique C. Creel, former ambassador to the United States, governor of Chihuahua, and secretary of foreign affairs, also appears to have served a similar role: he sat on the board of directors of one of the largest silver mining enterprises in his state, the Batopilas Mining Company.[37] These kinds of relationships, however, do not appear to be generalized across all mining companies. In fact, the very largest companies, such as ASARCO, did not award seats on their boards to Porfirian insiders. The major trade journal of the time, the *Engineering and Mining Journal*, also does not make mention of the need to pay off Díaz's cronies.[38]

The reason for the limited use of cronies as third-party enforcers was that the miners already had two powerful mechanisms at their disposal to monitor and constrain the Díaz government. The first was a producers' association, the Mexican Chamber of Mines. The chamber had been founded after the government's 1905 decision to abandon the silver standard, and was made up of powerful domestic and foreign mine owners. Its president, José Luis Requena, was in a very good position to signal the chamber's collective decisions to the government: he was a deputy in the federal Congress. The second mechanism that the miners had was a very powerful third-party enforcer: the U.S. government. This sanction did not require the use of force. Virtually all of Mexico's industrial metal production was exported to the United States. This meant that all the U.S. government had to do to sanction Mexico was apply a retaliatory tariff, thereby killing the industry, and taking the tax revenues of the Mexican government with it. The threat of such action was very real. In point of fact, in 1907 the United States imposed a 20 percent ad valorum duty on Mexican zinc ores in order to protect U.S. domestic producers from the rapid growth of zinc mining in Mexico. The tariff effectively killed the Mexican zinc mining industry until World War I.[39]

The need for these monitoring and enforcement mechanisms was very real indeed. In fact, from 1907 to 1909, the Díaz government and the foreign miners faced off over an attempt by the government to reform the

[37] *Mexican Yearbook*, 1909–10, pp. 493, 496; 1912, pp. 156, 157, 163.
[38] Fear of the Díaz government does not explain their silence on this matter. The *Engineering and Mining Journal* was openly critical about the fact that the Compañía Nacional Mexicana de Dinamita y Explosivos (the dynamite monopoly) was earning monopoly rents from its special concession and made no secret of the fact that these rents were shared with government officials. See *Engineering and Mining Journal*, April 9, 1905, p. 475; December 17, 1903, p. 918; March 23, 1905, p. 575; December 9, 1905, pp. 1074, 1077–78.
[39] *Engineering and Mining Journal*, January 5, 1907; March 13 and October 2, 1909. Zinc output figures (see Table 7.1) indicate that in 1911 zinc output was only 7 percent of its 1907 level.

property rights system. The first draft of the proposed law, written by a committee that had been appointed by Development Minister Olegario Molina, was made public in February 1907. Molina worked on it for another year, during which time Díaz secured permission from Congress to enact the law by decree (without congressional approval). The revised draft, presented in 1908 by Molina, contained many of the same provisions as did the 1892 mining code but also contained several dramatic changes to earlier laws. In the new law, foreign individuals would be prohibited from acquiring mining properties in the northern border states, and foreign *companies* would be prohibited from acquiring mining properties *anywhere* in the Mexican republic. Not even Díaz, according to the draft of the law, could authorize foreign companies to operate in Mexico, although he was authorized to grant exemptions to foreign individuals in border states.[40] The law essentially said that there could be virtually no new foreign investment in Mexican mining because the vast majority of industrial metal production took place in the border states, and because all mining investment was from companies (not individual sole proprietors). The only way around the law would be for foreign companies to incorporate in Mexico.

What motivated the Díaz government is not entirely clear. One view often expressed in the literature is that Molina and other committee members were economic nationalists.[41] American ownership of three-quarters of the mining industry constituted a potential loss of sovereignty that needed to be checked. This view is a bit hard to buy on a number of grounds. In the first place, Olegario Molina, who appointed the original committee and then redrafted the law, was not only the minister of development; he was also the governor of the state of Yucatán and one of the richest men in that state. His immense wealth was a function, in fact, of his partnership with the International Harvester Company (IHC) to create a monopsony in the henequen market – the express purpose of which was to hold down the prices received by Yucatecan planters, for the joint benefit of Molina and the IHC.[42] It is difficult to reconcile a view

---

[40] *Mexican Year Book,* 1908, pp. 510–11; *Engineering and Mining Journal,* June 13, 1908, pp. 1210, 1214.

[41] See, for example, Bernstein (1964), p. 78.

[42] The basic deal between Molina and IHC was that Molina served as IHC's intermediary in the Yucatán. IHC provided capital to Molina so that his export house could make loans to the capital-starved planters. In return, the planters signed contracts with Molina stipulating that they would sell his firm all of their output. Molina y Compañía, as part of its contract with IHC, agreed to "use every effort within their

of Molina as a resolute economic nationalist when it came to mining and a partisan of foreign direct investment when it came to agriculture. Second, laying responsibility for the draft version of the law at the feet of Molina and his committee would require a very naive view of the way that the Mexican political system functioned during the latter years of the Porfiriato. There was an entire year between the initial committee report and Molina's presentation of the law to Díaz, during which time Díaz had obtained permission from Congress to pass the bill by decree. It stretches the imagination to believe that during this time Molina did not confer with Díaz about the specific features of the law, especially those that were almost certain to arouse the intense interest of some of the richest men in the United States.

A more plausible explanation for the government's attempt to redefine property rights is that the new law would have forced American companies to incorporate in Mexico *as Mexican companies*. This would have made it difficult for them to use the U.S. government as the enforcer of their property rights. By necessity, it would force the companies to seek third-party enforcement from domestic political interests, forcing them to share rents with domestic political elites.

Regardless of the motivation of the government, it met with stiff opposition. The exact details of the negotiations among the Mexican Chamber of Mines, the Díaz government, and the U.S. government are not available. Doubtless, much of it took place in smoke-filled rooms. We do know, however, that the Mexican Chamber of Mines protested vigorously against the proposed law and even sent a delegation directly to meet with Treasury Secretary Limantour.[43] We also know that once he began to meet resistance, Díaz began to backpedal. Díaz had the authority to enact the law by decree, but he chose not to do so. Instead, he called a meeting of the cabinet on June 25, 1908, to discuss the law and the opposition to it.[44] After meeting with his cabinet, Díaz decided to drop the article of

---

power to depress the price of sisal fiber" and that it would "pay only those prices which from time to time are dictated by the International Harvester Company." The results of the alliance between IHC and Molina should not be surprising. Molina's merchant house gained a continually larger share of the expanding henequen market. Before 1902 Molina never controlled more than 35 percent of henequen exports. In 1903, one year after it affiliated with IHC, Molina's market share jumped to 46 percent – and then continued growing. By 1913 Molina controlled 74 percent of henequen exports. Wells (1985), pp. 48, 51, 72–75.

[43] That delegation included Federal Deputy José Luis Requena and Senator Ramón Alcazár. *Engineering and Mining Journal*, June 20, 1908, p. 1267; October 23, 1909.

[44] *Engineering and Mining Journal*, August 1, 1908, p. 252.

the proposed law that made it unlawful for foreign companies to acquire mines in Mexico.[45] The revised law also relaxed the provisions of the law that conditioned the circumstances under which foreign individuals could acquire property in frontier states.[46]

We also know that Diaz then decided not to enact the revised bill by decree, but instead had it move through both houses of Congress.[47] Díaz then delayed the law's passage through Congress so that he could travel to El Paso, Texas, to meet with U.S. president Taft.[48] The bill was not finally approved by the Senate until November 20, 1909, and did not go into effect until January 1, 1910, nearly three years after it was initially drafted and without the clauses that had limited the activities of foreigners. The only restriction that remained in the bill was the 80-kilometer exclusion zone along the border, in which foreign companies could not hold mining titles. Foreign individuals could hold titles in this zone, with the permission of the president. This restriction, however, had long been a provision of Mexican mining law, going all the way back to 1856.[49] Finally, we know that Díaz granted these exemptions. The Mining Law of 1909 specified that *existing foreign claims* in the exclusion zone that did not obtain special presidential permission would be auctioned off.[50] None were – the implication being that Díaz granted whatever special permits were required. In short, the evidence strongly indicates that the foreign miners were able to force Díaz to beat a strategic retreat.

THE REVOLUTION

The very same features of the industry that limited Díaz's ability to re- form the property rights system also prevented revolutionary factions and postrevolutionary governments from doing so either. Governments, and

---

[45] *Engineering and Mining Journal*, October 24, 1908, p. 833.
[46] The revised law only restricted their activities to an 80-kilometer strip along the border. Individual miners could obtain concessions within this strip but only after receiving the approval of the president. Foreign companies could not hold mines in this area, even with presidential permission. This was, in fact, a continuation of previous restrictions that dated back to 1856. *Engineering and Mining Journal*, November 21, 1908, p. 1025.
[47] Bernstein (1964), pp. 79–80.
[48] *Engineering and Mining Journal*, October 23, 1909.
[49] *Mexican Yearbook*, 1909–10, pp. 520–21; *Engineering and Mining Journal*, June 13, 1908, p. 1214.
[50] *Mexican Yearbook*, 1909–10, pp. 520–21; *Engineering and Mining Journal*, February 19, 1910, pp. 416–19.

factions that aspired to be governments, had strong incentives to raise taxes or threaten the property rights of the miners. They were blocked, however, by the fact that they were incapable of running the industry themselves. Even if they could have run a mine, they would have had no way to refine the ore without the assistance of the owners or senior managers of the smelting firms. This meant that the government could not increase tax rates. Miners could simply shut down their operations until tax rates were reduced to their former levels. The government could (and did) threaten to confiscate the mines and smelters if they were not operated, but the miners could simply ignore those threats.

The overthrow of Díaz by Madero and the overthrow of Madero by Huerta caused only the smallest perturbations in the mining industry. Rail service was interrupted, which caused shortages of fuel and ore at smelting plants. There were also robberies of paymasters or company offices. To the degree that this curtailed mining operations, the impact was predominantly felt at small, isolated gold or silver mining camps; larger operations tended not to be disturbed. For the most part, Mexico's mines and smelters worked without interference.[51] As Table 7.1 shows, Mexico's output of lead and copper in 1910, 1911, and 1912 was higher than the average for the decade 1900–9. Its output of silver in 1910–12 actually set an all-time production record.

Once the fight against Huerta began, and once the victors of that fight turned to fighting among themselves, the incentives of governments and factions changed. They needed revenues, and they needed them badly. They therefore tried to treat the mines the way they treated cattle ranches, beer breweries, or banks. The quickly found out that they could not do so.

The first Mexican politician to learn this lesson was Victoriano Huerta, who attempted to extort funds for his government from foreign miners in Durango, under pain of death. The American miners responded by shutting down their mines and leaving the state en masse.[52]

The Villistas, who controlled most of Mexico's major mining regions from 1913 to 1915, learned a similar lesson – again and again. As

[51] Meyers (1991), p. 346; *Engineering and Mining Journal*, January 28, 1911, p. 243; March 11, 1911, p. 536; March 18, 1911, p. 584; April 1, 1911, p. 680; April 8, 1911, p. 731; April 15, 1911, p. 780; May 20, 1911, p. 1033; June 10, 1911, p. 175; October 7, 1911, pp. 685–90; January 6, 1912, pp. 77–79; November 30, 1912, pp. 1017–18; January 11, 1913, pp. 136–39; November 2, 1912, p. 832; March 15, 1913, p. 582; December 7, 1912, p. 1096.
[52] *Engineering and Mining Journal*, October 18, 1913, p. 763.

Table 7.1. *Mexico's Major Mining Products*

| Year | Index of | | | | |
	Gold	Silver	Copper	Lead	Zinc
1900	31	73	47	51	60
1901	35	74	70	76	49
1902	36	79	75	86	38
1903	39	84	96	81	55
1904	46	82	107	76	44
1905	59	78	136	81	109
1906	66	75	128	59	1,231
1907	70	81	119	61	1,266
1908	77	92	79	102	854
1909	83	92	119	95	164
1910	100	100	100	100	100
1911	90	104	116	94	87
1912	78	105	119	85	69
1913	62	91	109	55	52
1914	21	35	55	5	43
1915	18	51	43	16	317
1916	28	38	59	16	2,043
1917	57	54	106	52	2,465
1918	61	80	146	80	1,129
1919	57	85	109	57	631
1920	55	86	102	66	854
1921	51	83	32	49	69
1922	56	104	56	89	335
1923	58	117	111	123	1,008
1924	60	118	102	133	1,345
1925	59	120	107	144	2,826
1926	58	126	112	170	5,749
1927	54	135	122	196	7,514
1928	52	140	135	190	8,824
1929	49	140	167	200	9,495
1930	50	135	152	194	7,796
1900–10	58	83	98	79	361
1911–20	53	73	96	53	769
1921–30	55	122	110	149	4,496

Notes: Indices of volume of output (1910 = 100).

Absolute values for 1910 are as follows: gold, 41,420 kilograms; silver, 2,417 metric tons; copper, 48,160 metric tons; lead, 124,292 metric tons; zinc, 1,833 metric tons. Other absolute volumes can be recalculated by multiplying the index by the 1910 volume and dividing by 100.

Source: Bernstein (1964), pp. 128–29.

William Meyers has shown, Villa at first tried to form a coalition with the mine owners. His initial strategy was to improve conditions for mine owners so that they could produce revenues that he could tax – much in the same way that Díaz had. No company benefited more from this than ASARCO. As one ASARCO official put it: "We are on the most friendly terms with Villa and his men. . . . On several occasions they have gone out of their way to extend assistance to our company."[53] This explains why, in the early years of the revolution, U.S. mining interests actually urged the Wilson administration to support Villa and why some of the mining companies covertly provided financial support to Villa.[54]

Try as he might, Villa could not jump-start the mining industry. The fundamental problem was the lack of railway transport. Mexico was in the midst of a modern war, and that meant that troops and equipment had to be moved on the railroads. Railroads thus became strategic targets for demolition.[55] The result was that from 1913 until 1917 the railways were in ruin.[56] Miners could not get ore to the smelters. Even when they succeeded, the smelters could not obtain coal to fire the furnaces. The result was that many mines and smelters sat idle for months at a time. This is not to say that they completely ceased operations. Reports by contemporary observers indicate that mining and smelting companies continued to work their properties throughout 1913–17, although they did so on an intermittent or extremely curtailed basis.[57] Bernstein's data on the output of Mexico's major mineral products reflect this. By 1914 (when production of most metals was at its lowest point), the output of most products was significantly below their 1910 volume: copper dropped 45 percent, silver 65 percent, gold 79 percent, and lead 95 percent (see Table 7.1).

Mexico's unstable polity was not, however, the only problem faced by miners. Even had there not been a revolution in Mexico, the industry would have been hammered by the sharp decline in demand for copper and lead that was caused by the onset of World War I. The price of copper,

---

[53] Meyers (1991), p. 346.

[54] Meyers (1991), p. 347.

[55] *Engineering and Mining Journal*, February 15, 1913, p. 394; November 15, 1913, p. 916.

[56] *Engineering and Mining Journal*, January 8, 1916, p. 95.

[57] *Engineering and Mining Journal*, January 10, 1914, pp. 137–39; May 2, 1914, p. 928; January 9, 1915, pp. 122–23; January 8, 1916, pp. 116–18; June 24, 1916, p. 1123; January 6, 1917, pp. 76–78; Cleland (1922), p. 277; Cárdenas García (1998), p. 94.

Table 7.2. *Prices of Mexico's Major Mineral Products, 1900–1929*

Year	Copper (cents/lb)	Lead (cents/lb)	Zinc (cents/lb)	Silver (cents/oz)
1900	16.2	4.4		61.3
1901	16.1	4.3		58.9
1902	11.6	4.1		52.2
1903	13.2	4.2	5.2	53.6
1904	12.8	4.3	4.9	57.2
1905	15.6	4.7	5.7	60.4
1906	19.3	5.7	6.0	66.8
1907	20.0	5.3	5.8	65.3
1908	13.2	4.2	4.6	52.9
1909	13.0	4.3	5.4	51.5
1910	12.7	4.4	5.4	53.5
1911	12.4	4.4	5.6	53.3
1912	16.3	4.5	6.8	60.8
1913	15.3	4.4	5.5	59.8
1914	13.6	3.9	5.1	54.8
1915	17.3	4.7	13.1	49.7
1916	27.2	6.9	12.6	65.7
1917	27.2	8.8	8.7	81.4
1918	24.6	7.4	7.9	96.8
1919	18.7	5.8	7.0	111.0
1920	17.5	8.0	7.7	100.9
1921	12.5	4.5	4.7	62.7
1922	13.4	5.7	5.7	67.5
1923	14.4	7.3	6.6	64.9
1924	13.0	8.1	6.3	66.8
1925	14.0	9.0	7.6	69.1
1926	13.8	8.4	7.3	62.1
1927	12.9	6.8	6.2	56.4
1928	14.6	6.3	6.0	58.2
1929	18.1	6.8	6.5	53.0

Source: México, Secretaría de Industria, Comercio y Trabajo (1932), p. 3, 64–65.

which had been at 16.3 ¢ (U.S.) per pound in 1912, fell to 15.3 ¢ in 1913, and to 13.6 ¢ in 1914. Lead prices moved in a similar direction, from 4.5 ¢ per pound in 1912 to 3.9 ¢ in 1914 (see Table 7.2). It was simply uneconomical to mine and smelt ore at this price, even had there been adequate rail transport.

Some Villista officials believed that the mining companies could be forced to resume production, even in the face of low international prices and the absence of railway transport. In May 1914, for example, Tomás Urbina, the Villista governor of Durango, ordered foreign mining companies to resume work or face confiscation. Other local and state leaders seized a number of Mexican-owned mines.[58] Two months later (July 1914) General Fidel Avila, governor general of Chihuahua and Silvestre Terrazas, Villa's secretary of state, issued a decree giving companies one month to renew "mining, industrial, and other operations which might have been closed by war" and threatened confiscation "if they persist in the continued closure of their operations."[59]

This strategy was doomed from the start. First, mine owners had a set of scarce skills – and they knew it. This meant that the Villistas could confiscate whatever ore had been mined but not yet shipped. They could not, however, run the mines in any serious way. Second, this ore was valueless to the Villistas because they had no way to smelt or chemically refine it. Virtually all of the smelting capacity in Villista Mexico was in the hands of ASARCO, and ASARCO simply refused to buy or smelt ore believed to have come from a confiscated mine.[60] Third, any attempt to confiscate an ASARCO smelter would have failed, because the Villistas could no more run a smelter than they could a mine. In fact, the Villistas tried on one occasion to fire up one of ASARCO's smelters but quickly realized that they lacked the knowledge to actually do so.[61] Finally, any attempt to ship unsmelted ore to the United States for smelting would have been blocked by the U.S. government, which worked with the mine owners to establish special offices to warn customs officials when "stolen" ore reached the border.[62] In short, ASARCO and the Customs Service could effectively enforce the property rights of miners.

The result was that Villa renewed his strategy of conciliation with the miners in late 1914 and on that basis was able to get some mines and smelters back into production in 1915. In fact, as Meyers has shown, Villa abandoned any redistributive goals he had regarding higher wages and better working conditions for miners and instead worked with the Miners and Smelters Owner's Association (MSOA) to get the mines back into production. The MSOA, founded in February 1915 by the largest

---

[58] Meyers (1991), p. 349.

[59] Meyers (1991), pp. 350–51.

[60] Meyers (1991), p. 350.

[61] This experiment took place in September 1915, when the Villistas were losing the war against Obregón and were desperate for any source of revenue. Meyers (1991), p. 358; *Engineering and Mining Journal*, January 8, 1916, p. 116.

[62] Meyers (1991), p. 351.

mining companies in Mexico, immediately set to work with the Villistas to hammer out a set of policies regarding taxation, labor rights, and the currency exchange rate. The Villistas were highly conciliatory on the labor issue (they did not try to reform the Porfirian labor system to any significant degree), the exchange rate (it would be determined by the market, not decreed by Villa), and the tax rate (it was the same as under Díaz). The only concession that Villa extracted from the MSOA was that American mine owners agreed to pay a onetime, extraordinary war tax of 5 percent of revenues. Even this extraordinary tax was later reduced by Villa, who declared (under pressure from the U.S. State Department) that it would not be collected "where impracticable."[63]

Villa's conciliatory stance vis-à-vis the MSOA did not mean that he no longer tried to behave opportunistically. Villa simply could not find a way around the fact that running a smelter is not like running a cattle ranch, that any ore he confiscated from mines was worthless because he could neither run a smelter nor export the ore to the United States, and that the MSOA could send a cable to the State Department at close to the speed of light. Thus, in mid-March 1915, losing the war and desperate for revenue, Villa decreed that mines that were not being worked would be subject to forfeiture. The MSOA and the State Department swung into action, and Villa backed down.[64] In July 1915 Villa needed funds to purchase a shipment of 250,000 cartridges that awaited him in El Paso. Lacking the cash, his finance secretary demanded a loan of $300,000 dollars from the MSOA representative in Chihuahua. The miners refused. Villa responded by decreeing that all mining companies in Chihuahua had to resume operations at once and turn over their ore to his administration. The MSOA, predictably, cabled the State Department, which dispatched General Hugh Scott to see Villa. We do not know what Scott told Villa. We do know, however, that Villa dropped all of his demands in exchange for 1,000 tons of coal.[65]

The high drama of Villa's attempts to increase taxes under threat of confiscation was replicated under Carranza. The first of Carranza's tax decrees came on March 1, 1915. Carranza, desperate for funds to fight the Villistas and Zapatistas, doubled the parcel tax on small properties and increased the parcel tax on large properties eightfold (the exact rate depending on the size of the mining claim). This increase in the parcel tax

[63] Meyers (1991), pp. 355–56.
[64] *Engineering and Mining Journal*, April 10, 1915, pp. 668–69; Meyers (1991), p. 356.
[65] Meyers (1991), pp. 357–58.

was accompanied by an export tax equal to 6.5 percent on bullion and 8.5 percent on ore. On April 16, 1916, Carranza revised these taxes. He slightly lowered the rate on the parcel tax (on a sliding scale, depending on the number of hectares in a claim), and lowered the export tax on industrial metals to 5 percent. He simultaneously raised the export tax on gold and silver to 10 percent. Moreover, he increased the tax that states could charge from 1.5 percent to 2.0 percent of revenues, and he raised the federal surtax from 25 percent to 60 percent.[66] The Buena Tierra Mining Company calculated that the combined effect of these taxes was to raise the total tax rate fourfold since 1912.[67]

These tax increases, however, generated little revenue for Carranza, because the mining companies were shutting down their operations all over the areas under his control and were evacuating as many of their employees from Mexico as they could. Some firms continued working on a very limited basis with their Mexican employees only. In the latter case, they ceased all work that could not be done without the supervision of the American engineers.[68]

Carranza followed the same predictable course as Villa. First, he attempted to be conciliatory toward the mining companies, appealing to them, as the *Engineering and Mining Journal* put it, "to please come back and reopen their mines and metallurgical works."[69] When that failed, he again followed Villa's lead and threatened the miners with expropriation if they did not reopen. Carranza decreed on September 14, 1916, that idle mining properties would become subject to operation by the government or would be thrown open for denouncement by third parties.[70]

---

[66] Under Díaz and Madero, the parcel tax had been 3 pesos per hectare for claims exceeding 25 hectares and 6 pesos for smaller claims. Under the new decree, the parcel tax was 18 pesos per hectare for properties of 21 to 50 hectares and 24 pesos per hectare for properties above 50 hectares. Thus, the rate was 6 to 8 times its Porfirian level. Even small properties were hit with a tax increase: parcels of 10 hectares or less paid 12 pesos per hectare (double the earlier level) and parcels of 11 to 20 hectares paid 15 pesos per hectare (2.5 times the earlier level). *Engineering and Mining Journal*, May 6, 1916, p. 827; Cleland (1922), pp. 277–78.

[67] *Engineering and Mining Journal*, November 3, 1917, p. 810.

[68] *Engineering and Mining Journal*, January 8, 1916, p. 95; June 24, 1916, p. 1123; September 16, 1916, p. 529.

[69] *Engineering and Mining Journal*, July 15, 1916, p. 151.

[70] The decree specified that any mine that had been idle for two consecutive months, or that was idle at various times for a total of three months in one year, could be denounced or confiscated and worked by the government. *Engineering and Mining Journal*, October 14, 1916, p. 729; March 3, 1923, p. 403; Bernstein (1964), pp. 112–13.

The mining companies appealed to the State Department, and the State Department immediately protested. It also advised miners to file statements explaining why their mines were closed. Carranza responded, on November 14, 1916, by giving the miners an extension until February 14, 1917, to resume work. The fact that Carranza had to make the threat twice (September 14, 1916, and again on November 14, 1916), and that he gave the companies until February 1917 to comply, indicates that he himself knew that he could not actually expropriate the mines. The government could not operate the mines, and the mine owners knew it.[71]

Not surprisingly, Carranza beat a strategic retreat: he did not rescind the law, but he did not enforce it either. The reports about conditions in Mexico by the *Engineering and Mining Journal*, which tended to portray Carranza in the most negative light imaginable, do not mention a single case of confiscation under this law.[72] The extension that Carranza granted, in fact, made the whole issue moot, because by early 1917 many of the major mining companies were back at work, earning tremendous profits from astronomically high metals prices.[73] By 1917 prices of copper, lead, and silver were double what they had been just four years earlier, and now stood at record levels (see Table 7.2). Carranza therefore quietly

---

[71] Later events provide us with two natural experiments to test the proposition that the Carrancistas could not actually run a mine profitably. The first occurred in early 1917 when the managers of the Chispas mine in Arizpe, Sonora, refused orders from the government to raise wages, employ more men, and increase production. Carranza's government jailed the manager and seized the mine. The government soon found, however, that without the foreign managers it could not run the mine at a profit and had to close down the operation entirely. The government also found out that it could not effectively imprison the mine's manager, who escaped from jail and fled to Arizona. The second experiment occurred later that same year, in the state of Coahuila, when, as a result of a labor dispute, the federal government decided to take over the state's coal mines and work them on its own account. The government quickly found out, however, that it could not unwater the mines and restart production – unless it had the cooperation of the mining companies' skilled staff, which was not forthcoming. The government therefore dropped its plans to confiscate the mines. *Engineering and Mining Journal*, May 19, 1917, p. 909; November 27, 1920, p. 1056.

[72] See, for example, *Engineering and Mining Journal*, January 11, 1919, pp. 112–13; Bernstein reaches a similar conclusion: "It appears that no property was declared forfeit under the law of 9/16/1916." Bernstein (1964), p. 114.

[73] There continued to be interruptions of output, particularly in the state of Chihuahua, because of the ongoing guerrilla war against Villa and because of the perceived danger to Americans that had been caused by Pershing's punitive expedition against Villa, but for the most part operations began to return to normal by the middle of 1917. *Engineering and Mining Journal*, November 24, 1917, p. 940; Bernstein (1964), pp. 113–14.

retreated. In March 1917 he once again demanded that firms that had not already done so restart production. He dropped, however, any mention of confiscation. Instead, his decree simply stated that the government would enforce its demand by "the means which may be judged convenient."[74]

INSTITUTIONAL REFORM

The specific features of the mining industry and the credible threat of third-party enforcement by the United States meant that the reform of property rights in the Constitution of 1917 was a dead letter. On paper, Article 27 of the Constitution severely reduced the property rights of the foreign companies that dominated the mining industry. It followed the mining code of 1909 by stating that the ownership of all minerals in the subsoil belonged to the federal government. It departed from Porfirian legislation, however, in three crucial respects. First, Article 27 reiterated Carranza's earlier decrees by stating that miners had to work their claims in order to maintain their usufruct property rights. It was the case, of course, that most companies only worked a small portion of their claims and had done so since Porfirian times. Article 27 therefore implied that they could be expropriated. Second, Article 27 stated that only Mexican citizens and Mexican companies had the right to acquire concessions to develop mines. It went on to say that the government might grant this right to foreigners, provided that they agreed to be considered Mexican in respect to such property and therefore not to invoke the protection of their governments. Third, Article 27 stated that all contracts and concessions made by former governments since 1876 that resulted in the monopoly of lands, waters, and natural resources of the nation were subject to revision. The president was authorized to declare such contracts and concessions null and void.[75]

The Mexican government could not, however, actually enforce any of these de jure changes in property rights, and the miners knew it. How little an impact Article 27 actually had is revealed by the subsequent actions of Mexico's governments from 1917 to 1929. In fact, Carranza, Obregón, and Calles *lowered* taxes. The process of downward revision in tax rates began less than one year after the constitution went into effect. In April 1918, facing a mining industry that was still not running at full capacity,

---

[74] Bernstein (1964), p. 114.
[75] Bernstein (1964), appendix 1, p. 288; *Engineering and Mining Journal*, March 3, 1923, pp. 401–3.

Carranza dramatically reduced just about every specific and ad valorum tax that he had declared just two years earlier. In June 1919 he lowered taxes yet again. Obregón drove down tax rates even further and, in fact, even invited the miners to help draft the tax code. As we shall see in the next section, tax rates declined monotonically throughout the 1920s. By 1923 the tax rate was lower than it had been before Díaz's 1905 reform of the tax code – and it continued dropping. By 1929 it approximated the rate charged by Díaz circa 1907.

In addition, none of the post-1917 governments was able to collect millions of pesos in back taxes that they were owed – despite the fact that even under Porfirian law these properties could have been legally confiscated. Many mines sat idle during the revolution. Indeed, many of them were located in areas outside of Carranza's control and had paid taxes to opposing factions, or had taken advantage of the disarray caused by the 1910–20 conflict to stop paying taxes at all. The result was that many mining properties were seriously in arrears on their parcel tax payments.[76]

The back tax issue was raised as early as Carranza's March 1, 1915, mining decree, which specified that the government would grant the miners who were in arrears on the parcel tax a grace period until June 30, 1915, to pay their debts. On June 19, 1915, Carranza staged his first retreat on the back-tax issue, declaring the legality of tax payments that had been made to other revolutionary factions.[77] On August 31, he retreated again, giving miners until September 30, 1915, to pay taxes on properties that were unworkable. It was not, however, possible for the government to enforce these decrees, and thus virtually no property was actually confiscated. Carranza admitted as much on March 31, 1917, when he decreed that back taxes would henceforth simply accumulate.[78] On June 27, 1919, Carranza issued a mining tax law and once again addressed the issue of back taxes, granting a period of three months for mine owners to *begin* paying taxes that were in arrears (payment of the taxes could be made in installments over a period of years).[79] Some of Mexico's miners took advantage of these various decrees to pay their back taxes and protect their

---

[76] Technically, mining property taxes that were in default were subject to a 50 percent fine after one month, a 100 percent fine after two months, and were forfeited after the third month. At this point, they could be denounced by a third party, who would receive title granting him the right to work the property. *Engineering and Mining Journal*, October 14, 1916, p. 729.

[77] *Engineering and Mining Journal*, September 10, 1921, p. 407.

[78] *Engineering and Mining Journal*, September 10, 1921, pp. 406–7.

[79] *Engineering and Mining Journal*, August 2, 1919, p. 186.

titles. Many others, however, took advantage of the fact that the government's tax records were in complete disorder and simply declined to pay. In fact, in many parts of the country mining records had been destroyed and the mining offices had no way of actually checking on ownership except where the owners voluntarily presented their tax payments. Not surprisingly, as late as October 1920, three-quarters of Mexico's miners had "not paid taxes in years."[80] The interim government of Adolfo de la Huerta (May–November 1920) rescinded all previous decrees confiscating properties for failure to pay back taxes and permitted owners (once again!) to pay those back taxes in easy installments.[81]

In 1922 the Obregón government, desperate to receive whatever tax revenues it could, gave up on collecting back taxes from the revolutionary period. It decreed that all back taxes on mining properties would be canceled if miners would pay, before September 1, 1922, the full amount of parcel taxes due for the previous 20 months – the clear implication being that the taxes due for all of 1921 and the first three months of 1922 had also not been made.[82] Even this amnesty was not enough to get companies to pay their taxes. On June 13, 1923, Obregón retreated even further. He decreed that all pending arrears from 1910 through the first trimester of 1923 would be canceled if mine owners would pay the *current mine parcel tax* (for the second third of the year 1923), plus a 25 percent surcharge.[83] That is to say, the government was willing to give up all claims on more than a decade of back taxes in exchange for five months of tax revenue.

Many mining companies rejected even this offer and continued to ignore the laws that required them to pay a parcel tax because the government's hand was so weak. Thus, in April 1924 the Calles government decreed that it would annul payment of back taxes prior to 1920 and would permit payment of the taxes for 1921, 1922, and 1923 in special "Employee Bonds" (which could be bought at a steep discount), provided that taxes for 1924 and 1925 were paid in cash. The clear implication was that parcel tax payments for many companies were not only in arrears for 1911–20, they were also in arrears for 1921–23.[84]

---

[80] *Engineering and Mining Journal*, August 7, 1920, p. 280.
[81] *Engineering and Mining Journal*, August 7, 1920, p. 280; *Engineering and Mining Journal*, September 4, 1920, p. 441.
[82] Tax payments were supposed to be made in three yearly installments, each one covering four months of the year. *Engineering and Mining Journal*, March 18, 1922, p. 462.
[83] *Engineering and Mining Journal*, September 15, 1923, p. 451.
[84] *Engineering and Mining Journal*, April 4, 1926, p. 577.

A final indication of the government's weakness vis-à-vis the mining companies was that neither Carranza nor Obregón promulgated enabling legislation to Article 27. The reform of mining property rights embodied in the Constitution of 1917 was therefore nothing more than a wish list; it had no practical application in law. It was not until 1926 that enabling legislation was actually promulgated.

Had it actually applied to the mining companies that were operating in Mexico, the 1926 mining law would have dramatically reduced the property rights of the foreign mining companies in Mexico. First, it stated that, instead of being perpetual, mining concessions had a duration of 30 years. Second, the law established that mining claims had to be continually worked. This requirement could be met by producing a specified amount of ore per hectare of surface covered by a claim (the exact output depending on the product being mined, the distance of the claim from a railroad, and the size of the claim). It was now no longer sufficient, as it was under Porfirian law, for a mining company simply to pay a parcel tax in order to maintain its claim. Third, the law required that 90 percent of mining engineers be of Mexican birth.[85] Fourth, the law stated that refining companies could not dismantle their works without government permission. Fifth, the law stated that foreigners could not obtain concessions in a "forbidden zone" 100 kilometers wide along the border and within 50 kilometers of the coast. Finally, the law limited the ability of foreigners to appeal to their home governments in property rights disputes with the Mexican government. Foreigners and foreign companies could only obtain concessions in Mexico if they formally renounced all protection of their own governments in respect to their holdings in Mexico.[86]

Calles already knew that he could not actually enforce the 1926 mining law, even before the final draft was completed. Indeed, the National Mining Chamber (Cámara Nacional de Minería) and the U.S. State Department wasted no time in signaling their displeasure at the early drafts.[87] Calles knew that when push came to shove, the mining companies would

---

[85] The intent of the law was obvious. Unless there was a trained cadre of Mexican mining engineers, who could actually run the mines and refining works, it would not be possible to threaten foreign companies with confiscation. The government had learned this lesson throughout the 1910s and early 1920s, and wished to deny foreign companies the ability to resist future tax increases and institutional reforms by shutting down production.

[86] *Engineering and Mining Journal*, October 31, 1925, p. 683; March 19, 1927, pp. 486–87.

[87] Sariego, Reygadas, et al. (1988), p. 70.

cite Article 14 of the Constitution, which stated that laws could not be retroactive. He also knew that in a showdown they would curtail production and deprive him of the tax revenues he desperately needed to fight the Cristeros and to maintain the loyalty of the army. Calles therefore did what any rational politician would have done under the circumstances: first, he obtained from Congress the right to promulgate the law by decree (without the need for a congressional debate and vote on the specific features of the law); and, second, he then grandfathered in all of the existing mining claims under whatever set of institutional arrangements had been made before the law went into effect.[88] The property rights held by foreign mining companies were not abrogated. Foreign companies were not forced to declare that they would not seek the protection of their governments in disputes with Mexico. The clauses of the law regarding minimum levels of production and the obligation to work a claim actively were declared to be not applicable to those properties already patented. The only components of the law that were applied to existing operations were the requirements that a proportion of the engineering personnel had to be Mexican and that mining and refining operations had to obtain the permission of the government to shut down or dismantle their operations.[89] Even these clauses of the law were eventually dropped. In August 1930 the entire law was abolished.[90]

In short, in postrevolutionary Mexico the government and the mining companies quickly came to an agreement similar to the one they had reached under Díaz: the government would not interfere with the property rights of the companies and the companies would agree to pay the government a reasonable tax for the right to work their concessions. From the point of view of the mining companies, the changes in Mexico's formal institutions were, during the 1910s and 1920s, easily mitigated.

DATA ANALYSIS

Survival

One clear implication of our analysis is that the mining and smelting industry survived the years of revolutionary violence intact. Fortunately

---

[88] *Engineering and Mining Journal*, January 23, 1926, p. 180; September 25, 1926, p. 509.

[89] *Engineering and Mining Journal*, May 8, 1926, p. 777; May 14, 1927, p. 815; February 12, 1927, p. 300; January 22, 1927, p. 163; Bernstein (1964), chap. 14.

[90] Sariego, Reygadas, et al. (1988), p. 71.

Table 7.3. *The State of Mexican Mining Companies in 1922*

Category by State of Conservation	Number of Firms in Category	Number of Mining Claims	Total Hectares	Average Size of Firms (hectares)
Paralyzed	221	1,398	15,600	71
Working	153	2,178	58,868	385
In Exploration	11	44	656	60
No Information	40	49	551	14
ALL FIRMS	425	3,669	75,675	178

Source: Mexico, Secretaria de Industria, Comercio y Trabajo (1924), "pull-out pages" between pp. 132 and 133.

for us, the Mexican government was also interested in the question of survivorship – for obvious taxation reasons. It therefore carried out a census of all mining, smelting, and chemical refining operations in Mexico in 1922 and directly inquired as to the physical state of each enterprise.

The 1922 census of mines canvassed 425 mining companies, which controlled 3,669 mining claims. Of these, 221 companies (with 1,398 claims) reported themselves as paralyzed. The census does not indicate whether this paralysis was the consequence of physical destruction, low mineral prices, or the exhaustion of a mine's ores. The data are clear, however, that the paralyzed mines tended to be small operations. The average size of the paralyzed firms' claims was only 18 percent that of working mines – 71 hectares compared to 385 hectares. The result was that the total area withdrawn from production in 1922 was only 21 percent – 15,600 hectares of paralyzed claims out of a total of 75,675 hectares included in the census (see Table 7.3).

One might argue that the census of mines in 1922 captured only a small part of the industry and therefore underestimates the extent of physical damage caused by the revolution. Such an argument would turn on the fact that in 1922 there were 370,220 hectares under concession, of which the census covered only 75,675. It is not clear, however, how far one would want to push this argument. Even under Díaz, firms worked only a small portion of their total claims; and we do not know how many hectares were actually worked prior to 1911. Thus, we do not have a metric by which to determine whether the proportion of mined to total property in 1922 was different from that which prevailed before the revolution.

The evidence regarding the survivorship of refining plants allows us to cross-check the evidence on mines. Indeed, when it comes to smelting

Table 7.4. *The State of Mexico's Cyanide Refining Plants in 1922*

Category by State of Conservation	Number of Firms in Category	Total Capacity (tons/day)	Average Firm Size (tons/day)
Destroyed	7	320	46
Bad	14	1,131	81
Regular	6	1,170	195
Good	70	20,823	297
In Construction	3	350	117
No Information	12	435	36
ALL FIRMS	112	24,229	216

Source: Mexico, Secretaria de Industria, Comercio y Trabajo (1924), p. 101.

plants, we can also cross-check Mexican sources against U.S. sources. Let us first consider Mexico's cyanide refining plants. The 1922 census revealed 112 cyanide reduction works in Mexico, with a total capacity of 24,229 tons per day. Only 7 firms listed their capacity as "destroyed," and that capacity totaled only 320 tons – 1.3 percent of total capacity. Another 14 firms listed their reduction works as being in "bad condition," but these represented only an additional 1,170 tons per day (4.7 percent of capacity). Thus, an upper-bound estimate of damaged capacity would only be 6 percent. As was the case with the mines, the average size of the affected firms was quite small: firms listing their capacity as destroyed had an average size of 46 tons per day; firms listing their capacity as being in bad condition had an average size of 81 tons per day; and firms that listed their capacity as being in good condition had an average size of 297 tons per day (see Table 7.4).

The evidence regarding the limited effects of revolutionary violence is stronger still when we turn our focus to copper and lead smelting companies. The 1922 census covered 57 firms operating 125 smelters. Of these, only 2 smelters were reported as being "destroyed." These were extremely small smelters; their combined capacity of 50 tons was equal to only one-quarter of 1 percent of the industry's total capacity (19,506 tons per day). Even if we treat firms that listed their smelters as being in "bad condition" as not surviving, the highest estimate we can produce of revolutionary loss was 4.2 percent of the industry's total capacity (50 tons per day destroyed, plus 760 tons per day in bad condition). The evidence, once again, indicates that these nonsurviving firms tended to be small operations: firms that reported their smelters as destroyed had an average capacity of 17 tons per day; firms that reported their smelters as in "bad condition" had an average capacity of 190 tons per day; firms

Table 7.5. *Lead and Copper Smelters in 1922*

Category by State of Conservation	Number of Firms in Category	Number of Furnaces	Total Capacity (tons/day)	Average Size of Firms (tons/day)
Destroyed	3	2	50	17
Bad	4	7	760	190
Regular	16	25	1,808	113
Good	25	85	16,416	657
No information	9	6	472	52
ALL FIRMS	57	125	19,506	342

Source: Mexico, Secretaria de Industria, Comercio y Trabajo (1924), pp. 106–9.

that reported their smelters as being in "good condition" had an average capacity of 657 tons per day (see Table 7.5).

We can cross-check these results on the survivorship of Mexican smelting operations with data from U.S. sources. In December 1913 and again in December 1919, the *Engineering and Mining Journal* published a census of the major lead and copper smelting operations in North America. It reported that in 1913 there were five silver-lead smelting companies operating in Mexico. These firms controlled 49 blast furnaces, with a total capacity of 2,297,000 tons per year. By 1919 Mexico's total capacity had actually grown: there were now 52 smelters with 2,424,000 tons per year in capacity. All of the smelting works in existence in 1913 were still in operation (see Table 7.6).

The implication is that the industrial structure of the lead smelting industry changed scarcely at all as a result of the revolution. The four-firm ratio in 1913 was 0.90. In 1919 it was 0.96. The ownership structure had also scarcely changed: ASARCO, the Compañía Metalúrgica Mexicana, and the Compañía Metalúrgica de Torreón were still the dominant players. The only difference was that the Compañía Minera de Peñoles was now a subsidiary of a new firm, the Compañía de Minerales y Metales (see Table 7.6).

An analysis of the journal's data on North America's copper smelters produces similar results. At the end of 1913 there were six companies in Mexico, operating 38 blast furnaces, with a total blast furnace capacity of 3,676,000 tons per year.[91] All six of those companies were still operating at year's end in 1919. Many, such as ASARCO, Cananea Consolidated Copper, and the Compagnie du Boleo, had increased their capacity

---

[91] These firms also operated three reverberatory furnaces.

Table 7.6. *Mexico's Lead Smelting Companies, 1913 and 1919*

Company	Location	Furnaces 1913	Furnaces 1919	Annual Capacity (thousand tons) 1913	Annual Capacity (thousand tons) 1919
ASARCO	Monterrey	10	7	475	410
ASARCO	Aguascalientes	2	1	100	50
ASARCO	Chihuahua	5	7	274	400
ASARCO	Valardeña	3	3	140	150
Cia Metalúrgica Mexicana	San Luís Potosí	11	10	385	360
Cia Metalúrgica de Torreón[a]	Torreón	8	8	360	286
Cia Minera de Peñoles[b]	Mapimi	6	6	325	310
Cia Fundidora y Afinadora de Monterrey[c]	Monterrey	4	4	238	238
Mazapil Copper Co.	Saltillo		3		105
Cia de Minerales y Metales[d]	Cerralvo		2		38
Cia de Minerales y Metales[e]	Guadalupe		1		77
TOTAL CAPACITY		49	52	2,297	2,424

[a] Not in operation as of February 1919.
[b] Subsidiary of Cia de Minerales y Metales in 1919.
[c] Smelter under lease to Cia de Minerales y Metales in 1919.
[d] Not in operation since January 23, 1919.
[e] Not in operation in 1919.
Source: *Engineering and Mining Journal*, January 10, 1914, p. 67; January 17, 1920, p. 119.

since 1913. In addition, there were several new market entrants. Thus, the industry's total blast furnace capacity actually grew during the revolution (by 21 percent), to 4,464,000 tons per year (see Table 7.7).

The ownership and industrial structure of the copper smelting industry was little altered by the revolution, as had been the case with the silver-lead smelting industry. In 1913 the four-firm concentration ratio was 0.86. In 1919 it was 0.83. The same firms that had dominated the industry in 1913 were still the industry leaders: ASARCO, Cananea Consolidated, the Compagnie du Boleo, Mazapil Copper, and Teziutlán Copper (see Table 7.7).

Investment

One implication of our analysis of survivorship is that there was considerable new investment in plant and equipment in the years during and after the revolution. This hypothesis is consistent with a broad range of evidence.

Table 7.7. *Mexico's Copper Smelting Companies, 1913 and 1919*

Company	Location	Blast Furnaces 1913	Blast Furnaces 1919	Blast Furnace Capacity (thousand tons) 1913	Blast Furnace Capacity (thousand tons) 1919
ASARCO (American Smelters Securities)[a]	Valardeña	3	3	228	250
ASARCO	Aguascalientes	8	6	730	480
ASARCO	Matehuala	3	4	325	400
ASARCO	Monterrey		1		80
ASARCO	Valardeña		3		250
Cananea Consolidated Copper Co.	Cananea	8	8	868	1,198
Cia Metalúrgica de Torreón	Torreón	2	1	175	55
Compagne du Boleo	Santa Rosalia	8	7	650	700
Mazapil Copper Co.	Saltillo	4	4	350	278
Teziutlán Copper Mining & Smelting Co.	Teziutlán	2	2	350	328
Democrata Cananea Sonora Copper Co.	Cananea		3		320
El Fuerte Mining and Smelting Co. 2	Choix		1		36
Cia Metalúrgica Mexicana	San Luis Potosi		1		72
Cia de Minas de Mexico SA[b]	Mina Mexico		1		17
TOTAL		38	45	3,676	4,464

[a] The Valardeña works are listed as belonging to ASARCO in 1913 and the American Smelter's Securities Corp. in 1919. The American Smelter's Security Corp. was, however, controlled by ASARCO.
[b] Not in operation in 1919.
Sources: *Engineering and Mining Journal*, January 10, 1914, p. 63; January 17, 1920, p. 117.

In Table 7.8 we present estimates of the real value of mining equipment and machinery imported into Mexico from the United States and Great Britain. These estimates measure the flow of new investment, not the stock of existing investment. This is an excellent proxy for capital spending by mining companies, because Mexico produced no mining equipment domestically. All machinery had to be imported from abroad.

We report both the absolute values (in real 1929 dollars) and index numbers (base year 1910 = 100) to assess change over time. Prior to 1922 the U.S. Department of Commerce did not disaggregate petroleum machines from mining machines. We have estimated the 1907–21 mining

Table 7.8. *Estimates of Mining Equipment Exported to Mexico from the United States and the United Kingdom, 1907–1929 (in thousands of 1929 U.S. dollars)*

Year	Estimated U.S. Mining Machinery[a]	Reported U.K. Mining Machinery	Total Mining Machinery	Index (1910 = 100)
1907	961	25	986	166
1908	693	27	720	121
1909	525	40	565	95
1910	494	101	595	100
1911	527	105	632	106
1912	411	76	487	82
1913	525	45	570	96
1914	404	21	425	71
1915	60	6	66	11
1916	83	1	84	14
1917	115	2	117	20
1918	361	7	369	62
1919	394	36	430	72
1920	1,111	106	1,217	205
1921	1,063	83	1,146	193
1922	1,277	108	1,386	233
1923	1,267	29	1,296	218
1924	1,437	6	1,443	242
1925	1,940	0	1,940	326
1926	1,937	0	1,937	326
1927	1,419	0	1,419	239
1928	1,658	0	1,658	279
1929	1,767	3	1,770	297

Note: The final results of these calculations are not sensitive to the ratios chosen.

[a] From 1907 to 1921, the estimated total is 45 percent of reported mining and petroleum machinery. The 45 percent ratio is derived from the ratio of reported oil line pipe and casings plus reported petroleum machinery to the the total of those categories plus mining machinery from 1922 to 1929. For total mining and petroleum machinery in these years, see Table 6.4. From 1922 to 1929, the estimated total is the reported total (the source disaggregated petroleum from mining machinery).

Sources: United States: United States, Department of Commerce (various years). United Kingdom: United Kingdom, Customs and Excise Dept. Statistical Office (1900–34).

machinery imports from the United States under the reasonable assumption that the proportion of mining machinery imports in total mining and petroleum equipment imports was the same from 1907 to 1921 as it was from 1922 to 1929, 45 percent. We also note that our results would not be sensitive to the ratio chosen. Even if we make the completely unrealistic assumption that 100 percent of Mexico's pre-1922 mining and petroleum machinery imports went to mining, Mexico's average imports of mining machinery from 1922 to 1929 would still have been higher than average imports from 1907 to 1911, or 1907 to 1921.

The investment data are unambiguous. First, from 1913 to 1915 rates of new investment fell in a dramatic fashion, so much so that in 1915 virtually no new machinery was being imported into Mexico. Because there was little in the way of rail service, this stands to reason. By 1918, however, companies were once again making significant investments in new equipment, the index taking a value of 64. The rate of new investment then increased rapidly. By 1920 Mexico was investing record amounts in new mining equipment (the index standing at 209). Mexico's mining companies then continued to import new mining equipment at record levels all through the 1920s. In fact, our estimates indicate that, on average, new expenditures during the period 1920–29 were 70 percent higher than they had been in the years 1907–10.

These estimates are consistent with data we have retrieved on another major imported input into mining production: pumps and pumping equipment. Pumping equipment is a good proxy for mining investment for three reasons: pumping equipment was a vital input (without a means to pump out groundwater, mines are unworkable); most pumping equipment imported into Mexico would have been used by mining companies, not other users;[92] and Mexico produced no pumping equipment of its own, importing all such equipment. Thus, using U.S. Department of Commerce records, we have constructed a data set on pumps and pumping equipment exported from the United States to Mexico. As is the case with the data on mining machines, the pumping equipment data are flows, not stocks.

As Table 7.9 demonstrates, U.S. exports of pumping equipment declined during 1913–16. This should hardly be surprising, because many of Mexico's mines sat idle during this period. Pumping equipment exports to Mexico then rose in a dramatic fashion beginning in 1918. In 1919 they were an order of magnitude higher than their 1901–10 average. During 1920–29 they averaged more than three times their level for 1901–10.

---

[92] Petroleum companies and agriculturalists also employed pumping equipment, but the single biggest user of pumps was the mining companies, which used them to unwater mines. Mexico's oil fields did not have to pump the oil out of the ground: it came out under pressure. Pumping equipment would therefore have been necessary only to move the oil through pipelines. Agriculturalists would have used pumps to bring groundwater to the surface for irrigation. Most agriculture in Mexico was, however, rain-fed and did not rely on the pumping of groundwater.

Table 7.9. *Pumps and Pumping Machinery
Exported from the United States to Mexico,
1900–1929 (in thousands of 1929 U.S. dollars)*

Year	Value	Index (1910 = 100)
1900	73	23
1901	79	25
1902	123	38
1903	167	52
1904	219	68
1905	396	123
1906	654	203
1907	725	225
1908	263	82
1909	243	76
1910	322	100
1911	320	99
1912	268	83
1913	285	89
1914	221	69
1915	107	33
1916	77	24
1917	297	92
1918	715	222
1919	1,369	425
1920	3,762	1,168
1921	2,973	923
1922	641	199
1923	372	116
1924	545	169
1925	588	183
1926	481	149
1927	350	109
1928	421	131
1929	490	152

Source: United States, Department of Commerce (various
years).

One might argue that this jump was the product of the replacement
of pumping equipment that had been destroyed during the years of civil
war. Such an interpretation is not consistent with the evidence. First, in
the three years 1918 1919, and 1920, the combined value of pump exports from the United States to Mexico exceeded the combined value of all
pumps exported to Mexico from 1900 to 1918. Even had all of Mexico's

pumps been destroyed as of the end of 1917, exports from the U.S. in 1918–20 would have replaced them, and still left a very wide margin (on the order of 21 percent!) for new investment. Second, even if we make the unreasonable assumption that all U.S. exports for 1918–20 were replacements of destroyed or damaged equipment, the level of U.S. exports for the period 1921–29 was, on average, more than twice the levels for 1901–10. The clear implication is that mining companies were investing well beyond their pre-1911 productive capacity in order to expand production.

These estimates are consistent with the observations of contemporaries. In 1923 the *Engineering and Mining Journal* noted that "more mining machinery is going into Mexico at this time than for ten years. The machinery is going chiefly to supply mines in the states of Chihuahua, Sinaloa, Sonora, and Durango. Considerable new equipment for ore-reduction mills is also being imported from the United States."[93] Later that same year, the journal noted that "Not in many years has there been so heavy a demand for mining machinery, and some of the border forwarding agencies are employing night shifts of men, in order to load cars and dispatch promptly freight consigned to the various mining districts of Mexico."[94] The journal further noted that during 1925 "much energy was devoted to the development and equipment of mines that recently have been idle or have been worked on only a comparatively small scale. About fifteen important construction projects were either financed during the year or were well advanced toward completion; and a number of others have been started."[95]

The evidence on the flow of new machinery and the observations of contemporaries are consistent with what we know about new investment by two of Mexico's largest mining and smelting companies. In 1924, for example, ASARCO (the largest mining and smelting enterprise in Mexico) committed $10 million to the upgrading and expansion of its existing plants, as well as the construction of new smelters. This included a new zinc smelter, a coal-mining operation, a by-product coke plant, a copper smelter, an arsenic plant, and a flotation plant.[96] The Compañía Minera de Peñoles (which controlled one-third of Mexico's lead output and one-fourth of its silver output) also undertook major new investments in the early 1920s. This included the installation of electric generators to supply

---

[93] *Engineering and Mining Journal*, April 28, 1923, p. 770.
[94] *Engineering and Mining Journal*, November 3, 1923, p. 784.
[95] *Engineering and Mining Journal*, January 16, 1926, p. 122.
[96] *Engineering and Mining Journal*, November 15, 1924, pp. 786–87.

power to its mines and smelting plants, the expansion of its mining operations, the construction of a lead refining plant, the renovation of its copper and lead smelting operations in Torreón, and the purchase of additional mining properties.[97]

These observations are consistent with what we know about the introduction of new refining technologies into Mexico in the 1920s – particularly the rapid construction of flotation plants for the treatment of silver-lead-zinc ores.[98] In 1926, 2.1 million tons of ore was treated in Mexico by flotation. This grew to 3.6 million tons by 1927, and to 4.1 million tons by 1928. In that year, there were 33 flotation plants in operation, treating 32 percent of the ores mined.[99]

Evidence on the number of hectares under exploitation also indicates that there was new investment taking place in the 1920s (see Table 7.10). In 1922, the first year for which we have good data, there were 961 mining sites working 37,529 hectares.[100] The number of sites and the number of hectares roughly doubled in the next five years, reaching 2,337 sites and 74,359 hectares in 1927. The number of hectares exploited then declined in 1928 and 1929. This post-1927 decline was the result of low metals prices (see Table 7.2), which pushed many firms to unprofitability. As the *Engineering and Mining Journal* noted in early 1929, "the low metal prices which have prevailed for the last two years for lead and zinc are principally blamed for the situation, but it is believed that a radical reduction in taxation and more favorable transportation prices might ameliorate the situation."[101]

This expansion during the 1920s of the number of mining claims is consistent with what we know about the consumption of dynamite – one of the most crucial inputs in mining exploration and exploitation. In 1918, the first year for which we have data, total dynamite consumed was only 286 thousand metric tons. Within a year, that figure had more than doubled (to 586 thousand metric tons), and then continued climbing. By 1929, dynamite consumption had increased 20-fold since 1918 (see Table 7.11).

---

[97] The Compañía Minera de Peñoles was, by the mid-1920s, a subsidiary of the American Metals Company. *Engineering and Mining Journal*, January 31, 1925, pp. 217–20.

[98] *Engineering and Mining Journal*, February 13, 1926, p. 278.

[99] *Engineering and Mining Journal*, October 10, 1929, p. 577.

[100] The Mexican government did not begin to record the number of hectares actually worked, rather than the number of hectares taxed, until 1922.

[101] *Engineering and Mining Journal*, January 26, 1929, p. 175.

Table 7.10. *Mining Properties (in hectares)*

Year	Hectares under Concession	Hectares Being Worked	Applications for New Concessions	Concessions Granted	Concessions Revoked[a]
1892	34,999				
1905	256,243				
1917				5,243	
1918			21,298	3,262	
1919	446,549		42,526	7,091	
1920	398,513		40,400	10,930	58,967
1921	284,561		25,436	7,459	21,022
1922	370,220	37,529	25,601	24,928	39,669
1923	361,098	40,738	33,727	20,534	29,656
1924	333,204	47,091	25,006	11,764	39,659
1925	276,629	44,770	39,722	29,771	86,346
1926	276,583	48,886	32,947	19,751	19,798
1927	259,141	74,359	212,257	7,772	25,213
1928	213,539	62,057	234,350	16,668	30,477
1929	218,988	48,653		15,378	9,929

[a] Concessions were revoked (Caduca) for failure to pay taxes. Our estimate of hectares revoked adjusts for those concessions that were reinstated by the payment of back taxes.

Sources: Bernstein (1964), pp. 28–29; México, Secretaría de Industria, Comercio y Trabajo (1924), pp. 132, 133, 145; (1925), pp. 63, 116; (1927), pp. 250, 257, 290, 292, 295, 296; (1928), p. 83; (1929), pp. 136–38, 146, 581; (1930), pp. 71, 368, 441, 445, 447; (1932), pp. 306, 354–56.

Table 7.11. *Dynamite Consumption in Mexico, 1918–1929*

Year	Metric Tons Consumed	Index (1918 = 100)
1918	285,519	100
1919	585,711	205
1920	741,114	260
1921	565,004	198
1922	647,242	227
1923	633,362	222
1924	721,428	253
1925	1,202,653	421
1926	1,463,975	513
1927	3,072,732	1,076
1928	4,671,643	1,636
1929	5,620,138	1,968

Source: México, Secretaría de Industria, Comercio y Trabajo (1932), p. 358.

In sum, the data on investment all point the same way: there was considerable new investment in Mexican mining, smelting, and other refining technologies in the years after 1918. One would be hard put to argue that political instability and institutional change caused producers to cease making new investments.

Output

The output of mineral products displays the exact same pattern as do the data on investment. In Table 7.1 we present estimates of the production, by volume, of Mexico's major mineral products: silver, lead, copper, gold, and zinc. The basic pattern is that output declined during 1913–17 and then recovered at a brisk pace. By the early 1920s (the exact year depending on the product) output of most minerals regained their Porfirian levels. In point of fact, the average volume of output for the 1911–20 decade as a whole was not all that much lower than for 1900–10. During the decade 1921–30, the only product that did not exceed its average Porfirian level was gold, which was not an important mineral product for Mexico. The output of silver during 1921–30 was, however, 47 percent higher than it had been from 1900 to 1910. The same is true for lead production, which was 88 percent higher than its prerevolutionary average. The production of zinc, which had been unimportant during the Porfiriato, went through the roof, reaching a level 12 times that of its 1900–10 average (see Table 7.1).

A skeptical reader might argue that even though the production of virtually all of Mexico's mineral products exceeded their pre-instability levels during the 1920s, this does not indicate that political instability did not impose a cost on the Mexican mining industry. Implicit in this view is a hypothetical Mexico in which output levels in the 1920s would have been even higher than those we observe.

Subjecting this argument to empirical verification is, in the case of mining, a fairly straightforward affair. One can posit either of two counterfactual cases. The first is the rest of the mineral-producing countries of the world as a group. They faced the same world prices and same technological constraints as Mexico, except that those other countries did not endure 20 years of revolutions, counterrevolutions, civil wars, and political assassinations. The second counterfactual is the United States, whose western states were geologically contiguous with the Mexican north. Comparing Mexico's actual performance with its potential performance is therefore a straightforward exercise. In the first counterfactual, Mexico would have lost world market share. In the second counterfactual, Mexico would have lost world market share to the United States.

In Table 7.12 we present data on Mexico's world market share in silver, lead, and copper, its three most important mineral exports by both value and volume. We also present data on market share captured by the United States. The data do not support the hypothesis that political instability caused Mexico to produce less than it would have had it not been unstable. In fact, in some mineral products, Mexico outperformed the United States. For example, Mexico accounted for 34 percent of world silver production from 1900 to 1910. This fell slightly during the civil war years (Mexico's average market share for 1911–19 was 27 percent) but then quickly recovered and continued growing. During the decade 1920–29, Mexico accounted for 40 percent of world output. During the 1920s, the United States actually underperformed Mexico: its share of the world market declined monotonically from 33 percent in 1920 to 22 percent in 1929.

Mexico also outperformed the rest of the world in lead production. Its market share increased from 9 percent on average in the five years 1906–10 to 13 percent on average in the period 1922–29. During the same eight years, the United States lost market share to Mexico, its proportion of the world market falling from 41 percent in 1922 to 36 percent in 1929.

In only one case, copper, was Mexico's average market share lower in the 1920s than it was in the period before 1910. Mexico produced an average of 7 percent of the world's copper from 1900 to 1910. It then lost market share during the years of revolution and civil war, averaging 5 percent of world production from 1911 to 1918. Its market share from 1922 to 1929 (we lack 1919–21 data) was, on average, even lower – only 4 percent. Even in the case of copper, however, Mexico's market share was rising in the 1920s. In 1922 Mexico had a 3 percent market share. By 1929 it had doubled its market share to 6 percent.

If we posit the U.S. copper industry as the appropriate counterfactual to Mexico, the evidence is even weaker regarding the underperformance hypothesis. The United States also lost market share during the 1920s. The United States accounted for 56 percent of world copper output during 1900–10 and 52 percent from 1922–29.

Taxes

One of the reasons why Mexico maintained output and its world market shares was because the mining companies were able to resist attempts by

Table 7.12. *Market Shares of Mexico and the United States in Silver, Lead, and Copper (%)*

Year	World Silver		World Lead		World Copper	
	Mexico's Share	U.S. Share	Mexico's Share	U.S. Share	Mexico's Share	U.S. Share
1900	32	32			5	55
1901	33	32			6	52
1902	37	34			7	54
1903	37	31			9	53
1904	35	32			8	56
1905	34	31			10	57
1906	32	31	6	32	9	58
1907	34	31	7	33	8	55
1908	34	25	11	27	5	57
1909	31	24	11	30	7	58
1910	32	24	11	31	7	56
1911	32	24	11	32	7	55
1912	32	25	10	31	7	55
1913	32	30	5	32	6	55
1914	17	45			4	56
1915	21	40			3	59
1916	18	44			4	63
1917	24	41			3	61
1918	32	34			5	61
1919	37	31				
1920	40	33				
1921	39	33				
1922	39	27	11	41	3	52
1923	39	28	13	41	3	53
1924	38	27	12	40	3	54
1925	38	25	12	41	4	54
1926	39	24	12	39	4	54
1927	41	23	15	36	4	50
1928	42	22	14	35	5	49
1929	42	23	14	36	6	48

Sources: Mexico, Secretaria de Industria, Comercio y Trabajo (1924), pp. 37–38; (1927), pp. 37, 41; (1932), pp. 18, 20, 22; *Engineering and Mining Journal*, May 4, 1901, p. 556; June 20, 1903, p. 935; January 7, 1904, p. 8; March 20, 1907, p. 627; June 20, 1908, p. 1253; May 10, 1909, p. 764; May 1, 1909, p. 907; September 22, 1917, p. 531; May 25, 1912, p. 1044; January 11, 1919, p. 47.

the government to raise taxes. Every government that came to power (and every faction that hoped to be a government) from 1913 onward looked at Mexico's mining industry as a crucial source of tax revenue. As we have already seen, however, the government's very desperation limited its ability to raise taxes. The government needed tax income more than the miners needed operating revenues. Lacking the ability to run the mines, and fearing retaliation from the United States, the government could not credibly threaten to confiscate the mines.

The only advantage that the Mexican government had, and it was ephemeral, was that for a brief period during and immediately after World War I mineral prices were astronomically high. The price of copper, for example, rose from 13.6 ¢ per ounce in 1914 to 27.2 ¢ per ounce in 1917, and then gradually declined to 18.7 ¢ per ounce by 1919. The price of lead also doubled, rising from 3.9 ¢ per pound in 1914 to 8.8 ¢ per pound in 1917. It was still trading at close to 8 ¢ per pound as late as 1920. The price of silver rose even more dramatically, increasing from 49.7 ¢ per troy ounce in 1915 to $1.11 per ounce in 1919. In 1920 it was still trading at $1.01 per ounce (see Table 7.2).

The increase in metals prices almost certainly produced windfall profits for the mining companies. What is particularly remarkable, therefore, is that in April 1918, the Carranza government *lowered taxes*. Precious metals were now taxed at an ad valorum rate of 8 percent (instead of the previous level of 10 percent), while most industrial metals were taxed at 3 percent and zinc at 1 percent (instead of the previous level of 5 percent). Copper was taxed on a complex sliding scale. The property tax was reduced to 18 pesos for claims over 100 hectares, sliding downward to 6 pesos per hectare for claims of 5 hectares or less. The export of gold or silver required special permission unless an equal amount of gold coins was reimported.[102] The tax rates underwent a further downward revision in June 1919, when taxes on industrial metals other than copper were reduced from 3 to 2 percent.[103]

The resulting tax rates, while lower than those in effect during 1914–17, were still higher than those in effect under Díaz. Data from the *Anuario de Estadística Minera* allow us to calculate the effective tax rate on mining in 1919 (Carranza's last full year in office). Total federal taxes came to 6.8 percent of output. State taxes added another 2 percent, producing a

---

[102] Bernstein (1964), p. 122.
[103] Assay fees remained basically unchanged from Porfirian levels. Cleland (1922), pp. 285–87.

total tax rate of 8.8 percent, roughly double the tax rate of 4.3 percent that had existed in 1907 (see Table 7.13).

The collapse of metals prices beginning in mid-1920, however, brought the bonanza enjoyed by the mining companies and the Mexican government to an end. By 1921 the price of copper was less than half of what it had been in 1917 (it now stood at 12.5 ¢ per pound), and the price of lead had fallen nearly as far (to 4.5 ¢ per pound) (see Table 7.2). The interim government of Adolfo de la Huerta (May–November 1920) and later the Obregón government therefore reformed the tax code. They did so, in fact, through a mechanism that they would later use to set import tariffs and establish banking laws: they let the asset holders play a large role in writing the laws. In August 1920 de la Huerta appointed a commission composed of government officials and mining company representatives to establish a new tax code. The new code essentially made the tax on copper and silver a function of the metal's price in New York. Under certain thresholds, 60 ¢ per ounce for silver and 15 ¢ per pound for copper, there were no production taxes at all. They then increased on a sliding scale. Assay fees continued as under Díaz, and the parcel tax remained unchanged. States could levy a production tax, but it was capped at 2 percent of the value of output.[104]

The net result was that effective tax rates declined monotonically throughout the 1920s. In 1920 total federal and state taxes on mining came to 10.2 percent of the value of output. By 1922 the new sliding-scale tax system yielded total federal and state taxes of 7.5 percent, and by 1926 they were yielding 6.0 percent. By 1929 the combined federal and state tax rate was only 5.2 percent, which was lower than the tax rate that prevailed in 1905 (7.7 percent) and was close to the rate in effect in 1907 (4.3 percent)[105] (see Table 7.13).

CONCLUSIONS

This chapter has studied the impact of political instability on Mexico's mining industry. In terms of the underlying institutions, we have established that, prior to the revolution, mining companies had been able to craft a very favorable environment that persisted throughout the

---

[104] Cleland (1922), pp. 285–88.
[105] Taxes were lowered still further in 1930. In fact, the authority of states to levy any mining taxes at all was removed in the 1930 tax law. This move alone would have dropped the implicit tax rate, all other things being equal, to only 3.7 percent. *Engineering and Mining Journal*, February 24, 1930, p. 210.

Table 7.13. *Estimated Taxation Rates for Mexican Mining (taxes as a percentage of the gross value of production)*

	Tax Rate		
Year	Federal	State	Combined
1905	5.7	2.0	7.7
1907	2.8	1.5	4.3
1919	7.3	2.0	9.3
1920	8.7	2.0	10.7
1921	5.2	2.0	7.2
1922	5.9	2.0	7.9
1923	4.9	2.0	6.9
1924	4.8	2.0	6.8
1925	5.2	2.0	7.2
1926	5.0	1.3	6.3
1927	4.0	1.3	5.3
1928	4.2	1.4	5.6
1929	3.5	1.2	4.7

Notes: Taxes include state and federal production, export, assay, and parcel taxes and surtaxes.

See notes 14 and 17 in Chapter 7 for sources and methods for 1905 and 1907.

For 1919–29 we proceeded in several steps. We took the value of mining production for taxable mineral products and the value of federal production taxes directly from México, Secretaría de Industria, Comercio y Trabajo, 1924–32.

Federal parcel taxes and federal title taxes for 1923–29 were taken directly from México, Secretaría de Industria, Comercio y Trabajo, 1924–32.

For 1919–22 federal parcel taxes were estimated, by multiplying the number of hectares under concession (from Table 7.10) times the average parcel tax per hectare from 1923 to 1925 (7.31 pesos per hectare).

We recognize that many firms did not actually pay the parcel tax. The tax rate we compute is the tax they legally owed, not the tax they actually paid.

For 1919–22 we estimated title taxes by multiplying the number of new hectares under concession (from Table 7.10) by the average title tax per hectare from 1923 to 1925 (10.66 pesos per hectare).

State taxes were estimated in several steps. Prior to 1926, state taxes were capped at 2 percent of the value of all mineral products. We assumed that states taxed at the maximum (2 percent) rate.

For 1926–29 we estimated state taxes by multiplying the value of gold and silver produced by 2 percent (the maximum allowable under law). State taxes for other mineral products were fixed at 50 percent of the federal production tax on those products. We assumed that states taxed at the maximum allowable rate.

revolutionary period. We can specify three hypotheses regarding the quantitative impact of political instability on the mining industry: that instability should have brought investment and production to a grinding halt; that investment and production might have continued but at a reduced level; that investment and production might have continued to rise but did so at a slower rate than it would have otherwise. The empirical evidence we have analyzed indicates that none of these hypotheses holds. Mexican mining and smelting firms not only increased output; they gained world market share. This was accomplished by an aggressive program of new investment.

The reason why output and investment grew amid an unstable polity was that the mining companies knew that they could mitigate any reform of their property rights. No government, or faction that aspired to be a government, wanted a confrontation with the United States. In addition, potential predators who might have disregarded the threat of U.S. intervention confronted major obstacles on the technological front. They lacked the necessary technical know-how to run the industry themselves. In the medium run they could have hired foreign engineers and managers. The relevant time horizon for unstable governments and factions that wanted to be governments was not, however, the medium term. That meant that tax increases could be met by the threat of production cutbacks. The commitment mechanisms that supported mining activity in Mexico under Díaz thus remained intact throughout the revolution and the 1920s.

8

Agriculture

Agriculture played a dominant role in the Mexican economy from precolonial times until well into the 20th century. In 1910 two-thirds of the population earned its livelihood from farming or farm work.

Agriculture's importance is perhaps matched only by the relative dearth of quantitative evidence about it. Because virtually all agricultural production took place in family-owned enterprises, there are no corporate financial data on which to draw. In addition, agricultural output was not subject to the excise taxes that were levied on producers in other sectors, so we cannot develop the range of firm-level data sets that we can for other sectors of the Mexican economy. We are, however, able to use U.S. and British trade records to put together data sets on Mexico's importation of capital and intermediate goods for agricultural use. We are also able to use those sources to estimate the net imports and exports of Mexican agricultural products to the United States. This means that we can develop data sets on the flow of new investment and on the economic performance of Mexican staple and export agriculture.

The data sets we have developed, when coupled with the extant secondary literature, allow us to capture the basic outlines of Mexico's agricultural history. Before the revolution, the federal government played an important role in the *specification* of agricultural property rights. The federal government played a very small role, however, in the *enforcement* of the property rights system. Agricultural property rights were enforced not by vertical political integration (VPI) coalitions, such as those that characterized manufacturing or banking, but by coalitions between large landowners and local political bosses, who almost always included the state governor. These coalitions used federal land laws to take predatory actions against other landowners, particularly small farmers. At times they preyed on other large landowners who happened to have the misfortune of backing the wrong side in a political battle.

Property rights in prerevolutionary Mexico were therefore selectively enforced, and that enforcement was largely a matter of personal connections between local governors (and other local officials) and their political allies in the landowning class. Once these local political officials were removed from power by the revolution, property rights in agriculture were, for a time, in the public domain. Properties could be seized by any group with the violence potential to take them. Not surprisingly, in the short run, the Mexican Revolution had a negative impact on agricultural investment and output. Passing armies confiscated crops and destroyed farm buildings and other land improvements. Sometimes output or property would be spared, but only if landowners would pay protection money. At other times, particularly when an army perceived that it would hold an area for a prolonged period, an armed faction would settle down and work the land themselves, appropriating the income for the benefit of the movement. This meant, of course, that the revolution did not produce widespread and enduring food shortages.

In the medium term, the political instability of 1911–29 did not produce a fall in investment and output. The evidence indicates that staple crop production quickly recovered its pre-1911 levels. The evidence is even clearer that Mexican export agriculture boomed. Not only did most agricultural exports continue growing even in the midst of the civil war, but Mexico entered into the production of a much broader range of export crops during the 1920s. Finally, the data indicate that there was substantial investment in agricultural machinery and chemical fertilizers in the 1920s. In short, the evidence strongly suggests that commercial agriculturalists were not particularly worried about the security of their property rights in the late 1910s and the 1920s.

This result may strike readers as surprising. After all, the Mexican Revolution is often portrayed as a peasant revolution. In addition, the Mexican Constitution of 1917 provided for an agrarian reform. Article 27 of the Constitution declared null and void the alienations of village lands that had taken place since June 25, 1856.[1] This article also made the federal government the residual claimant on property rights in land and established that the redistribution of land would be an administrative, rather than judicial, procedure. One would not normally expect landowners

---

[1] Parcels less than 50 hectares were not affected by this provision. Tannenbaum (1968), p. 524.

to invest in new technologies and to expand production under these conditions.

Large-scale agriculturalists in the 1910s and 1920s were able to mitigate the effects of political instability and formal institutional change by creating political institutions that enforced *their* property rights. Indeed, the very fact that the polity was unstable in the 1910s and 1920s allowed them to form coalitions with political and military actors who could prevent an agrarian reform – even a constitutionally mandated one – from taking place. During the late 1910s and the 1920s, agricultural property rights in some areas of the country were enforced by VPI coalitions composed of the federal government, large landowners, and revolutionary "generals" – who enforced the coalition in exchange for protection rents. In some cases of commercial agriculture, such as sugar production, third-party enforcement also came from the CROM, which organized sugar workers much in the way it did manufacturing workers.

These coalitions effectively reversed the de facto land reforms that had occurred during 1914–17. They also blocked the de jure agrarian reform that was specified by the Constitution of 1917. In fact, Carranza had begun to hand back large swathes of land to their prerevolutionary owners even before the constitution was enacted. His successors, Álvaro Obregón and Plutarco Elias Calles, followed Carranza's lead. The enabling legislation to Article 27, enacted during the Obregón administration, was, in fact, crafted so as to complicate the reform process: it gave state governors a veto on any reform in their states; it excluded sharecroppers and tenants from receiving land under the reform program, thereby turning them into allies of the landlords; and it provided a series of loopholes that allowed large landholders to retain their best lands even in those cases where reform occurred.

Not surprisingly, the federal government redistributed land to peasants in a very limited fashion. Markiewicz estimates that by 1928 only 4 percent of all agricultural land had been distributed as a result of agrarian reform.[2] Soon thereafter (1930), former president Calles (who still ruled through puppet presidents) declared the agrarian reform a failure and called for an end to land redistribution.[3]

Secure commitment mechanisms were regional in scope. In some regions of Mexico property rights were *more* secure after the revolution than before, despite constitutional changes that allowed for land redistribution.

---

[2] Markiewicz (1993), p. 55.
[3] Markiewicz (1993), p. 59.

Property rights were strongest in those areas with the potential for agricultural exports, because those regions had the ability to generate the rents necessary to share with third parties. Thus, Mexican agricultural exports boomed in the 1920s.

In regions producing staple crops for the domestic market there were fewer rents to distribute. These regions also contained peasant constituencies that had supported President Obregón against the Delahuertistas and President Calles against the Cristeros. These peasant militias did not face down the army in 1923–24 and the Cristeros in 1926–29 because of some vague commitment to democracy. They did so in exchange for land. Thus, in the heavily settled, corn-growing regions of central Mexico, some agrarian distributions took place, even though the presidents who carried them out were not, in fact, believers in land reform.

These limited redistributions did not seriously affect Mexico's ability to feed its population during the 1920s. In the first place, they covered only a very small portion of Mexico's cropland. In the second place, Mexican staple crop production, even on large farms, was extremely inefficient. There had been, in essence, two Mexican agricultural sectors since Porfirian times: a vibrant, hard-driving commercial sector that produced high-value crops for distant markets; and a staple sector characterized by labor-intensive production methods and slow productivity growth. The available descriptions of the technologies used in staple agriculture indicate that the prerevolutionary standard was simply not very high. As long as the peasants believed that their new lands were not likely to be seized in turn, they produced as efficiently as the previous owners.

In the late 1930s, Mexico underwent a dramatic agrarian reform that had strongly negative consequences for agricultural productivity in the long run.[4] The land distributions under President Lázaro Cárdenas were targeted precisely at those regions that produced export revenues, particularly the Laguna cotton region and the Yucatán peninsula. These expropriations occurred precisely when it was no longer possible to maintain the VPI coalitions of the 1920s. One of the requirements for VPI to work is that the third-party enforcers and the government be of roughly equal strength. Otherwise, the third party cannot lodge a credible threat against the government. By the mid-1930s, the third parties that enforced the coalition between government and landlords could no longer meet this requirement. The revolutionary generals who had protected private

---

[4] For the best discussion of the problems generated by the agrarian reform, see Yates (1981).

agriculture throughout the 1910s and 1920s were not the men they had been 20 years before. Time and gravity had taken its toll on them and on their men. At the same time, the federal government had grown stronger: it was no longer wracked by coups, assassinations, and civil wars. The government could now carry out a sweeping agrarian reform – something it could not do when the polity was unstable.

AGRICULTURE BEFORE THE REVOLUTION

Early History

Prior to the Mexican Revolution, agriculture's perennial problem was the insecurity of property rights. During the colonial era, the Spanish crown deliberately ignored the need to provide secure property rights.[5] Independence changed little. Some individuals and groups had primordial deeds from the Spanish crown. Some had fee simple titles, but these did not necessarily demarcate the boundaries of their properties. Some had nothing at all, save their claim that the land had been theirs since time immemorial.

The problem of poorly defined property rights could not be solved easily. First, there were vested interests in preserving the existing system, however inefficient. Many large landowners (who included political bosses) did not, in fact, have legal title to the lands that they had appropriated. Second, Mexico's wide climactic and topographical variation, poor transport and communications, and divergent interests among the growers of different crops meant that creating organizations to coordinate their political actions was extremely difficult, if not impossible.

Third, the government(s) of Mexico actively contributed to the insecurity of property rights through predatory actions against their political opponents.[6] Even the "liberals" who formed the Republican movement and espoused the virtues of private property plundered their political enemies when they could. For example, in 1865 Republican forces under Benito Juárez ousted strongman Santiago Vidaurri from his virtually independent

---

[5] Razo (1998). Also see Melville (1997).

[6] Much of this predation took place in the context of state-level political battles, which produced, over time, an increase in the number of Mexican states. To cite one example, the present-day states of Yucatán, Quintana Roo, and Campeche were originally a single state. In 1857, the western portion of the state violently seceded, forming the present-day state of Campeche. Opponents of the secession lost their land and had to flee for their lives. See Wells (1985), pp. 68–69.

fiefdom in northeastern Mexico. They then expropriated the properties of his supporters.[7] Much the same happened in Chihuahua. There, Governor Luis Terrazas acquired his largest estate by expropriating another hacendado who had chosen the wrong side during the French intervention.[8] Similar fates befell prominent Conservative supporters of Maximilian's empire. For example, in 1867 the Republicans seized the lands belonging to Juan Nepomuceno Flores and Leonardo Zuloaga. These lands, which included holdings spread across the states of Durango, Coahuila, and Nuevo León, were then parceled out among officers in the Republican army.[9]

This is not to say that all agricultural producers suffered predation. The interaction between weak federal and strong local governments gave rise to various arrangements that enforced property rights on a selective basis. These arrangements took the form of coalitions between groups of large landowners and local political bosses, who themselves were – or became – large landowners. The coalitions were held together by kinship networks or business dealings.[10] The very nature of the enforcement mechanism, a set of personal ties between particular individuals who were part of a social network, meant that coalitions were usually restricted to small groups of people. It also meant that any commitments made by state or local governments were unstable. If the local boss was replaced, property rights would again be up for grabs.

The upshot was underinvestment in staple agriculture. Consider corn, Mexico's most important staple. Even on haciendas, yields were stunningly low and techniques rudimentary. Seeds were untested and crop rotation almost unheard of.[11] As late as 1900, in Mexico's most productive corn-growing region (Mexico State), corn production took place on unirrigated and generally unimproved lands. Fallow lands were broken with hand plows, which dug perpendicular furrows approximately six inches deep. Laborers then sowed the seeds by hand, situating themselves at the intersection of the furrows, where they dug a three-inch-deep hole and dropped in approximately three seeds. This technique varied from that

---

[7] Plana (1996), pp. 32–33.
[8] Katz (1998), p. 15.
[9] Plana (1996), pp. 73–74. The branch of the Zuloaga family in Chihuahua would do better than their northeastern compatriots, forming an alliance through marriage and cheap credit with the Liberal leader Luis Terrazas. Wasserman (1984), p. 15.
[10] For a discussion of informal networks in 19th-century Mexico, see Wells and Joseph (1996), chaps. 2, 3.
[11] Sterret and Davis (1928), p. 72.

described by Sahagún in the 16th century only in the number of seeds dropped in each hole.[12] A more "modern" technique involved following an ox-drawn plow, dropping seeds at the new furrows' intersection with older furrows, and having another ox-team follow to cover up the ditches. This was less common, since it required more seeds. Harvesting was typically done by peasants with sickles, who then divided the crop into seed corn and corn for immediate sale in the local vicinity. Nothing as simple as the scythe was in use, let alone mechanical reapers.[13]

Agriculture in Porfirian Mexico

Effective VPI requires that there be a single unitary government and that asset holders and third-party enforcers be able to coordinate their actions. In addition, VPI arrangements are easier to create and sustain when the number of asset holders in the coalition is small and when the competitive structure of the industry is concentrated.

None of these conditions held in Porfirian agriculture. First, the agricultural sector was characterized by hundreds of thousands of proprietors spread over millions of square miles. The ability of agriculturalists – even the very largest ones – to coordinate their actions at the national level would have been difficult, if not impossible. Second, the federal government was weak relative to the states. Third, the state of internal transport and communications, even after the advent of the railway, was poor. These factors meant that the relevant government, from the point of view of agriculturalists, was not the one sitting in Mexico City but the one located in the state capital. This meant in turn that no single third party was likely to be able to enforce the commitments made by individual state governors. In short, VPI arrangements of the type we have already seen in banking or manufacturing were not likely to occur in agriculture.

There were only two limits to the predatory behavior of the state-level political bosses. The first was the threat of federal intervention, which grew stronger over time. Certain groups close to the president – or certain foreigners – could call on Díaz to enforce their property rights. The second was the threat of rebellion by large landowners outside the governing coalition, should predation on their property rights occur on such a scale as to prompt them to coordinate a military response. Small farmers, of course, offered no such threat. They were fair game.

---

[12] Tortolero (1995), pp. 220–22.
[13] Tortolero (1995), pp. 222–25.

Not surprisingly, the state governors and other members of the local political elite tended to ally with some subset of the large landowners in the state. They then used the de jure institutional reforms that had been written at the federal level to move against the property rights of those groups unintegrated into the local governance structure. That is to say, the *specification* of property rights was a federal affair. The *enforcement* of property rights, however, was a state-level affair. Property rights were therefore enforced as a private good – available only to those who were allied with the state governor and his cronies.

The Specification of Property Rights. There were two formal institutional reforms that were used to transfer massive amounts of land into the hands of coalition members: The Terrenos Baldíos (Vacant Lands) program; and the Ley Lerdo (Lerdo Act). The first was designed to privatize federally-owned lands. The second was designed to privatize municipally owned lands and the lands of the church.

The Terrenos Baldíos program had its origins in 1863, when the federal government – which was in rebellion against the French occupation at the time and not actually in control of the public lands – passed a law allowing individuals to submit claims for public lands, doing the surveying themselves and paying the federal government a set price.[14] This was, essentially, a homesteading act. The 1863 law failed to produce the desired results. Because few claims were actually filed, in 1883 the federal government passed a new law authorizing the award of concessions to private survey companies for a particular region. The companies would clarify (or "perfect," to use their terminology) existing land titles and establish exactly where boundary lines ran. One-third of the lands then certified as "vacant" would go to the survey company, which could resell the land. The federal government would sell off the rest. This would serve several purposes. The surveys would provide a basis for a national cadastral survey, allowing federal and state governments to levy uniform land taxes. The surveys would also force squatters on public lands to regularize their titles under the 1863 law, providing a stream of tax revenues.[15] Finally, revenue from land sales would provide a welcome source of income for the government.[16]

---

[14] Holden (1994), p. 9.
[15] Holden (1994), p. 12.
[16] Holden (1994), p. 14.

The Terrenos Baldíos law of 1883 was tremendously successful – if the measure of success is the amount of land that was passed into the hands of a small number of individuals. The programs surveyed 32 percent of Mexico's *total* land area, resulting in the privatization of 13 percent of the country's total territory – the balance held by the federal government as public lands. In some northern states, such as Chihuahua and Baja California, the proportion of privatized land exceeded 30 percent.[17] In addition, approximately 7,000 claims under the 1863 "homesteading" law privatized another 8.6 percent of the national territory.[18] Purchasers apparently considered property rights on surveyed federal lands to be *relatively* secure compared to other properties. According to Robert Holden, surveyed federal land in 1888–1900 sold for a premium ranging from 50 to 81 percent compared with unsurveyed land.[19]

Not all cultivable land in Porfirian Mexico was vacant or designated as such. In fact, few survey companies were ever active in the heavily populated states of Colima, Guanajuato, Guerrero, Hidalgo, Michoacán, Puebla, Oaxaca, and Tlaxcala. In these states, the relevant property rights reforms were undertaken under the Ley Lerdo of 1856, named for the law's Liberal author, Miguel Lerdo de Tejada. The act proclaimed that all property in the hands of either the Catholic Church or other communal organizations (such as municipal governments) would be seized and privatized, either by being turned over to its occupants or by being auctioned off by federal authorities. Some traditional village lands were exempted.[20] The Ley Lerdo, among other changes, was a large part of what triggered the War of the Reform (1857–60) and ultimately enabled the French to install a puppet regime in Mexico City between 1862 and 1867. Therefore, the law had little effect until the Porfiriato.

In many parts of Mexico, the land redistribution and titling program authorized by the Ley Lerdo did not produce clearly defined property rights. The law putatively exempted village lands proper (the *fundo legal*), as well as lands used for foraging (the *ejido*). As a practical matter, however, distinguishing between exempt properties and nonexempt

---

[17] The balance, 19 percent, was held as public lands. Calculated from figures in Holden (1994), pp. 16–17.

[18] Calculated from data in Holden (1994), pp. 16–17, 129.

[19] Holden (1994), p. 105. Holden's data come from the states of Sonora, Sinaloa, and Chiapas. In his analysis, "the value of newly surveyed land is compared to the government-administered price for the land (terreno baldío) before it was surveyed."

[20] Schenk (1995), p. 4.

communal lands and religious properties was not straightforward. The law provided no clear guideposts to determine where one type of land stopped and another started. Disputes over the extent of the *fundo legal*, the boundaries between village lands and the properties of various haciendas, and disputes among the peasants over which families would be entitled to which formerly communal lands held up the demarcation of individual property rights. In the areas of Mexico State studied by Frank Schenk, peasant villages routinely ignored petitions, decrees, or orders from higher levels of government.[21] In some cases, villages surreptitiously "privatized" land by turning communal properties over to their own designated representatives. When such representatives tried to enjoy their new position as "landowners," they found that local political leaders refused to support them and enforce their claims.[22] In the state of Michoacán, the situation was much the same. Disputes over land first mentioned in 1877 still blocked adjudication in 1896.[23] In some cases state records indicated that a privatization had been carried out but that it had been done so poorly as to be useless.[24] The resulting lack of investment in land improvements in central Mexico was remarkable. An 1890 survey conducted in the Mexico State county of Ocoyoacac found little change from 1845 in either the condition of the land or the techniques used to cultivate it.[25]

In regions where they were effectively implemented, the Terrenos Baldíos program and the Ley Lerdo became vehicles to enable large-scale commercial farmers, in alliance with local political elites, to seize the lands of small farmers. Although the data on land tenure patterns for this period are rough, the evidence indicates that in 1910 54 percent of the national territory was held by large-scale farms, another 20 percent was held by ranchers and small-scale agriculturalists, and 6 percent was held by Indian communities. The remaining 20 percent was classified as either unimproved or vacant national lands. An estimated 95 percent of rural heads of families had no land of their own.[26]

What had driven this process of land concentration was an alliance of local political bosses with the large landholders in their states. In order to illustrate how these local-level coalitions were able to use the Porfirian

[21] Schenk (1995), p. 23.
[22] Schenk (1995), pp. 25–26.
[23] Knowlton (1995), pp. 126–27.
[24] Knowlton (1995), pp. 128–29.
[25] Menegus Bornemann (1995), p. 168.
[26] Markiewicz (1993), p. 15.

land laws to prey on smallholders, we present two geographically dispersed examples: the states of Morelos and Chihuahua.

Morelos. The state of Morelos, just south of Mexico City, is one of the most striking cases in which a subset of the local planter class captured the state government and used its political power to seize the land of the state's smaller farmers. Sugar had been grown in Morelos since colonial times, but the sugar plantations had coexisted with haciendas growing staple crops, peasant villages, and independent small farms. During the Porfiriato, these other producers were swallowed up by the sugar estates. By 1908, 17 sugar planters controlled 25 percent of the state's total surface, most of its cultivable land, and almost all of its good land.[27]

As John Womack has described in detail, a crucial factor in the transformation of Morelos was the alliance between the state's governors and the local planter class. Two governors in particular, Manuel Alarcón (1894–1908) and Pablo Escandón (1908–11), were crucial to the land grab. Alarcón got his start as the district chief of a rural police garrison. In 1876, when Díaz declared against Lerdo de Tejada, Alarcón joined the revolt. As a reward, he was appointed the chief of Morelos's rural police. Alarcón quickly became the most powerful man in the state. He was appointed *jefe político* of the Cuautla district in 1883 and was "elected" to the state legislature in 1884. He served simultaneously as the state's lieutenant governor. All the while he retained his post as state police chief. In 1894 Díaz named him governor. Not surprisingly, Alarcón became a plantation owner himself, quite an achievement for someone born a *peón* whose entire career had been in "public service."[28] When Alarcón died in 1908 (after serving four consecutive terms as governor), the local planters engineered the election of Díaz's chief of staff (and local sugar planter) Pablo Escandón.[29]

Under both governors, the Ley Lerdo and the Terrenos Baldíos program were brought to bear against small farmers and peasant villages. The planters even developed tools, such as the reallocation of water rights, to use against small farmers who could demonstrate their property rights.[30] Other acts lowered the taxes paid by the plantations, by devaluing their assessments, while simultaneously increasing the assessments on small

[27] These 17 individuals owned 36 haciendas. Womack (1969), pp. 45, 49.
[28] Womack (1969), p. 15.
[29] Womack (1969), pp. 14–18.
[30] Womack (1969), pp. 50–52.

and midsized farmers.[31] When foreign sugar imports threatened the profitability of the Morelos plantations, the federal government doubled the import duty on sugar.[32]

As Womack has shown, attempts by groups of small farmers to resist the onslaught of the planters were dealt with by state-administered brutality. To cite one of the most notorious examples, in 1903 Pablo Escandón seized the pasture lands of the village of Yautepec. The villagers took their case to Morelos courts, which not only ruled against them but also fined them 100 pesos. The village, undaunted, then filed suit in the federal Supreme Court and sent a delegation, led by a local farmer (Jovito Serrano) to appeal directly to Porfirio Díaz. The Supreme Court ruled in favor of Escandón. Serrano never made it home alive. He was arrested and deported to a labor camp in the federal territory of Quintana Roo, where he died a little move than a year later.[33]

Chihuahua. The case of Chihuahua, on the border with Texas and New Mexico, provides an equally dramatic case of local political bosses using their power to abrogate the property rights of smallholders. Throughout the colonial period and much of the nineteenth century, land in Chihuahua had little value because markets were distant and transport costs were high. In addition, properties were subject to raids by the Apaches. The state was thus settled by military colonists, who were given land rights in exchange for keeping the Apaches at bay. Once the Mexican economy began to grow, however, and particularly once Chihuahua became crisscrossed by railroad trunk lines that ran north from Mexico City to the United States, Chihuahuan land began to be valuable.

As was the case in Morelos, a small elite abrogated the property rights of the smallholders. Indeed, as Wasserman has demonstrated, the state was run almost as a family business by the Terrazas-Creel clan. Luis Terrazas served as governor in 1860–73, 1879–84, and 1903–4. In 1904, Terrazas stepped down as governor in favor of his son-in-law, Enrique Creel. Creel ruled until 1910. The Terrazas-Creel holdings ran across banking, ranching, agriculture, manufacturing, food processing, mining and smelting, dry goods retailing, railroads, and public utilities. By 1910 the clan was the single largest employer in the state. They controlled the state's largest bank, 70 percent of the flour market, and

---

[31] Womack (1969), p. 53.
[32] Womack (1969), p. 49.
[33] Womack (1969), pp. 50–51.

50 percent of its meat-packing operations. Their agricultural holdings ran to 15 million acres. Terrazas was reputedly the wealthiest man in Mexico.[34]

The core of the Terrazas-Creel empire was its agricultural holdings. As Friedrich Katz has shown, one of the first things that Luis Terrazas did as governor in the 1860s was to expropriate the property of another hacendado, Pablo Martínez del Rio, who had made the political error of supporting the French over Benito Juárez. Terrazas then allocated this property to himself.[35] Other properties were obtained by buying them at steep discounts from hacendados who had abandoned them during the instability of the 1860s and could not settle them again because they could not guarantee that their work forces would be protected against Indian raids. Terrazas, of course, did not have this problem. As state governor, he controlled the militia.[36]

As Friedrich Katz has demonstrated, Terrazas and Creel, along with other large landowners in Chihuahua, used federal land policies to gradually whittle away at the vast tracts of land held by small farmers.[37] They also engaged in a range of swindles. Typical of these is the case of the village of Bachiniva, in which a neighboring hacienda attempted to claim some of the village's land. The mayor of the town, who was also a hacendado, told the villagers that in order to protect their rights he needed their deeds and other documents that proved their ownership of the land. The mayor then conveniently "lost" the documents. The neighboring hacienda obtained the lands, and the mayor received a bribe. Opponents of the mayor were then murdered.[38]

The Terrazas-Creel offensive against smallholders gathered momentum after 1904, when Terrazas stepped down in favor of Creel. Creel quickly carried out two reforms that allowed him to accelerate the attack on small farmers. The first was a 1904 law that replaced the elected heads of municipalities with officials appointed by the state governor. This eliminated an important obstacle to the land grab, because local elected officials had often served as the first line of defense of a community's lands. These elected officials were now replaced with Creel's cronies, who used their positions to grab village lands or to sell them to other outsiders.[39] In

[34] Wasserman (1984), chap. 3; Wasserman (1993), pp. 74–75.
[35] Katz (1998), pp. 14–15.
[36] Katz (1998), p. 15.
[37] Katz (1998), pp. 18–19, 27.
[38] Katz (1998), p. 41.
[39] Katz (1998), pp. 32–35.

fact, Terrazas-Creel "family members or close allies filled nearly every important political office in state government."[40]

Creel's second reform was a state land law promulgated in 1905. This law replaced the federal government as the arbiter of land questions with the state government – which is to say, with Creel. The law also eliminated restrictions in federal land law that protected municipal lands from expropriation and increased the range of individuals who could bid on those privatized lands.[41]

One particularly striking feature of this land law was that it was completely unconstitutional. The adjudication and distribution of public lands fell under federal, not state, jurisdiction. Even more striking, once this fact was pointed out (in a grievance filed by the village of Janos), the federal government did nothing about it. At one point, the undersecretary of the Secretaría de Fomento (Ministry of Development) wrote Creel complaining about the unconstitutionality of the law and informing the governor that the federal government was sending a surveyor to Janos to sort out the land dispute. Creel responded with an open threat of rebellion by Chihuahua's large landowners. "Revoking that law," Creel wrote, "was a grave matter" that could cause "serious disorders" and "great harm," because approximately 10,000 people had benefited from it. The federal government backed down. The Ministry of Development did not send the promised surveyor to the village. It also did not inform the village that the law was unconstitutional. Liberated from the threat of federal intervention, the Creel-appointed mayor of the village (who was behind the landgrab in the first place) cut off the village's water supply and began to charge the villagers for access to the pastures that they had previously used for free.[42]

The existence of unconstitutional state land laws indicates the weakness of the federal government vis-à-vis the states. As the exchange between Creel and the Secretaría de Fomento makes clear, even had the Díaz government wanted to, it could not have enforced its own laws without the assistance of local political bosses. In point of fact, not only was Creel's land law unconstitutional; his very possession of the governor's office was unconstitutional. The Constitution of 1857 required that state governors be born in Mexico of parents who were Mexican citizens. Creel's father

---

[40] Wasserman (1993), p. 74.
[41] Katz (1998), pp. 28–29.
[42] Katz (1998), pp. 35–37.

was an American who had served as the U.S. consul in Chihuahua City.[43] In Porfirian Mexico, however, this was nothing more than an inconvenient fact. The federal government never tried to remove Creel. Instead, Díaz appointed him secretary of foreign affairs.

THE IMPACT OF THE REVOLUTION

Violent Conflict

One might easily imagine that the revolution would have completely destroyed Mexican agriculture. To be sure, there was plenty of mayhem and murder in the Mexican countryside. Armies slaughtered livestock, commandeered crops, and turned farm buildings into barracks. Agricultural properties were confiscated by every armed faction, regardless of their stated ideology.

Yet when all was said and done, the years of civil war had less of an impact on agricultural output than one might imagine. The violence did not completely disrupt the productive apparatus of the country's agricultural system. The reason is obvious: farms and ranches were a source of finance for passing armies. Thus, most factions, with the notable exception of the Zapatistas of Morelos, continued operating the ranches and plantations they occupied, employing their work forces and oftentimes even their former administrators. This strategy implied that factions could not carry out the agrarian reforms that they had promised their followers. Even factions with strong agrarian ideologies, such as the Villistas, forwent agrarian reform in favor of generating income for their armed movement.

Friedrich Katz's monumental study of Pancho Villa indicates that the Villistas were perhaps among the most capable of Mexico's revolutionary factions when it came to diverting the revenues of haciendas to the cause of the army. Even though Villa had promised to carry out an agrarian reform, he soon decided that this lofty goal would have to wait until the end of the war. He also quickly realized that the most efficient way to administer the large estates he had confiscated was to run them just as they had been run by the oligarchy he had dispossessed.[44]

---

[43] Katz (1998), p. 47.
[44] Katz (1998), p. 404.

Some captured haciendas were administered by a specially created state agency, the Administración General de Confiscaciones del Estado de Chihuahua (General Administration of Confiscations of the State of Chihuahua). Others were controlled by various local and regional boards. Then there were the haciendas allocated to Villa and his generals, 12 in all; 2 of these were administered for Villa himself. It is not clear whether the generals were supposed to support their armies out of the proceeds from these haciendas, whether they had turn over part of their revenues to the state government for this purpose, or whether the revenues were theirs alone. In the one case we know about, that of General Tomás Urbina, 50 percent of the profits had to be turned over to the Villista central administration.[45]

Not all haciendas in Chihuahua were occupied by the Villistas. Villa was both politically astute and personally loyal. Thus, he exempted two classes of properties. The first were foreign-owned properties, with the exception of those belonging to Spaniards. The reason is clear: he wanted to maintain good relations with the United States. His only action against American interests was to impose a tax on cattle exports.[46] The second exemption were properties owned by the family of Francisco Madero, who Villa had followed during the early years of the revolution. His personal loyalty prevented him from seizing either properties belonging to the Madero family or to families that had intermarried with them, such as the wealthy Zuloagas.[47]

Villa continued the strategy of financing his movement with captured estates when he moved outside the state of Chihuahua. In the spring of 1914 he took control of Mexico's most important cotton-growing region, the Laguna, which overlaps the states of Durango and Coahuila. Villa at first tried to run the Laguna's cotton plantations through a centralized agricultural commission. This proved more difficult than anticipated. Villa therefore devolved the management of the plantations to favored "generals." Sometimes the properties were rented out for fixed rates, but sharecropping agreements were more common. For example, Villa rented the El Carrizal property to General Roque González Garza in return for 30 percent of production, a typical rental rate for these arrangements.[48] At times, rather than seize properties, Villa allowed the old owners to

---

[45] Katz (1998), pp. 404–5.
[46] Katz (1998), p. 413.
[47] Katz (1998), p. 443.
[48] Vargas-Lobsinger (1999), p. 37.

remain in control in exchange for a specific tax of 15 pesos per bale of cotton (230 kilograms).[49]

Other armies in northern and central-north Mexico followed a strategy similar to that of the Villistas. As Alan Knight has shown, confiscated estates were often kept intact and worked for the good of the cause, either directly or through commercial contracts. This was the case, for example, in Carrancista controlled Sonora. It was also the case in Durango, where "confiscated estates were placed in 'public' hands and the haciendas were either worked 'directly for the benefit of all' or parceled out among friends and retainers of rebel commanders."[50] In Zacatecas, General Pánfilo Natera appears to have tried to follow the Villista strategy of establishing a state commission to administer the 150 captured haciendas in his possession. It is unlikely that Natera was able to successfully run the estates in a centralized manner. He probably had to devolve these to his retainers and friends. He may also have had to distribute at least some of the property to local peasants.[51]

In the state of San Luis Potosí, the strategy of the state's most important revolutionary faction, led by the Cedillo brothers, evolved along with their ability to retain control over the territories they occupied. At the beginning of their campaign in 1913 the Cedillos and their allies simply sacked haciendas. By 1914, however, they were militarily capable of holding onto the estates that they had captured and thus started to exploit them commercially.[52] For both ideological and practical political reasons, the Cedillos distributed at least some haciendas to the local populace.[53] Nevertheless, on balance, the Cedillos operated much in the same way as other revolutionary factions. Romana Falcón has summed up the evidence as follows: "In the end, and in spite of all the variations, the seizure of haciendas, ranchos, and houses in San Luis Potosí basically had, during the bloodiest years of civil strife, a military objective: to sustain the armed bands and the Revolution. The distribution of confiscated lands was, most of the time, an entirely secondary objective in comparison to the more important one of preserving the estates as an economic unit."[54]

---

[49] Vargas-Lobsinger (1999), p. 39, citing unpublished work by Mario Cerutti. In 1914, 15 pesos per bale came to 14 percent of the gross value of production; in 1915 and 1916 it came to 21 percent. Calculated from data in México, INEGI (1994), p. 448.
[50] Knight (1986b), p. 187.
[51] Knight (1986b), p. 187.
[52] Falcón (1990), pp. 147–48.
[53] Knight (1986b), p. 188.
[54] Falcón (1990), p. 146.

Even in Morelos, where the agrarian radicalism of the Zapatistas called for the immediate return of confiscated plantations to peasant villages, there were attempts by the military leadership to run the sugar estates on a commercial basis. The problem was that the Zapatistas could not sell their production after 1915. Before the revolution, Morelos sugar was primarily sold in Mexico City, which was now under the control of the Carrancistas. Exporting sugar to the United States or Europe was not an option: the Carrancistas controlled the port of Veracruz. Thus, cut off from markets and starved for capital, the Zapatistas succeeded in getting only eight sugar mills back into operation.[55] Most of the estates were therefore divided up among the peasant-soldiers who backed Zapata. Morelos's sugar fields reverted to corn and beans.[56]

Because crops and livestock do not mature overnight, armies would operate plantations or ranches only if they were reasonably certain that they would be in control of the property at least until the next harvest. Otherwise, their incentives were not to plant but to plunder. The net result in these cases was the collapse of agricultural production. In the states of Guanajuato and Querétaro (and parts of Jalisco and Michoacán), for example, José Inés Chávez García rampaged freely between 1914 and 1918, looting and kidnapping for ransom. Occasionally, Chávez's men would temporarily occupy a plantation and plant some corn for their own consumption, but they never attempted to restart cash crop production or preserve the plantations' infrastructure.[57] The Carrancistas fighting Chávez behaved no differently. One observer wrote, "The government troops went up there [Arcadia County] and began stealing the animals, goods, chattels, the owners resisting were called bandits, their homes were burnt, everything was stolen and many killed."[58]

Carranza realized that uncertainty discouraged landowners from investing and producing. He therefore aggressively asserted that his movement had nothing to with the "depredatory seizures" carried out by other factions.[59] The problem was that these assertions were not credible. The evidence, impressionistic as it is, is that when the Carrancistas began to emerge triumphant on the battlefield at the end of 1915, the de facto property rights system established by occupying armies began to

---

[55] Bartra (1993), pp. 69–70. Knight puts the number of mills at four. Knight (1986b), p. 188.
[56] Womack (1986), p. 157; Knight (1986b), pp. 188–89; Katz (1998), pp. 403–4.
[57] Knight (1986b), pp. 400–1.
[58] Quoted in Knight (1986b), p. 397.
[59] Falcón (1990), p. 138.

break down. Time horizons became short; the incentive to cultivate was low.[60]

Thus, there began a period of food shortages. How widespread these were is not clear. We know that areas of the north-central region of the country in some years operated at only 10 to 20 percent of their capacity.[61] The government of Mexico State reported hunger in 1915.[62] Food riots hit Mexico City in that same year.[63] In 1916 foreign diplomats in Querétaro reported that food was scarce.[64] In 1917 the governor of Mexico State again reported food shortages. "The loss of last year's harvests produced terrible misery . . . especially among the inhabitants of the small villages, whose members invaded the state's most important cities with the objective of pleading for public charity."[65]

That there were periodic shortages in some regions is undisputable. Alan Knight's chronicling of a wide variety of observations by contemporaries makes this abundantly clear.[66] What is less clear is whether these shortages were a sustained and generalized phenomenon. The available quantitative evidence suggests that they probably were limited in geographic and temporal extent. First, we know that there were sizable swathes of Mexico almost completely unaffected by revolutionary violence, including the states of Oaxaca, Tabasco, the Yucatán, and parts of Chiapas.[67] Second, to the extent that we can proxy domestic production shortfalls by food imports from the United States, the evidence does not indicate widespread and sustained declines in crop output. Imports of corn, for example, increased during the revolution – but the net increase in imports over their Porfirian levels was only one-tenth of a bushel per inhabitant per year. Increases in rice and bean imports were of even smaller per capita magnitudes than in corn. In the case of rice, net imports, at their highest level, were on the order of half a pound per year. In the case of beans, net imports were on the order of a cup per

---

[60] In the Laguna region, for example, agriculture collapsed when the Villistas were forced on the run in late 1915. The Constitutionalists seized the cotton crop but did not restore production. In fact, Villa returned in December 1916, but he too did not restore production. Instead, he exacted a forced loan of 2 million pesos from local planters. Vargas-Lobsinger (1999), pp. 43–45.

[61] Knight (1986b), p. 414.

[62] Castellanos Suárez (1998), pp. 115–16.

[63] Knight (1986b), p. 416.

[64] Knight (1986b), p. 415.

[65] Castellanos Suárez (1998), p. 145.

[66] Knight (1986b), pp. 412–16.

[67] Katz (1998), p. 451.

person per year. (We return to the analysis of this data in detail in the next section.)

One might argue that staple crop imports are not a good proxy for domestic production shortfalls. The cost of imported corn might have been prohibitive for many Mexicans. If that were the case, however, we would expect to see a decline in adult heights of children born in the 1910s.[68] A height-by-age study carried out by Moramay López Alonso on Mexican army recruits (who tended to be from Mexico's poorest classes, and who therefore would have been the most strongly affected by a spike in food prices) does not, however, indicate any decline in heights for men born in the 1910 decade. In fact, her research indicates that men born during 1910–20 reached adult heights that exceeded those of men born during the decade 1900–10. These results are not sensitive to geographic region of birth or to markers of social class (such as literacy).[69]

When taken together, the evidence on staple imports and heights indicates that, to the extent that food shortages occurred, they were probably local in nature or of short duration. How, then, can we reconcile the "impressionistic" (to use Knight's term) evidence with the available quantitative data? One potential explanation is sample bias in the impressionistic evidence: when food was scarce, people wrote about it; when food was plentiful, it did not merit mention by contemporary observers.

As the civil war ended and Carranza consolidated power, what was the state of Mexican agriculture? Mexico's large landowners survived the revolution as a social class. Few were hauled before firing squads.[70] Much of the physical capital of agriculture also escaped the fighting. This was particularly the case for haciendas owned by foreigners. It was also true in those states unaffected by the fighting (predominantly in the south and southwest of the country), but was true in the northern states of Coahuila and Sonora as well.[71] There was, however, plenty of devastation elsewhere in the countryside. In addition, the Mexican peasantry had emerged as a powerful political force. The peasants had fought a revolution and had been militarily defeated. Their defeat had not, however,

---

[68] Average adult heights in any native-born population are the product of two variables: diet and disease exposure during childhood. One would expect that a period of widespread food shortages would produce malnourishment and increased incidence of diseases associated with malnourishment.

[69] López-Alonso (2000), chap. 4.

[70] Katz (1998), p. 448.

[71] Katz (1998), p. 449.

been total. They could make demands on the political system, and they knew it.

Institutional Change

Carranza was well aware that the experience of the revolution made it impossible to go back to the status quo ante. He was going to have to go with the tide, which in the late 1910s was strongly rising in favor of land redistribution. At the same time, however, Carranza also needed the support of Mexico's large landowners. First, he needed to get the economy in gear again, and to do that he needed to make a commitment to private property rights. Second, Carranza could not afford the risk that a widespread land reform would push large landowners into open revolt. Because his military campaign against the Zapatistas and Villistas actually dragged on until 1919 and 1920, respectively, he could hardly afford any additional enemies. Carranza therefore walked a tightrope and did so in an unbalanced, zigzag gait: he enacted formal laws that on paper benefited the peasantry; then he actively worked to forestall any of the laws from taking effect.

Carranza's zigzag land policies can be traced back to the Plan de Guadalupe of 1913, in which he refused to include a call for an agrarian reform. During the course of the anti-Huerta campaign, he tried to pressure Villa to return confiscated estates to their former owners.[72] By late 1914 Carranza had been driven from Mexico City by Villa and Zapata. Looking for support, he began to court radical peasants. A decree of December 12, 1914, stated that he would work for "agrarian laws favoring the formation of small property, dissolving the large estates, and restoring to the villages the lands of which they were unjustly deprived."[73] One month later, on January 6, 1915, Carranza issued another decree ordering the return of stolen lands to Mexico's villages.[74]

By 1916 Carranza's military fortunes were rising. The Villistas and Zapatistas were on the run. Carranza now changed course again and began to court the nation's large landowners. In January 1916 he established the Comisión Nacional Agraria (National Agrarian Commision), whose purpose was not to redistribute land but to reverse distributions

---

[72] Katz (1998), p. 400.
[73] Quoted in Tannenbaum (1968), p. 167, n. 29.
[74] Tannenbaum (1968), p. 171.

undertaken by local authorities.[75] In fact, Carranza returned the vast majority of the lands that had been "intervened" by various revolutionary factions in the preceding years. He even sought, not completely successfully, to return the lands of the Terrazas-Creel family.[76]

Carranza's commitment to protect private property rights was, however, not credible. Carranza's agrarian reform decree of 1915 still hung over the heads of large landowners, and Carranza himself seized lands belonging to his political enemies, including the Madero family.[77] Also, Carranza had tried to introduce much weaker agrarian measures into the original draft of the Constitution of 1917, but the radicals at the convention successfully rewrote the provisions.[78] Article 27 declared null and void the land transfers that had taken place since 1856, called for the breakup of Mexico's large estates in the interest of the public good, made the government the residual claimant on property rights in land, and made decisions about land distribution an administrative rather than judicial procedure.

Carranza did his best to ignore Article 27. In April 1917 he issued a decree prohibiting provisional grants of lands.[79] This decree effectively halted land redistribution. Markiewicz's estimates indicate that from 1915 until November 1920, only 400,000 hectares were distributed, 0.3 percent of all agricultural land. Only 67,193 small farmers benefited.[80]

Obregón, after he overthrew Carranza, walked the same tightrope. He could not afford to ignore organized peasants. At the same time, he and many of his generals had become big landowners or had gone into business with big landowners.[81] These circumstances forced him to continue Carranza's zigzag course regarding the agrarian question. In one region of Mexico, the government armed peasants and gave them land. In other parts of the country, the government ordered the army to expel peasants occupying hacienda lands.

There was one crucial difference between Obregón and Carranza: Obregón understood the need to form durable coalitions with property

[75] Falcón (1990), p. 137; Simpson (1937), table 17.
[76] Carranza was overthrown by Obregón before this could be successfully carried out. Katz (1998), p. 749.
[77] Womack (1986), p. 179; Falcón (1990), p. 138; Markiewicz (1993), p. 43.
[78] Tannenbaum (1968), p. 174.
[79] Tannenbaum (1968), p. 184.
[80] Markiewicz (1993), pp. 179, 184.
[81] For a discussion of Obregón's own successes as an agricultural entrepreneur, see Hall (1981), pp. 200–2.

owners. He therefore allowed antireform governors to arrange that landowners and their allies would be elected to the Senate.[82] The Senate provided a forum for the landowners to negotiate the terms and extent of whatever agrarian reform was to take place. The agreement reached in 1922 provided that landowners would retain a *minimum* of 150 hectares of irrigated land, 250 hectares of good-quality rain-fed land, or 500 hectares of poor-quality rain-fed land. States often set even higher minimums. If properties marked for expropriation formed part of an "agroindustrial unit," the proprietors could cede equivalent land in another location. In addition, grants would not include buildings, gardens, orchards, irrigation works, or plantations that produced coffee, cacao, vanilla, rubber, or other "similar" products.[83]

In addition, the law gave the state governor a veto over any land redistributions within his state. The law specified that petitions for a land grant had to be made to the state governor, who would judge its merit before forwarding it on to the federal authorities. If he did not approve the request, it died then and there.

Finally, the law created strong incentives for sharecroppers and agricultural workers to side with the landlords and oppose any agrarian reform. The law specified that only villagers whose lands had been taken during the prerevolutionary period would be eligible to receive an ejidal grant. Agricultural workers and sharecroppers were not, therefore, legally eligible to receive land. Until the law was revised in the early 1930s, a huge percentage of Mexico's rural population had little reason to make common cause with the peasants in the villages. In fact, an agrarian reform would redistribute the lands they worked, thereby depriving them of a livelihood.

Enforcement of the Property Rights System

The existence of a law was not in and of itself a credible commitment to property owners. The Mexican government was not limited. The Constitution gave the president extraordinary powers to act by decree. Congress did not limit his actions, and everyone knew it (see Chapter 3). The only genuine limit on the actions of state governors within their territories was the threat of federal military intervention, not the dictates of the federal Congress. The governors, in fact, had every incentive to redistribute land

[82] Markiewicz (1993), p. 38.
[83] Markiewicz (1993), p. 38.

to peasants who could be organized into armed militias that would support the governor in the event of an armed confrontation with the federal government. Also, everyone knew that even Obregón might need these militias to remain in power in the event of a coup. In fact, during the de la Huerta revolt of 1923–24, Obregón turned to the radical state governors and their peasant militias to fight the federal army. Their loyalty, however, came at a price: land distribution.[84]

What then made the agreement hammered out in the Senate credible? The answer is third-party enforcement by revolutionary generals – some "irregular," some "retired," some active duty officers in the newly reconstituted federal army.[85] These generals either received a stream of rents directly from large landowners, or became large landowners themselves. Often, both mechanisms were at work. Regardless of the mechanism, their interests were aligned not with the peasants and agricultural day laborers but with the landlords. They therefore actively worked to thwart anyone – the federal government included – who actually tried to implement the agrarian reform specified in the 1917 Constitution. As Dudley Ankerson has observed: "Many military chiefs in particular, either as hacendados or through their commercial activities, already had a vital interest in checking widespread local distribution. Having acquired a stake in the rural economy, they were naturally concerned with protecting it."[86]

The enforcers of private property rights even included generals who had fought on the side of landless workers and peasants. Pancho Villa, for example, was given the Canutillo hacienda in the state of Durango in order to get him to lay down his arms in 1920. Villa was allowed to keep an escort of 50 armed men on the hacienda. An additional 750 of Villa's soldiers were settled on two neighboring properties.[87] Other landowners in the region transferred rents to Villa, by, for example, buying farm machinery for him and his men.[88] The federal government appears to

[84] Markiewicz (1993), p. 43.
[85] During the revolution, most generals were essentially warlords who commanded irregular armies. In fact, the federal army disappeared as of 1914, when Huerta was overthrown. To an extent, the federal army was reconstituted when Carranza came to power in 1917, but this was not a professional, regular army in the normal sense of the word. Indeed, the warlord nature of its leadership is precisely what fueled many of the military uprisings of the 1920s. In addition, many of the warlords of the 1910s, who were not integrated into the regular army after 1917, continued to command large numbers of militiamen whom they could easily mobilize.
[86] Ankerson (1984), p. 111.
[87] Katz (1998), pp. 726, 735.
[88] Vargas-Lobsinger (1999), p. 57.

have also transferred rents to the Villistas. The Mexican consul in the United States spent $60,000 dollars in 1921–22 alone to buy agricultural equipment for Canutillo. Other payments, one for $40,000 dollars and another for 25,000 pesos, were made to Villa as well.[89]

The logic of the situation was not lost on Villa: he quickly allied himself with local landowners and began to behave like they did on agrarian issues. In 1921, for example, Villa had his retinue of soldier-farmers occupy lands adjacent to Canutillo, even though those lands had been legally allocated to peasants in the region. Obregón, fearing that Villa would react violently, refused to send federal troops to force the Villistas to leave. In 1922 Villa sent Obregón a letter urgently asking him to pressure the governor of Chihuahua to return lands to a hacendado friend of his.[90] Ultimately, in Villa's case, Obregón came to believe that Villa might revolt, and therefore had Villa assassinated. Indeed, there is evidence that Villa was preparing to side with de la Huerta in 1923. The evidence was a cache of arms at Villa's hacienda that included 6,400 Winchester carbines, 1,100 Mauser rifles, 800 Mauser carbines, and 550,000 rounds of ammunition, as well as grenades and bombs.[91]

Villa was not the only former general providing third-party enforcement in the 1920s. Landowners diverted rents to former (and current) generals, their retinues, and organized agricultural workers. These arrangements would, of course, reduce the total amount of rent received by landowners, but they created a set of allies who could help prevent expropriation.

There were essentially two mechanisms to divert this stream of rents. One was simply the payment of protection rents to the military zone commander. Ernest Gruening, for example, informs us that virtually all regional zone commanders demanded money from landowners to protect them from expropriations.[92] The other mechanism was for revolutionary generals to become sharecroppers – *very big sharecroppers* – on the properties of large landholders. This linked the fate of the generals with that of the landlords. In the Laguna, for example, Carlos González's extensive properties were placed under the management of various agents in return for a percentage of the profits. The share ranged anywhere from 3 to 65 percent, depending on the parcel. General

---

[89] Katz (1998), p. 740.
[90] Katz (1998), p. 747.
[91] Katz (1998), p. 780.
[92] Gruening (1928), p. 319.

Cesáreo Castro, Obregón's cavalry chief and the "liberator" of Gómez Palacio, for example, received a contract for 33 percent of the production of the La Partida plantation. Should anything threaten Castro's stream of rents from González, he stood ready to revolt.[93] By 1920 more than 60 percent of the Laguna was worked under rental or large-scale share-cropping agreements.[94]

Similar sharecropping arrangements between generals and landowners can be found in a number of other states. The purpose of these arrange-ments, as Tobler makes clear, was to align the interests of the generals with those of the landowners. In the state of Hidalgo, for example, General Enrique Espejel received a share of the benefits from the state's maguey plantations via a tenancy contract. On the border of the nearby states of Puebla and Tlaxcala, the troops of General Fortunato Maycotte ran a lucrative pulque business. Despite repeated orders from Mexico City to leave, they stayed put. These arrangements between the military and pri-vate actors were so well developed in Puebla that as late as 1933 soldiers prevented peasants from occupying ejido lands near Chiquahuapan, even though the ejido had been legally granted to them. This took place right under the nose of the federal government: the soldiers were "stationed" in the Federal District but only appeared once a month to receive their salaries. The rest of the month they provided protection for Puebla's ha-cendados. Their officers worked on the haciendas as "administrators." Similar accounts come to us from the state of Guanajuato. As late as 1934, landless peasants in that state complained about a landholder who had "placed his rights under the protection of Señor General Domínguez, who has changed from a revolutionary into a landholding protector of the latifundistas."[95]

In many cases, active duty generals became major landowners. One of the most notable of these was General Guadalupe Sánchez, the fed-eral military zone commander in Veracruz. General Sánchez acquired sugar-growing properties throughout the counties of Córdoba, Jalapa, Orizaba, and Pánuco. Not surprisingly, he became one of the state's most outspoken – and violent – opponents of land redistribution. Sánchez al-lied himself with Veracruz's other landlords and even allowed federal troops under his command to supplement the landowner's private militias.

---

[93] Castro joined the de la Huerta revolt against the government in 1923. Vargas-Lobsinger (1999), p. 55.
[94] Vargas-Lobsinger (1999), pp. 54–55.
[95] All of these examples are taken from Tobler (1988), pp. 494–96.

Military engagements between peasant activists and Sánchez's troops were a constant throughout the state.[96]

An example of how, exactly, Mexico's generals protected their newfound interests comes to us from Aguascalientes in 1925. The military zone commander, General Rodrigo Talamantes, formed an alliance with the local landowners. When a official from the CROM arrived to investigate the murder of local peasant leaders by the army and to demand protection for the local peasantry, Talamantes simply had him shot as he stepped off the train. While he was at it, Talamantes also shot several of the peasants who had gathered to greet the CROM representative. The murders were never investigated.[97]

Another example of how property rights enforcement worked on the ground comes from southwest Tamaulipas. Here General Carrera Torres had settled down as a local cacique (local political boss) along with his troops on confiscated farms. These men had seized their property by force and would defend it by force. When Governor Portes Gil sent Lieutenant Colonel José Dolores Álvarez to try to undercut Carrera Torres by organizing petitions for land restitution, Carrera Torres simply ordered his military farmers to shoot Colonel Álvarez.[98]

In addition to current and "retired" generals, private militias formed whose purpose was to head off attempts to carry out a land reform. These private militias usually consisted of armed resident workers, sharecroppers, or tenants.[99] In some cases, these militiamen were deployed alongside federal troops. In Veracruz, for example, private militias and federal troops under the command of General Guadalupe Sánchez clashed with agrarian radicals supported by the state civil guard. Sánchez, it should be noted, was financed by the local landowners, not federal taxes. To end the fighting, President Obregón ordered that the civil guard and all agrarian radicals be disarmed "to prevent further bloodshed."[100] General Sánchez's troops – *and the private militias* – were, of course, exempt from the disarmament decree.[101] Clashes between radicals and militias occurred in Guanajuato, Guerrero, and Michoacán, with similar results.[102] In Mexico State, landowners even succeeded in co-opting armed *peasant*

---

[96] Plasencia de la Parra (1998), pp. 25, 27, 31.
[97] Gruening (1928), p. 324.
[98] Fowler-Salamini (1990), p. 207.
[99] Tobler (1988), p. 506.
[100] Markiewicz (1993), p. 39; Fowler-Salamini (1978), p. 36.
[101] Fowler-Salamini (1978), p. 132.
[102] Simpson (1937), p. 349; Friedrich (1977), p. 56; Wasserman (1987), p. 92.

militias (the so-called defenses sociales or social defenses) and mobilized them to defend their property rights against the peasantry whose interests they were presumably meant to protect.[103]

What motivated Mexico's rural poor to join militias whose purpose was to block land redistribution? Rental or sharecropping arrangements were one motivation. Such arrangements increased the number of people who would stand to lose should the government unilaterally attempt to alter the owner's property rights. In the state of Tlaxcala, for example, an attempted land distribution in 1918 provoked violent clashes with share-croppers.[104] This explains why land companies in northern Mexico that had worked the lands directly during the Porfiriato converted themselves into absentee landlords in the 1920s. By 1928 the Compañía Algodonera Industrial de la Laguna, for example, had subdivided all its extensive properties into smaller ranches, without officially transferring a single title of ownership.[105] The renters and sharecroppers stood to gain little from an agrarian reform. In fact, they were legally ineligible to receive land as part of the agrarian reform. Any agrarian reform that took place would come at their expense. In addition, in many cases renters could sublet their lands, creating even more interests in maintaining the status quo.[106]

The resident work force also served to support the status quo. Its de-mands extended only to higher wages and better working conditions. In Puebla, for instance, owners and workers clashed over wages, holidays, privileges, and piece work, but not land.[107] In fact, resident workers or sharecroppers often aided their bosses in defending their properties.[108]

When they were established, agricultural unions ironically aided in in-stitutionalizing the landowners' position. In the 1920s at least 40 differ-ent unions represented agricultural workers in the Laguna district *alone*. They eventually affiliated with the CROM, the same organization that represented factory workers. These unions were not interested in lands but in distributing benefits to their members and leaders. In 1927, for example, the Durango boss of the Sindicato de Campesinos Agraristas declared that his exclusive goal was not the subdivision of the latifundia but the "intensification of agricultural production."[109] In other words,

---

[103] Tobler (1988), p. 506.
[104] Buve (1988), pp. 370–71.
[105] Vargas-Lobsinger (1999), p. 103.
[106] Vargas-Lobsinger (1999), p. 117.
[107] Nickel (1988), p. 406.
[108] Tobler (1988), p. 508.
[109] Vargas-Lobsinger (1999), p. 95.

they wanted higher wages (and more revenue and influence for the union), and they would presumably oppose anything that would negatively affect those benefits. In Veracruz, in fact, sugar mill owners actively encouraged unionization in order to protect themselves against the threat of expropriation.[110]

The net result of these maneuvers was that Obregón and Calles distributed very little land. Markiewicz estimates that during Obregón's four years in office, he distributed only 1.7 million hectares, or 1.3 percent of Mexico's agricultural land. These distributions benefited only 158,000 farmers.[111] In fact, during Obregón's presidency, many of Mexico's prominent Porfirian families were able to reconstitute a good part of their landed empires. This even included the notorious Terrazas-Creel clan.[112] The policies followed by Calles were little different. The total land area distributed by Calles was 3.2 million hectares, only 2.4 percent of Mexico's total agricultural land. The 1930 agricultural census provides a strong idea of how inconsequential the reform had been to that point. Even though Article 27 had mandated the distribution of large private farms, 83 percent of private farmland in 1930 was held in farms larger than 1,000 hectares. These farms were owned by only 1.5 percent of farmers. An additional 12 percent was held in farms of from 101 to 1,000 hectares.[113] The implication is clear: only 5 percent of farmland was held by the small farmers who were supposed to have benefited from the agrarian reform.[114] Moreover, much of this land consisted of hills and woodlands, not prime cropland.

In short, stable coalitions formed in some regions of Mexico, particularly the North. Former generals, members of the government, and large landowners found it in their mutual interest to forge alliances that allowed them to share rents. Even Presidents Obregón and Calles participated. Obregón became a major landowner and cornered the export of chickpeas from Mexico to the United States.[115] Calles became a sugar baron. In 1926 he formed the El Mante sugar company and opened a large milling operation in the state of Tamaulipas. Calles, his sons, and Foreign Secretary Aáron Sáenz, all sat on the board.[116] Not surprisingly,

---

[110] Aurrecoechea and Paz Paredes (1993), p. 107.
[111] Markiewicz (1993), pp. 179, 184.
[112] Katz (1998), p. 755; Wasserman (1993), pp. 74–90.
[113] Markiewicz (1993), p. 188.
[114] Markiewicz (1993), p. 184.
[115] Hall (1981), pp. 200–2; Okada (2000), pp. 134–36.
[116] Saenz was Calles's brother in law. Aurrecoechea and Paz Paredes (1993), p. 93.

they received extensive financial support from the Banco de México. In addition, the federal government built a publicly funded irrigation network in the same district as El Mante's lands. As Aurrecoechea and Paz Paredes have put it: "In practical terms, the state constructed for the Compañía Azucarera del Mante an irrigation district for its private use."[117]

The coalition of large landowners and military men turned farmers used federal policy to its own purposes. These were threefold: to prevent the redistribution of their properties, to use the federal government to provide them with subsidized credit, and to use the federal government to build road and irrigation programs that would lower their costs of production and distribution.

Subsidized credit was obtained via the Banco Nacional de Crédito Agrícola, founded in 1926. The bank was originally capitalized at 20.3 million pesos, almost all of which (89 percent) came from the federal government. Its nominal purpose was to lend to cooperatives of small farmers.[118] In 1926, the bank's first year of operation, it made virtually no attempt to provide any credit to cooperatives of small farmers. Of the 16.7 million pesos lent by the bank, 98 percent went to private parties. Until Obregón's assassination in 1928, the story was much the same: in 1927, 86 percent of credit went to private parties; in 1928, 78 percent went to private parties. From 1929 to 1931 the proportion of new credit going to private parties versus cooperatives dropped to about half, but the vast majority of the bank's capital had already been lent out. The volume of new loans in 1929–31 was less than 25 percent of what it had been from 1926 to 1928, when the large farmers swallowed up all the credit.[119]

The lion's share of the bank's lending went to private landowners, the largest of whom were politically integrated into the governing faction.[120] Special loans were made to generals or other government officials for the purchase of new lands or for the improvement of the haciendas already in their hands. These included General Abundio Gómez, governor of Mexico State from 1921 to 1925, and General José Gonzalo Escobar, who would lead the last violent revolt against the government in 1929. Loans also went to Secretary of War Joaquín Amaro, Secretary of Industry Luis León, and Interior Secretary (Gobernación) Valenzuela. None other than former president Álvaro Obregón was at the top of the list of loan recipients.[121]

[117] Aurrecoechea and Paz Paredes (1993), pp. 91–92.
[118] Krauze, Meyer, et al. (1977), p. 149.
[119] Markiewicz (1993), p. 193.
[120] Krauze, Meyer, et al. (1977), pp. 157–58.
[121] Markiewicz (1993), p. 50; Krauze, Meyer, et al. (1977), pp. 157–58.

Tracts obtained with the Banco Agrícola's help could be massive: Luis León, who had worked for the Comisión Local Agraria in Sonora (and had therefore been putatively in charge of redistributing land to small-holders in the state), came to control over 100,000 acres of land that had previously belonged to the Terrazas family in Chihuahua.[122]

Roads, irrigation, and hydroelectricity were also subsidized by federal infrastructure projects.[123] The federal government constructed four large dams in Durango, Aguascalientes, Tamaulipas, and Coahuila, which directly irrigated over 100,000 hectares of land.[124] An additional 550,000 hectares were irrigated by less dramatic federal projects, which extended existing private irrigation systems at public expense in the states of Hidalgo, Mexico, and Sonora. By 1928 funds for irrigation accounted for 6.7 percent of all federal spending.[125]

ECONOMIC PERFORMANCE

What was the outcome of these arrangements? Did Mexican political instability, and its concomitant threat of dramatic institutional change, cause investment and output to collapse? Or, did the commitment mechanisms created by third-party enforcement of the implicit contract between the federal government and the large landowners produce positive rates of investment and output growth?

In answering these questions, we need to be careful to discriminate between staple crops and export agriculture. There had been, at least since Porfirian times, two Mexican agricultural sectors: one producing low-value staples largely for local markets and another producing high-value commercial crops for distant markets. The former was dominated by the production of corn and beans (and, to a lesser extent, rice), and the latter was dominated by crops such as henequen (sisal), tampico (ixtle) cotton, coffee, bananas, and sugar. The revolution and its ensuing period of political instability and institutional reforms did little to help staple agriculture, although it does not, on balance, appear to have done much to hurt it either. In staple agriculture, the productivity standard that had to be met was plain and simply not very high. Export-oriented commercial agriculture is another issue entirely. The quantitative evidence indicates

---

[122] Wasserman (1987), p. 99; Krauze, Meyer, et al. (1977), pp. 156–57; Markiewicz (1993), p. 50.
[123] Krauze, Meyer, et al. (1977), pp. 100–6; Sterret and Davis (1928), pp. 162–78.
[124] Krauze, Meyer, et al. (1977), pp. 140–42.
[125] Sterret and Davis (1928), p. 171.

not only that exports grew but also that Mexico increased its share of the U.S. market; in addition, Mexico entered into the exportation of a number of new agricultural products in the 1920s (notably chickpeas and fresh tomatoes) and quickly came to be the most important exporter of those products to the United States.

Staple Production

Measuring the output of Mexican staple agriculture is not easy. The first agricultural census did not take place until 1930. Prior to that, the Mexican government made some estimates of output for various crops in various years, but these are not comprehensive series and are of very doubtful reliability.

Lacking direct observations of staple crop production, we employ a second-best method to detect dramatic downturns or upturns in production: we estimate Mexico's net imports of staple crops from the United States. The underlying idea behind this method is as follows: under the reasonable assumption that the demand for basic foodstuffs is inelastic with respect to price, drops in domestic production should produce a concomitant increase in imports.[126] We also operate on the reasonable assumption that the vast majority of Mexico's imported food came from the United States. The absolute advantages that the United States had in staple crop production and the proximity of the United States to Mexico make it extremely unlikely that Mexico imported food in significant quantities from any of its other trade partners.

We can therefore use data on exports and imports of the United States, gathered by the U.S. Department of Commerce, as a way to proxy Mexican production shortfalls of staple crops. We note that Mexico was simultaneously an importer and an exporter of most staples (one Mexican region might export a crop to the United States, while another region might import that same crop from the United States). Our estimates are therefore of *net imports* (total imports from the United States minus total exports to the United States). Rising net imports would indicate a domestic production shortfall.

In looking at these data we need to be mindful that the output of crops can vary widely on a year-to-year basis for reasons of climate and blight.

---

[126] In theory, a sudden import spike could be caused by a positive shock that suddenly made the cost of foreign produce much cheaper. In practice, there is no evidence that American corn gluts drove changes in Mexico's net imports of its most important staple crop.

For that reason, we look at the staple crop data by comparing decadal averages. Even with the use of averaging, however, we should keep in mind that one or two spectacularly bad years can drive the results for an entire decade. In these cases, we recur to the accounts of contemporaries to try to isolate the effects of institutions and instability from the effects of drought and frost.

Table 8.1 presents estimates of Mexico's net corn imports from the United States. Mexico had been, even during the Porfiriato, a net corn importer. During the period 1894–1900 net imports averaged 1.7 million bushels per year. During the decade 1901–10 net imports averaged 1.1 million bushels per year. During the decade 1911–20, net corn imports nearly doubled (to 1.9 million bushels per year) over their 1901–10 level. The fact that the years 1915, 1916, 1917, and 1918 were all significantly above the 1901–10 average suggests that at least part of the need to import additional corn was caused by the inability of domestic producers to meet demand for reasons other than annual fluctuations in climate. The evidence, in short, supports the hypothesis that the civil war years were accompanied by a disruption in corn production. How serious this disruption was is another matter. At their highest level during the revolution (1918) net corn imports were 3 million bushels per year. This is a very small amount of corn to import compared with the amount consumed by Mexico's population. It suggests that, at worst, Mexico had to import one-fifth of a bushel per inhabitant per year (roughly twice the level of 1901–10). This hardly suggests a dramatic collapse of domestic corn production.

The evidence also suggests that the enduring effects of political instability and institutional change were similarly small. During the period 1921–29 Mexico continued to import corn in quantities well above its 1901–10 average. Net imports for the 1920s averaged 2.7 million bushels per year. Much of the difference, however, was caused by climate. Close to half of Mexico's net corn imports for the period 1921–29 occurred in a single year (1921), and we know from contemporary sources that the harvest was small that year because the crop failed.[127] If we exclude 1921, average net imports fall to 1.5 million bushels per year, roughly midway between the average for 1901–10 and 1911–20. Moreover, the data for the 1920s neither display any kind of trend (annual figures bounce around randomly), nor do they indicate a clustering of bad years as occurred in 1915–18. Even if these figures do indicate that Mexican corn production

---

[127] Sterret and Davis (1928), p. 150.

Table 8.1. *Mexico's Net Corn Imports from the United States,*
1894–1929

Year	Volume (in thousands of bushels)	Value (in thousands of nominal dollars)
1894	432	220
1895	180	108
1896	1,677	672
1897	8,826	3,234
1898	125	44
1899	155	63
1900	580	244
1901	1,566	803
1902	747	478
1903	134	77
1904	457	273
1905	503	301
1906	1,647	992
1907	1,926	1,177
1908	686	479
1909	64	48
1910	3,254	2,486
1911	7,041	4,851
1912	1,168	913
1913	543	408
1914	460	366
1915	1,569	1,379
1916	3,056	2,607
1917	2,065	2,820
1918	2,673	5,704
1919	126	237
1920	712	851
1921	11,667	9,921
1922	2,997	2,038
1923	97	109
1924	788	948
1925	2,411	2,901
1926	4,212	3,982
1927	1,058	1,013
1928	420	453
1929	354	404
1894–1900	1,710	655
1901–10	1,098	711
1911–20	1,941	2,014
1921–29	2,667	2,419

Note: Net imports are gross imports from the United States minus Mexico's exports
to the United States.

Source: United States, Department of Commerce (various years).

was underperforming its prerevolutionary levels, the shortfall in production would have been very small – on the order of one-tenth of a bushel per year per person.

We also gathered data on Mexico's net imports of dried beans, another major staple of the Mexican diet. We note that our analysis is made complicated by the fact that through 1921 the United States recorded the volume of its bean imports and exports in bushels. Beginning in 1922, however, it recorded exports to Mexico in bushels and imports from Mexico in pounds. This means that we can only produce a volume series that runs from 1905 to 1921. We can, however, produce a value series that runs until 1929.

The data, presented in Table 8.2, do not support the hypothesis that the revolution caused much in the way of a collapse of the bean crop. Mexico was a *net exporter* of dried beans to the United States during the Porfiriato, and it continued to be a net exporter in the 1910s. In fact, 1914 and 1915, arguably two years that should have been characterized by predatory behavior and uncertainty among agriculturalists, were record years for Mexican net exports to the United States. Average net exports of beans from Mexico to the United States for the decade 1911–20 were 30 percent above the average for 1905–10. Much as was the case with corn, the (limited) evidence we have about dried beans indicates that Mexico probably underperformed in the 1920s relative to the years before 1911. Beginning in 1916, Mexico started to be a net importer of dried beans. Data on the value of net imports indicate that Mexican producers failed to satisfy domestic demand for beans in 1916, 1918, 1919, 1921, 1924, 1925, 1926, and 1927. The available volume and value data do not indicate, however, that the production shortfalls were particularly large. In 1918, at the highest level of net bean imports, Mexico's total production shortfall was 67,000 bushels. On a per capita basis, we are talking about a cup of beans per person per year.

We gathered data on a third major staple in the Mexican diet, rice. We present the data in Table 8.3. During the years 1901–10 Mexico was a net exporter of rice, sending, on average, close to 750,000 pounds of rice per year to the United States. The data are unambiguous that Mexican rice production fell during the years of revolution. From 1914 to 1921 Mexico was a *net importer* of rice. The average for the decade 1911–20 is 2.5 million pounds per year. In 1916 and 1917 net imports hit 5.9 and 7.5 million pounds per year, respectively. We must be careful, however, not to draw the conclusion from these data that Mexican rice production must have declined dramatically during the revolution. Even at its peak of

Table 8.2. *Mexico's Net Bean Imports from the United States, 1905–1929*

Year	Volume (in thousands of bushels)[a]	Value (in thousands of nominal dollars)
1905	122	108
1906	90	106
1907	133	193
1908	54	97
1909	66	129
1910	37	54
1911	110	204
1912	150	298
1913	31	29
1914	367	449
1915	412	593
1916	(22)	(127)
1917	144	355
1918	(67)	(336)
1919	(57)	(223)
1920	1	(45)
1921	(39)	(141)
1922		71
1923		85
1924		(25)
1925		(228)
1926		(252)
1927		(5)
1928		157
1929		38
1905–10	84	115
1911–20	107	120
1921–29		(33)

Note: Net imports are gross imports from the United States minus Mexico's exports to the United States. Negative numbers (in parentheses) indicate that Mexico was a net exporter.

[a] From 1910 to 1916 U.S. exports to Mexico also include peas, but these are insignificant amounts. From 1905 to 1909 Mexican bean exports to the United States include peas. From 1915 to 1921 Mexican bean exports to the United States also include lentils.

Source: United States, Department of Commerce (various years).

Table 8.3. *Mexico's Net Rice Imports from the United States,*
1894–1929

Year	Volume (in thousands of pounds)	Value (in thousands of nominal dollars)	Gross Rice Exports from Mexico as % of Total U.S. Rice Imports (by value)[a]
1894	(1)	(0)	0
1895	(348)	(8)	0
1896	(20)	(1)	0
1897	(92)	(4)	0
1898	(224)	(6)	0
1899	(575)	(25)	1
1900	(729)	(20)	1
1901	(760)	(20)	1
1902	(1,439)	(54)	3
1903	(1,925)	(55)	3
1904	(937)	(25)	1
1905	2,529	59	1
1906	(660)	(25)	3
1907	(961)	(48)	3
1908	(1,122)	(46)	2
1909	(1,159)	(44)	2
1910	(1,038)	(35)	2
1911	8	1	1
1912	(85)	(1)	0
1913	(528)	(11)	1
1914	874	37	0
1915	329	33	1
1916	5,920	223	0
1917	7,511	340	0
1918	2,874	243	0
1919	2,309	205	1
1920	5,405	393	0
1921	6,278	180	4
1922	(1,766)	(47)	4
1923	(3,108)	21	8
1924	(508)	(7)	8
1925	(2,635)	(158)	1
1926	(17,509)	(665)	13
1927	(15,719)	(637)	27
1928	(2,698)	(148)	15
1929	(9,247)	(473)	37

(*continued*)

Table 8.3 (continued)

Year	Volume (in thousands of pounds)	Value (in thousands of nominal dollars)	Gross Rice Exports from Mexico as % of Total U.S. Rice Imports (by value)[a]
1894–1900	(284)	(9)	0
1901–10	(747)	(29)	2
1911–20	2,462	146	0
1921–29	(5,212)	(215)	13

Note: Net imports are gross imports from the United States minus Mexico's exports to the United States. Negative numbers (in parentheses) indicate that Mexico was a net exporter.

[a] These figures are gross, not net of U.S. imports to Mexico. We use gross values in order to estimate the percentage of U.S. imports accounted for by Mexican exports.

Source: United States, Department of Commerce (various years).

7.5 million pounds (in 1917), we are talking about net imports of roughly half a pound per person per year. We estimate that this accounted for approximately 8 percent of rice production in normal years.[128]

The data also indicate that Mexican rice production recovered in a dramatic fashion in the 1920s. By 1922 Mexico was once again a net exporter of rice. Average net exports for 1921–29 were roughly seven times the level for the decade 1901–10. In point of fact, by the late 1920s Mexico accounted (on average) for 23 percent of total U.S. rice imports.

The increase in Mexico's total net exports conceals an important geographical redistribution in rice production. Before the revolution, almost all Mexican rice was grown in Morelos. By the time of the 1930 agricultural census, the state of Sonora produced 38 percent of the nation's production and almost all of its exports.[129] This shift in the locus of production is consistent with what we know about the political history of the

---

[128] Mexico's Departamento de Estadística Nacional (Department of National Statistics) began to collect data on rice production in 1920 and estimated that production in that year was 86 million pounds. Mexico imported 5.4 million pounds in 1920 (see Table 8.3), meaning that consumption was on the order of 91.4 million pounds. If we assume that consumption was stable from 1917 to 1920, we estimate that at its peak net rice imports accounted for 8 percent of consumption. Production data from México, INEGI (1994), pp. 451–52; import data from table 8.3.

[129] México, Ferrocarriles Nacionales (1989), pp. 26, 29.

two states. Morelos had been the focal point of the Zapatista movement and was one of the few Mexican states to undergo a substantial agrarian reform. Sonora, on the other hand, was the political power base of the revolutionary generals who took power in the 1920s. Indeed, Obregón and Calles were both Sonorans. Not surprisingly, large-scale agriculturalists in Sonora perceived that their property rights were more secure than did their counterparts in Morelos. They therefore invested and produced accordingly.

Export Agriculture

Measuring Mexico's production of nonstaple crops (henequén, tampico fiber, cotton, chickpeas, sugar, bananas, and coffee) is comparatively easy. Virtually all of Mexico's exports of these crops were destined for the United States, and U.S. imports from Mexico can be measured by putting together data sets from Department of Commerce records.[130] This is an excellent proxy for Mexican output for two reasons. First, for a number of crops, particularly hard fibers such as henequén and tampico, there was very little domestic Mexican consumption: U.S. imports therefore capture the vast majority of Mexican production. Second, to the degree that there was domestic Mexican consumption of some nonstaple goods (coffee, bananas, sugar, chickpeas, tomatoes, and cotton), we can reasonably assume that Mexican demand for these products did not vary widely over time: increases in exports to the United States represent an increase in total output. In one important crop, cotton, we have linked our data sets on net exports from Mexico to a data set on domestic consumption. This allows us to estimate Mexico's total production of raw cotton.

The data sets we have developed on nonstaple crops allow us to specify three hypotheses regarding Mexico's agricultural export sector. The first hypothesis is that Mexican output collapsed as a result of political instability. The second is that output stagnated as a result of instability. The counterfactual case for both hypotheses is Mexico itself during the

---

[130] We note that Sandra Kuntz Ficker has developed data sets on some of the same agricultural products that we have, using sources for Mexico's European trading partners as well as those for the United States. She has also compared these data sets against those she has developed from available Mexican sources. The inclusion of Mexico's European trading partners produces similar qualitative conclusions to those we offer here: Mexico underwent a substantial agricultural export boom in the late 1910s and 1920s. See Kuntz Ficker (2001).

period when the polity was stable (1901–10). The third hypothesis is that political instability caused Mexico to underperform what it might have produced had the polity been stable. That is, even if the production of an agricultural export exceeded its pre-instability levels, this does not indicate that political instability did not impose a cost on Mexican export agriculture. Implicit in this view is a hypothetical Mexico in which output levels in the 1920s would have been even higher than those we observe. The counterfactual in this case is other countries that exported those same crops to the United States as a group. They faced the same world prices and same technological constraints as Mexico, except that those other countries did not endure 20 years of revolutions, counterrevolutions, civil wars, and political assassinations. Comparing Mexico's actual performance with its potential performance is therefore a straightforward exercise. It simply involves calculating Mexico's share of total U.S. imports of a particular commodity. If Mexico lost its share of the U.S. market over time, the implication is that Mexico could have potentially produced more (thereby maintaining its market share), had it not been for some intervening institutional factor. If Mexico gained market share, on the other hand, the implication is that institutional factors specific to Mexico did not significantly affect Mexico's economic performance.

When we examine the data on individual crops, the evidence does not support any of the hypotheses. Levels of output of most crops actually increased – even during the years of civil war. In fact, in the 1920s Mexico became a major exporter of a whole range of crops that it had not exported previously, including chickpeas, tomatoes, and bananas. Moreover, in most product lines, Mexico also increased its share of the U.S. market in the 1920s. There is little support for the argument that Mexico underperformed its potential production in the 1920s.

One of the clearest examples of the Mexican agricultural export boom was bananas. In the last three years of the Porfiriato, Mexico began to export bananas to the United States in commercial quantities. The evidence indicates that the revolution did nothing to halt the growth in banana exports. By 1915 banana exports were 10 times their average level for the years 1908–10. Even with a sharp downturn in exports in 1917–19 average exports for the decade 1911–20 were more than 5 times their Porfirian levels. In the next decade, banana exports boomed. Average exports were close to 19 times their Porfirian level. Mexico, in fact, actually outperformed its major competitors. It had 0 percent of the U.S. market during the Porfiriato, a 2 percent average market share in the 1910s, and a 7 percent market share in the 1920s (see Table 8.4). By 1929 bananas

Table 8.4. *Mexican Banana Exports to the United States,*
1905–1929

Year	Volume (in thousands of bunches)	Value (in thousands of nominal dollars)	Mexico's Share of U.S. Imports by Value (%)
1905		5	0
1906		6	0
1907		11	0
1908	120	19	0
1909	212	35	0
1910	241	53	0
1911	585	117	1
1912	817	227	2
1913	1,542	413	3
1914	2,697	702	4
1915	2,041	525	4
1916	1,527	425	4
1917	217	36	0
1918	0	0	0
1919	175	82	1
1920	728	512	3
1921	1,429	1,157	6
1922	739	456	2
1923	2,098	1,016	5
1924	3,047	1,399	6
1925	3,241	1,656	6
1926	4,592	2,658	8
1927	5,721	3,380	10
1928	5,526	3,121	9
1929	5,700	3,219	9
1908–10	191	36	0
1911–20	1,033	304	2
1921–29	3,566	2,007	7

Source: United States, Department of Commerce (various years).

made up 19 percent of Mexico's agricultural exports by value. This result should not be surprising, given the geographic locale of Mexican banana production. For climatological reasons, banana cultivation in Mexico is concentrated in the isthmus of Tehuantepec, where the southern states of Veracruz, Tabasco, Chiapas, and Oaxaca border each other.[131] This

---

[131] México, Ferrocarriles Nacionales (1989), p. 30.

region was almost entirely unaffected by revolutionary violence or land redistribution.

A somewhat similar story can be told about Mexican coffee exports (see Table 8.5). The quantitative evidence clearly indicates that coffee exports were unaffected by the revolution. In fact, average coffee exports from Mexico to the United States were 50 percent higher during the decade 1911–20 than during the decade 1901–10. Coffee production was concentrated in southern Veracruz and Chiapas, which were not characterized by intense military action during the revolution. Coffee growing appears to have been unaffected by the fact that Veracruz was under the rule of one of Mexico's most radical state governors in the 1920s. Average export levels during 1921–29 were roughly 30 percent above their average levels for 1901–10. The strongest argument that one can make about the negative effects of political instability and institutional change on the performance of the Mexican coffee sector is that Mexico underperformed its competitors in the 1920s. Mexico controlled, on average, 4 percent of the U.S. market in the decades 1901–10 and 1911–20. During the period 1921–29, its market share fell to 3 percent. This coincides with the expansion of the Colombian coffee sector.

Even areas of the country that did experience revolutionary violence were not negatively affected in terms of their export performance. One such case is the cotton-growing regions. Until the late nineteenth century, most Mexican cotton had been grown in the lowlands of Veracruz, not far from the cotton textile mills in that state and the neighboring state of Puebla. During the Porfiriato, massive irrigation projects allowed cotton production to shift to the states of Coahuila and Durango (the La Laguna district). Nevertheless, even with the growth of this new, highly productive area, Mexico continued to be a net cotton importer throughout the Porfiriato. Mexico's cotton textile industry grew even more rapidly than its ability to produce raw cotton.

The Laguna cotton district was wracked by violence during both the revolution and the de la Huerta rebellion. Because cotton production was highly capital intensive and depended upon the maintenance of extensive irrigation and flood control works along the Nazas and Aguanaval Rivers, one might have expected that the fighting and uncertainty about property rights would have reduced output. The evidence is clear, however, that quite the opposite happened: Mexico became a *net exporter* of cotton as of 1914 (see Table 8.6). The reasons for this surprising outcome are two. First, as we discussed earlier, armies financed themselves by exporting cotton to the United States from the plantations under their control.

Table 8.5. *Mexican Coffee Exports to the United States,*
1894–1929

Year	Volume (in thousands of pounds)	Value (in thousands of nominal dollars)	Mexico's Share of U.S. Imports by Value (%)
1894	38,161	6,964	8
1895	35,262	5,971	6
1896	23,975	4,040	5
1897	28,834	4,592	6
1898	34,721	3,599	6
1899	27,325	2,686	5
1900	35,328	3,313	6
1901	20,433	1,960	3
1902	30,846	2,837	4
1903	22,207	1,998	3
1904	23,216	2,222	3
1905	21,958	2,163	3
1906	24,581	2,650	4
1907	14,726	1,697	2
1908	29,012	3,339	5
1909	35,004	3,755	5
1910	21,205	2,299	3
1911	25,233	2,983	3
1912	34,156	5,212	4
1913	26,121	4,091	3
1914	49,386	8,028	7
1915	52,706	6,898	6
1916	49,833	6,222	5
1917	54,908	6,383	5
1918	19,849	2,104	2
1919	29,567	5,435	2
1920	19,520	3,873	2
1921	26,895	3,475	2
1922	37,801	5,130	3
1923	38,933	6,177	3
1924	27,590	5,070	2
1925	27,532	7,049	2
1926	26,934	7,206	2
1927	22,559	6,162	2
1928	38,877	10,193	3
1929	31,267	7,858	3
1894–1900	31,944	4,452	6
1901–10	24,319	2,492	4
1911–20	36,128	5,123	4
1921–29	30,932	6,480	3

Source: United States, Department of Commerce (various years).

Table 8.6. *Mexican Cotton Consumption, Production, and Net Imports, 1895–1929*

Year	Mexican Cotton Consumption (in thousands of pounds)[a]	Mexican Net Imports Volume (in thousands of pounds)[b]	Estimated Mexican Cotton Production (in thousands of pounds)[b]	Mexican Net Imports Value (in thousands of nominal dollars)	Gross Cotton Exports from Mexico to the U.S. as % of Total U.S. Cotton Imports by Value[c]
1895	47,388	37,976	9,412	2,352	0
1896	48,374	19,405	28,968	1,643	0
1897	53,238	15,101	38,137	1,236	0
1898	55,147	21,222	33,925	1,322	0
1899	58,340	17,887	40,453	1,030	0
1900	63,767	9,261	54,506	814	0
1901	66,576	17,459	49,118	1,749	0
1902	60,782	13,768	47,014	1,275	0
1903	60,526	33,394	27,132	3,189	0
1904	63,450	28,182	35,269	3,338	0
1905	68,706	39,541	29,165	3,768	0
1906	78,377	14,643	63,735	1,620	0
1907	80,639	(10,542)	91,181	(1,216)	6
1908	79,288	(826)	80,114	(100)	3
1909	77,957	21,279	56,678	2,207	0
1910	76,419	14,680	61,740	1,941	0
1911	76,050	2,179	73,871	330	0
1912	72,939	7,571	65,368	856	0
1913	72,206	9,670	62,536	1,251	0
1914		(19,903)		(1,607)	21

Year					
1915	44,735	(22,253)		(1,968)	16
1916	68,409	(6,593)		(196)	4
1917	69,727	(13,780)		(2,153)	6
1918	79,033	(21,001)	65,736	(5,297)	14
1919	76,239	(30,551)	98,960	(10,057)	14
1920	71,155	(14,785)	84,511	(5,433)	7
1921	67,137	(25,868)	104,901	(4,022)	18
1922	90,193	(23,630)	99,869	(5,760)	12
1923	91,348	(460)	71,614	89	3
1924	90,574	(27,451)	94,589	(7,797)	16
1925	86,583	(10,706)	100,900	(2,641)	5
1926	86,761	(35,126)	126,475	(5,934)	13
1927		(21,653)	112,227	(2,941)	6
1928		(22,160)	108,743	(4,141)	10
1929		(26,603)	113,364	(4,881)	9
1895–1900	54,376	20,142	34,233	1,400	0
1901–10	71,272	17,158	54,114	1,777	1
1911–20		(10,945)		(2,427)	8
1921–29	82,114	(21,518)	103,631	(4,225)	10

Note: Net imports are gross imports from the United States minus Mexico's exports to the United States. Negative numbers (in parentheses) indicate that Mexico was a net exporter.

a Raw cotton consumed by Mexico's textile industry.

b Consumption minus net imports. This means that when Mexico was a net exporter, production is consumption plus net exports.

c These figures are gross, not net, of U.S. imports to Mexico. We use gross values in order to estimate the percentage of U.S. imports accounted for by Mexican exports.

Sources: Cotton consumption data from Haber (1989), pp. 125, 158. Trade data from United States, Department of Commerce (various years).

Irrigation, storage, and transportation infrastructure were therefore rarely damaged.[132] Second, civil war blocked transport links to central Mexico, where most of the country's cotton textile plants were located. What had formerly been domestically consumed was now exported.[133]

The Mexican cotton export boom was not, however, a short-lived phenomenon, produced by a temporary increase in world demand and a temporary decrease in domestic demand. Mexico continued to be a net cotton exporter even after these conditions changed: average net exports for the years 1921–29 were 23 million pounds per year, roughly double their 1911–20 level. In fact, Mexico continually gained a larger share of total U.S. raw cotton imports, which is to say it outperformed other countries that exported cotton to the United States. In the decade 1901–10 *gross exports* from Mexico (not netting out U.S exports to Mexico) only made up 1 percent of total U.S. raw cotton imports. During the decade 1911–20 gross exports from Mexico made up 8 percent of total U.S. imports, and during the years 1921–29 gross exports from Mexico accounted for 11 percent of U.S. imports.

A skeptical reader might argue that this increase in exports was not a result of increased cotton production; it was caused by the redirection of domestic consumption of raw cotton to export markets. This alternative interpretation does not, however, stand up to the evidence we have retrieved on the domestic consumption of raw cotton, as reported by Mexican textile manufacturers. On average, Mexico consumed 15 percent more cotton during 1921–29 than during 1901–10 (see Table 8.6). When we link our data set on cotton consumption to our data set on net imports, the result is clear: total Mexican production was increasing dramatically in the late 1910s and the 1920s. Our estimates indicate that, on average, Mexico produced almost twice as much cotton in 1921–29 as in 1901–10.

One would, in short, have a hard time arguing that political instability and institutional change had a negative effect on Mexican cotton cultivation. In point of fact, the evidence clearly indicates that there was substantial new investment in land and irrigation systems in the 1920s. In the Laguna, the 1921 discovery of underground aquifers prompted heavy investment in wells and expanded the amount of land under cultivation.[134] In addition, cultivation also expanded to states where cotton had never been grown before. The most important of these was Baja California,

---

[132] Cerutti and Flores (1997), p. 199.
[133] Cerutti and Flores (1997), p. 233.
[134] Vargas-Lobsinger (1999), p. 73.

where the Valle de Mexicali, near the state's borders with California and Sonora, boomed.[135] By 1930 the Valle de Mexicali accounted for 42 percent of Mexican raw cotton output.[136] In short, Mexico's cotton growers do not appear to have been particularly worried about their property rights.

Of course, some export sectors were shut down by the violence and uncertainty that accompanied the Mexican Revolution – sugar, for example, which before 1911 had been centered in the state of Morelos. Morelos, as the center of the Zapatista movement, had experienced some of the most prolonged and destructive fighting of 1911–20. During the years 1910–14 Mexican sugar exports to the United States almost completely collapsed (see Table 8.7).

What is equally striking, however, is the fact that in 1915 Mexican sugar exports boomed. During the short time that the Zapatista-Villa alliance had Carranza on the ropes, the Zapatistas were able to export production from the mills they controlled in Morelos, as well as export the reserves of existing sugar that they had confiscated from the state's haciendas. We know for a fact that during 1915 they actually succeeded in putting eight mills back into production.[137] In 1916–17, however, the Carrancistas closed a noose around Morelos. From this point on, the Morelos sugar estates were broken up and given over to the production of corn and beans.

How can we then explain the fact that in the 1920s Mexico was exporting more sugar than ever before? Average exports during 1921–29 were more than five times the level of 1901–10. Mexico had even succeeded in increasing its share of the (highly protected) U.S. market. It controlled, on average, 0 percent of the U.S. market in the periods 1894–1900, 1901–10, and 1911–20. During the period 1921–29, it accounted, on average, for 2 percent of U.S. imports.

The expansion of sugar exports was a product of the migration of the sugar industry out of Morelos and into new areas of the country. The industry moved to the Gulf Coast states of Tamaulipas and Veracruz, and to the northwestern state of Sinaloa. The migration of the industry implies that there had to be significant new investment in fields, irrigation, and mills. This, in turn, implies that the landowners making those investments were not particularly worried about their property rights.

---

[135] México, Ferrocarriles Nacionales (1989), p. 29.
[136] México, Ferrocarriles Nacionales (1989), p. 27.
[137] Bartra (1993), pp. 69–70.

Table 8.7. *Mexican Sugar Exports to the United States, 1894–1929*

Year	Volume (in thousands of pounds)	Value (in thousands of nominal dollars)	Mexico's Share of U.S. Imports by Value (%)
1894	2,923	68	0
1895	3,000	54	0
1896	3,680	58	0
1897	1,412	19	0
1898	2,893	45	0
1899	3,088	53	0
1900	1,892	41	0
1901	1,358	36	0
1902	337	9	0
1903	2,196	94	0
1904	868	17	0
1905	18,788	628	1
1906	2,196	50	0
1907	6,361	195	0
1908	28,114	899	1
1909	3,767	101	0
1910	405	14	0
1911	241	8	0
1912	510	21	0
1913	494	19	0
1914	2,033	75	0
1915	75,788	2,767	2
1916	14,632	483	0
1917	9,287	586	0
1918	2,332	357	0
1919	20,646	2,442	1
1920	62,178	9,932	1
1921	23,701	2,343	1
1922	41,803	2,831	1
1923	28,640	1,883	0
1924	66,397	5,012	8
1925	28,254	2,002	1
1926	58,130	2,637	1
1927	25,035	1,285	0
1928	12,730	636	0
1929	30,787	1,263	1
1894–1900	2,698	48	0
1901–10	6,439	204	0
1911–20	18,814	1,669	0
1921–29	35,053	2,210	2

Source: United States, Department of Commerce (various years).

Table 8.8. *Mexican Fresh Tomato Exports to the United States,*
1924–1929

Year	Volume (in thousands of pounds)	Value (in thousands of nominal dollars)	Mexico's Share of U.S. Imports by Value (%)
1924	44,444	1,334	71
1925	61,176	1,875	77
1926	67,048	2,042	77
1927	105,027	3,207	71
1928	88,300	2,715	71
1929	87,855	2,791	73

Source: United States, Department of Commerce (various years).

In point of fact, there is abundant evidence that Mexico's landowners, particularly in the North, were so confident about their ability to mitigate institutional reforms that they moved into the production of a whole new range of export crops. One example of this was the cultivation and export of fresh tomatoes from the northwestern state of Sinaloa. Beginning in 1924, exports began a vertiginous increase. On average, from 1924 to 1929 Mexico exported 75 million pounds of tomatoes per year to the United States, accounting for 73 percent of U.S. tomato imports (see Table 8.8). By 1929 fresh tomato exports accounted for 18 percent of total Mexican agricultural exports to the United States.

A similar phenomenon occurred in chickpeas. Mexico had not been a major producer or exporter of chickpeas prior to 1911. In the early 1920s Mexican landowners moved aggressively into chickpea production for export. Practically all this production took place in the northwestern state of Sonora.[138] Most of that was controlled by none other than Mexico's revolutionary general turned president turned landlord, Álvaro Obregón.[139] On average, from 1924 to 1929 Mexico exported 42 millon pounds of chickpeas per year to the United States. By 1929 Mexico had a virtual lock on U.S. chickpea imports, accounting for 96 percent of U.S. imports by value (see Table 8.9).

Only one major agricultural export underwent a serious long-term deterioration: hard fibers (henequén and tampico). That deterioration was not caused by revolutionary violence, agrarian reform, or investor

---

[138] México, Ferrocarriles Nacionales (1989), p. 29.
[139] Hall (1981), pp. 200–2.

Table 8.9. *Mexican Chickpea Exports to the United States,*
1924–1929

Year	Volume (in thousands of pounds)	Value (in thousands of nominal dollars)	Mexico's Share of U.S. Imports by Value (%)
1924	43,858	2,466	85
1925	19,745	987	62
1926	52,592	2,718	91
1927	36,958	1,922	93
1928	51,575	3,126	93
1929	49,410	3,129	96

Source: United States, Department of Commerce (various years).

uncertainty caused by political instability, nor as is often suggested, by the Carranza government's attempt to create a government-run marketing board in henequén – although the marketing board clearly hastened Mexico's relative decline as a hard-fiber producer. Rather, it was caused by the near impossibility of maintaining a monopoly on any agricultural product in the long run. Mexican hard fibers were no exception.

Henequén, also known as sisal, is a leafy cactus native to the Yucatán peninsula.[140] Its leaves provide a very tough fiber. After the invention of the McCormick grain binder in 1878, the demand for henequén seemed almost unlimited. Plantation owners and merchants in the Yucatán peninsula, in particular Olegario Molina (governor of the state of Yucatán and Díaz's minister of development), quickly capitalized on the fact that the state's soil and climate were well suited to henequén production. The result was that the Yucatán had a world monopoly on henequén, and most output was handled by Olegario Molina's merchant house.[141]

Exports of henequén rose in an almost uninterrupted fashion through the Porfiriato and through the revolution. In point of fact, 1914, 1915, and 1916 were all record years. Of course, there was virtually no revolutionary activity in the Yucatán. From 1911 to 1915 life went on much as it had under Díaz.

From 1917 onward, however, henequén exports began to trend downward, and Mexico began to lose its world market share. By 1929 henequén exports were approximately 40 percent of their 1916 peak. Mexico had

---

[140] At the time, henequén was often referred to as sisal. Sisal, however, is also used to refer to similar species that will grow in most other tropical regions.
[141] For a full discussion, see Wells (1985), pp. 48, 51, 72–75.

also lost its monopoly, accounting for only 57 percent of U.S. imports (see Table 8.10).

What happened is that producers in Africa and Asia had been attracted by the high prices received by Mexican henequén producers and were grabbing market share from Mexico. The expansion of these rival producers began at the turn of the century. By the 1910s they were emerging as serious rivals.[142]

Hastening Mexico's loss of market share was an ill-advised attempt by the Carranza government to create a marketing board: the Comisión Reguladora del Mercado de Henequén. The marketing board operated as a monopsonist vis-à-vis henequén producers, and as a monopolist vis-à-vis the purchasers of henequén. It then pushed the price it charged for henequén through the roof. In the presence of potential competitors, however, this could only succeed in the short run. All that the marketing board succeeded in doing was to attract even more producers into the market.

We wish to underline that Mexico would have lost control of its dominance in hard fibers even had it not had a marketing board for henequén. Two facts sustain this hypothesis. First, henequén requires five to seven years to mature.[143] Had the Henequén Board been the cause of the industry's demise, Mexico would not have begun to lose market share until the early to mid-1920s. Table 8.10 indicates, however, that its market share began to erode in 1917. Rival producers were already entering the market in force well before the advent of the marketing board. Second, Mexico's other major hard-fiber export – tampico (a variety of hemp, also known as ixtle) – underwent a similar decline, even though the government did not attempt to curtail its output and raise its price. As Table 8.11 shows, the output of tampico increased all through the years of civil war and then began to decline in the 1920s.[144]

Fertilizer and Machinery Imports

One way to cross-check our analysis of Mexican agricultural output is to look at data on agricultural inputs. We have therefore retrieved data on the exportation of chemical fertilizers and agricultural machinery from the United States and Great Britain to Mexico.

---

[142] Joseph (1982), p. 181.
[143] Joseph (1982), p. 181.
[144] We do not include U.S. market share because, by definition, Mexico always took 100 percent of the U.S. market for tampico fiber (tampico is only grown in Mexico). There were, however, numerous fibers that could substitute for tampico.

Table 8.10. *Mexican Henequén (Sisal) Exports to the United States,*
1894–1929

Year	Volume (in thousands of tons)	Value (in thousands of nominal dollars)	Mexico's Share of U.S. Imports by Value (%)
1894	48	3,691	99
1895	47	2,735	100
1896	51	3,339	98
1897	63	3,809	99
1898	68	5,104	99
1899	70	8,902	97
1900	75	11,534	98
1901	70	7,901	99
1902	87	11,609	97
1903	86	13,074	98
1904	108	15,733	99
1905	98	14,896	98
1906	95	14,884	97
1907	96	14,662	98
1908	101	13,702	98
1909	87	9,802	96
1910	95	10,894	95
1911	111	11,466	95
1912	104	10,734	90
1913	137	15,496	87
1914	195	22,980	89
1915	176	19,236	94
1916	221	24,697	96
1917	131	23,191	89
1918	139	50,897	93
1919	134	36,660	93
1920	164	29,201	87
1921	105	11,700	86
1922	66	6,452	79
1923	75	7,169	66
1924	85	11,413	70
1925	109	17,710	76
1926	83	14,264	66
1927	91	13,072	72
1928	97	12,950	66
1929	85	12,083	57
1894–1900	60	5,588	98
1901–10	92	12,716	98
1911–20	151	24,456	91
1921–29	88	11,868	71

Source: United States, Department of Commerce (various years).

Table 8.11. *Mexican Tampico (Ixtle Fiber) Exports to the United States,*
1894–1929

Year	Volume (in thousands of tons)	Value (in thousands of nominal dollars)
1894	5	257
1895	10	457
1896	12	718
1897	6	336
1898	3	130
1899	4	284
1900	6	475
1901	2	164
1902	8	495
1903	15	1,083
1904	13	1,155
1905	15	1,384
1906	14	1,283
1907	15	1,369
1908	10	893
1909	10	676
1910	9	643
1911	7	469
1912	10	775
1913	10	923
1914	11	1,036
1915	12	1,214
1916	30	2,809
1917	33	2,913
1918	32	3,649
1919	21	2,516
1920	23	3,159
1921	9	745
1922	11	808
1923	10	997
1924	12	1,373
1925	17	1,933
1926	13	1,926
1927	13	1,876
1928	14	1,630
1929	12	1,274
1894–1900	7	379
1901–10	11	915
1911–20	19	1,946
1921–29	12	1,396

Note: We do not present market share data because ixtle is only grown in Mexico.
By definition, Mexico had 100 percent of the ixtle market. It was, however, possible
to substitute various other types of hemp for ixtle.

Source: United States, Department of Commerce (various years).

Table 8.12. *U.S. Fertilizer*
Exports to Mexico, 1900–1929
(in 1929 dollars)

Year	Total Fertilizers
1900	392
1901	90
1902	881
1903	
1904	411
1905	989
1906	1,095
1907	5,866
1908	29,217
1909	8,551
1910	20,717
1911	14,326
1912	18,391
1913	17,247
1914	5,415
1915	2,544
1916	740
1917	10,960
1918	223
1919	54,758
1920	105,826
1921	57,381
1922	22,890
1923	43,993
1924	76,605
1925	27,585
1926	153,880
1927	109,888
1928	17,988
1929	141,752

Note: Price deflator is the U.S. whole-sale price index.

Source: United States, Department of Commerce (various years).

We present our estimates of U.S. fertilizer exports to Mexico in Table 8.12. The data on fertilizer imports are consistent with the hypothesis of rising agricultural output. Mexico began to import chemical fertilizers from the United States during the Porfiriato. The civil war of 1914–17 interrupted the upward trend of the Porfiriato but only temporarily. When substantial imports resumed in 1919, they did so at twice Porfirian levels. Fertilizer imports then continued to rise all through the 1920s.

The evidence also indicates that Mexican agriculturalists made considerable new investments in agricultural machinery. In Table 8.13 we present data on the real value of U.S. and British exports of agricultural machinery to Mexico. For exports from the United States, we are able to break down agricultural machines into different subcategories: cultivating and harvesting machinery, sugar mill machinery, cotton gins, and tractors, and other machinery.

The series on Mexican imports of agricultural machinery display a clear pattern. The first few years of political instability (1911–13) had no effect. Not only did levels of machinery imports rise; they rose *faster* than during the 1901–10 decade. During the years of civil war (1914–17) new investment collapsed. In 1914 imports of agricultural machinery were barely a third of their 1913 level. In 1915 they halved again. Imports climbed rapidly, however, once the civil war began to subside. By 1917 they were twice the level of 1913 and then continued growing. In fact, in 1920 Mexico imported enough agricultural machinery to replace seven years of Porfirian imports. Throughout the 1920s imports remained on average four to five *times* the level of the late Porfiriato. The implication is that Mexican agriculturalists were importing agricultural machines at a level well beyond the need to replace machinery that might have been depreciated or destroyed during the revolution. Moreover, this general result is not driven by one or two specific types of machines: machinery of every type, from harvesters to cotton gins, from cultivators to sugar milling equipment, all expanded precipitously. The evidence is therefore clear: Mexican agriculturalists were investing in order to take advantage of opportunities to expand production in lucrative commercial crops.

CONCLUSIONS

Mexico ultimately had an agrarian reform that redistributed tens of millions of acres of land and that had strongly negative consequences for agricultural production. That agrarian reform occurred, however, not during the politically unstable 1920s but during the politically stable 1930s. Under conditions of political instability, the incentives for factions and governments – even those ideologically predisposed to carry out a land reform – were not to disrupt existing production systems. The very fact that the government was weak meant that landowners could call upon third parties to lodge credible threats against the government. The result was

Table 8.13. *Combined U.S. and U.K. Agricultural Machinery Exports to Mexico, 1900–1929 (in 1929 U.S. dollars)*

Year	Cultivating Machinery	Harvesting Machinery	Oil Mill Machinery	Sugar Mill Machinery	Tractors	Cotton Gins	Other Agricultural Machinery	U.S. Total	U.K. Total	Grand Total
1900	103	2					151	256	137	393
1901	63	9					121	193	138	331
1902	29	8					99	136	157	293
1903	66	6					125	197	50	247
1904	76	16					128	221	7	228
1905	70	7					142	219	7	226
1906	127	14					195	336	22	357
1907	117	7					201	324	41	366
1908	97	22					157	276	30	306
1909	66	23					172	260	9	270
1910	118	9					186	312	9	321
1911	127	5		55			308	496	30	525
1912	133	18		59			324	534	26	559
1913	170	15		103		12	242	543	112	655
1914	46	8		46		2	81	182		182
1915	12	6		22		5	54	100		100
1916	46	5		51		5	65	172	1	173
1917	196	21		44		48	118	426	3	429
1918	524	62		241		0	606	1,432	2	1,434
1919	734	106		277		82	1,297	2,497	31	2,528
1920	1,063	277		646		163	1,557	3,707	108	3,814
1921	285	32		752	96	29	751	1,944	243	2,187
1922	316	58	28	501	340	57	217	1,517	116	1,633
1923	438	112	12	367	253			1,182	6	1,188
1924	518	111	15	481	388			1,512	52	1,564
1925	828	168	101	354	654			2,104	17	2,121
1926	715	166	71	224	736	118		2,032	30	2,062
1927	402	185	183	205	418	67		1,460	22	1,482
1928	582	154	41	298	461	217		1,753	14	1,766
1929	610	131	33	853	574	66		2,267	42	2,309

Note: The price deflator is the wholesale price index.

Sources: United States: United States, Department of Commerce 1902–30. United Kingdom: United Kingdom, Customs and Excise Dept. Statistical Office (1900–30).

that they were able to mitigate the formal institutional reforms that were embodied in the Constitution. Thus, it was precisely during the period when the government was under threat from rival factions that agriculturalists invested at prodigious rates and that Mexican export agriculture boomed.

9

Conclusions

This book has addressed the puzzle of how economies can grow amid political violence and disorder. In order to resolve this puzzle, we employed a somewhat heterodox approach, combining methods from history, economics, and political science. We concluded that political instability does not have a systematic impact on economic performance.

The resulting approach to evidence and theory – what some researchers call an analytic narrative – involved three steps:[1] we built a theoretical framework; we gathered systematic quantitative and qualitative data about a polity – Mexico from 1876 to 1929 – that passed from a long period of political stability into a prolonged period of instability; and we used our theoretical framework, coupled to analytic techniques drawn from economics, to analyze the historical evidence in a coherent manner. We specified explicit hypotheses and the counterfactual propositions that emanate from them and then compared the results that one should expect from theory with the results that were obtained in the real world. The result is a book that offers, on the one hand, an analytic economic history of Mexico and, on the other, a generalizable model of the interaction of political institutions and economic performance.

We would venture that the combination of methods and evidence that we have employed is outside the mainstream of research in all three fields on which we have rather shamelessly trespassed. Our trespassing across disciplinary boundaries requires that we say something at this point about the implications of our substantive findings for each of these disciplines.

---

[1] Bates, Greif, et al. (1998).

Conclusions

HISTORY

A major portion of the trespassing we did in this book was through territory that has long been the province of Mexican historians. We found that the analytic tools and approaches to evidence that we brought to bear from the social sciences caused us to revise many of the accepted interpretations in Mexican history. In other cases, the evidence and methods that we brought to bear allowed us to confirm arguments that had been made by historians but had not been fully substantiated.

In order to understand the economic effects of Mexico's long period of political instability, we first had to understand the commitment mechanisms that underpinned growth during the long peace of the Porfiriato. The first implication of our research regarding the Porfiriato is that, contrary to the conventional wisdom, Porfirian Mexico was *not* a laissez-faire economy. Until recently, historians have stressed the public pronouncements of the Díaz regime, which echoed 19th-century liberal notions about the free play of the market. This view goes back as far as Frank Tanenbaum's classic works on Mexico and became embedded in countless monographs and textbooks. The consensus view is, in fact, articulated in the *Cambridge History of Latin America*: "The Díaz government had no plans for developing particular industries, no programme to stimulate the import of technology, no policies for protecting infant industries."[2]

Members of the Díaz government did, of course, espouse the virtues of the free market, often in stentorian tones. As a practical matter, however, the Díaz regime could not and did not honor the principles of classical liberalism. Entry into banking was tightly regulated. Manufacturers received high tariffs to protect them from foreign competition. Some received quasi-official monopolies, to protect them from domestic competition. Property rights in land were allocated to insiders. Those who could not afford to buy political protection lost their lands.

The Porfiriato's rent seeking served a purpose. It allowed a weak central government facing potential violent opposition to restore political order and simultaneously to encourage economic growth. The dilemma facing Díaz when he assumed power was to encourage growth while making a credible commitment to protect property rights. If he safeguarded property rights, however, he would deny himself the resources he needed to either defeat or buy off his political opposition. Every government

---

[2] Cited in Beatty (1996), pp. 1, 55.

that had preceded him since independence had been faced with this same dilemma, and every one of those governments had failed to solve it.

Díaz had an advantage that earlier Mexican governments did not have: by the last two decades of the 19th century, the growth of the United States economy, coupled with a depreciating exchange rate and a dramatic decrease in the cost of long-distance transport, created an opportunity for Mexico to earn rents from its privileged position next to the United States. Díaz realized that in order to attract foreign capital he needed to create credible commitments to protect property rights, even if such protection was restricted to a select group of asset holders. Some of these asset holders were foreigners, predominantly in the oil and mining industries. Some of them were domestic capitalists or expatriate foreigners. Selective protection particularly characterized agriculture, banking, and manufacturing. Díaz's use of selective commitments in banking, for example, allowed the government to obtain the credit it needed to establish political order and subsidize the construction of a national railway network. In exchange, Díaz created one of the most segmented and concentrated banking systems in the world.

Much the same was true in manufacturing. By the standards of less developed countries, Mexico had developed a large and modern manufacturing sector by 1911. In order to do this, however, Díaz provided levels of protection to selected industries that were extraordinarily high. Some of his policies, particularly those regarding patents and those that created selective exemptions from taxes, also protected some manufacturers against domestic competition. Much the same could be said about Mexico's largest economic sector, agriculture. A series of insider deals between state governors and large landowners allowed a boom to take place in the production of cash crops. The cost was, however, that asset holders outside of the coalition lost much of their land. In short, none of the mechanisms by which Díaz created incentives to invest and by which he turned his potential political opposition into enforcers of a selectively enforced property rights system, had anything to do with the precepts of laissez-faire.

Porfirian Mexico's insider deals were very sweet for those who could get them, but they were not giveaways. By the standards of the time, federal taxes were *not* low. The cotton textile and mining industries, for example, were rather heavily taxed. Those industries that have been identified as the most infamous giveaways – steel and petroleum being the most prominent – were new industries during the Porfiriato. They were highly risky for their owners, and, more important, *they made little or no money before 1910.*

344

The final implication of our research for the history of Mexico under Díaz was that Porfirian Mexico did not grow as fast as at it *could have*. Mexico saw rapid investment across the board, in almost all economic sectors. That investment and the resulting economic growth, however, was prompted by barriers to entry, protectionist tariffs, federal tax subsidies, and – most clearly in agriculture – the ability to infringe upon the property rights of asset holders outside the governing coalition. All this rent seeking could not have been good for economic efficiency. In short, the deals needed to underpin Porfirio Díaz's commitments slowed growth in the long-term relative to a system in which property rights were specified so as to maximize externalities and were enforced as public goods.

Our research also has implications for the history of the Mexican Revolution. The revolution, and the years of political violence, coups, assassinations, and civil wars that followed it, did not destroy the economy. Two decades ago John Womack argued that a theoretically informed reading of the available secondary literature suggested that the years 1910–20 were not characterized by economic collapse.[3] The notion that most of the economy escaped damage from the events of 1910–20 was offered by Womack not so much as a definitive finding but as a hypothesis to be tested. Unfortunately, the generation of historians who came after Womack chose not to test hypotheses against data but to engage in other pursuits.

Our sector-by-sector analysis of the economy makes it clear that the early years of the revolution (1910–13) had little effect at all on economic performance. The years of civil war of 1914–17 were far more disruptive. They were not, however, characterized by the destruction of fixed assets or the elimination of the owners of those assets. Except for *agriculture in some regions*, assets and asset holders survived intact.

That is not to say that the civil war of 1914–17 had no effects. Investment and output declined in most sectors during its three years, but for *different* reasons in *different* economic sectors. Output in manufacturing and mining declined for one simple reason: the national transportation network shut down during the war. Mexico's manufacturing and mining industries found themselves cut off from necessary inputs to production and from the most important markets for their output. In the mining industry, for example, it was near impossible to obtain dynamite to blast new shafts or coal to fire smelters. It was also extremely difficult to transport ore from the mines to the smelters, or transport refined ore from the

[3] Womack (1978).

smelters to the U.S. border. In the cotton textile industry, to cite an example from manufacturing, there were long periods when it was not possible to transport raw cotton from the Laguna cotton fields in the North to the cotton mills in central Mexico. Indeed, the two areas were under the control of opposing armies. Once the railroads resumed operation, however, manufacturing and mining recovered rapidly – even though the polity continued to be unstable.

Banking and agriculture also suffered during the civil war but for a different reason than manufacturing and mining: factions saw them as easy sources of funds for their military efforts and targeted them for predation. Not surprisingly, the banking sector was almost entirely destroyed and had to be rebuilt almost from scratch in the 1920s. Agriculture was much less negatively affected by predation, because, unlike banks, farms do not have significant liquid assets: most of their value is tied up in fixed assets (land and improvements to land). Because their value lay in the income that they could produce, there were strong incentives for armies to continue to run agricultural operations, often employing the same managers and workers as before. The evidence indicates, in fact, that agricultural properties were only destroyed in those areas of the country where no single faction was able to establish its control for a prolonged period. The only exception to this general pattern was the state of Morelos. Here the Zapatistas, who controlled Morelos, had no way to get the state's sugar to market. The Constitutionalists controlled Mexico City, the largest market for Morelos's sugar, as well as Veracruz, the port city from which sugar could have been exported.

Petroleum was the only sector unaffected by the civil war. Wells and pipelines were not destroyed in combat, and production did not depend on the availability of the railroad network. Mexico's petroleum output, therefore, rose monotonically in 1914–17.

Why wasn't the civil war more destructive? The reason is that factions had few incentives to destroy productive assets, and every incentive to use them to finance their armies. They could do this either by taking over those enterprises themselves or by demanding protection rents. This held true for manufacturing, mining, petroleum, and agriculture. The one exception is banking. There, the incentives were to simply take whatever was in the vault. The reason for the difference between banking and other sectors is that the assets of the banks were highly liquid. The assets of other enterprises, however, were illiquid: machines, land, and buildings had little ready value except for what could be earned from their productive use. That is, in banking factions could expropriate the stock of capital. In other sectors, they could only expropriate the flow of income that capital produced.

We would also suggest that a revision to the way that historians tend to think about the periodization of Mexico's political history might be in order. Historians tend to date the end of the revolution at 1920, when Obregón, Calles, and de la Huerta overthrew Carranza. This was the last actual violent change of the national government in Mexico. Our point is this: the last *successful* overthrow of a government and the last *credible attempt* to overthrow the government are not one and the same. Ex post, we know that Álvaro Obregón's accession to power in 1920 was the last violent change of government in Mexico, and the political system that he and Calles created lasted, with some subsequent refinement and modification, until the election of July 2000. It would not be correct, however, to draw from this fact the notion that Mexico was politically stable from 1920 onward. This confuses ex ante conditions and ex post results. Ex ante, it was not clear to someone in December 1923 – when Secretary of the Treasury Adolfo de la Huerta declared against Obregón – that the political system created by Obregón and Calles would survive until January 1924, let alone July 2000. In fact, the de la Huerta rebellion came very close to success. Calles was also confronted by serious coup attempts in 1927 and 1929, as well as by the Cristero War of 1926–29. The Cristeros, in fact, were never beaten on the battlefield, succeeded in assassinating Obregón in 1928, and nearly brought down Calles's regime. In short, the 20 years between Madero's call to arms against Díaz and the establishment of the Partido Nacional Revolucionario in 1929 form one long period of political instability. In some important senses the Mexican Revolution did not end until 1929, with the defeat of the Escobar revolt, the negotiated settlement of the Cristero War, and the creation of the PNR.

Our research indicates that the instability of the 1920s had almost no discernible effect on the growth of Mexico's economy. All the evidence we have gathered indicates that investment in all sectors recovered rapidly after 1917 and soon *exceeded* Porfirian levels by a substantial margin. Although all sectors recovered both in terms of the levels and rate of growth, the nature of the mechanisms that underpinned recovery and growth differed from sector to sector.

In manufacturing, a vertical political integration (VPI) coalition under-pinned the commitment not to prey upon or unilaterally alter property rights. After 1916 no government could exclude organized labor from the country's ruling coalition. The initial coalition was with anarchist unions, but an alliance of conservative landowners and anarchists was, for obvious reasons, unsustainable. The anarchists were, in short order, replaced with the Confederación Regional Obrera Mexicano, a more orthodox labor federation. Mexican industrialists – whatever they might have thought about the CROM and its gangster leadership – shared rents with organized labor by paying high wages to workers and by making payoffs to CROM leaders. The CROM served as the third-party enforcer of the agreement between Mexico's industrialists and the government. The industrialists knew that no government would reduce the high tariffs that protected them from foreign competition, because doing so would prompt organized labor to defect from the coalition. This could bring down the weak governments of the 1920s. In short, manufacturing is one of the sectors where the theoretical framework we develop in Chapter 2 most closely fits the empirical outcomes in the Mexican case.

A similar coalition also emerged in agriculture in the 1920s, where "retired," irregular, and active-duty generals and their armed coteries received a stream of rents from landowners. No government could afford to risk a rebellion by these generals brought about by a frontal attack on the property rights of the country's large landowners. The result was that property owners in many areas of the country were able to mitigate the institutional reforms that had been mandated in the constitution. In these areas, agriculture boomed. The country became a net exporter of sugar and cotton for the first time. It also began to export large quantities of new crops such as seasonable vegetables and bananas. Only hard-fiber production suffered, but this was due not to insecure property rights in Mexico but to competition from new producers in Africa and Asia, who had been attracted by the rents that Mexico had been earning from its henequén monopoly since the 1890s. Indeed, these overseas competitors had begun to invest in sisal plantations even before the Mexican Revolution broke out. In sum, Mexico was going to lose market share in hard fibers whether or not it had a revolution.

In banking, Mexico's postrevolutionary governments relied on a hostage in order to create a credible commitment. The hostage was the Banco de México (Banxico) and the profits it generated. If the government changed the rules in the future, its 50 million peso investment in Banxico would be threatened. The reason the government had to resort to using a hostage was that there was no clear third-party enforcer of the bankers' implicit contract with the Obregón and Calles governments. The experiences of the early 1920s (particularly the failure of the Caja de Préstamos – see Chapter 4) suggested that the government would not hesitate to behave opportunistically with respect to the financial system. In fact, at the same time that the government was attempting to form a coalition with the country's domestic bankers, by letting them fashion the laws governing new entry into banking, it was also abrogating its foreign debt. The government therefore needed to proffer a hostage in order to make its commitment credible.

In mining and petroleum, the main protection mechanism was third-party enforcement by the United States. Thus, our theoretical framework about credible commitments without either limited government or stationary banditry captures how credible commitments were made to asset holders in both of these sectors. There is one important difference between the mechanism we describe in theory and the actual empirical outcome: the U.S. government did not enforce property rights because it received a direct stream of rents from the asset holders. Rather, the United States enforced property rights because it was a limited government that had made a commitment to protect the property rights of its citizens overseas. No U.S. administration could easily renege on this commitment without suffering electoral consequences or difficulties in Congress.

Mexican governments used VPI to make credible commitments before 1910 and after 1917. Commitments were based on the generation and sharing of rents in both periods. This created a property rights system capable of growth – *but it was an inefficient system both before and after the revolution.* That is not to say that there were *no* economic differences between the Porfirian coalition and the postrevolutionary Obregón-Calles coalition. Evidence from the cotton textile industry, where we have gathered more detailed data than are available for other sectors, suggests that the postrevolutionary VPI coalition may have been less efficient than the Porfirian coalition in sustaining long-term growth. The labor unions used their position as third-party enforcer to prevent the introduction of labor-saving technologies. Productivity continued to rise, and new investment was substantial – but the machines were obsolete and the rise in productivity was entirely due to higher work effort prompted by the shift from hourly wages to piece rates. It is to say, however, that the detailed examination of the evidence does not indicate that Porfirian Mexico was on a path of rapid long-run growth that was brought to an end by the events of 1911–29. In point of fact, some economic sectors (mining, export agriculture, and petroleum) actually grew faster after 1911 than they had before.

One implication of these results is that historians should exercise caution when thinking about the political and economic consequences of the revolution. It is, perhaps, quite natural to view the events of the 1910s and

1920s through lenses colored by our knowledge of the attack on property rights that took place under Lázaro Cárdenas (1934–40). This produces a seamless narrative that connects the civil war of 1914–17 with reforms carried out two decades later. Friedrich Katz, for example, suggests that: "To a large extent, they [Mexico's hacendados] would manage to survive the revolution as a class.... But they came out of it so weakened that in 1934, 24 years after the outbreak of the Mexican Revolution, the administration of President Lázaro Cárdenas decided to expropriate most of Mexico's large landholdings, and the hacendados would be unable to put up any decisive resistance."[4] This view, however, is not consistent with what we know about new investment in agricultural machinery or with the boom in export agriculture we observe in the 1920s. It is hard to reconcile the kind of upswing we observe with an agricultural sector owned by a class of "weakened" landowners who thought that they were about to lose their property rights.

The agrarian reform of the 1930s and the nationalization of the oil industry notwithstanding, the property rights system created by Obregón and Calles proved long-lasting. In 1929 Calles formed the PNR to mediate disputes among the remaining politically ambitious generals who had survived the 1910s and 1920s. In the 1930s Lázaro Cárdenas transformed the PNR from a talking shop designed to distribute spoils among a few leaders into a genuine corporatist party and, in many ways, a branch of the federal government. He therefore completed the process begun by Obregón. The structure that emerged remained stable until the late 1980s, and the direct descendent of the PNR – the Partido Revolucionario Institucional (PRI) – did not fall from power until the election of 2000.

There were three differences between the post-Cárdenas equilibrium and its predecessors. First, large landowners, who had been part of the Díaz and Obregón-Calles coalitions, were no longer part of the ruling coalition. Second, third-party enforcement of the contract between government and asset holders was institutionalized. Under Díaz, the third parties had been powerful individuals or groupings of individuals. Under Obregón-Calles, and more so after Cárdenas, the third parties were institutionalized entities such as labor or peasant federations. Indeed, post-Cárdenas, they were directly embedded into the country's governance structure through their official incorporation into the ruling party. Third, there was now a selection mechanism by which a president appointed his successor and then permanently and completely retired from the political

---

[4] Katz (1998), p. 448.

arena. While we do not discount the importance of these changes, the basic logic of the system remained unchanged from the Porfiriato.

POLITICAL SCIENCE

There has been, in recent years, a great deal of interest in the political foundations of economic growth. Most of the recent literature has focused on the role of limited government as a solution to the commitment problem. A government limited by sets of self-enforcing institutions can credibly commit that it will not arbitrarily engage in predatory actions against the property rights of its citizens. An alternate notion of credible commitment is known as "stationary banditry." These are despotic governments that can credibly commit to protect property rights because breaking their commitments would lead to lower revenue for them in the future. While less efficient than limited governments, stationary bandits are far more common in history. In fact, most governments since the discovery of agriculture have been stationary bandits of one form or another.

Neither notion of credible commitment is consistent with the empirical phenomenon of economic growth amid political instability. For both theoretical and empirical reasons, the group of countries that are typically characterized as unstable and the group of countries that are ruled by limited governments do not overlap. As a theoretical matter, unstable polities cannot be ruled by limited governments. In a limited government, by definition, the selection mechanism for choosing government officials is based on the rule of law. If you can shoot your way into office, it means that the mechanisms of limited government have ceased to function. As an empirical matter, until the 1990s, the set of limited governments was very small, and the set of limited governments that fell into instability was even smaller still. As a matter of history, limited government is, in fact, a very rare phenomenon.

Unlike limited government, stationary bandits *can* exist in an unstable polity. What they cannot do is make a credible commitment to protect property rights. In an unstable polity, where governments change hands violently and unpredictably, the expected life-span of a stationary bandit will be short. A despotic government with a short expected life-span will heavily discount the future. Knowing that the government cannot credibly commit to refrain from predation, the population will heavily discount the future as well. Asset holders in such a situation would only invest their wealth in activities where the rate of return exceeded the rate at which they discount the future. Satisfying this constraint would be difficult – rates of

351

return would have to be extraordinarily high to justify investment. The amount of new investment that one would expect would be extremely modest. Under these circumstances, the stock of preexisting capital would likely depreciate at a faster rate than the additions of new capital. The result would be economic contraction. Even if new investments could match the rate at which preexisting capital depreciated, the best that could be hoped for would be economic stagnation.

The theoretical framework we advance expands the notion of credible commitment in two respects and thereby allows us to explain the puzzle of growth amid instability. First, we relax the requirement that governments need to commit to the enforcement of property rights for everyone in society. Second, we have explicitly differentiated between the players in the polity. The government does not face a single commitment problem – it faces multiple commitment problems with multiple asset holders. The government is therefore able to make selective credible commitments to some subset of asset holders. The government's actions, however, are influenced by the fact that there are other groups in society who can affect the strategic behavior of asset holders and governments – even if those other groups are not directly involved in economic activity or the exercise of government.

By expanding the number of players in the polity, we have connected the security of property rights with the degree of rent seeking in polities lacking limited government. Rent seeking is often viewed as unambiguously negative. There is little doubt in our minds that compared with limited government, VPI is inefficient. The point we seek to make is that limited government is often not a feasible option. Indeed, the historical record does not offer us even a single case of a country that moved directly from an episode of political instability directly to limited government. The reason is not hard to divine: under political instability any government that tried to protect the property rights of the entire society would quickly be overthrown by a faction that did not hesitate to usurp property rights. When the first-best solution is infeasible, the second-best solution is the Pareto-improving solution. VPI may be theoretically second best to limited government, but it beats the empirically possible counterfactual outcomes, a despotic stationary bandit or chaos.

Creating and distributing rents gives a government facing instability three advantages over its opponents. First, it compensates those asset holders that join the government's coalition for the risk of doing so. Second, it allows the government to buy off potential opposition by allowing the asset holders to transfer rents to the government's potential opponents, who become the third-party enforcers of the VPI coalition. Third, because the third party has the ability to bring down the government, integrated asset holders will have confidence in the government's commitment to protect their property rights *and* insure their access to a steady stream of rents from the rest of society.

The implication is that VPI can provide a rapid exit from political instability in terms of economic growth. A faction fighting for its life cannot make a credible commitment to limit its own actions, because it will then face defeat from factions that are not so constrained. Thus, limited government cannot provide an exit from political instability. A stationary bandit can make a credible commitment to protect property rights following instability, but only if it can satisfy one crucial constraint: it must eliminate *all* actual and potential sources of political opposition. Unless this constraint is satisfied, the population will continue to discount the future at a high rate. There will be little (or no) new investment. In addition, there will a reduction in the amount of economic exchange, because economic agents will perceive that contracts they enter into today may not be honored, or cannot be honored, tomorrow. A VPI coalition, in contrast, can credibly commit to protect some asset holders' property rights without destroying all its enemies, and that commitment will remain credible even after stability has returned.

The obvious corollary is that a VPI coalition can sustain economic growth even in a polity where there is a high probability that the government will fall violently. In fact, should any government that may come to power be perceived to need the support of the existing third-party enforcers, then political instability may have no effect whatsoever on economic growth. Neither the identity nor the expected life-span of the government will matter.

The identity and the life-span of the third-party enforcers, on the other hand, matter a great deal. The less capable the third party is of punishing the government, the *more* rents the government must extract in order to make the coalition credible. In other words, the more likely it is that the third party will collapse or disappear, the weaker the government's commitment will be and the more it will be constrained solely by its own long-run self-interest.

The most effective way to ensure the permanency of the third party is to replace individuals or groups of individuals with an institutional-ized entity that can outlive any of its particular members. We offer two hypotheses about the effect of institutionalized third parties. Our first hypothesis is a prediction derived from our theoretical framework. An institutionalized third party will lower or eliminate the ability of any government, no matter how selected, to change policies in any way that threatens the rents of the integrated asset holders. This will, by definition, reduce political competition. Institutionalized third parties may make it much more difficult for a polity governed by VPI to make the transition to limited government.

Our second hypothesis is more speculative. Institutionalizing the third-party enforcer may, perversely, generate a negative impact on economic efficiency. In a repeated game, third parties who permit (or abet) predation by the government will not be invited into future coalitions with other asset holders. Institutionalized third parties will therefore have a valuable reputation that they will want to preserve. A stable third party with a good reputation, however, may be able to "charge" more for integration into a VPI coalition. The amount of rent seeking may rise. This will depress the amount of investment and, by implication, future growth. On the other hand, institutionalized third parties increase the security of property rights. This will have a positive effect on investment. Resolving how these two factors balance out requires both the construction of theoretical models that endogenize the demands of the third party and the careful analysis of empirical evidence beyond the case we have analyzed here.

ECONOMICS

The basic argument we advance is that economic growth does not require governments to protect property rights at the global level. Asset holders are first and foremost concerned with *their* particular property rights. It follows that economic growth does not automatically require limited government – a government that is constrained from preying upon property rights because sets of self-enforcing institutions constrain its agents from acting arbitrarily. It only requires that governments make selective credible commitments to some *subset* of asset holders. This is possible under various kinds of political systems.

Our model of how sovereign governments can make credible commitments has several implications for research into economic growth under political instability. Most immediately, our framework explains why researchers cannot find a statistically robust, causal relationship between instability and growth. Implicit in their research is the notion that instability must be bad for growth because property rights will become insecure. This will cause investment to fall and, as a consequence, output and productivity to decline. Our point is that political instability does not *necessarily* translate into instability of the property rights system, and this can be the case for any of three reasons.

First, political instability will affect the property rights of different industries to varying degrees depending on specific technological and organizational features of those industries. In fact, political instability may actually make the property rights of some asset holders *more* secure. This occurs when an industry provides a significant portion of government tax revenues, the government cannot nationalize and run the industry in the short run because there is knowledge of specific technologies that cannot be easily obtained, and the owners of firms can easily coordinate their actions. Precisely because an unstable government values current revenues more than the asset holders, and precisely because any attempt to nationalize the industry would cause at least a temporary shortfall in tax revenues, the government will be in a very weak bargaining position with the asset holders. Indeed, the more unstable the political situation, the more the government needs the tax revenues generated by the industry, and hence the more secure the property rights of the asset holders in that industry.

Consider, for example, the case of Mexican petroleum. During the period when the polity was unstable, attempts by the government to alter property rights in this industry were easily thwarted by the oil companies. Thus, even though the Mexican Constitution of 1917 established the government as the owner of Mexico's subsoil, government control of the oil industry did not take place until 1938 – that is, until the polity was stable. The fragile governments of the 1910s and 1920s could not successfully challenge the foreign oil companies.

Second, the specific features of the political coalitions that enforce property rights in different industries will have an important effect on whether changes in government can have any effect on the policies that affect property rights. In a system such as the one we outline in Chapter 2, in which property rights are enforced as private goods, the commitment mechanism that constrains government opportunism is the threat that crucial political supporters of government will defect from the coalition because their rents have been interrupted or reduced. If it is the case that any government that may come to power needs the political support of that particular group, then asset holders who share rents with that group will not fear that governments will try to reduce their property rights. From their point of view, governments may come and go, and may even do so at gunpoint, but the underlying property rights system will be unchanged. As long as instability does not result in the elimination of the third-party enforcers, asset holders will know that their property rights cannot be abrogated. Even if the enforcers are eliminated, property rights may not be disrupted for long. The rules of the game are common knowledge among all of the consequential players. Asset holders, factions aspiring to be governments, and potential third-party enforcers will seek one another out and may reconstitute the system in short order.

Whether or not the third-party enforcers of the property rights system are eliminated will be a function of a third factor: there is political instability, and there is *political instability*. The cross-country regression literature tends to code instability as a binary variable – you are either stable or not stable – but the truth of the matter is that not all unstable polities are alike. There is a tremendous difference between recurrent bloodless coups and civil wars so violent that they destroy productive assets and interdict markets. This is clearly seen in the Mexican case. During 1910–13 and 1918–29, political assassinations, coup attempts, and even civil wars such as the de la Huerta revolt (1923–24) and the Cristero War (1926–29) had minimal effects on investment and production. The full scale civil wars of 1913–17 (first against Huerta and then among the victors) were quite another story. In this period, investment and output collapsed. The reason for this difference in outcomes was that during the 1913–17 period factor and product markets could not function because the railways were unavailable for civilian and commercial transport. In addition, there was no single national currency. As we have shown, even the extreme violence of 1913–17 produced little destruction of fixed assets: armies viewed them as sources of income to be protected. Thus, once the railways were up and running and a single currency restored, the economy recovered rapidly, and was dominated by the same firms (and the same owners!) as before 1911.

Lest we be misunderstood, we are not arguing that political instability is never bad for growth. Rather, our point is that the effects of political instability will vary depending on the degree to which the polity is unstable, the specific technological and organizational features of the economy, and the nature of the political system that specifies and enforces property rights.

We also wish to be clear that we are not arguing that the kind of robust-to-instability political system that we have outlined – a set of implicit contracts between a weak authoritarian government, a set of asset holders, and a politically crucial third group that receives rents from the asset holders – is economically efficient compared with limited government. Our framework predicts, in fact, that VPI encourages economic inefficiency. The whole point of joining a VPI coalition is to earn rents. Indeed, a coalition cannot be sustained if no rents are produced. Thus, the government has to provide an environment that can produce rents, which implies that it will restrict competition. This will almost certainly lead to a misallocation of resources in the economy. Countries governed by VPI systems may display impressive economic growth for a time, but will not catch up with advanced economies ruled by limited governments. It is not clear, however, whether excessive rent seeking will slow factor accumulation, growth in total factor productivity, or both. In addition, because the identity of the actors in VPI coalitions can take numerous forms, it is not clear if certain types of third-party enforcers or integrated asset holders may produce more efficient outcomes than others. Only additional theoretical and empirical research beyond the case analyzed here can fully address this question.

Testing our hypotheses about VPI's economic efficiency will require the careful analysis of historical evidence of a quantitative and institutional nature. Although all VPI systems share the same basic framework, the details of the coalition will necessarily vary. Those details, moreover, may have profound effects on long-term growth. More study, both theoretical and empirical, of the political foundations of rent seeking and how rent seeking affects economic growth is clearly needed. That will require, however, that social scientists be willing to engage in careful historical analysis, and that historians be willing to ask social science questions, employ social science tools, and be willing to meet social science standards of evidence.

References

Adelman, M. A. (1995). *The Genie Out of the Bottle: World Oil since 1970*. Cambridge, MA: MIT Press.

Albert, Bill (1988). *South America and the First World War: The Impact of the War on Brazil, Argentina, Peru, and Chile*. Cambridge: Cambridge University Press.

Alesina, Alberto, Sule Özler, et al. (1996). "Political Stability and Economic Growth." *Journal of Economic Growth*, 1: 189–211.

Alston, Lee J., Thráinn Eggertsson, et al. (1996). *Empirical Studies in Institutional Change*. Cambridge: Cambridge University Press.

Anderson, Rodney O. (1976). *Outcasts in Their Own Land: Mexican Industrial Workers, 1906–1911*. DeKalb: Northern Illinois University Press.

Ankerson, Dudley (1984). *Agrarian Warlord: Saturnino Cedillo and the Mexican Revolution in San Luis Potosí*. Dekalb: Northern Illinois University Press.

Arrow, Kenneth Joseph (1974). "Organization and Information." In Kenneth Joseph Arrow (ed.), *The Limits of Organization*, pp. 33–43. New York: Norton.

Atack, Jeremy (1985). *Estimation of Economies of Scale in Nineteenth Century United States Manufacturing*. New York: Garland Press.

Aurrecoechea, Juan Manuel, and Lorena Paz Paredes (1993). "El nuevo despegue de la agroindustria y la crisis de los años veintes." In Juan Manuel Aurrecoechea (ed.), *De haciendas, cañeros y paraestatales: Cien años de historia de la agroindustria cañero-azucarera en México, 1880–1980*, pp. 82–124. Mexico City: Universidad Nacional Autonoma de México: ENEP Acatlán.

Banamex (1929). *Examen de la situación económica de México*. Mexico City: Banamex.

——— (1931). *Examen de la situación económica de México*. Mexico City: Banamex.

Banker's Magazine. Boston.

Barragán, Juan (1993). *Juan F. Brittingham y la industria en México, 1859–1940*. Monterrey, Nuevo León: Urbis Internacional.

Barrera Pages, Gustavo Adolfo (1999). "Industrialización y revolución: El desempeño de la cervecería Toluca y México, S.A. (1875–1926)." B.A. thesis, ITAM, Mexico City.

References

Barro, Robert J. (1991). "Economic Growth in a Cross Section of Countries." *Quarterly Journal of Economics*, 106(2): 407–43.

(1997). *Determinants of Economic Growth: A Cross-Country Empirical Study.* Cambridge, MA: MIT Press.

Barro, Robert J., and David Gordon (1983). "Rules, Discretion, and Reputation in a Model of Monetary Policy." *Journal of Monetary Economics*, 12(1): 101–21.

Bartra, Armando (1993). "La industria cañero-azucarera y la Revolución de 1910." In Juan M. Aurrecoechea (ed.), *De haciendas, cañeros y paraestatales: Cien años de historia de la agroindustria cañero-azucarera en México, 1880–1980.* Mexico City: Universidad Nacional Autonoma de México: ENEP Acatlán.

Barzel, Yoram (1997). *Economic Analysis of Property Rights.* Cambridge: Cambridge University Press.

Bates, Robert H. (2001). *Prosperity and Violence: The Political Economy of Development.* New York: W. W. Norton.

Bates, Robert H., Avner Greif, et al. (1998). *Analytic Narratives.* Princeton: Princeton University Press.

Beatty, Edward (2001). *Institutions and Investment: The Political Basis of Industrialization in Mexico before 1911.* Stanford, CA: Stanford University Press.

(2002). "Commercial Policy in Porfirian Mexico: The Structure of Protection." In Jeffrey L. Bortz and Stephen H. Haber (eds.), *The Mexican Economy, 1870–1930: Essays on the Economic History of Institutions, Revolution, and Growth,* pp. 205–52. Stanford, CA: Stanford University Press.

Benjamin, Thomas, and Mark Wasserman (eds.) (1990). *Provinces of the Revolution: Essays on Regional Mexican History, 1910–1929.* Albuquerque: University of New Mexico Press.

Bernard, A. B., and C. I. Jones (1996). "Productivity across Industries and Countries: Time Series Theory and Evidence." *Review of Economics and Statistics,* 78(1): 135–46.

Bernstein, Marvin D. (1964). *The Mexican Mining Industry, 1890–1950: A Study of the Interaction of Politics, Economics, and Technology.* Albany: State University of New York.

Boletín Financiero y Minero. Mexico City.

Bortz, Jeffrey L. (1997). "'Without Any More Law Than Their Own Caprice': Cotton Textile Workers and the Challenge to Factory Authority during the Mexican Revolution." *International Review of Social History,* 42(2): 253–88.

(2002). "The Legal and Contractual Limits to Private Property Rights in Mexican Industry during the Revolution." In Jeffrey L. Bortz and Stephen H. Haber (eds.), *The Mexican Economy, 1870–1930: Essays on the Economic History of Institutions, Revolution, and Growth,* pp. 255–88. Stanford, CA: Stanford University Press.

Brennan, Geoffrey, and James M. Buchanan (1985). *The Reason of Rules: Constitutional Political Economy.* Cambridge: Cambridge University Press.

Brown, J. W. (1927). *Modern Mexico and Its Problems.* London: Labour.

Brown, Jonathan C. (1985). "Why Foreign Oil Companies Shifted Their Production from Mexico to Venezuela during the 1920's." *American Historical Review,* 90(2): 362–85.

(1993). *Oil and Revolution in Mexico.* Berkeley: University of California.

References

Brunetti, Aymo (1997). *Politics and Economic Growth: A Cross Country Data Perspective*. Paris: Organisation for Economic Cooperation and Development.

Buve, Raymond Th. J. (1988). "The Peasant Movement in Tlaxcala." In Friedrich Katz (ed.), *Riot, Rebellion, and Revolution: Rural Social Conflict in Mexico*. Princeton: Princeton University Press.

Cámara Nacional de Cemento (n.d.). *Medio siglo del cemento en México*. Mexico City: Cámara Nacional de Cemento.

Camp, Roderic A. (1991). *Mexican Political Biographies, 1884–1935*. Austin: University of Texas Press.

Campos, Nauro F., and Jeffrey B. Nugent (2000). "Investment and Instability." University of Southern California, Department of Economics, Los Angeles.

——— (2002). "Who Is Afraid of Political Instability?" *Journal of Development Economics*, 67(1): 157–72.

Cárdenas, Enrique, and Carlos Manns (1989). "Inflación y estabilización monetaria en México durante la Revolución." *Trimestre Económico*, 56(221): 57–79.

Cárdenas García, Nicolás (1988). *Empresas y trabajadores en la gran minería mexicana (1900–1929): La Revolución y el nuevo sistema de relaciones laborales*. Mexico City: Instituto Nacional de Estudios Históricos de la Revolución Mexicana.

Careaga, Maite (1998). "King for Six Years: The Political Economy of Presidencialismo and Corruption in Post-1940 Mexico." Unpublished manuscript, Department of Political Science, Stanford University, Stanford, CA.

Carmagnani, Marcello (1994). *Estado y mercado: La economía pública del liberalismo mexicano, 1850–1911*. Mexico City: El Colegio de México and Fondo de Cultura Económica.

Carr, Barry (1976). *El movimiento obrero y la política en México, 1910/1929*. Mexico City: Edición Era.

Carter, Susan B., and United States Bureau of the Census (1997). *Historical Statistics of the United States on CD-ROM: Colonial Times to 1970*. Cambridge: Cambridge University Press.

Castellanos Suárez, José Alfredo (1998). *Empeño por una expectativa agraria: experiencia ejidal en el municipio de Acolman, 1915–1940*. Mexico City: Instituto Nacional de Estudios Históricos de la Revolución Mexicana; Chapingo, Mexico: Universidad Autónoma Chapingo.

Cerutti, Mario (1992). *Burguesía, capitales, e industria en el Norte de México*. Monterrey, Mexico: Universidad Autónoma de Nuevo León.

Cerutti, Mario, and Oscar Flores (1997). *Españoles en el Norte de México: Propietarios, empresarios y diplomacia, 1850–1920*. Monterrey, Mexico: Universidad Autónoma de Nuevo León.

Clark, Gregory (1987). "Why Isn't the Whole World Developed? Lessons from the Cotton Mills." *Journal of Economic History*, 47(1): 141–74.

Cleland, Robert Glass (1921). "The Mining Industry of Mexico: A Historical Sketch II." *Mining and Scientific Press* 123 (November 5, 1921): 638–42.

——— (1922). *The Mexican Yearbook: The Standard Authority on Mexico, 1920–21*. Los Angeles: Mexican Yearbook Publishing Company.

——— (1924). *The Mexican Yearbook: The Standard Authority on Mexico, 1922–24*. Los Angeles: Mexican Yearbook Publishing Company.

Coatsworth, John H. (1978). "Obstacles to Economic Growth in Nineteenth Century Mexico." *American Historical Review*, 83(1): 80–100.

(1981). *Growth against Development: The Economic Impact of Railroads in Porfirian Mexico*. Dekalb: Northern Illinois University Press.

Collado Herrera, María del Carmen (1987). *La burguesía mexicana: El emporio Braniff y su participación política, 1865–1920*. Mexico City: Siglo XXI Editores.

(1996). *Empresarios y políticos, entre la Restauración y la Revolución 1920–1924*. Mexico City: Instituto Nacional de Estudios Históricos de la Revolución Mexicana.

Compañía Fundidora de Fierro y Acero de Monterrey (1900–30). *Informe Anual*. Monterrey, Mexico: Compañía Fundidora de Fierro y Acero de Monterrey, S.A.

Conant, Charles A. (1910). *The Banking System of Mexico*. Washington, DC: Government Printing Office.

Connolly, Priscilla (1997). *El contratista de don Porfirio: Obras públicas, deuda y desarrollo desigual*. Mexico City: Fondo de Cultura Económica.

Cosío Villegas, Daniel (1989). *La cuestión arancelaria en México*. Mexico City: Universidad Nacional Autónoma de México.

Davis, Harold E. (1932). "Mexican Petroleum Taxes." *Hispanic American Historical Review*, 12(4): 405–19.

de la Fuente Piñeirua, Alberto (2001). "El desplazamiento de México como productor de petroleo en los años veinte." B.A. thesis, ITAM, Mexico City.

DeLong, Bradford, and Andrei Shleifer (1993). "Princes and Merchants: European City Growth before the Industrial Revolution." *Journal of Law and Economics*, 36(2): 671–702.

Díaz Dufoo, Carlos (1921). *La cuestión del petroleo*. Mexico: Eusebio Gomez de la Puente, Editor.

(1922). *Limantour*. México: Imprenta Victoria.

Dye, Alan (1998). *Cuban Sugar in the Age of Mass Production*. Stanford, CA: Stanford University Press.

Economista Mexicano. Mexico City.

Eggertsson, Thráinn (1990). *Economic Behavior and Institutions*. Cambridge: Cambridge University Press.

El Demócrata. Mexico City.

El Economista Mexicano. Mexico City.

El Universal. Mexico City.

Engineering and Mining Journal. New York.

Falcón, Romana (1977). *El agrarismo en Veracruz: La etapa radical, 1928–1935*. Mexico City: El Colegio de México.

(1984). *Revolución y caciquismo: San Luis Potosí, 1910–1938*. Mexico City: El Colegio de México.

(1990). "San Luis Potosí: Confiscated Estates-Revolutionary Conquest or Spoils?" In Thomas Benjamin and Mark Wasserman (eds.), *Provinces of the Revolution: Essays on Regional Mexican History, 1910–1929*, pp. 133–62. Albuquerque: University of New Mexico Press.

Fowler-Salamini, Heather (1978). *Agrarian Radicalism in Veracruz, 1920–38*. Lincoln: University of Nebraska Press.

References

(1990). "Tamaulipas." In Thomas Benjamin and Mark Wasserman (eds.), *Provinces of the Revolution: Essays on Regional Mexican History, 1910–1929*, pp. 185–217. Albuquerque: University of New Mexico Press.

Friedrich, Paul (1977). *Agrarian Revolt in a Mexican Village*. Chicago: University of Chicago Press.

Fuentes Mares, José (1976). *Monterrey, una ciudad creadora y sus capitanes*. Mexico: Editorial Jus.

Gambetta, Diego (1993). *The Sicilian Mafia: The Business of Private Protection*. Cambridge, MA: Harvard University Press.

Gamboa Ojeda, Leticia (1985). *Los empresarios de ayer: El grupo dominante en la industria textil de Puebla, 1906–1929*. Puebla, Mexico: Universidad Autónoma de Puebla.

García Naranjo, Nemesio (1955). *Una industria en marcha*. Monterrey, Mexico.

Gilly, Adolfo (1994). *La revolución interrumpida*. Mexico City: Ediciones Era.

Goldstone, Jack (1991). *Revolution and Rebellion in the Early Modern World*. Berkeley: University of California Press.

Gómez Galvarriato, Aurora (1997). "El desempeño de la Fundidora de Hierro y Acero de Monterrey durante el Porfiriato. Acerca de los obstáculos a la industrialización en México." In Mario Cerutti and Carlos Marichal (eds.), *Historia de las grandes empresas en México, 1850–1930*, pp. 201–44. Mexico: Universidad Autónoma de Nuevo León and Fondo de Cultura Económica.

(1999). "The Impact of Revolution: Business and Labor in the Mexican Textile Industry, Orizaba, Veracruz, 1900–1930." Ph.D. dissertation, Harvard University, Cambridge, MA.

(2002). "Measuring the Impact of Institutional Change on Capital Labor Relations in the Mexican Textile Industry, 1900–1930." In Jeffrey L. Bortz and Stephen H. Haber (eds.), *The Mexican Economy, 1870–1930: Essays on the Economic History of Institutions, Revolution, and Growth*, pp. 289–323. Stanford, CA: Stanford University Press.

Gómez Galvarriato, Aurora, and Aldo Musacchio (1998). "Un nuevo índice de precios para México, 1886–1930." Working Paper 113, CIDE, Mexico City.

Graham-Clark, W. A. (1909). *Cotton Goods in Latin America, Part I*. Washington, DC: USGPO.

Green, Edward, and Richard Porter (1984). "Non-Cooperative Collusion under Imperfect Price Information." *Econometrica*, 52(1): 87–100.

Greif, Avner (1989). "Reputation and Coalitions in Medieval Trade: Evidence on the Maghribi Traders." *Journal of Economic History*, 49(4): 857–82.

(1997). "Contracting, Enforcement, and Efficiency: Economics beyond the Law." In Michael Bruno and Boris Pleskovic (eds.), *Annual World Bank Conference on Development Economics*, pp. 239–66. Washington, DC: World Bank.

(1998). "Informal Contract Enforcement Institutions: Lesson from Late Medieval Trade." In Peter Newman (ed.), *Dictionary of Economics and the Law*, pp. 287–95. London: Macmillan Press.

Greif, Avner, Paul Milgrom, et al. (1994). "Coordination, Commitment, and Enforcement: The Case of the Merchant Guild." *Journal of Political Economy*, 102(4): 745–76.

References

Gruening, Ernest (1928). *Mexico and Its Heritage*. New York: Century.

Grunstein, Arturo (1994). "Railroads and Sovereignty: Policy-Making in Porfirian Mexico." Ph.D. dissertation, University of California, Los Angeles.

Gutiérrez Alvarez, Coralia (2000). *Experiencias contrastadas: Industrialización y conflictos en los textiles del centro-oriente de México, 1884–1917*. Mexico: El Colegio de México Centro de Estudios Históricos; Benemérita Universidad de Puebla Instituto de Ciencias Sociales y Humanidades.

Haber, Stephen H. (1989). *Industry and Underdevelopment: The Industrialization of Mexico, 1890–1940*. Stanford, CA: Stanford University Press.

(1991). "Industrial Concentration and the Capital Markets: A Comparative Study of Brazil, Mexico, and the United States, 1830–1930." *Journal of Economic History*, 51(3): 559–80.

(1992). "Assessing the Obstacles to Industrialization: The Mexican Economy." *Journal of Latin American Studies*, 24(1): 1–32.

(1997). "Financial Markets and Industrial Development: A Comparative Study of Governmental Regulation, Financial Innovation, and Industrial Structure in Brazil and Mexico, 1840–1930." In Stephen H. Haber (ed.), *How Latin America Fell Behind: Essays on the Economic Histories of Brazil and Mexico, 1800–1914*. Stanford, CA: Stanford University Press.

(1998). "The Efficiency Consequences of Institutional Change: Financial Market Regulation and Industrial Productivity Growth in Brazil, 1866–1934." In John H. Coatsworth and Alan M. Taylor (eds.), *Latin America and the World Economy since 1800*. Cambridge, MA: David Rockefeller Center for Latin American Studies, Harvard University.

(Forthcoming). "It Wasn't All Prebisch's Fault: The Political Economy of Latin American Industrialization." In Victor Bulmer-Thomas, John Coatsworth, and Roberto Cortes Conde (eds.), *The Cambridge Economic History of Latin America*. Cambridge: Cambridge University Press.

Haber, Stephen H., and Armando Razo (1998). "Political Instability and Economic Performance: Evidence from Revolutionary Mexico." *World Politics*, 51(1): 99–143.

Hall, Linda B. (1981). *Álvaro Obregón: Power and Revolution, 1911–1920*. College Station: Texas A&M University Press.

(1995). *Oil, Banks, and Politics: The United States and Postrevolutionary Mexico, 1917–1924*. Austin: University of Texas Press.

Hall, Michael M., and Hobart Spalding (1986). "The Urban Working Class and Early Latin American Labour Movements, 1880–1930." In Leslie Bethell (ed.), *The Cambridge History of Latin America*, vol. 4, *1870–1930*, pp. 325–66. Cambridge: Cambridge University Press.

Hart, John Mason (1987). *Revolutionary Mexico: The Coming and Process of the Mexican Revolution*. Berkeley: University of California Press.

Hart, Oliver (1995). *Firms, Contracts, and Financial Structure*. Oxford: Oxford University Press.

Hoffman, Phillip, and Katherine Norberg (eds.) (1994). *Fiscal Crises and the Growth of Representative Institutions*. Stanford, CA: Stanford University Press.

Holden, Robert H. (1994). *Mexico and the Survey of Public Lands: The Management of Modernization, 1876–1911*. Dekalb: Northern Illinois University Press.

References

Johnson, Ronald D., and Allen Parkman (1983). "Spatial Monopoly, Non-Zero Profits, and Entry Deterrence: The Case of Cement." *Review of Economics and Statistics*, 65(3): 431–39.

Joseph, Gilbert M. (1982). *Revolution from Without: Yucatan, Mexico, and the United States, 1880–1924*. Cambridge: Cambridge University Press.

Journal of the American Chamber of Commerce of Mexico, 1918–30.

Kane, Nancy F. (1988). *Textiles in Transition: Technology, Wages, and Industry Relocation in the U.S. Textile Industry*. Westport, CT: Greenwood.

Kasper, Wolfgang, and Manfred E. Streit (1999). *Institutional Economics: Social Order and Public Policy*. Northampton, MA: Edward Elgar.

Katz, Friedrich (1981). *The Secret War in Mexico: Europe, the United States, and the Mexican Revolution*. Chicago: University of Chicago Press.

(1998). *The Life and Times of Pancho Villa*. Stanford, CA: Stanford University Press.

Kemmerer, Edwin Walter (1940). *Inflation and Revolution: Mexico's Experience of 1912–1917*. Princeton: Princeton University Press.

Keremetsis, Dawn (1973). *La industria textil mexicana en el siglo XIX*. Mexico City: Secretaría de Educación Pública.

Khan, B. Zorina, and Kenneth L. Sokoloff (2002). "The Innovation of Patent Systems in the Nineteenth Century: A Comparative Perspective." Paper presented at the International Economic History Congress, Buenos Aires.

Klein, Benjamin, Robert G. Crawford, et al. (1978). "Vertical Integration, Appropriable Rents, and the Competitive Contracting Process." *Journal of Law and Economics*, 21(2): 297–326.

Knight, Alan (1986a). *The Mexican Revolution: Porfirians, Liberals, and Peasants*. Cambridge: Cambridge University Press.

(1986b). *The Mexican Revolution: Counter-Revolution and Reconstruction*. Cambridge: Cambridge University Press.

Knowlton, Robert (1995). "La división de las tierras en el siglo XIX: El caso de Michoacán." In Margarita Menegus Bornemann and Brian R. Hamnett (eds.), *Problemas agrarios y propiedad en México, siglos XVIII y XIX*. Mexico City: El Colegio de Mexico. 11.

Krauze, Enrique, Jean Meyer, et al. (1977). *Historia de la Revolución Mexicana, 1924–1928: La reconstrucción económica*. Mexico City: El Colegio de México.

Kuntz Ficker, Sandra (1995). *Empresa extranjera y mercado interno: El Ferrocarril Central Mexicano, 1880–1907*. Mexico City: El Colegio de México.

(2000). "Economic Backwardness and Firm Strategy: An American Railroad Corporation in Nineteenth-Century Mexico." *Hispanic American Historical Review*, 80(2): 267–98.

(2001). "The Mexican Revolution Export Boom: Characteristics and Contributing Factors." Unpublished manuscript, Universidad Autónoma Metropolitana-Xochimilco, Mexico City.

(2002). "Institutional Change and Foreign Trade in Mexico, 1870–1911." In Jeffrey L. Bortz and Stephen H. Haber (eds.), *The Mexican Economy, 1870–1930: Essays on the Economic History of Institutions, Revolution, and Growth*, pp. 161–204. Stanford, CA: Stanford University Press.

References

Kuntz Ficker, Sandra, and Paolo Riguzzi (eds.) (1996). *Ferrocarriles y vida económica en México, 1850–1950: Del surgimiento tardío al decaimiento precoz.* Mexico: Colegio Mexiquense.

Lamoreaux, Naomi (1994). *Insider Lending: Banks, Personal Connections, and Economic Development in Industrial New England.* Cambridge: Cambridge University Press.

Lear, John (2001). *The Revolution in Mexico City.* Lincoln: University of Nebraska Press.

Lenz, Hans, and Federico Gómez de Orozco (1940). *La industria papelera en México: Bosquejo histórico.* Mexico: Editorial Cultura.

Levi, Margaret (1988). *Of Rule and Revenue.* Berkeley: University of California Press.

Levine, Ross, and David Renelt (1992). "A Sensitivity Analysis of Cross-Country Growth Regressions." *American Economic Review*, 82(4): 942–63.

Levy, Brian, and Pablo T. Spiller (1996). *Regulations, Institutions, and Commitment: Comparative Studies of Telecommunications.* Cambridge: Cambridge University Press.

Lewis, George King (1959). "An Analysis of the Institutional Status and Role of the Petroleum Industry in Mexico's Evolving System of Political Economy." Ph.D dissertation, University of Texas, Austin.

Lobato López, Ernesto (1945). *El crédito en México, esbozo histórico hasta 1925.* Mexico: Fondo de Cultura Económica.

Londregan, John B., and Keith T. Poole (1990). "Poverty, the Coup Trap, and the Seizure of Executive Power." *World Politics*, 42(2): 151–83.

   (1992). "The Seizure of Executive Power and Economic Growth: Some Additional Evidence." In Alex Cukierman, Zvi Hercowitz, and Leonard Leiderman (eds.), *Political Economy, Growth, and Business Cycles*, pp. 51–80. Cambridge, MA: MIT Press.

López-Alonso, Moramay (2000). "Height, Health, Nutrition and Growth: A History of Living Standards in Mexico, 1870–1950." Ph.D. dissertation, Stanford University, Stanford, CA.

Ludlow, Leonor (1986). "La construcción de un banco: El Banco Nacional de México (1881–1884)." In Leonor Ludlow and Carlos Marichal (eds.), *Banca y poder en México (1880–1925)*, pp. 299–346. Mexico City: Grijalbo.

   (1998). "La formación del Banco de México: Aspectos institucionales y sociales." In Leonor Ludlow and Carlos Marichal (eds.), *La banca en México, 1820–1920*, pp. 142–80. Mexico City: Instituto Mora; El Colegio de Michoacán; El Colegio de México; Instituto de Investigaciones Históricas-UNAM.

Madero, Francisco I. (1911). *La sucesión presidencial en 1910.* Mexico City: La Viuda de C. Boret.

Manero, Antonio (1958). *La reforma bancaria en la Revolución Constitucionalista.* Mexico City: Instituto Nacional de Estudios Históricos de la Revolución Mexicana.

Mantzavinos, Chrysostomos (2001). *Individuals, Institutions, and Markets.* Cambridge: Cambridge University Press.

References

Marichal, Carlos (1986). "El nacimiento de la banca mexicana en el contexto latinoamericano: problemas de periodización." In Leonor Ludlow and Carlos Marichal (eds.), *Banca y Poder en México (1800–1925)*, pp. 231–66. Mexico City: Grijalbo.

Marichal, Carlos (1995). "Foreign Loans, Banks and Capital Markets in Mexico, 1880–1910." In Reinhard Liehr (ed.), *La deuda pública en América Latina en perspectiva histórica*, pp. 337–74. Frankfurt: Vervuet; Madrid: Iberoamericana.

(1997). "Obstacles to the Development of Capital Markets in Nineteenth-Century Mexico." In Stephen H. Haber (ed.), *How Latin America Fell Behind: Essays on the Economic Histories of Brazil and Mexico, 1800–1914*, pp. 118–45. Stanford, CA: Stanford University Press.

(1998). "El nacimiento de la banca mexicana en el contexto latinoamericano: Problemas de periodización." In Leonor Ludlow and Carlos Marichal (eds.), *La banca en México, 1820–1920*, pp. 231–66. Mexico City: Instituto Mora; El Colegio de Michoacán; El Colegio de México; Instituto de Investigaciones Históricas-UNAM.

(2002). "The Construction of Credibility: Financial Market Reform and the Renegotiation of Mexico's External Debt in the 1880's." In Jeffrey L. Bortz and Stephen H. Haber (eds.), *The Mexican Economy, 1870–1930: Essays on the Economic History of Institutions, Revolution, and Growth*, pp. 93–119. Stanford, CA: Stanford University Press.

Marichal, Carlos, and Mario Cerutti (eds.) (1997). *Historia de las grandes empresas en México, 1850–1930*. Mexico: Universidad Autónoma de Nuevo León and Fondo de Cultura Económica.

Markiewicz, Dana (1993). *The Mexican Revolution and the Limits of Agrarian Reform, 1915–1946*. Boulder, CO: Lynne Rienner Publishers.

Márquez, Graciela (2001). "Protección y cambio institucional: La política arancelaria del Porfiriato a la Gran Depresión." Unpublished manuscript, El Colegio de México, Mexico City.

(2002) "The Political Economy of Mexican Protectionism, 1868–1911." Ph.D. dissertation, Harvard University.

Maurer, Noel H. (1999). "Banks and Entrepreneurs in Porfirian Mexico: Inside Exploitation or Sound Business Strategy?" *Journal of Latin American Studies*, 31(2): 331–61.

(2002a). "Banking Regulation and Banking Performance in Porfirian Mexico." In Jeffrey L. Bortz and Stephen H. Haber (eds.), *The Mexican Economy, 1870–1930: Essays on the Economic History of Institutions, Revolution, and Growth*, pp. 50–92. Stanford, CA: Stanford University Press.

(2002b). *The Power and the Money: The Mexican Financial System, 1876–1928*. Stanford, CA: Stanford University Press.

Maurer, Noel, and Stephen H. Haber (2002). "Institutional Change and Economic Growth: Banks, Financial Markets, and Mexican Industrialization." In Jeffrey L. Bortz and Stephen H. Haber (eds.), *The Mexican Economy, 1870–1930: Essays on the Economic History of Institutions, Revolution, and Growth*, pp. 23–49. Stanford, CA: Stanford University Press.

References

McCaleb, Walter F. (1920). *Present and Past Banking in Mexico*. New York: Harper and Brothers.

McCubbins, Mathew D., Roger G. Noll, et al. (1987a). "Administrative Procedures as Instruments of Political Control." *Journal of Law, Economics, and Organization*, 3: 243–77.

McCubbins, Mathew D., Roger G. Noll, et al. (1987b). "Structure and Process, Politics and Policy: Administrative Arrangements and the Political Control of Agencies." *Virginia Law Review*, 75: 431–82.

McCubbins, Mathew D., and Thomas Schwartz (1984). "Congresional Oversight Overlooked: Police Patrols versus Fire Alarms." *American Journal of Political Science*, 28: 165–79.

McGuire, Martin, and Mancur Olson (1996). "The Economics of Autocracy and Majority Rule: The Invisible Hand and the Use of Force." *Journal of Economic Literature*, 34: 72–102.

Melville, Elinor (1997). *A Plague of Sheep*. Cambridge: Cambridge University Press.

Méndez Reyes, Jesús (1996). *La política económica durante el gobierno de Francisco I. Madero*. Mexico City: Instituto Nacional de Estudios Históricos de la Revolución Mexicana.

(2001). "Lealtad e infidencia a la causa revolucionaria: Préstamos a los generales mexicanos, 1917–1934." *Sólo Historia*, 3(11): 21–26.

Menegus Bornemann, Margarita (1995). "Ocoyoacac: una comunidad agraria en el siglo XIX." In Margarita Menegus Bornemann (ed.), *Problemas agrarios y propiedad en México, siglos XVIII y XIX*. Mexico City: El Colegio de Mexico, pp. 144–89.

Mexican Herald. Mexico City.

Mexican Yearbook: A Financial and Commercial Handbook Compiled from Official and Other Returns, 1908 (1908). London: McCorquodale and Company.

Mexican Yearbook: A Financial and Commercial Handbook Compiled from Official and Other Returns, 1909–1910 (1910). London: McCorquodale and Company.

Mexican Yearbook: A Financial and Commercial Handbook Compiled from Official and Other Returns, 1911 (1911). London: McCorquodale and Company.

Mexican Yearbook: A Financial and Commercial Handbook Compiled from Official and Other Returns, 1912 (1912). London: McCorquodale and Company.

Mexican Yearbook: A Financial and Commercial Handbook Compiled from Official and Other Returns, 1913 (1913). London: McCorquodale and Company.

Mexican Yearbook: A Financial and Commercial Handbook Compiled from Official and Other Returns, 1914 (1914). London: McCorquodale and Company.

México. Banco Central Mexicano (1908). *Las sociedades anónimas en México*. Mexico City: Banco Central Mexicano.

México. Comisión Nacional Bancaria (1928). *Boletín de la Comisión Nacional Bancaria*. Mexico City: Comisión Nacional Bancaria.

(1929). *Boletín de la Comisión Nacional Bancaria*. Mexico City: Comisión Nacional Bancaria.

(1930). *Boletín de la Comisión Nacional Bancaria*. Mexico City: Comisión Nacional Bancaria.

References

(1932). *Boletín de la Comisión Nacional Bancaria*. Mexico City: Comisión Nacional Bancaria.

México. Departamento de la Estadística Nacional (1921–32). *Estadística Nacional, Revista Mensual*. Mexico City: Departamento de la Estadística Nacional.

México. Dirección General de Estadística (1894). *Anuario estadístico de la República Mexicana 1893–94*. Mexico City: Dirección General de Estadística.

(1926). *Anuario estadístico, 1923–1924*. Vol. 2. Mexico City: Dirección General de Estadística.

(1930). *Anuario estadístico, 1930*. Mexico City: Dirección General de Estadística.

México. Ferrocarriles Nacionales (1989). *México económico 1928–1930*. Mexico City: Oficina de Estudios Económicos, Ferrocarriles Nacionales.

México. INEGI (1994). *Estadísticas Históricas de México*. Aguascalientes, Mexico: Instituto Nacional de Estadística Geografía e Informática.

México. Secretaría de Hacienda (1893). *Reglamento para el cobro de los derechos de amonedación, timbre, afinación, fundición, ensaye, y apartado con que la ley de ingresos grava los metales preciosos y las substancias minerales que los contienen*. Mexico City: Secretaría de Hacienda and F. P. Hoeck.

(1895). *Reglamento para el cobro de los derechos de amonedación, timbre, afinación, fundición, ensaye, y apartado con que la ley de ingresos grava los metales preciosos y las substancias minerales que los contienen*. Mexico City: Secretaría de Hacienda and F. P. Hoeck.

(1924–29). *Estadísticas del ramo de hilados y tejidos de algodón y de lana, 1924–1929*. Mexico City: Secretaría de Hacienda, Departamento de Impuestos Especiales.

(1936). *El problema actual de la industria papelera en México*. Mexico City: Secretaría de Hacienda.

(Various years). *Boletín de estadística fiscal*. Mexico City: Secretaría de Hacienda.

México. Secretaría de Hacienda y Crédito Público (1897). *Memoria 1896–1897*. Mexico City: Secretaría de Hacienda y Crédito Público.

(1912). *Anuario de estadística fiscal, 1911–1912*. Mexico City: Talleres Gráficos de la Nación.

(1924). *Comisión Permanente de la Convención Bancaria*. Mexico City: Secretaría de Hacienda y Crédito Público.

(1951). *La hacienda pública a través de los informes presidenciales*. Mexico City: Secretaría de Hacienda y Crédito Público.

México. Secretaría de Industría, Comercio y Trabajo (1924). *Anuario de estadística minera 1922*. Mexico City: Talleres Gráficos de la Nación.

(1925). *Anuario de estadística minera 1923*. Mexico City: Talleres Gráficos de la Nación.

(1926). *Anuario de estadística minera 1924*. Mexico City: Talleres Gráficos de la Nación.

(1927). *Anuario de estadística minera 1925*. Mexico City: Talleres Gráficos de la Nación.

(1928). *Anuario de estadística minera 1926*. Mexico City: Talleres Gráficos de la Nación.

(1929). *Anuario de estadística minera 1927*. Mexico City: Talleres Gráficos de la Nación.

(1930). *Anuario de estadística minera 1928*. Mexico City: Talleres Gráficos de la Nación.

(1932). *Anuario de estadística minera 1929–1930*. Mexico City: Talleres Gráficos de la Nación.

México. Secretaría del Estado y del Despacho de Fomento, Colonización, Industria y Comercio (1885). *Código de mineria de la República Mexicana y su reglamento*. Mexico City: Secretaría del Estado y del Despacho de Fomento, Colonización, Industria y Comercio.

(1893). *Mining Code of the Mexican Republic, with Treasury Regulations, Tariff of Fees, Taxes, Circulars, and Decrees. In English and Spanish*. Mexico City: Secretaría del Estado y del Despacho de Fomento, Colonización, Industria y Comercio and F. P. Hoeck.

Meyer, Jean (1973). *La Cristiada*. Mexico City: Siglo XXI editores.

Meyer, Lorenzo (1977). *Mexico and the United States in the Oil Controversy, 1916–1942*. Austin: University of Texas Press.

Meyer, Lorenzo, Rafael Segovia, et al. (1978). *Historia de la Revolución Mexicana, 1928–1934: Los inicios de la institucionalización*. Mexico City: El Colegio de México.

Meyer, Michael C., William L. Sherman, et al. (1999). *The Course of Mexican History*. New York: Oxford University Press.

Meyers, William K. (1991). "Pancho Villa and the Multinationals: United States Mining Interests in Villista Mexico, 1913–1915." *Journal of Latin American Studies*, 23: 339–63.

Middlebrook, Kevin J. (1995). *The Paradox of Revolution: Labor, the State, and Authoritarianism in Mexico*. Baltimore: Johns Hopkins University Press.

Miller, Gary J. (1992). *Managerial Dilemmas: The Political Economy of Hierarchies*. Cambridge: Cambridge University Press.

Monaldi, Francisco (2002). "Rent Seeking, Institutions, and Commitment: The Political Economy of Foreign Investment in the Venezuelan Oil Industry." Ph. D. dissertation, Stanford University, Stanford, CA.

Moody's Manual of Investments. New York: Moody's Investment Services.

Moore, Barrington (1967). *Social Origins of Dictatorship and Democracy: Lord and Peasant in the Making of the Modern World*. Boston: Beacon.

Musacchio, Aldo, and Ian Read (2001). "Bankers, Industrialists and Their Cliques: Elite Networks in Mexico and Brazil, 1890–1915." Unpublished manuscript, Department of History, Stanford University, Stanford, CA.

Nickel, Herbert (1988). "Agricultural Laborers in Puebla-Tlaxcala." In Friedrich Katz (ed.), *Riot, Rebellion, and Revolution: Rural Social Conflict in Mexico*, pp. 376–416. Princeton: Princeton University Press.

North, Douglass C. (1981). *Structure and Change in Economic History*. New York: Norton.

(1990). *Institutions, Institutional Change, and Economic Performance*. Cambridge: Cambridge University Press.

North, Douglass C., William Summerhill, et al. (2000). "Order, Disorder, and Economic Change: Latin America versus North America." In Bruce Bueno

References

de Mesquita and Hilton L. Root (eds.), *Governing for Prosperity*, pp. 17–58. New Haven: Yale University Press.

North, Douglass C. and Robert Paul Thomas (1973). *The Rise of the Western World: A New Economic History*. Cambridge: Cambridge University Press.

North, Douglass C., and Barry R. Weingast (1989). "Constitutions and Commitment: the Evolution of Institutions Governing Public Choice in Seventeenth-Century England." *Journal of Economic History*, 49(4): 803–32.

Okada, Atsumi (2000). "El impacto de la Revolución Mexicana: La compañía Richardson en el Valle del Yaqui (1905–1928)." *Historia Mexicana*, 197: 191–244.

Olson, Mancur (1993). "Dictatorship, Democracy, and Development." *American Political Science Review*, 87(3): 567–76.

(2000). *Power and Prosperity : Outgrowing Communist and Capitalist Dictatorships*. New York: Basic Books.

Patiño Rodríguez, Raúl (1964). "La industria del cemento en México." Unpublished manuscript, Banco de México, Mexico City.

Pejovich, Svetozar (1990). *The Economics of Property Rights: Towards a Theory of Comparative Systems*. Dordrecht: Kluwer Academic Publishers.

(1998). *Economic Analysis of Institutions and Systems*. Boston: Kluwer Academic Publishers.

Peltzman, Sam (1976). "Towards a More General Theory of Regulation." *Journal of Law and Economics*, 19(2): 211–40.

Perry, Laurens Ballard (1978). *Juárez and Díaz: Machine Politics in Mexico*. Dekalb: Northern Illinois University Press.

Plana, Manuel (1996). *El reino del algodón en Mexico: La estructura agraria de La Laguna (1855–1910)*. Monterrey, Mexico: Universidad Autónoma de Nuevo León.

Plasencia de la Parra, Enrique (1998). *Personajes y escenarios de la Rebelión Delahuertista, 1923–1924*. Mexico City: Instituto de Investigaciones Históricas, Universidad Nacional Autónoma de México.

Potter, Neal, and Francis T. Christy (1962). *Trends in Natural Resource Commodities: Statistics of Prices, Output, Consumption, Foreign Trade, and Employment in the United States, 1870–1957*. Baltimore: Published for Resources for the Future by Johns Hopkins Press.

Qian, Yingyi, and Barry R. Weingast (1997). "Federalism as a Commitment to Preserving Market Incentives." *Journal of Economic Perspectives*, 11(4): 83–92.

Ramirez Rancaño, Mario (1987). *Burguesía textil y política en la Revolución Mexicana*. Mexico City: Instituto de Investigaciones Sociales, Universidad Nacional Autónoma de México.

Razo, Armando (1998). "Land Policy and Property Rights in Colonial Mexico." Unpublished manuscript, Department of Political Science, Stanford University, Stanford, CA.

Razo, Armando, and Stephen H. Haber (1998). "The Rate of Growth of Productivity in Mexico, 1850–1933: Evidence from the Cotton Textile Industry." *Journal of Latin American Studies*, 30(3): 481–517.

Reed, John (1969). *Insurgent Mexico*. New York: International Publishers.

References

Reynolds, Clark W. (1970). *The Mexican Economy*. New Haven: Yale University Press.

Rickard, T. A. (1924). "The Mexican Primary." *Engineering and Mining Journal*, 117(4): 173.

Riker, William H. (1964). *Federalism: Origin, Operation, Significance*. Boston: Little Brown.

Riordan, Michael (1990). "What Is Vertical Integration?" In Masahiko Aoki, Bo Gustafsson, and Oliver E. Williamson (eds.), *The Firm as a Nexus of Treaties*, pp. 94–109. Newbury Park, CA: Sage.

Rippy, Merrill (1972). *Oil and the Mexican Revolution*. Leiden: Brill.

Robinson, James A. (Forthcoming). "Implications of Shleifer-Treisman Deals: Lessons from the Porfiriato." *Studies in Comparative International Development*.

Rodríguez López, María Guadalupe (1995). "La banca porfiriana en Durango." In Mario Cerutti (ed.), *Durango (1840–1915)*, pp. 7–34. Monterrey, Nuevo León, Mexico: Impresora Monterrey.

Rojas Alonso, Angel (1967). "Aspectos económicos de la industria del cemento en México." Universidad Nacional Autónoma de México, Mexico City.

Root, Hilton L. (1989). "Tying the King's Hands: Credible Commitments and Royal Fiscal Policy during the Old Regime." *Rationality and Society*, 1(2): 240–48.

Saragoza, Alex (1988). *The Monterrey Elite and the Mexican State, 1880–1940*. Austin: University of Texas Press.

Sariego, Juan Luis, Luis Reygadas, et al. (1988). *El estado y la minería mexicana: Política, trabajo, y sociedad durante el siglo XX*. Mexico City: Fondo de Cultura Económica.

Schelling, Thomas (1956). "An Essay on Bargaining." *American Economic Review*, 46(3): 281–306.

Schenk, Frank (1995). "La amortización de las tierras comunales en el Estado de México (1856–1911)." *Historia Mexicana*, 45(1): 3–37.

La Semana Mercantil. Mexico City.

Shepsle, Kenneth (1991). "Discretion, Institutions, and the Problem of Government Commitment." In Pierre Bourdieu and James Coleman (eds.), *Social Theory for a Changing Society*, pp. 245–63. Boulder: Westview Press.

Shleifer, Andrei, and Daniel Treisman (2000). *Without a Map: Political Tactics and Economic Reform in Russia*. Cambridge, MA: MIT Press.

Simpson, Eyler N. (1937). *The Ejido: Mexico's Way Out*. Chapel Hill: University of North Carolina Press.

Skocpol, Theda (1979). *States and Social Revolutions: A Comparative Study of France, Russia, and China*. Cambridge: Cambridge University Press.

Sokoloff, Kenneth L. (1984). "Was the Transition from the Artisanal Shop to the Nonmechanized Factory Associated with Gains in Efficiency? Evidence from the U.S. Manufacturing Censuses of 1820 and 1850." *Explorations in Economic History*, 21(4): 351–82.

(2002). "The Evolution of Suffrage Institutions in the New World: A Preliminary Look." In Stephen Haber (ed.), *Crony Capitalism and Economic Growth: Theory and Evidence*, pp. 75–107. Stanford, CA: Hoover Institution Press.

References

Sterret, Joseph E., and Joseph E. Davis (1928). *The Fiscal and Economic Condition of Mexico*. New York: International Committee of Bankers on Mexico.

Stigler, George J. (1971). "The Theory of Economic Regulation." *Bell Journal of Economics and Management Science*, 2: 3–21.

Summerhill, William R. (1997). "Transport Improvements and Economic Growth in Brazil and Mexico." In Stephen Haber (ed.), *How Latin America Fell Behind: Essays on the Economic Histories of Brazil and Mexico, 1800–1914*, pp. 93–117. Stanford, CA: Stanford University Press.

Suzigan, Wilson (1986). *Indústria Brasileira: Origen e Desenvolvimento*. São Paulo: Editora Brasiliense.

Tannenbaum, Frank (1968). *The Mexican Agrarian Revolution*. New York: Archon Books.

Tennenbaum, Barbara (1986). *The Politics of Penury: Debt and Taxes in Mexico, 1821–1856*. Albuquerque: University of New Mexico Press.

Tobler, Hans Werner (1988). "Peasants and the Shaping of the Revolutionary State." In Friedrich Katz (ed.), *Riot, Rebellion, and Revolution: Rural Social Conflict in Mexico*, pp. 487–518. Princeton: Princeton University Press.

Tortolero, Alejandro (1995). *De la coa a la máquina de vapor: Actividad agrícola e innovación tecnológica en las haciendas mexicanas, 1880–1914*. Mexico City: Colegio Mexiquense; Siglo XXI Editores.

Turrent Díaz, Eduardo (1982). *Historia del Banco de México*. Mexico City: Banxico.

Uhthoff Lopez, Luz Maria (1998). *Las finanzas públicas durante la Revolución: El papel de Luis Cabrera y Rafael Nieto al frente de la Secretaría de Hacienda*. Mexico City: Universidad Autónoma Metropolitana, Unidad Iztapalapa.

(2001). "La dificil concurrencia fiscal y la contribución federal." Unpublished manuscript, Universidad Autónoma Metropolitana-Iztapalapa, Mexico City.

United Kingdom. Customs and Excise Dept. Statistical Office (Various issues). *Annual Statement of the Overseas Trade of the United Kingdom*. London: H. M. Stationery Office.

United States. Department of Commerce (various years). *Foreign Commerce and Navigation of the United States*. Washington, DC: Treasury Dept.

Vargas-Lobsinger, María (1999). *La Comarca Lagunera: De la Revolución a la expropiación de las haciendas, 1910–1940*. Mexico: Universidad Nacional Autónoma de México, Instituto Nacional de Estudios Históricos de la Revolución Mexicana.

Velasco Avila, Cuauhtémoc, Eduardo Flores Clair, et al. (1988). *Estado y minería en México, 1767–1910*. Mexico City: Fondo de Cultura Económica.

Veugelers, Reinhilde (1993). "Reputation as a Mechanism for Alleviating Opportunistic Host Government Behavior against MNEs." *Journal of Industrial Economics*, 41(1): 1–17.

Walker, David (1986). *Kinship, Business, and Politics: The Martinez del Rio Family in Mexico, 1824–1867*. Austin: University of Texas Press.

Wall Street Journal. New York.

Wasserman, Mark (1984). *Capitalists, Caciques, and Revolution: Elite and Foreign Enterprise in Chihuahua, Mexico, 1854–1911*. Chapel Hill: University of North Carolina Press.

(1987). "Strategies for Survival of the Porfirian Elite in Revolutionary Mexico: Chihuahua during the 1920s." *Hispanic American Historical Review,* 67(1): 87–107.

(1993). *Persistent Oligarchs: Elites and Politics in Chihuahua, Mexico, 1910–1940.* Durham, NC: Duke University Press.

Weingast, Barry R. (1997a). "The Political Foundations of Limited Government: Parliament and Sovereign Debt in 17th- and 18th-Century England." In John N. Drobak and John V. C. Nye (eds.), *The Frontiers of the New Institutional Economics,* pp. 213–46. San Diego: Academic Press.

(1997b). "The Political Foundations of Democracy and the Rule of Law." *American Political Science Review,* 91(2): 245–63.

Weldon, Jeffrey (1997). "The Political Sources of Presidencialismo in Mexico." In Scott Mainwaring and Matthew Soberg Shugart (eds.), *Presidentialism and Democracy in Latin America,* pp. 225–58. Cambridge: Cambridge University Press.

Wells, Allen (1985). *Yucatán's Gilded Age: Haciendas, Henequen, and International Harvester, 1860–1915.* Albuquerque: University of New Mexico Press.

Wells, Allen, and Gilbert M. Joseph (1996). *Summer of Discontent, Seasons of Upheaval: Elite Politics and Rural Insurgency in Yucatán, 1876–1915.* Stanford, CA: Stanford University Press.

Williamson, Oliver E. (1985). *The Economic Institutions of Capitalism: Firms, Markets, Relational Contracting.* New York: Free Press; London: Collier Macmillan.

Womack, John (1969). *Zapata and the Mexican Revolution.* New York: Alfred A. Knopf.

(1978). "The Mexican Economy during the Revolution, 1910–1920: Historiography and Analysis." *Marxist Perspectives,* 1(4): 80–123.

(1986). "The Mexican Revolution, 1910–1920." In Leslie Bethell (ed.), *The Cambridge History of Latin America,* vol. 5, *1870–1930,* pp. 79–154. Cambridge: Cambridge University Press.

Wood, Gordon (1998). *The Creation of the American Republic, 1776–1787.* Chapel Hill: University of North Carolina Press.

Yates, Paul Lamartine (1981). *Mexico's Agricultural Dilemma.* Tucson: University of Arizona Press.

Yergin, Daniel (1991). *The Prize: The Epic Quest for Oil, Money, and Power.* New York: Simon and Schuster.

Index

Index

Index

Other Books in the Series (*continued from page iii*)